Comparative Semitic Linguistics

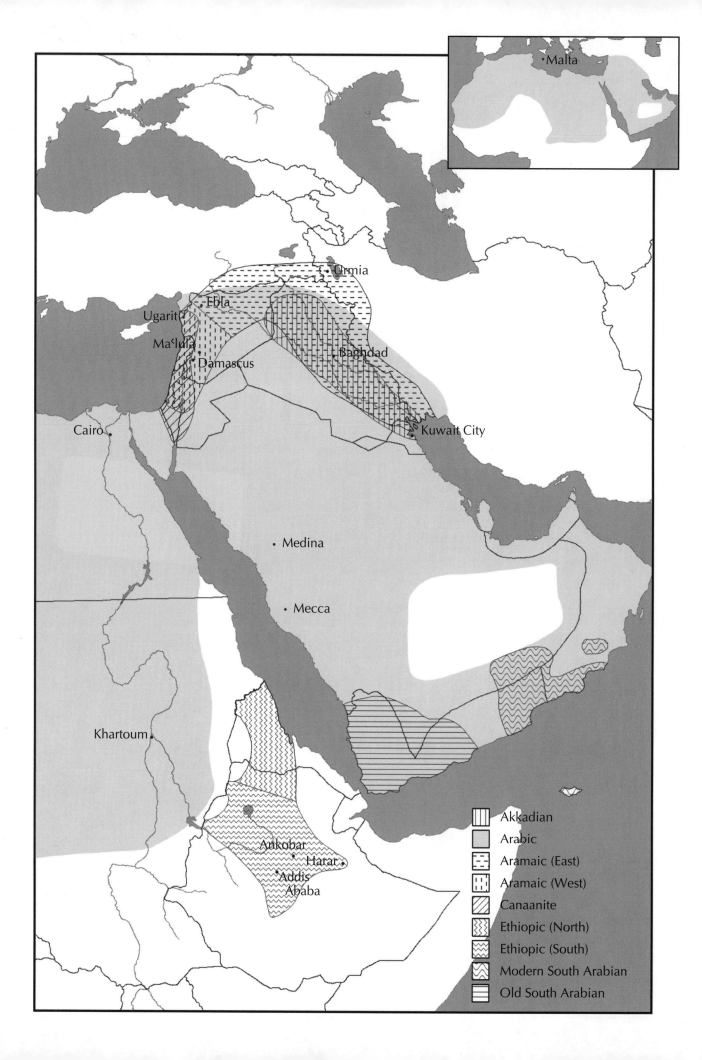

Malta

Urmia

Ebla

Ugarit

Ma'lula

Damascus

Baghdad

Cairo

Kuwait City

Medina

Mecca

Khartoum

Ankobar

Harar

Addis
Ababa

▯▯▯	Akkadian
▨	Arabic
⋰⋰	Aramaic (East)
▨	Aramaic (West)
▨	Canaanite
▨	Ethiopic (North)
∿∿	Ethiopic (South)
▨	Modern South Arabian
═══	Old South Arabian

Comparative Semitic Linguistics

A Manual

Patrick R. Bennett

Winona Lake, Indiana
Eisenbrauns
1998

Library of Congress Cataloging-in-Publication Data

Bennett, Patrick R.
    Comparative semitic linguistics : a manual / Patrick R. Bennett.
       p. cm.
    Includes bibliographical references and index.
    ISBN 1-57506-021-3 (pbk. : alk. paper)
    1. Semitic languages—Grammar, Comparative.   2. Semitic languages—
Glossaries, vocabularies, etc.   3. Comparative linguistics.
I. Title.
PJ3021.B36   1998
492—dc21
                                            98-17772
                                           CIP

Contents

List of Tables ix
List of Exercises xi
Shukran xii

To the Reader 1

Part 1: Basics of Descriptive Linguistics 3

What's in a Name? 3

Phonology 5

Phonetics 5

Vowels 5;   Semivowels 7;   Consonants 7;
Type of closure 8;   Voicing 9;   Nasality 9;   Coarticulation 9;
Release 10;   Syllabic Continuants 10;   Other Features 10

Phonemics 11

Morphophonemics 12

Metathesis 12;   Assimilation 12;   Dissimilation 12;
Epenthesis 12;   Elision 12

Transcription 12

Morphology and Syntax 14

Morphemes 14

Words 15

Word Marking 16

Phrases 17

Clauses 17

Hierarchy 18

Part 2: A General Introduction to the Semitic Language Family 19

What Is a Semitic Language? 19

Internal Relationships 20

External Relationships 21

Part 3: An Outline of Comparative Linguistics 23

Sources and Their Use 23

Assumptions and Techniques of Diachronic Linguistics 24

The Linguistic List 26

Cognacy and Regularity 26

Skewing 30

Part 4: Lexicostatistics: Some Alternatives **34**

    Appendix: The Swadesh 200-Word Basic Vocabulary List 40

Part 5: Linguistic Reconstruction: Comparative and Internal **41**

    Comparative Reconstruction: Phonology 42

    Comparative Reconstruction: Lexicon 47

    Comparative Reconstruction: Semantics 49

    Internal Reconstruction 49

    Comparative /Internal Reconstruction 52

Part 6: Various Less-Common Techniques **56**

    Loan Analysis 56

    Geographic Analysis 57

    Cultural Reconstruction 60

Part 7: Onward and Beyond **61**

    Semitic and Afroasiatic 61

    Evading the Triconsonantal Root 62

    Ebla and What Next? 65

Conclusion **67**

Paradigms A: Phonology **68**

    Proto-Semitic 68

    Old Babylonian 69

    Syriac 69

    Urmi 70

    Ugaritic 70

    Hebrew 71

    Classical Arabic 71

    Egyptian Arabic 72

    Geʿez 72

    Tigre 73

    Jibbali 73

Paradigms B: Morphology: Nouns and Pronouns **74**

    Old Babylonian 75

    Syriac 76

    Urmi 78

    Ugaritic 79

Hebrew 80

Classical Arabic 82

Egyptian Arabic 84

Geʿez 86

Tigre 88

Jibbali 90

Coptic 91

Ghadamsi 92

Paradigms C: Morphology: Verbs **94**

Old Babylonian 95

Syriac 98

Urmi 100

Ugaritic 101

Hebrew 102

Classical Arabic 104

Egyptian Arabic 107

Geʿez 109

Tigre 111

Jibbali 113

Coptic 115

Ghadamsi 117

Bibliography **119**

General Semitic and Afroasiatic 119

Akkadian 121

Arabic 121

Aramaic 121

Canaanite 122

Ethiopic 123

Modern South Arabian 124

Old South Arabian 124

Writing 124

Wordlist A: Cognates and Skewed Reflexes **127**

Wordlist B: Pair-Referenced Lexicostatistics and Subgrouping **130**

Wordlist C: Norm-Referenced and Pair-Referenced Lexicostatistics **143**

Wordlist D: Diglossia and Language Contact **153**

Wordlist E: Isoglosses **161**

Wordlist F: Berber and Semitic **222**

Wordlist G: Proto-Semitic A **232**

Wordlist H: Proto-Semitic B **233**

Wordlist I: Proto-Semitic C **233**

Appendix: Classical Semitic Scripts, by Peter T. Daniels **251**

    A Bit of History 251

    Abjads 252

        Hebrew 254

        Syriac 254

        Arabic 255

    Maltese 255

    Ethiopic 257

    Akkadian 258

Index 1: Languages of Glosses **261**

Index 2: Glosses **263**

List of Tables

Table 1. Vowel Symbols 7

Table 2. Semivowel Symbols 7

Table 3. Consonant Symbols 8

Table 4. Phonetic Identity 28

Table 5. Phonemic Identity 28

Table 6. Neither Phonetic nor Phonemic Identity 28

Table 7. Conditioned Correspondences 28

Table 8. Additional Correspondences 28

Table 9. Phonemic vs. Phonetic Correspondences 29

Table 10. Pattern Correspondence 29

Table 11. Identity in Form and Meaning 30

Table 12. Difference in Form/Identity in Meaning 30

Table 13. Frequent but Unconditioned Skewing 31

Table 14. Skewed Correspondence 32

Table 15. Semitic Number Words 35

Table 16. Lexicostatistical Investigation of Number Words in Four Semitic Languages . . 36

Table 17. Phonological Reconstructions 42

Table 18. Reconstructions of Dead Languages 42

Table 19. "Checklists" for Exercises 7–10 45

Table 20. Modern Arabic Correspondence Sets 47

Table 21. Modern Arabic Phonological Reconstructions 47

Table 22. Proto-Modern Arabic Reconstructions Compared with Classical Arabic 48

Table 23. Semantic Development 49

Table 24. Semantic Ranges 50

Table 25. Hebrew Nominal Paradigms 50

Table 26. Arabic Case and Number Endings 51

Table 27. Internal Reconstruction of Arabic Case and Number Endings 51

Table 28. Semantic Internal Reconstruction 52

Table 29. Basics of Semitic Verbal Derivation 54

Table 30. Reconstructed Semitic Verbal Derivation 55

Table 31. Loanwords in Egyptian Arabic 57

Table 32. Semitic Verbal Patterns, Base Form: Perfect/Imperfect/Subjunctive 58

Table 33. Proto-Semitic Verbs with *n-* 64

Table 34. Proto-Semitic Verbs with *-m* 64

Table 35. Proto-Semitic Verbs Relating to 'cutting'   65
Table 36. Some Periodicals to Check Through (with recognized abbreviations) 125
Table 37. Northwest Semitic Scripts 252
Table 38. Vocalization Systems of the Abjads 253
Table 39. Arabic 256
Table 40. Geʿez 257
Table 41. Phonetic Arrangement of Neo-Assyrian Cuneiform Syllabary 260

List of Exercises

Exercise 1. Compiling Vocabularies 27
Exercise 2. Discovering Cognates and Correspondences 30
Exercise 3. Determining Cognates and Skewed Reflexes 33
Exercise 4. Pair-Referenced Lexicostatistics (General Semitic) 38
Exercise 5. Norm-Referenced Lexicostatistics 38
Exercise 6. Pair-Referenced Lexicostatistics (Ethiopic) 38
Exercise 7. Phonological Reconstruction A 43
Exercise 8. Phonological Reconstruction B 43
Exercise 9. Phonological Reconstruction C 44
Exercise 10. Phonological Reconstruction D 44
Exercise 11. Phonological Reconstruction E 46
Exercise 12. Phonological Reconstruction F 46
Exercise 13. Regular Correspondences and Reconstruction 48
Exercise 14. Semantic Ranges 49
Exercise 15. Reconstructing Morphology 52
Exercise 16. Reconstructing Verbal Inflection 55
Exercise 17. Identifying Loanwords 58
Exercise 18. Drawing Isoglosses 59
Exercise 19. Cultural Reconstruction 60
Exercise 20. Critical Reading in Afroasiatic Studies 62
Exercise 21. Reconstructing Proto–Berber-Semitic 63
Exercise 22. Identifying a Prefix 64
Exercise 23. Identifying a Suffix 64
Exercise 24. Identifying Roots and Affixes 65
Exercise 25. Reconstructing Proto-Semitic with Classical, Ancient, and Modern Data 66

Shukran

Gratitude and appreciation are due to many, but especially to Emmett Bennett, Jr., and Malcolm Guthrie, who put my attempts at language comparison on the right path; to Muhammad Alwan and Menahem Mansoor, who first led me into Semitic; to the students of the Comparative Semitic seminar at the University of Wisconsin–Madison, who showed me the need for these materials; to my colleagues in the Department of African Languages and Literature, who insisted that I put other projects aside and produce this manual: among them most particularly Neil Skinner for many discussions on Afroasiatic, Dustin Cowell for Arabic expertise, and J. H. Carter for much support.

Nor must I forget Jim Eisenbraun and his crew, who, I fear, have worked more intensely on this project than I have myself, singling out Beverly Fields, who has plowed through a great deal of my prose, and Jennifer Ortega and Jason Horst, who labored long over the maps (p. ii and inside cover). And a special *salaam* to Peter Daniels, not only for contributing the appendix on writing systems, but for sharp-eyed, sharp-edged, sharp-witted, and always constructive criticism, for sifting and winnowing much of the chaff out of this book, and for positive input in countless sections.

Not least, I have had the support and patience of my family throughout the process, urging me to see it through, living with the late hours, stacks of books, heaps of papers, and long discourses that it has entailed, and providing insights and feedback again and again.

I must acknowledge that any errors of fact or interpretation, anything misleading or incomprehensible remaining in this work come from my oversight, ignorance, or refusal to hear excellent advice. The ultimate credit for all good that has gone into the manual or will come out of it goes to Him who *was* before the speakers of Proto-Semitic first came up with the word *ʾil-*; to Him all glory.

PATRICK BENNETT

To the Reader

This modest book is not a source for comparative Semitic grammar and lexicon. Though the wordlists and appendixes would be useful adjuncts to a comparative Semitic handbook, this is designed rather as a collection of tools for Semitic reconstruction. Nor does this work claim to be adequate to turn you into a competent comparative Semitist. It will give you a chance to try your hand at some of the techniques most useful to the comparative linguist. It will provide you with some insights into the interrelationships of a select subset of Semitic languages. It may inspire you to carry on and delve deeper into one of the richest fields for the comparative linguist.

I have not written for the seasoned comparativist or the advanced Semitist. The former can easily apply standard comparative techniques to Semitic data; the latter may well be developing innovative techniques. There are some minimum expectations. If you are going to make the best use of this text, you should have at least one year's study of a Semitic language behind you (it will probably be Arabic or Hebrew, though a solid grounding in any other Semitic language will do); it would also be helpful to have had a general course in comparative linguistics. Of course, it would be best to have had both. I have not assumed a reading knowledge of any language other than English or of any script other than Roman. If you are already familiar with any system of phonetic symbols, especially one commonly used in transliterating Semitic languages, it will help; but even this will not be assumed.

If you are sufficiently involved in Semitic linguistics to be using this book and are likely to want to go deeper into comparative Semitic linguistics, you will want to have a reading knowledge of as many as possible of the languages in which Semitic scholarship is published. Probably the most important are German, French, English, Italian, and Latin. Russian, Hebrew, and Arabic are increasingly important; this list is not exhaustive.

It would also be good to widen your range of Semitic languages. It is not necessary to delve equally into all of them, but it would be good to be familiar with the structure and most essential vocabulary of one language from each of three of the major branches. If at least one of them were Ugaritic or Akkadian, it would help. And, of course, you need to be able to read a few of the major Semitic scripts and be able to use dictionaries and consult grammars. Without them, most of the major data sources and much of the discussion in the literature will be closed to you.

Part 1

Basics of Descriptive Linguistics

What's in a Name?

Before proceeding with the comparison of Semitic languages, the reader will need to understand the meanings of some basic linguistic terminology. The study of LINGUISTICS encompasses many different fields. Linguistics may be the study of "language"—the human communication process, focusing on what we all share: the organs involved in speech, the speech areas in the brain, whatever language structures are "wired in" and universal. Linguistics may also be the study of "languages"—the specific culture-bound systems of speech behavior. We will assume the latter definition.

This type of linguistics studies languages synchronically or diachronically. SYNCHRONIC LINGUISTICS examines a single language as spoken at a given time. DIACHRONIC LINGUISTICS is the study of a single language, tracing its development through time, looking at the similarities and differences in several languages at the same time, or combining the two, studying the development of a language family from its common ancestor to the languages of today. Most of what we do in this manual will be diachronic, though the Semitist may have to do a synchronic study of a Semitic language at some point.

Some of the activities that can be grouped as diachronic linguistics have their own names. DIALECTOLOGY is the diachronic study of dialects of a single language. COMPARATIVE LINGUISTICS applies to studies of two or more related languages; CONTRASTIVE LINGUISTICS describes differences between languages (related or not).

It is important to note here that there are many schools of linguistics and many different traditions of diachronic linguistics, even within Semitics. Semitic languages are described in different traditions with very different terminology. Even when we eliminate the differences reflecting national origin (the Italians and the English, for example, differ in approach) and the differences reflecting theoretical training, we find descriptions of Ethiopic to be written very differently from sketches of Arabic dialects.

It would be impossible—and confusing—to represent all of the variations of linguistic terminology. Here we employ one set of definitions. Readers with previous background in general linguistics will probably recognize that this presentation is old-fashioned and simplistic. It is old-fashioned because most of the language descriptions Semitists will read are older, and

3

even the more recent are rarely written to reflect the rapidly changing "state of the art" of theoretical linguistics. It is simplistic because the intent is to employ language that can be understood by students who have little or no general linguistic training.

Languages are very complex systems. They must be, in order to communicate adequately and flexibly. It is very common—especially in diachronic linguistics—to treat just one subsystem at a time. We will discuss the major subsystems, each of which has its own set of terminology, in the following sections.

To begin with, let us attempt to define a language. A LANGUAGE is a complex system of culturally transmitted behaviors used for oral communication. It consists of a set of units of form and meaning and a set of rules specifying how these units are combined and modified to convey messages. However, this definition leaves out some essential information. For instance, if we were to ask the question, who speaks the Arabic language? the precise answer would be, nobody; Arabic speakers all speak Arabic IDIOLECTS.

An idiolect is the system of behaviors used for oral communication by one person. It will be seen that it is not identical with the system used by any other person. Since it is not useful to have a separate linguistic description of every idiolect in the world, we take a set of idiolects that have more in common with one another than they have with anything else and call it a language, assigning to the language the common elements and ignoring the individual differences.

Often a given language community can be seen to be subdivided into sets of idiolects that have more in common with one another than with other idiolects belonging to the same language. We recognize these as DIALECTS of the language. Often it can be seen that two or more languages show similarities that lead one to recognize them as belonging to the same LANGUAGE FAMILY (or LANGUAGE GROUP, or LANGUAGE CLUSTER).

The problem we face is that this is open-ended. Consider one Arabic speaker, who speaks an idiolect that we class with a group of idiolects spoken in Cairo, which we will call Cairene Arabic. This group is similar to other groups that we classify as Egyptian Arabic. Egyptian Arabic is joined with other groups in what we will simply call Arabic, which is one component of North Arabian, which may be classed as Central Semitic, which is part of Semitic, which is a constituent of Afroasiatic, which some would include in an even larger unit.

The status of the idiolect as a linguistic entity is clear. There is no problem with the highest level of language family we are willing to recognize. But it is by no means clear where to draw the lines in between. Is Egyptian Arabic a language one of whose dialects is Cairene? Or is Egyptian Arabic a dialect of the language Arabic? Or is Arabic a dialect of the North Arabian language? Is Semitic a language, a dialect, a dialect cluster, or a language family? I do not have the answers. At various times linguists have tried to set criteria, to say that two idiolects are members of the same dialect if they have this much in common or are to this degree mutually intelligible, but they pertain to the same language if there are greater differences. But all of the cutoff points are arbitrary.

The result is that one author will refer to Egyptian Arabic as a dialect of Arabic, while another (or the same author in another publication) may treat Cairene as a dialect of the Egyptian Arabic language. Though perhaps confusing to the beginner, this is acceptable variation. We need some flexibility. At the same time, there are practical limits to variation. Although there may be no agreement on criteria, it is highly unlikely that we will find anyone describing Arabic and Hebrew as two dialects of a single language, for example.

Because a language (however defined) is a complex system, it is normal to look at only one subsystem at a time. The major subsystems are PHONOLOGY, having to do with the sounds of speech and their interactions; MORPHOLOGY, which refers to the smallest meaningful units and the way they combine to make words; SYNTAX, or the patterns in which words combine to build phrases and clauses; and the LEXICON, which is not, in this use of the term, a synonym for "dictionary," but rather the inventory of meaningful units of the language.

Phonology

Phonetics

This section introduces phonetic concepts and some of the very specific terminology used in the study of phonetics, if only because many of the correspondences we find and the changes they indicate are understandable only if one can look behind the symbol to the sound.

In what follows we will associate the most useful phonetic symbols with the sounds they represent—or rather, with the positions and actions of the vocal apparatus that produce the sounds. Although it is true that sounds can be described as sounds (ACOUSTICALLY), and that essentially identical sounds can be produced in different ways, it is conventional to describe phonological units in terms of ARTICULATION. Articulations will be described in terms of the diagrams below. It will be useful for the reader to become familiar with the organs and the sounds produced. I recommend trying out the sounds; it is easier to understand how sounds change if one knows what they feel like in the mouth.

VOWELS. We will begin with vowels, which are a little easier to describe than consonants. Vowels, generally speaking, involve vibration of the vocal cords caused by a flow of air from the lungs. The air flows through the mouth, whose shape determines the sound. The lower jaw, tongue, lips, and velum are used to adjust the shape and resonating characteristics of the mouth. These distinctions between, for example, *e* and *i*, *i* and *ü*, and *ü* and *u* are referred to as distinctions in QUALITY.

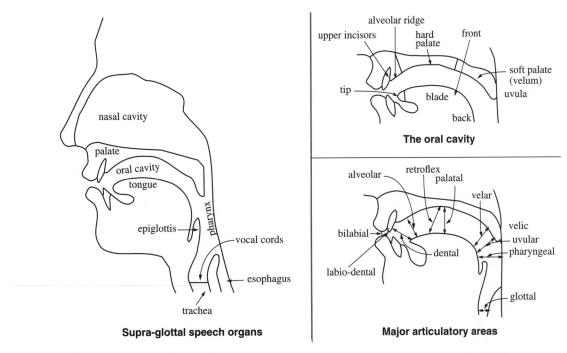

Diagrams after J. D. O'Connor, *Phonetics* (Harmondsworth: Penguin, 1973).

Perhaps the most important characteristic of vowels is that they function as the resonant peak of a syllable—put more simply, the most audible part. Try saying a vowel by itself: *u*. Even if you speak softly with your back turned, someone listening can tell what you pronounced. Now try pronouncing *t* by itself. If your back is turned, your partner probably cannot identify what you said, and if you are doing it softly you may not even be heard. A consonant like *s* or *n* is more audible, but still not as prominent as the vowel.

• Vowels are described first in terms of jaw position. We will distinguish four degrees of jaw opening (more degrees are possible, but for Semitic we do not generally need them). LOW vowels have the widest possible jaw opening. Most Semitic languages have one low vowel, *a*. HIGH vowels involve narrowing the opening. Most Semitic languages have *i* and *u* as high vowels. Vowels between high and low are MID vowels. Typical mid vowels are *e* and *o*. Not all Semitic languages have mid vowels (Classical Arabic is analyzed as having only high and low vowels); but to balance this out, some (Jibbali is an example) have two levels between high and low. When necessary, we distinguish UPPER MID (*e*, *o*) from LOWER MID (*ε*, *ɔ*). The lower mid vowels involve a somewhat wider jaw opening.

• The second parameter in characterizing vowels is tongue position. For some vowels, the tongue is shaped in such a way that it is closest to the roof of the mouth toward the front. We describe *i* as a high (tight jaw) FRONT (tongue pushed forward) vowel.

For BACK vowels, the tongue is pulled back and shaped to come closest to the roof of the mouth back toward the throat end. You may test this with *u*, a high back vowel. CENTRAL vowels are located between the two ends of the mouth; the tongue tends to be flat, as in *a*.

• A third parameter is the shape of the lips, which may be either spread or rounded. The lips are spread for UNROUNDED vowels like *i*, *a*. ROUNDED vowels are made with rounded lips. Observe that the lower a rounded vowel is, the weaker the rounding. The jaw can only be dropped so far in producing a low vowel before pulling on the muscles of the lips.

For most languages—certainly most Semitic languages—there is a correlation between rounding and tongue position. Back vowels are normally rounded, front and central vowels normally unrounded. However, many languages—including some Semitic languages—have front rounded vowels and/or back unrounded vowels.

In a few of the Semitic languages, we need also to discuss PHARYNGEALIZED vowels and NASAL vowels. Both are articulated exactly like the oral plain vowels, as far as what goes on in the mouth. Pharyngealized vowels add a constriction at the pharynx. In most Semitic languages where they exist, they are allophones (see "Phonemics" on page 11) in the environment of emphatic consonants. In a few languages they have come to be phonemically distinct from plain vowels. Nasal vowels involve an opening into the nasal cavity, adding a nasal resonance to the vibrations that make up the vowel. These too are often allophones heard in the environment of nasal consonants. Again, in a few languages they are phonemically distinct.

Table 1 presents the symbols used here for the most commonly found vowels.

In addition to the qualitative distinctions discussed above, vowels may differ in QUANTITY, the length of time it takes to pronounce the vowel. In Arabic, for example, كَتَبَ *kataba* 'write' contrasts with كَاتَبَ *kātaba* 'correspond with' in that the initial syllable in the former is short while that of the latter is long. While we will discuss the issue of vowel and consonant quantity elsewhere (see page 10), we need to mention here the interaction between quantity and quality. In many languages, the placement of long vowels is noticeably different from the placement of the corresponding short vowels. This has resulted, for example, in the general shift from **ā* to *ō* in Hebrew (compare the Hebrew participle pattern *pōʿēl* with the Arabic pattern *fāʿil*). (The asterisk (*) is conventionally used to mark reconstructed or hypothetical forms.)

Table 1. Vowel Symbols

	Front unrounded	Central unrounded	Back rounded
High	*i*		*u*
Upper mid	*e*		*o*
Lower mid	*ε*	*ə*	*ɔ*
Low		*a*	

Table 2. Semivowel Symbols

	Front unrounded		Back rounded
High	*y*		*w*

Over time, in some languages the qualitative differences have come to be at least as important in the system as the quantitative, and length may cease to be contrastive as such. This has occurred in several modern Semitic languages, as in Amharic and some dialects of Arabic. A similar contrast based on quality rather than quantity may be seen in Hebrew and Geʿez, for example, where the writing system and traditional pronunciation would support such an interpretation.

SEMIVOWELS.   Semivowels (see Table 2) may be described as sounds with the articulatory characteristics of vowels and the functions of consonants. Like vowels, they involve tongue placement and lip shape; unlike vowels, the degree of jaw opening is rarely an issue, and they do not function as the nucleus of a syllable. While other semivowels are possible, most Semitic languages use the two most common: a front unrounded semivowel *y*, which is related to the high front unrounded vowel *i*, and a back rounded semivowel *w*, related to the high back rounded vowel *u*.

Since semivowels are equivalent in acoustic and articulatory terms to nonsyllabic vowels and most frequently occur juxtaposed to vowels, there may be problems of interpretation. A sequence *ay* may be as readily heard and transcribed as *ai*. Should we recognize it in a given context as a sequence of a vowel and a consonant parallel, for example, to *ab*, or as a DIPHTHONG? The decision will normally be based on functional criteria. If *ai* occurs in contexts where one would normally expect a short or long vowel, it will be analyzed as a diphthong. If it occurs in patterns where one would find vowel plus consonant, the interpretation as vowel plus semivowel is more appropriate.

CONSONANTS.   Consonants (see Table 3) are much more diverse than vowels and in most languages will outnumber vowels at least two to one (the average is rather higher in Semitic). Consonants involve bringing two of the speech organs close enough together to shut off or restrict the flow of air. They function, generally speaking, as the boundaries between syllables.

Consonants are described first in terms of point of articulation. It should be a help to readers to remember that the labels assigned to points of articulation are related to the names of the organs brought together to produce the sound.

BILABIALS: The two lips are brought together. Examples are *p*, *m*.

LABIODENTALS: One lip and one row of front teeth are involved. These are always the lower lip and the upper front teeth. Examples are *f*, *v*.

INTERDENTALS: The tongue tip is placed between the two rows of teeth, touching or close to the upper set. Examples are *θ*, *δ*.

Table 3. Consonant Symbols

			Bilabial	Labiodental	Interdental	Alveolar	Lateral	Alveolopalatal	Palatal	Velar	Labiovelar	Uvular	Pharyngeal	Glottal
Stop	Voiceless	Plain	p			t ת		č	c	k	kʷ	q		ʾ
		Emphatic	ṗ			ṭ ט		č̣		ḳ	ḳʷ			
	Voiced	Plain	b			d		ǰ	j	g	gʷ			
		Emphatic				ḍ								
Fricative	Voiceless	Plain	υ	f	θ	s	ś	š	ç	x	xʷ	χ	ḥ ח	h ה
		Emphatic			θ̣	ṣ	ṣ́							
	Voiced	Plain	β	v	δ	z	ź	ž		γ		ʁ	ʿ	
		Emphatic			δ̣	ẓ	ẓ́							
Approximant		Plain				r	l		y		w			
		Emphatic				ṛ	ḷ							
Nasal			m			n								

ALVEOLARS: the tongue tip contacts or approaches the roof of the mouth at or near the alveolar ridge behind the upper teeth. Examples are *t, z.*

LATERALS: As with the alveolars, the tongue tip contacts or approaches the roof of the mouth behind the teeth, but the airflow passes by at least one side of the tongue, rather than over the top as with alveolars and dentals. Examples are *l, ś.*

ALVEOLOPALATALS: The point of closest approximation is between the center of the tongue and the roof of the mouth, somewhat behind the alveolar ridge. Examples are *š, č.*

PALATALS: The back of the tongue contacts or approaches the center—or a bit back from center—of the roof of the mouth. Examples are *j, ç.*

VELARS: The back of the tongue contacts or approaches the soft palate (velum). Examples are *k, g.*

LABIOVELARS: These show lip rounding or closure simultaneous with a velar articulation. Labiovelars with lip closure are not reported for Semitic. Examples are *kʷ, xʷ.*

UVULARS: The back of the tongue contacts or approaches the uvula. Examples are *q, χ.*

PHARYNGEALS: Here we have a constriction—not closure—of the pharynx. Examples are *ʿ* and *ḥ*, which, while not limited to Afroasiatic, nor found in all Afroasiatic languages, are very characteristic of the family.

GLOTTALS: These involve closing or narrowing of the glottis, the vocal cords. Examples are *ʾ, h.*

A number of other parameters are involved in the production—and therefore in the description—of consonants. We will list only those that are important in the study of Semitic.

TYPE OF CLOSURE. STOP: The flow of air is completely cut off. Examples are *p, d.* Trills and affricates also meet this description, but the closure is not complete throughout the duration of the consonant.

FRICATIVE: The flow of air through the mouth is constricted enough to be audible. Examples are *θ, ḥ*.

APPROXIMANT: The oral passage is narrowed in such a way that the resonance characteristics are changed, though the air flow will not normally be audible. An example is *l*.

TRILL: The flow of air is cut off, as in a stop. The organs involved in the closure are pushed apart by air pressure, then spring back to stop the flow again, for a varying number of cycles. Because the airflow continues with brief interruptions, these tend to pattern with fricatives or approximants. An example is *r*.

AFFRICATE: The flow of air is cut off, as in a stop, but the closure is then partially released, to give the audible friction of a fricative. Affricates are often transcribed as sequences of stop and fricative. It is only language-specific patterns of syllable structure that allow one to decide whether a sequence is an affricate (a single unit) or a sequence (two units). An example is *č* (approximately *tš*). Affricates normally pattern with stops. For example, in Iraqi Arabic *č* and *ǰ* occur in the following positions that are restricted to single consonants:

a. after long vowel (*čākūč* 'hammer', *zōǰ* 'pair')
b. geminated (*wučč* 'face', *raǰǰa* 'return')
c. in consonant clusters (*čfūf* 'gloves', *maǰnūn* 'crazy')

Note also that *č* frequently alternates with *k*: *čān/ykūn* 'be'. Contrast this with the situation in Moroccan Arabic, where *tš* and *dž* pattern as clusters:

a. stop prefixed (*išuf/tšuf* 'he/she sees', *iži/dži* 'he/she comes')
b. fricative suffixed (*ma-bγit-š* 'I don't want')
c. prefixes take a vowel (*metša'em* 'skeptical'; cf. *mṣafeṛ* 'traveling')

In addition, restrictions on consonant sequences make the clusters rare in roots, especially verb roots. Perhaps the only common instance is *džadža* 'chicken'.

VOICING.   There are two alternatives that concern the Semitist.

VOICED: Air forced through the vocal cords produces a vibration simultaneously with the consonant. Examples are *ʿ, g*.

VOICELESS: There is no vibration from the vocal cords. Examples are *ḥ, k*.

NASALITY.   Again there are two alternatives.

NASAL: The soft palate is lowered, leaving the nasal passages open. Examples are *m, n*.

ORAL: The soft palate blocks access to the nasal passages. Examples are *p, d*.

COARTICULATION.   There are three types of consonant to consider here.

PLAIN: No articulation is added to the basic consonant. Examples are *t, z*.

EJECTIVE: A glottal stop (*'*) is made simultaneously with an oral stop or fricative (the latter being often heard as an affricate). If a stop, the oral closure is released shortly before the release of the glottal stop. Ejectives are always voiceless. They may be transcribed with a symbol representing the oral consonant followed by *'*. Examples are *t', s'*.

PHARYNGEALIZED: A pharyngeal constriction is made simultaneously with an oral or nasal consonant. Neighboring vowels are affected much as they are by *ʿ*. Pharyngealized consonants could be transcribed with *ʿ* following the oral or nasal consonant, but Semitic studies almost exclusively mark pharyngealized consonants with a subscript dot. Examples are *ṭ, ṃ*.

RELEASE.   We again recognize three types.

PLAIN: The consonant ends, followed immediately by a vowel, another consonant, or pause. Examples are *p*, *δ*.

ASPIRATE: The consonant (usually a voiceless stop or affricate) is followed by a small puff of air. Aspirates may be transcribed with a symbol representing the stop or affricate followed by *h*. Examples are *p^h*, *č^h*.

GLOTTALIZED: The consonant is followed by a glottal stop ('). These differ from ejectives in that the glottal closure is not in place during the articulation of the oral consonant, and, consequently, they may be voiced. They rarely (if ever) contrast with ejectives and like ejectives may be transcribed with the oral consonant followed by '. Examples are *d'*, *ź'*.

In Table 3 on page 8, presenting the most common symbols we will be using, the reader will find some simplifications. Affricates are aligned with stops, and most trills are classed with fricatives. The alveolar trill *r*, however, is placed with the approximants. Note, by the way, that the inventory of approximants includes the semivowels already discussed. Ejective, pharyngealized, and glottalized consonants are not distinguished but are lumped as emphatic, transcribed here and elsewhere as underdotted. The rationale is simple—in (most? all?) Semitic languages they are not found to contrast, and they are clearly historically related: Amharic ejective *ṣ* (*ts'*) corresponds regularly to Arabic pharyngealized *ṣ* (*s'*) and to Jibbali glottalized *ṣ* (*s'*).

SYLLABIC CONTINUANTS.   As we have seen, semivowels stand between vowels and consonants, having the articulatory characteristics of vowels but functioning as syllable boundaries rather than peaks. There are also sounds that have the articulatory characteristics of consonants but are found as the peak of a syllable. Most commonly they are continuants, usually voiced. Syllabic nasals and laterals are the most frequent. Syllabic consonants are usually transcribed with a subscript circle added to the consonant symbol.

OTHER FEATURES.   QUANTITY: In most Semitic languages, both consonants and vowels have two contrasting quantities. Single, short consonants and vowels contrast with double (long, or in the case of consonants, "geminate") units. The distinction is important in morphology, as is shown by examples like Arabic كَتَبَ *kataba* 'write', كَتَّبَ *kattaba* 'make write', كَاتَبَ *kātaba* 'write to one another'.

Semitic long consonants are normally transcribed by doubling the symbol: short *t*, long *tt*. If the consonant is transcribed with two symbols, as is the case with the labiovelars, e.g. *k^w*, it is normal to double only the first symbol to indicate a long consonant: *kk^w*. Semitic long vowels are normally transcribed with a diacritic, either a following colon or raised dot or a superscript macron: short *a*, long *a:*, *a·*, or *ā* (we will use the last option).

Long vowels and long consonants have much in common structurally (we will use the colon to mark length just for this set of examples).

a. They may result from assimilation of sequences (Arabic *al-tibn* > اَلتِّبْن *at:ibn* 'the straw', *yamwutu* > يَمُوت *yamu:tu* 'he will die').

b. They may appear as the result of morphological processes (as in Arabic كَتَبَ *kataba* 'write', كَتَّبَ *kat:aba* 'make write', كَاتَبَ *ka:taba* 'write to one another', quoted above).

c. They may result from contraction (Arabic *mawata* > مَات *ma:ta* 'he died', *ḥa:rir* > حَارّ *ḥa:r:* 'hot').

d. Long vowels differ from diphthongs (surface or underlying sequences of vowel and semivowel, like *aw* ~ *ō*) in that they are not subject to the type of alternation seen in Hebrew בַּיִת *bayit* 'house', בֵּיתִי *be:ti:* 'my house', underlyingly *bayt* and *bayt-i:*; contrast סוּס *su:s* 'horse', סוּסִי *su:si:* 'my horse'. Long consonants differ from clusters in that they are not subject to the similar alternation seen in Hebrew כֶּלֶב *keleb* 'dog', כַּלְבִּי *kalbi:* 'my dog', underlyingly *kalb* and *kalb-i:*; contrast כַּף *kap* 'palm', כַּפִּי *kap:i:* 'my palm', underlying *kap:* and *kap:-i:*.

e. Long vowels resemble sequences of vowel plus consonant in that they are not subject to rules like Aramaic vowel deletion: Syriac *kitab* > ܟܬܰܒ *ktab* 'he wrote', *kitabat* > ܟܬܰܒ݂ܰܬ݂ *kitbat* 'she wrote', but *ka:tib* > ܟܳܬ݂ܶܒ݂ *ka:tib* 'writing' and *kita:b-a:k* > ܟܬ݂ܳܒ݂ܳܟ݂ *kta:ba:k* 'your book'. Long consonants resemble sequences of consonants in that they block rules like Aramaic vowel deletion: Syriac *dim* > ܕܶܡ *dim* 'blood', *dim-ih* > ܕܡܶܗ *dmih* 'his blood', but *pak:* > ܦܰܟ *pak:* 'cheek', *pak:-ih* > ܦܰܟܶܗ *pak:ih* 'his cheek', compare *kalb-ih* > ܟܰܠܒܶܗ *kalbih* 'his dog'.

f. In many Semitic languages, CVCC, CV:C, and CVC: are acceptable and essentially equivalent structures for monosyllabic words. Such structures as CCVC, CVVC, C:VC, and CV:C: are not normally allowed in monosyllables (though through contraction CCVC and CV:C: may occur).

PHARYNGEALIZATION: In those Semitic languages where the emphatic consonants are pharyngealized, neighboring vowels are frequently affected. In some cases it is most convenient to take pharyngealization as a feature of vowels, not consonants. In the Neo-Aramaic of Urmi, for example, there is a pharyngealization-based VOWEL HARMONY, such that in most cases all the vowels of a word will be either pharyngealized or plain (this is conventionally represented by underlining the pharyngealized segments). So we have <u>basmanta</u> 'publication', pharyngealized throughout, contrasting with *basmanta* 'healer', and <u>šraya</u> 'to judge' contrasting with *šraya* 'to dwell'.

NASALIZATION: In many languages, vowels in contact with nasal consonants are to some degree nasalized (indicated with a superscript tilde); that is, the nasal passage is open while the vowel is articulated. In most Semitic languages, such nasalization is not significant. However, in Jibbali, for example, the loss of the conditioning nasal consonant has resulted in contrasts such as *xēr* 'news', *x̃ēr* 'wine'.

STRESS: Most Semitic languages have stress patterns that are predictable in terms of syllable structure. Some languages, however, have a contrastive stress, here marked with ´. Hebrew, for example, contrasts אוֹרִי *'ōrí* 'my light' with אֹרִי *'órī* 'curse (feminine imperative)'.

Phonemics

We need to introduce the phonemic principle. In any language, some units in the phonology may be realized in several different ways, without changing the identity of the unit. Thus in Arabic *-a* is articulated toward the front of the mouth in كَلْب *kalb* 'dog', but in بَطّ *baṭṭ* 'duck' is pronounced much further back; in Syriac (at least in native material), *d* is a stop initially, when geminate, or after another consonant, but otherwise is a fricative *δ*. Such differences, which, although important to correct pronunciation, do not affect meaning, are called ALLOPHONIC; Syriac *d* and *δ* are said to be ALLOPHONES of a single unit. Differences are PHONEMIC, however, when contrast is involved. In Arabic, the contrast between *d* and *δ* is shown by pairs such as دَلَّ *dalla* 'show' and ذَلَّ *δalla* 'be lowly'; two PHONEMES are involved.

Many modern approaches to phonology have eliminated the concept of phoneme, or greatly modified it, but the principle remains. Most will describe phonological structure in terms of some type of abstract underlying unit—analogous to the phoneme even if not bearing that name—and phonetic realizations of that unit determined by context-sensitive rules—analogous to allophones. When using modern descriptions, do not be misled by differences in terminology and presentation. Rather, seek out the underlying forms and treat them as you would phonemes.

In most cases, a phonemic transcription provides all the detail we need for comparison; occasionally, however, the comparativist must examine allophones. Occasionally, as well, it is necessary to compare data from one language that are available only in a phonemic transcription, with phonetic data from another language.

Morphophonemics

Morphophonemics, so called because it has been seen as involving the interaction of phonology and morphology, involves conditioned alternations between phonemes. For example, in Arabic *u* and *i* are in contrast, but the 3ms possessive suffix *-hu* will be heard as *-hi* if suffixed to a noun ending in *i*: بَيْتُهُ *baytuhu* 'his house', but في بَيْتِه *fī baytihi* 'in his house'. Morphophonemics is a component of phonology which is very important to diachronic linguistics, since the morphophonemic processes in force today may give clues to past phonological states.

The following are some of the more common types of morphophonemic processes:

METATHESIS. Two sounds are transposed. When the Syriac reflexive prefix *ʾit-* precedes stem-initial *s*, *z*, *ṣ*, or *š*, the two consonants metathesize: ܐܬܦܬܚ *ʾit-ptaḥ* 'be opened', but ܐܫܬܡܥ *ʾi-š-t-maʿ* 'be heard' (not *ʾi-t-šmaʿ*).

ASSIMILATION. A sound changes to become more like another. An example is the Syriac reflexive prefix *ʾit-*, in which *t* is voiced when it follows *z*: ܐܣܬܬܪ *ʾi-s-t-attar* 'be hidden', but ܐܙܕܡܢ *ʾi-z-d-ammin* 'be invited'. Some linguists restrict the term ASSIMILATION to cases where the resulting consonant is identical to the conditioning consonant, as in the Arabic definite marker *al-*, in which *l* will assimilate to certain initial consonants of the following word: الْكِتَاب *al-kitāb* 'the book', but التَّاجِر *at-tājir* 'the trader', النُّور *an-nūr* 'the light'.

DISSIMILATION. A sound changes to become less like another. For instance, Classical Arabic has a morpheme *-nV* which is suffixed to dual or sound masculine plural nominals except in the construct. Following the high-voweled plural suffixes *-ū* and *-ī*, this suffix appears with the low vowel *a*, to give *-ū-na/-ī-na*. Following the low-voweled dual suffixes *-ā* and *-ay*, it takes the high vowel *i*: *-ā-ni/-ay-ni*.

EPENTHESIS. The insertion of a sound. In Semitic, epenthesis most commonly involves insertion of a vowel to break up an unacceptable cluster. In Iraqi Arabic final sequences of two unlike consonants are eliminated by insertion of a vowel: *rijil* 'foot', *šahar* 'month', *ʾuxut* 'sister' (Classical Arabic رِجْل *rijl*, شَهْر *šahr*, أُخْت *ʾuxt*).

ELISION. The deletion of a sound. In the perfective of the Hebrew base conjugation, two vowels are normally found in the stem with no suffix, or with a suffix of shape -C or -CV: כָּתַבְתִּי *kātabtī* 'I wrote', כָּתַבְתְּ *kātabt* 'you (f.s.) wrote', כָּתַב *kātab* 'he wrote'. With a vowel-initial suffix, the second vowel of the stem is deleted: כָּתְבָה *kātbāh* 'she wrote'. With a suffix of shape -CVC, the first vowel of the stem is lost: כְּתַבְתֶּם *ktabtem* 'you (m.p.) wrote'.

Transcription

It is important to remember that we have phonetic detail and phonemic analyses only for the living languages. For Maʿlula, Jibbali, Amharic, or Maltese we have only to locate a speaker or a phonetic description compiled by a competent linguist. For some other languages—Hebrew, Syriac, Classical Arabic, Geʿez—we have somewhat reliable information from reading traditions, and in some cases we have early phonetic descriptions written by native scholars.

For most of the ancient Semitic languages, our phonetic knowledge is based on extrapolation from the modern or the better-known ancient languages; on transcriptions in other languages (Punic in Latin-based transcription in Plautus's play *Poenulus*, Ugaritic in Akkadian transcription); or on internal evidence from morphophonemic changes, alternations in spelling, or changes over time.

The original scripts, other than cuneiform, are generally reliable for representing phonemic consonant contrasts, but vowels are often not represented at all. Vowel quality and quantity may be marked with diacritics, or (primarily long vowels) with *matres lectionis*, consonant symbols conventionally used for vowel marking (usually ' to mark *ā*, the semivowels *y* and *w* for *ī* and *ū* respectively). Consonant length may be marked with a diacritic like the Arabic *šadda*[t] or the Hebrew *dāgēš*; it is never marked in indigenous Semitic scripts by doubling the consonant symbol. Indication of stress placement is rare.

Fortunately, for our purposes, this lack of phonetic detail is not an insuperable problem; indeed, in some cases, like the retention of archaic consonantal spellings in Hebrew and Syriac, it may help us. Even without being able to specify the pronunciation of a given consonant in, say, Ugaritic, we can determine that it corresponds to a particular Proto-Semitic unit, since it occurs in corresponding positions in related words. Such a sound is said to be a REFLEX of the unit in the proto-language; reflexes will normally retain features of the earlier unit they reflect. Thus the Arabic *f*, which is a reflex of Proto-Semitic **p* (reconstructed items assumed to belong to the proto-language are marked with an asterisk), retains the voicelessness and labial articulation of **p*. In some cases, we can draw fairly detailed conclusions regarding probable pronunciation.

An example is the reflex of Semitic **ṣ́* in older Aramaic. In later Aramaic—Syriac, for example—this consonant has merged with **ʿ*: **'arṣ́* 'earth' > Syriac ܐܪܥܐ *'arʿā*. This pronunciation is confirmed by modern Aramaic languages: Maʿlula *arʿa*. In older Aramaic, however, it is often written with a *q*, as in Biblical Aramaic *'arqā*. We reason thus:

a. Languages outside the Aramaic group uniformly show an emphatic (pharyngealized or glottalized) alveolar or lateral as the reflex of **ṣ́*: Hebrew אֶרֶץ *'ereṣ*, Arabic أرض *'arḍ*, Jibbali *'ɛrẓ̂*.

b. In most languages for which we have phonetic documentation, the reflex of **q* in a word like **qabr-* 'tomb' is either a velar ejective (Mehri *ḳōbər*, Harari *ḳäbri*) or a uvular (Arabic قبر *qabr*, Modern Mandaic *qoβra*).

c. In later Aramaic, as in most of Semitic, ʿ is a voiced pharyngeal fricative: **ʿayn* 'eye' > Maʿlula *ʿayna*, Moroccan *ʿeyn*, Tigrinya *ʿayni*, Soqotri *ʿáyn*.

d. It would be consistent with the evidence to assume a pre-Aramaic Northwest Semitic pharyngealized lateral (voiced or voiceless) as the reflex of **ṣ́*.

e. Velarized laterals are known to have lost their lateral component in some languages, for example Polish, where *ł* is realized as *w*; Sicilian Albanian (*vaya* for Standard Albanian *valla*); or sporadic instances in English (*would* corresponding to German *wollte*). The pharyngealized lateral postulated for Semitic in (d) above seems to have undergone a similar change in early Aramaic, probably yielding a uvular fricative. Thus Semitic **'arṣ́-* would have become Aramaic **'rγ*.

f. Because there was no symbol for a uvular fricative in the northern Semitic alphabet then in use, early Aramaic used the symbol for the uvular **q* for it.

g. The skewing (see page 30) seen in Syriac ܓܚܟ *g̱ḥak* = Arabic ضحك *ḍaḥika* 'laugh' confirms a voiced consonant toward the back of the mouth.

h. Most instances of the uvular fricative resulting from *ś merged with *ʿ, just as the reflex of *γ did in most of Semitic. By the time of Biblical Aramaic, conventional spellings with *q* alternated with phonetic spellings with ʿ, as in אַרְקָא *ʾarqā* alternating with אַרְעָא *ʾarʿā*, both spellings attested in Jeremiah 10:11.

i. Occasional Aramaic reflexes with *ṣ*, as in Syriac ܨܡܕ *ṣmad* = Arabic ضَمَدَ *ḍamada* 'bind up', are either borrowings from non-Aramaic languages or instances of an alternative shift of *ś, merging with *ṣ as in Hebrew and Akkadian.

Nevertheless, such extrapolation has its limitations. It is not always possible to forge such chains of inferences, nor is it always possible to convince other scholars of their validity. The reading traditions, too, are problematic; not only are there variant reading traditions in some cases, but the traditions often stem from periods when the "classical" language was ceasing to be spoken and (like the English, German, and Italian traditional pronunciations of Latin) may reflect the languages of those carrying on the tradition.

Even when we have older transcriptions, we are limited by the lack of phonetic training of the transcriber and by the foreigner's limited knowledge of the language. In addition, we may not be sure of exactly how, for example, Greek was pronounced at the time. Thus we need to be careful in using phonetic evidence from languages not spoken today.

Morphology and Syntax

Some linguistic traditions separate morphology and syntax; others merge them. If they are kept separate, it is because morphology is concerned with units of form and meaning—*morphemes*—which combine to make words, while syntax is concerned with the arrangement of words to form phrases, clauses, and so on. If they are merged, it is because both deal with the arrangement of units of form and meaning to build higher-order units—morphemes building words, words building phrases, phrases building clauses, clauses building sentences, sentences building paragraphs, etc. We will distinguish MORPHOLOGY and SYNTAX, but treat them in a single section because of their relationship.

Morphemes

The MORPHEME is an indivisible unit that consists of a phonetic signal and a signaled meaning or function. These are combined in identifiable patterns to form words. Thus the Arabic word كَلْبَتُكُم *kalbatukum* 'your bitch' may be segmented *kalb-* 'dog' + *-at-* 'feminine' + *-u-* 'nominative' + *-k-* '2d-person possessive' + *-um* 'masculine plural possessor'.

It is common to distinguish between BOUND morphemes, which, like the Hebrew plural marker ◌ִים *-īm* or the Arabic noun stem شَمْس *šams-* 'sun', always occur attached to another morpheme; and FREE morphemes, which, like Geʿez ቤት *bēt* 'house', may occur independently. Somewhat more useful in Semitic is a distinction between AFFIXES, morphemes that are attached to other units, and BASES, the units to which they are attached. We will not worry too much about INDECLINABLES, units that stand on their own. In such an analysis, a base may consist of a single morpheme (like Arabic شَمْس *šams-* 'sun') or be complex, like Arabic تَتَكَلَّم *tatakallamu* 'you speak', which already consists of five morphemes, but serves as a base to which an object marker like *-hā* 'it (f.)' may be attached.

Formally, affixes may be divided into:

SUFFIXES: morphemes attached at the end of another morpheme, like the Hebrew plural marker *-īm* in נוּרִים *nūr-īm* 'lights' < נוּר *nūr* 'light'.

PREFIXES: morphemes attached at the beginning of another morpheme, like the Syriac causative marker *’a-* in ܐܠܒܫ *’a-lbiš* 'dress' < ܠܒܫ *lbiš* 'wear'.

INFIXES: morphemes sandwiched inside another morpheme, like the Arabic intransitive marker *-t-* in اِرْتَفَعَ *ir-t-afaʿa* 'rise' < رَفَعَ *rafaʿa* 'raise'.

Functionally, it is conventional to divide affixes into INFLECTIONAL and DERIVATIONAL. Inflectional morphemes are highly productive, are highly predictable in terms of form and meaning, tend to occur at the boundaries of words, tend to mark grammatical relationships, and usually do not change part of speech. Derivational morphemes are less productive, may be highly unpredictable in terms of form and meaning, will often occur in the interior of complex words, mark differences of meaning, and frequently change the part of speech to which the word belongs.

Thus, taking our examples from Akkadian:

Inflection: *bēl* 'lord' >

bēlu	⸢cuneiform⸣	'lord (nominative)'
bēla	⸢cuneiform⸣	'lord (accusative)'
bēlka	⸢cuneiform⸣	'your lord'
bēlēku	⸢cuneiform⸣	'I am lord'
bēlū	⸢cuneiform⸣	'lords (nominative)'

Derivation: *bēl* 'lord' >

bēltu	⸢cuneiform⸣	'mistress'
bēlūtu	⸢cuneiform⸣	'lordship'
ba’ūlu	⸢cuneiform⸣	'great'
bēlu	⸢cuneiform⸣	'rule'
bu’’ulu	⸢cuneiform⸣	'make powerful'

Unfortunately, the inflectional/derivational distinction is not very useful, because it is hard to apply logically and consistently. Arabic noun pluralization (usually assumed to be inflectional) is highly unpredictable and often involves infixation or multiple affixes; the formation of Arabic *nisbe* adjectives is quite productive and predictable, involving a single suffix, but would usually be classed as derivational. Rather than using any set of criteria to distinguish which term is appropriate, you will find it more practical to examine several grammars to see to which category a phenomenon is conventionally assigned.

Words

Somewhat surprisingly, there is no standard and satisfactory definition for *word*. Roughly, a word is the smallest unit that a speaker is willing to say on its own. If we try to get more specific, different languages have many different ways of building words and identifying units as words. And different linguists working on the same language may come up with different criteria.

A special problem is the status of CLITICS, words that cannot normally stand alone, but must precede (PROCLITICS) or follow (ENCLITICS) another word. In some cases, where we have to deal with CLITICIZED variants of independent words, analysis is relatively simple. The CONSTRUCT forms of nouns in many Semitic languages are simply forms modified by being accentually bound to a following word: in Hebrew יַד הָאִישׁ *yad ha’īš* 'the man's hand' we see a shortening of independent יָד *yād* 'hand'.

With a word like Arabic مِن *min* 'from', which is not found without an object, it is more difficult to determine whether it should be treated as a clitic word or an affix. A useful criterion is mobility—affixes attach to the word to which they relate grammatically, whereas clitics may be phonologically linked to another word. Thus the Arabic definite marker أَل *al-* is a prefix which may not be separated from its nominal, whereas the clitic مِن *min* may be separated by, for example, a demonstrative: مِن هٰذَا ٱلْـبَيْت *min hāδā lbayti* 'from this house'. This criterion, however, is not perfect: the Arabic future marker سَوْفَ *sawfa*, with accentually reduced alternant سَـ *sa*, is probably best analyzed as a clitic but seems never to be separated from the following verb.

Words are grouped on the basis of grammatical behavior into several PARTS OF SPEECH. The number of these and the precise definitions vary from language to language. The following are typical categories with generic descriptions:

NOUNS (or SUBSTANTIVES): words that typically function as subject or object in a clause, as the head of a nominal phrase, or in equational nonverbal predication.

ADJECTIVES: words that typically function as qualifiers of nouns or in descriptive nonverbal predication. In Semitic languages, DEMONSTRATIVES and NUMERALS are frequently formally differentiated from most adjectives.

NOMINALS: a cover term including nouns and adjectives. In many Semitic languages, there is no clear-cut difference in form or function. Words primarily functioning as modifiers may be used as if nouns, and words normally used as nouns may be found modifying another noun. In such cases, we group the two together as nominals.

PRONOUNS: words used as substitutes for nouns.

VERBS: words typically used as predicators. Note that while nouns and adjectives can serve as predicates, verbs will not usually function as subjects, objects, or modifiers.

ADVERBS: words used typically to modify verbs or adjectives. They often formally resemble or are related to nominals.

PREPOSITIONS/POSTPOSITIONS: words used typically with a noun to build adverbial phrases. If the item precedes the noun, it is called a PREPOSITION; if it follows, it is a POSTPOSITION. These words are often formally related to adverbs.

CONJUNCTIONS: words typically used to link words, phrases, or clauses into larger units, or to mark relationships between clauses.

Word Marking

In most if not all languages, words are marked to make their functions and interrelationships more explicit. In Semitic languages, nouns are typically marked for CASE. Verbs are marked for TENSE, ASPECT, and MOOD. Nouns, verbs, and adjectives bear CONCORD markings. Other parts of speech, such as adverbs and conjunctions, are typically unmarked.

It is important to recognize a distinction between the semantic categories marked and the affixal, clitic, or positional markings. Rarely is there a one-to-one relationship. In Ge'ez, *-a* suffixed to a noun marks both OBJECT and POSSESSED, but the object is marked both by the presence of the suffix and by its position relative to verb and subject. The categories discussed below are semantic; the ways they are marked, with affixes, clitics, or position, will vary considerably from one language to another.

CASE: a category normally marked on nouns, also marked through concord on adjectives. Case involves relationships between noun and verb or noun and noun. The distinctions between SUBJECT and OBJECT and between POSSESSOR and POSSESSED are apparently made in all languages.

TENSE/ASPECT: categories normally marked on verbs. Both deal with temporal relationships; as a result, they are often confused. The confusion is increased by the fact that they are often similarly marked. Whereas TENSE indicates a reference time prior to, simultaneous with, or subsequent to the present (PAST, PRESENT, and FUTURE tense, respectively), ASPECT specifies how the action time relates to the reference time. Thus in the Arabic كَانَ يَكْتُبُ *kāna yaktubu* 'he was writing', *kāna* marks tense, placing the reference time in the past, while *yaktubu* marks aspect, specifying the action as continuing after the reference time.

MOOD: a category normally marked on verbs. Mood generally marks the verb as appropriate to a particular type of clause. Thus the Akkadian *šuṭur* 'write' is used in direct commands, *išṭur* 'he wrote' in independent clauses, and *išṭuru* 'he wrote' in subordinate clauses.

CONCORD (or AGREEMENT): a category marked on several parts of speech. Nouns are divided into a number of sets, which may relate to meaning but do not always: the relationship between Arabic مُعَلِّم *muʿallim* 'male teacher' and مُعَلِّمَة *muʿallimaᵗ* 'female teacher' is not the same as that between مَكْتَب *maktab* 'office' and مَكْتَبَة *maktabaᵗ* 'library'. The nouns are usually marked to indicate which set they belong to, but are not always: Arabic مُعَلِّمَة *muʿallim-aᵗ* 'female teacher' and شَمْس *šams* 'sun' belong to the same set, feminine singular. Other words (usually including adjectives and verbs) bear markings to specify the set of the noun referred to.

Phrases

A phrase is a unit made up of one or more words, having a head (normally a noun or verb) and its modifiers. We may classify phrases by function.

NOUN PHRASE: a phrase functioning as a noun. The head is a nominal; modifiers include adjectives and nouns marked as possessives.

ADJECTIVE PHRASE: a phrase functioning as an adjective. The head is a nominal; modifiers include adverbs.

VERB PHRASE: a phrase whose head is a verb, functioning as a predication. Modifiers include subjects, objects, and adverbs. In many languages, subjects are considered to be outside the verb phrase; but in most Semitic languages, subjects in their unmarked position are best analyzed as within the verb phrase. Some languages differentiate two or more types of object.

ADVERBIAL PHRASE: a phrase functioning as an adverb. The head may be an adverb; in many cases it is a noun with a preposition or postposition. In either case, the head may be modified by an adverb.

Clauses

A clause is a unit made up of one or more phrases, including a predication and (usually) a subject. While languages vary as to what types of clause need to be recognized, the following are common.

INDEPENDENT CLAUSE: a clause that could stand by itself as the only clause in a sentence. Thus Arabic رَأَيْتُ أَخِي *raʾaytu ʾaxī* 'I saw my brother' is an independent clause.

CONSECUTIVE CLAUSE: a clause marking the second or subsequent action in a chain of events, semantically coordinate with an independent clause, but so marked by choice of verb form, deletion of subject, or otherwise that it could not stand alone. Thus in Hebrew וַיִּבֶן מִגְדָּלִים *wayyiben migdālīm* 'and he built towers' would not initiate a narrative.

SUBORDINATE CLAUSE: a clause functioning as a component of another clause. Such clauses may function as nouns, adjectives, or adverbs. An example is Geʿez ዘሞተ። *za-mōta* 'he who died', which may function as subject or object, or modify a noun.

QUOTATIVE CLAUSES: a quotation resembles a subordinate clause in that it functions as a component of another clause; normally it will be the object of a verb involving speech or thought. Quotatives differ from subordinate clauses in that they are usually restricted to specific positions in the sentence and may be composed of several sentences.

Hierarchy

Languages have a hierarchical structure such that units may include embedded within them units of equal or even greater rank. Consider a Syriac noun phrase consisting of a noun modified by an adjective:

ܡܠܟܐ ܛܒܐ

malkā ṭābā   'the good king'

The adjective may be replaced by a possessive that consists of the particle *d-* followed by a noun:

ܡܠܟܐ ܕܐܪܥܐ

malkā d-ʾarʿā   'the king of the land'

The possessor noun may be replaced by a noun phrase:

ܡܠܟܐ ܕܐܪܥܐ ܫܦܝܪܬܐ

malkā d-ʾarʿā šappīrtā   'the king of the beautiful land'

The adjective modifying the possessor noun may be replaced by an adjectival clause:

ܡܠܟܐ ܕܐܪܥܐ ܕܙܟܗ

malkā d-ʾarʿā da-zkāh   'the king of the land which he conquered'

For greater complexity, we add a subject noun phrase (including an adjective) and an adverbial clause to the adjectival clause:

ܡܠܟܐ ܕܐܪܥܐ ܕܙܟܐܘܗ ܦܠܚܐ ܚܝܠܬܢܐ ܟܕ ܐܬܘ

malkā d-ʾarʿā da-zkaʾūh pālḥē   'the king of the land which the mighty
  ḥayltānē kad ʾitaw*   soldiers conquered when they came'

In theory, we could go on to even greater levels of complexity. However, while there is no theoretical limit, practical considerations for speaker and listener keep levels of embedding relatively low.

Besides this, there is structuring beyond the clause level. Clauses may be arranged to form paragraphs, which have their own linguistic and logical structure, and paragraphs likewise are conjoined to form complete discourses. Studies of structure beyond the level of the clause are still rare and hardly ever enter into comparative discussions.

Part 2

A General Introduction to the Semitic Language Family

Unto Shem also, the father of all the children of Eber, the brother of Japheth the elder, even to him were children born.

—*Genesis 10:21*

What Is a Semitic Language?

At one level, "what is a Semitic language?" is a trivial question. Of the language families of the world, Semitic is one of the least controversial. The strong similarities between Hebrew, "Chaldee,"* Syriac, and Arabic (all Central Semitic languages) had been recognized at least since the Middle Ages. A. L. Schlözer originated the label *Semitic* in 1781, by which time the family was known to include Phoenician and Geʿez; Sabean, Soqotri, Akkadian, and Urmi were added by the middle of the next century. Remarkably, there do not seem to have been any disputed cases—no non-Semitic languages falsely included, or Semitic languages whose relationship was not readily accepted. Practically speaking, it might seem that we have a well-defined language family, readily distinguishable even from its nearer relatives in Afroasiatic.

We do not need to be concerned about the circularity involved. We are, to be sure, saying in effect that Hebrew, Aramaic, Arabic, Geʿez, Sabean, Soqotri, Akkadian, and Ugaritic are Semitic languages, and then defining Semitic as the set of languages whose grammatical and lexical features are more closely related to these languages than to any other. We assume that they share a common ancestor, whose characteristics we deduce from the presumed descendants, and then define a Semitic language as one that seems to be derived from that ancestor. But while we may frown on circular reasoning, it often works well enough, and the history of linguistic classification is full of cases where formal study has simply confirmed what was abundantly obvious to the eye.

If we do not assume Semitic status as a given, however, but attempt to delimit the Semitic family on a formal basis, we run into problems. When we look for diagnostic grammatical and

---

* *Chaldee* was the name given to the language of the parts of the Jewish scriptures that are not in Hebrew—portions of Ezra and Daniel and a few words elsewhere—and of various rabbinic writings; these, like Syriac, are now identified as forms of Aramaic, but the term *Aramaic* did not come into use in this sense until early in the 19th century.

19

lexical features that can be used to define a Semitic language, to differentiate Semitic from the remainder of Afroasiatic, we do not find them.

The Semitic languages do, indeed, share many grammatical features; but Ghadamsi, a Berber language (Afroasiatic, but not Semitic) shares more of these features with Classical Arabic (Semitic) than Chaha (an Ethiopic language) shares with Urmi (Neo-Aramaic). Chaha is linked with other Ethiopic languages by regular sound correspondence, by morphology, and by lexicon. Urmi is similarly linked with other Aramaic languages. Ghadamsi, on the other hand, is clearly part of Berber. Unless we choose to overlook the important differences which set Berber in general apart from Semitic in general, we cannot use features common to Ghadamsi and Arabic to define Semitic. Nor can features absent in Ghadamsi and Urmi be taken as diagnostic.

So, it comes to this. The most typical Semitic languages are easily recognizable as a coherent group, not for any particular features but by a gestalt compounded of phonological, morphological, and lexical elements. This is adequate to differentiate them from Berber, Cushitic, and other Afroasiatic groups, though no single feature or simple complex of features can be specified. The languages most drastically changed from the classic Semitic pattern, such as Urmi and Chaha, remain recognizable as Semitic. Their connection with other Aramaic and Ethiopian Semitic languages, respectively, may be established formally through their links in grammar and lexicon. But this connection is also clear when they are examined informally by someone familiar with the gestalt of classic Semitic.

Can there be a Semitic language that does not fit the pattern? Can a language descended from the common Semitic ancestor lose or modify enough features that it could not be recognized? If such a language existed, we might need to decide whether or not to include it and might need to come up with some principled criteria. Cases similar to Juba Arabic, a pidgin or creole used in Southern Sudan, with mostly Arabic lexicon but with greatly modified morphology, do exist. But pidgins generally pose a problem for the classifier and may best be excluded from any of the language families that have contributed to their structures.

Until a descendant of Proto-Semitic becomes unrecognizable and unless we uncover a language precisely intermediate between Semitic and Berber, we are entitled to keep things simple and recognize the Semitic status of our languages, even while admitting that we do not know what makes them Semitic.

Internal Relationships

Within Semitic we may recognize the following branches: Akkadian (Assyrian, Babylonian), Aramaic (Syriac, Mandaic, Samaritan, etc.; Ma'lula, Ṭur 'Abdin, Urmi, etc.), Canaanite (Ugaritic; Hebrew, Phoenician, etc.), North Arabian (Arabic, Thamudic, Safaitic, etc.; Moroccan, Sudanese, Iraqi, etc.), Ethiopic (Ge'ez; Tigre, Amharic, Chaha, etc.); Old South Arabian (Sabean, Minean, Qatabanian, etc.); Modern South Arabian (Soqoṭri, Meḥri, Jibbali, etc.). Modern South Arabian seems to be a separate branch, not a continuation of Old South Arabian, though the absence of modern material from Old South Arabian and ancient from Modern South Arabian makes it difficult to be certain.

With a few exceptions (the status of the boundary between Canaanite and Aramaic, the proper placement of Ugaritic, and the affiliations of Eblaite), these branches are as little in dispute as the Semitic family itself. Some difficulty arises, however, if one attempts to establish groupings intermediate between Semitic as a whole and the seven branches. There have been several different groupings. Most recognize a primary division between East Semitic (Akkadian) and West Semitic (the remaining branches). Most likewise split West Semitic into northern and southern subgroups. The two main classifications of this type are shown in the outline:

a. SEMITIC
    EAST SEMITIC   Akkadian
    WEST SEMITIC
        SOUTH SEMITIC   Arabic
                                    Ethiopic
                                    Old South Arabian
                                    Modern South Arabian
        NORTHWEST SEMITIC   Aramaic
                                    Canaanite

b. SEMITIC
    EAST SEMITIC   Akkadian
    WEST SEMITIC
        SOUTH SEMITIC   Ethiopic
                                    Old South Arabian
                                    Modern South Arabian
        CENTRAL SEMITIC   Aramaic
                                    Canaanite
                                    Arabic

The two schemes are, in fact, in agreement except on the issue of Arabic. The rather conservative phonetic structure of Arabic makes it appear closer to the southern languages than to the phonologically much-altered Hebrew and Aramaic. Its lexical affinities also point to the south. In morphology, however, Arabic is somewhat nearer to the northern languages, which may explain why most recent groupings are of the second type.

It is not only in the placement of Arabic that phonological, morphological, and lexical criteria point in different directions. Either subgrouping is vulnerable at many points. Even if one of them reflects the historical facts, the separation of the branches took place at an early period, and the seven groups have interacted and affected one another for millennia. It might be preferable to reject levels of relationship between Semitic and its branches and see early Semitic as a cluster of seven dialects gradually diverging. We would then attribute the similarities between Canaanite and Aramaic, or Ethiopic and Old South Arabian, to proximity and diffusion. Even the primary division into East and West Semitic, though the differences that support it are numerous, could be challenged. Modern South Arabian, though it shares some features with Ethiopic and Old South Arabian and has been heavily influenced by Arabic, may be as distinct as Akkadian.

External Relationships

Semitic is part of a larger family that has come to be known as Afroasiatic, a name suggested by Joseph Greenberg in 1950. The family was earlier known as Hamito-Semitic, and some people still use that term, as well as Semito-Hamitic, but it is becoming rarer. Part of the reason is that the older grouping Hamitic covered all but one of the Afroasiatic subgroups, the remaining group being Semitic. But there is no clear set of features defining the "Hamitic" subgroups as a unit, except that scholarship worked with Semitic first.

Six main branches are commonly recognized: Berber, Chadic, Cushitic, Egyptian, Omotic, and Semitic. Omotic is the most distinctive, most distantly related, most recently identified, and most disputed—some scholars still prefer to class it as Western Cushitic. Across the other branches, the structural similarities are easy to spot. Except for Omotic, most languages show a gender-based concord system, with a feminine marker reconstructible as *t* in both the nominal and the verbal system, and clearly related pronominal systems. Except for Omotic and Chadic, most languages show related systems of verbal derivation based on transitivity. Most languages show three series of stops corresponding to the Semitic voiceless, voiced, and emphatic, and most have (or show signs of having had) a number of postvelar consonants. Lexical similarities are relatively few and usually only extend across two or three of the branches, though some names of body parts occur in five of the six.

The subclassification of Afroasiatic is not agreed on any more than that of Semitic. It is clear that Omotic is only distantly related to the remainder. Semitic seems perhaps the second most distantly related. There is some reason to suspect a special relationship between Berber and Chadic, but except for the special case of Omotic, the branches of Afroasiatic could be seen as parallel divisions with no intermediate groupings.

There is a typological contrast between Berber, Egyptian, and Semitic (the three northern branches), and the southern branches, Chadic, Cushitic, Omotic: the southern languages show relatively full vowel systems, tonal contrasts, and roots of varied length that normally include a vowel; the northern languages generally have (or can be reconstructed as having had) three underlying vowels, no tonal contrasts (though stress apparently has been important), and typically triconsonantal roots that at least in the verbal system seem not to include vowels.

The question remains unresolved: Do these features of the northern languages reflect the original state of Afroasiatic? or an innovation shared by Semitic, Egyptian, and Berber that would justify recognizing them as a distinct subgroup? or a localized innovation that spread across linguistic boundaries? Of course, the same could be asked about the distinctive features of the southern groups. Given the apparently closer relationship of Chadic and Berber, and the very distinct status of Omotic, one might conclude that the three northern groups lost vocalic and perhaps tonal distinctions under the influence of a strong stress accent and that this took place after the branches were well differentiated.

Part 3

An Outline of Comparative Linguistics

Sources and Their Use

The computer programmer's GIGO axiom (Garbage In, Garbage Out) applies to linguistic comparison as well. Without adequate and accurate data, the best of techniques cannot hope to produce valid conclusions. The Semitic languages are among the best-documented language groups, equaled by few for quantity and quality of available data. But there are problems.

Perhaps the greatest frustration is the great disparity of documentation. Compare the wealth of literature on Akkadian with what we know of Phoenician or Nabatean. Among modern languages, the coverage of Arabic dialects is many times more thorough than the coverage of modern Aramaic or Ethiopic. In compiling vocabularies for comparative study, we are limited by the small extant vocabularies of several languages. When we wish to compare grammatical patterns, we are hindered by the scarcity of, for example, 2d-person feminine forms in ancient inscriptions. In some cases, we must extract vocabulary from a grammar or collection of texts because there is no published glossary. In others, our only source for grammatical features is the examples in a dictionary.

The factor of time depth is another problem. For some languages, like Ugaritic, we have only data millennia old; for others, like some Gurage dialects, we can find nothing prior to the latter half of the twentieth century. Our sources for Hebrew, for example, include several stages in the development of the language, which are not always kept separate from one another; in the case of Gafat, the materials come from a single period. How much easier the task would be if all Semitic subgroups were like Aramaic, with fair to good documentation of several dialects from each of three or more periods! How valid is it to base comparisons on Old South Arabian, with only ancient documentation, and Modern South Arabian, with only modern sources?

Then there is the far-from-trivial factor of writing systems. How are we to compare data from Akkadian, which records vowels with some reliability but does not clearly differentiate all consonants, with Sabean material, which records consonants but no vowels except in occasional non-Sabean transcriptions? If we are working from transcription, how fair is it to compare a mechanical transliteration like the one that is conventional for Mandaic, a more detailed transcription informed by the reading tradition as is normal for Geʿez, and a transcription such as is common in Akkadian which is far removed from the original shape? In working with Samaritan Aramaic, should we base our conclusions on the written text or the traditional pronunciation?

For the ancient languages in particular, there may be great discrepancy between sources. A Sabean inscription has to be read (and may be read differently by different scholars) and then translated (and interpreters will often disagree). Since there are no modern Sabean speakers to whom to appeal, we cannot determine which is correct. The equivalent problem for the modern languages may be illustrated from Modern Aramaic. One article may give us data on the verbal system but few nouns; if another scholar has written on the noun (saying little about verbs) in a closely related dialect, how legitimate is it to conflate the two? Again, in working with Hebrew, should we mix data from biblical and medieval sources?

Finally, there are the problems of grammatical and lexicographic traditions. A Phoenician grammar written by a Hebrew scholar, a Sabean grammar written by an Arabist, and an Amharic grammar written by a transformationalist will present different material in different arrangements, using different terminology. Even paradigmatic tables, if they are included, will be arranged differently. To compile comparative vocabularies, using only romanized material from Akkadian, Ugaritic, Geʿez, Jibbali, and Maʿlula, one must work with five distinct alphabetic sequences, remembering which dictionaries group words by root and which simply alphabetize.

There are a few principles that can make the process easier.

- FLEXIBILITY: If you are aiming for a 100-word comparative list, begin with 150 entries to allow for items that need to be dropped. If you want Tigre as your representative of modern Ethiopic, be prepared to switch to Amharic if you find you cannot locate enough of the type of material you need.

- ECONOMY: Since the size and complexity of a comparative study will be limited by the least-documented languages, do not begin by comparing the two best-documented. First extract all available information from your smallest sources.

- UNDERSTANDING: Before using a source for comparative purposes, get to know it. How is it arranged? What does it include and exclude? How does its transcription system compare with other sources? Practice locating information in it.

- REDUNDANCY: Whenever practical, consult multiple sources for each language. One will make up for deficiencies in the other.

- JUDGMENT: Check alternative sources for compatibility and accuracy. Use the most complete, up-to-date, and reliable sources available, recognizing that in some cases the most up-to-date may not also be the most reliable.

- FAIRNESS: Avoid the temptation to choose between alternatives on the basis of how well one suits your needs. The word drawn from a source because it matches entries from other languages may well reflect the author's misinterpretation.

Assumptions and Techniques of Diachronic Linguistics

All linguistic techniques may be reduced to a comparison of two sounds, two words, two symbols, two sentences, two paradigms, or whatever, and a determination of their similarities and differences. If we compare Arabic كَتَبَ *kataba* 'he wrote'/ يَكْتُبُ *yaktubu* 'he writes'/ اُكْتُب *uktub* 'write!' and determine that they share formally كتب *ktb* and semantically 'writing' and that they differ in prefixes, suffixes, and vocalic infixes correlated with meanings of 'past time', 'present time', and 'command', we are doing exactly what is needed for most of the techniques of diachronic linguistics.

We assume that patterned similarities between languages are not accidental. We assume three possible explanations, once chance is ruled out: mutual influence, parallel development from a similar base, or a common ancestor. It is not always easy to distinguish the three; in some cases we need to look to all three to explain the similarities between two languages. Thus, if we compare Semitic and Berber, we find some similarities that we may explain as being due to contact, such as Arabic loanwords in Berber and the reduction of short vowels in Moroccan Arabic. We further find that, in Berber and some parts of Semitic, a definite article arose that later came to be simply a marker of nominals; this developed independently long after Semitic and Berber were distinct. On the other hand, such features as the gender system, the inflectional and derivational morphology of the verb, and some basic vocabulary are shared through inheritance from Proto-Afroasiatic.

The principal techniques we will apply to Semitic data are as follows:

- LEXICOSTATISTICS: judging linguistic relationship by frequency of shared features, usually vocabulary.
- RECONSTRUCTION: deducing probable structures and morpheme shapes of an earlier stage of the language from regular correspondences across languages.
- INTERNAL RECONSTRUCTION: deducing probable structures and morpheme shapes of an earlier stage of the language from the morphophonemic processes of the language itself.
- LOAN ANALYSIS: deducing linguistic contacts and their timing relative to linguistic changes from borrowed vocabulary.
- LINGUISTIC GEOGRAPHY: mapping the distribution of linguistic features and drawing conclusions as to contacts and population movements.
- CULTURAL RECONSTRUCTION: drawing conclusions regarding the culture and environment of the speakers of an ancestral language from the reconstructible vocabulary.

The order in which these techniques are listed above, and in which they will be discussed, is not necessarily the order in which one will apply them in normal practice. In practice, they are applied in any order. Many linguists prefer not to practice lexicostatistics; some will never make formal reconstructions. In many cases, a spiral approach is useful: one may begin with a lexicostatistical analysis for rough determination of internal groupings, reconstruct major features of the protolanguage, map the distribution of diagnostic innovations, carry out internal reconstructions of major systems in several languages, refine one's reconstructions, and base a new lexicostatistical count on the insights gained. The order in which we will present the techniques is chosen because it gives a logical progression for the learner from the simple cognacy judgments of lexicostatistics through the process of making reconstructions to the more complex logic necessary in internal reconstruction. The remaining three techniques are placed last because they are less commonly practiced.

Most of what the diachronic linguist does—and most of what the comparative Semitist does—is technically linguistic prehistory: making deductions about what might have occurred, not recording what did occur. The comparative linguist, like Pygmalion, often comes to love what he has created and forgets that only the raw data are real. As some protection against the temptation to believe that one's analysis is a true statement and not a highly oversimplified story, we apply several techniques. If all or most yield similar results, then we may think of those results as highly likely. But if no two agree, we will not take the results seriously.

The Linguistic List

Vocabulary lists supply the raw material for most of the techniques we will use. It is, of course, possible to compare anything. One can (and does) compare phonological systems, or inflectional markers; one can (and does) compare syntactic patterns. But vocabulary is most often the focus because of the large number of items available and the manageable size of the items.

The total number of units in any phonological system is small; in the Semitic languages, the total for a specific language may be as low as 20 or as high as 35. Each unit is a single phoneme. An inflectional system is rather more complex; a Semitic verbal system will involve approximately 50 units, each being a morpheme of one or two syllables. We can increase this number somehat by comparing inflectional patterns involving more than one morpheme. This greater size, however, is offset by the frequency of irregular developments in inflectional morphemes. Syntactic units are even more numerous (though the precise count would vary with the analytic approach) and involve multiword units. But the stability of syntactic patterns over time is at least as low as that of inflectional morphology.

Lexicon, on the other hand, is open-ended and has the added advantage of being one of the first types of information collected when a new language is described. The units are long enough and varied enough to give a good basis for comparison, and their shapes are specific enough and constant enough to allow confident reconstruction even over greater periods of time.

We must begin, therefore, by making wordlists that can then be evaluated. Vocabulary compilation is usually a matter of selection. The available lexicon of even relatively poorly documented languages can be too large for convenient analysis. Most of the lists we will use will consist of between 100 and 300 items per language. A list of 1000 items, except when dealing with a small number of closely related languages, is beginning to be impractical.

The choice of items to be included will depend on the technique to be applied; the discussion of each technique will include a description of the ideal list for that technique. The availability of material is also a consideration. In the case of Semitic, some ancient languages are known to us from a rather small corpus of texts, and the topics covered even in a large corpus may be restricted. Some of the modern languages, likewise, are represented in the literature only by short grammatical sketches or travelers' vocabularies. In both cases, certain very important areas of vocabulary may not be attested.

The selection of languages to be represented is also important. Quantitatively, the more languages included, the more difficult the analysis. It is very difficult to compile and process a group of even 50 languages. On the other hand, if too few languages are included, there is a loss of time depth. Qualitatively, if the languages are too closely or too distantly related, it will be difficult to get meaningful results. Again, different techniques may require very different data.

Cognacy and Regularity

We need to understand the concepts of cognacy, regularity, and skewing before we can evaluate our lists. At the simplest level, judging that two items are cognate merely assumes that they have—somewhere, somehow—a common origin. In practice, definitions of cognacy are greatly

---

Exercise 1. Compiling Vocabularies

Although we have provided fairly extensive vocabularies that will serve as the basis for most of the practical exercises, it is important that you see for yourself what is involved in compiling such lists. Your instructor will assign you (or you will choose) three Semitic languages. The choice of languages will be based on your interests and the availability of appropriate documentation. The lexical resources you use will vary in size and arrangement. Probably at least one will be available to you only in a one-directional glossary or dictionary. The language into which the Semitic words are translated will vary. You may need to make your own transliterations.

Compile a comparative listing, alphabetized by English gloss, of 50 entries per language. Your instructor may choose to limit your semantic range to body parts, verbs of motion, or the like. You should end with exactly one entry per gloss per language. Pick the most appropriate word where there are multiple possibilities; for example, given Arabic ساق *sāq* and رِجْل *rijl* as alternatives for 'foot', you must make a principled choice (flipping a coin to ensure randomness is principled). It will also be necessary for you to eliminate glosses when you cannot, for example, find a Phoenician word for 'finger'.

Write a narrative to accompany your wordlist. Record the process; note any problems you encountered, and your solutions. Give your reasons for each choice between alternatives. Record glosses rejected. Discuss your finished wordlist and narrative with your instructor.

---

varied. Some studies are quite restrictive, recognizing as cognate only semantically equivalent items that show point-by-point regular correspondence in form and then only where borrowing is ruled out. By this standard, Hebrew אֹזֶן *'ōzen* 'ear' and Syriac ܐܕܢܐ *'idnā* 'ear' would not be cognate because of the unpredictable difference in vocalization. Others will recognize as cognate any two items that have some similarity in meaning and shape; in extreme cases, Arabic سَبْعَة *sab'aᵗ* 'seven' and English *seven* could be considered cognate.

In most cases, a moderate, somewhat flexible standard of cognacy is desirable. We generally restrict cognacy to items whose similarity in form and meaning is too great to be due to chance and where borrowing and onomatopoeia can be ruled out. While much rests of necessity on the linguist's judgment and cannot be quantified, regularity of correspondence, which *is* quantifiable, is an important factor.

Due to the nature of linguistic change, where two languages have developed from a single source, there will be patterns of correspondence. In some cases there will be correspondences that involve phonetic identity; that is, some sounds that correspond will be the same in both languages. We find, for example, that where Akkadian and Arabic have words similar in shape and meaning, as in Table 4, *m* in Akkadian will generally be matched by *m* in Arabic.

In other cases, there will not be phonetic identity, but there will be phonemic identity; that is, the corresponding sounds will not be identical but will fit into the sound systems of the languages in the same way. Comparing Arabic and Jibbali in Table 5, we find that Jibbali *ḳ* (a velar

Table 4. Phonetic Identity

	Akkadian	Arabic
blood	*dāmu*	*dam*
eight	*samānat*	*θamāniya*
leopard	*nimru*	*namir*
sun	*šamšu*	*šams*
water	*mū*	*mā'*

Table 5. Phonemic Identity

	Arabic	Jibbali
cut	*qaṭaʿa*	*ḳétaʿ*
fall	*saqaṭa*	*šɔ́ḳɔ́ṭ*
leaf	*waraqa*	*érɛ́ḳt*
lightning	*barq*	*bɛrḳ*
tomb	*qabr*	*ḳɔ̄r*

Table 6. Neither Phonetic nor Phonemic Identity

	Arabic	Syriac
careful	*ḥafīẓ*	*ḥpīṭā*
gazelle	*ẓaby*	*ṭabyā*
guard/watch	*naẓara*	*nṭar*
nail	*ẓifr*	*ṭiprā*
oppress	*ẓalama*	*ṭlam*
carry off	*xaẓifa*	*ḥṭap*

Table 7. Conditioned Correspondences

	Arabic	Syriac
egg	*bayḍa*	*bīʿǝtā*
earth	*'arḍ*	*'arʿā*
molar	*ḍirs*	*ʿaršā*
rib	*ḍilʿ*	*'ilʿā*
hyena	*ḍabʿ*	*'apʿā*
frog	*ḍifdaʿa*	*'urdʿā*

Table 8. Additional Correspondences

	Arabic	Syriac
cut	*qaṭaʿa*	*qṭaʿ*
drive off	*ṭarada*	*ṭrad*
gather	*laqaṭa*	*lqaṭ*
grind	*ṭaḥana*	*ṭḥin*
sin	*xaṭiʾa*	*ḥṭā*
mix	*xalaṭa*	*ḥlaṭ*

ejective) predictably corresponds to Arabic *q* (uvular). While not identical acoustically or in articulation, the two consonants function similarly in their respective phonologies.

One also finds correspondences where there is neither phonetic nor phonemic identity. For example, it will be found that, as in Table 6, where an Arabic word has *ẓ*, a corresponding Syriac word will have *ṭ*. When one finds a number of items showing the same patterned correspondence, one can decide that Arabic *ẓ* : Syriac *ṭ* is a regular correspondence. It is then normal to assume that the two consonants reflect a single element in the phonology of an ancestral language.

How many instances suffice to establish a correspondence as regular? The number chosen is arbitrary. If it is set high, we eliminate many red herrings but may also fail to include some valid information on the protolanguage; if it is set low, we may multiply the number of assumed protophonemes. We usually pick a number between three and five as the minimum.

Table 9. Phonemic vs. Phonetic Correspondences

	Arabic	Syriac		Arabic	Syriac
	d	*d*		*δ*	*d*
bear	*dubb*	*dibbā*	beard	*δiqn*	*daqnā*
blood	*dam*	*dəmā*	fly	*δubāba*	*diββā*
child	*walad*	*yaldā*	gold	*δahab*	*dahəβā*
	d	*δ*		*δ*	*δ*
breast	*θady*	*təδā*	ear	*ʾuδun*	*ʾiδnā*
kid	*jady*	*gaδyā*	lie	*kaδiba*	*kəδaβ*
one	*ʾaḥad*	*ḥaδ*	take	*ʾaxaδa*	*ʾiḥaδ*

Table 10. Pattern Correspondence

	Geʿez	Amharic
bear	*walada*	*wällädä*
hang	*saqala*	*säqqälä*
kick	*ragaṣa*	*räggäṭä*
milk	*ḥalaba*	*alläbä*
sew	*safaya*	*säffa*

The set of data in Table 7 yields two correspondences, Arabic *ḍ* : Syriac *ʿ* and Arabic *ḍ* : Syriac *ʾ*. There are three examples of each, which would allow us to recognize both as regular. Since in this case a single Arabic consonant corresponds to two different sounds in Syriac, we have to determine whether there were originally two sounds, as in Syriac, which merged in Arabic, or one sound, as in Arabic, which split in Syriac.

The determination is made by looking for conditioning. Is there something in the shape of the word—a neighboring vowel, a consonant, stress, syllable structure—that would make it reasonable to assume a split? In Table 7, there is a conditioning factor. Syriac consistently shows *ʾ* instead of *ʿ* corresponding to Arabic *ḍ* when another *ʿ* occurs later in the word. There is no need to postulate another consonant in the protolanguage.

When we compare the data in Table 8 with the data in Table 6, we again find two correspondences that may be taken as regular: Syriac *ṭ* corresponds to Arabic *ṭ* in Table 8 but to Arabic *ẓ* in Table 6. When we look for a conditioning factor for this set of correspondences, we find none. There is nothing in the shapes of the Syriac words containing *ṭ* to support a split in Arabic. We therefore postulate two source consonants, to which we assign the symbols *θ* and *ṭ* respectively. We assign *ṭ* to the set in Table 8 because the languages compared show identical reflexes. While we could use any symbol not already in use for the correspondence *ṭ* : *ẓ*, we pick *θ* to reflect the voicelessness of Syriac *ṭ* and the fricative nature of Arabic *ẓ* (an emphatic dental fricative for many speakers).

The correspondences in Table 9 are more complex. The Syriac forms (here in phonetic transcription rather than phonemic) show conditioning: *δ* appears after a vowel; otherwise the

---

Exercise 2. Discovering Cognates and Correspondences

Wordlist A provides material for your exercises in discriminating cognates and skewed reflexes. You are given a list of 52 glosses with entries for Classical **Ar**abic, **Eg**yptian Arabic, **Su**danese Arabic, **Ge**ʕez, **T**igriny**a**, and **T**igr**e**. All entries are nouns, and singular and plural are given in each case.

List and identify regular correspondences between Classical and Egyptian Arabic, Egyptian and Sudanese Arabic, Geʕez and Tigrinya, or Tigrinya and Tigre. Use three instances of a correspondence as the criterion for regularity.

Using your inventory of regular correspondences, identify the cognates shared by your languages. For this exercise, take one-to-one regular correspondence in stem consonants and vowels as your criterion for cognacy. Ignore gender markings and plurals at this stage. Your report should include an inventory of regular correspondences with supporting evidence, a list of cognates, and a commentary on the process.

---

reflex is *d*. Arabic has *δ* and *d* as phonemically distinct, with no conditioning. We only need to reconstruct two original consonants, *δ (Arabic *δ* : Syriac *d/δ*) and *d (Arabic *d* : Syriac *d/δ*).

As a final example, consider the correspondences in Table 10 between Geʕez and Amharic. Here we see a regular correspondence, not of one phoneme with another, but of one pattern with another. The verbs of this class in Geʕez, with a single medial consonant, correspond to Amharic verbs with a medial geminate in the citation form. This type of regularity is also important in evaluating cognacy.

Skewing

In evaluating cognacy, we must reckon with degrees of similarity. We may find that items in two languages are identical in form and meaning, as in Table 11. Or, as discussed above, we may find them with identical meaning but different shape, where all formal differences are regular, as in Table 12.

Frequently, two languages have items so similar in shape or meaning that we believe the two forms to be historically connected, though they do not show perfect regularity of correspondence. It is appropriate to consider such forms as reflecting the same item in the ancestral language, but we cannot treat them on the same basis as regularly corresponding items. These

Table 11. Identity in Form and Meaning

	Hebrew	Syriac
and	*w-*	*w-*
from	*min*	*min*
he	*hū*	*hū*
hear (imv.)	*šmaʕ*	*šmaʕ*
on	*ʕal*	*ʕal*

Table 12. Difference in Form/ Identity in Meaning

	Hebrew	Syriac
break	*šābar*	*tbar*
three	*šlōšā*	*tlātā*
parable	*māšāl*	*matlā*
garlic	*šūm*	*tūmā*
return	*šāb*	*tāb*

Table 13. Frequent but Unconditioned Skewing

	Hebrew	Syriac
beard	*zāqān*	*daqnā*
milk	*ḥālāb*	*ḥalbā*
river	*nāhār*	*nahrā*
lightning	*bārāq*	*barqā*
parable	*māšāl*	*matlā*
onion	*bāṣāl*	*biṣlā*
meat	*bāśār*	*bisrā*
rain	*māṭār*	*miṭrā*
lip	*śāpā*	*siptā*
wing	*kānāp*	*kinpā*

items, the result of random changes in one language or both, we call SKEWED reflexes of the protoform, borrowing the term from Malcolm Guthrie's treatment of Bantu (*Comparative Bantu*, Farnborough, Eng.: Gregg, 1967–71).

Skewing may be formal, involving replacements of phonological units, metatheses, expansions or truncations, or, frequently in Semitic, changes in the pattern of vowels and root consonants. It may be grammatical (which usually involves differences in shape as well), such as changes in gender or number of nouns, or in the type of verb, or in part of speech. Semantic changes of various types also occur. Some common types of skewing include:

- difference in a consonant: Hebrew בֵּן *bēn*, Syriac ܒܪܐ *brā* 'son'
- difference in a vowel: Hebrew מָטָר *māṭār*, Syriac ܡܛܪܐ *miṭrā* 'rain'
- metathesis: Hebrew נָשַׁךְ *nāšak*, Syriac ܢܟܬ *nkat* 'bite'
- truncation: Hebrew אֶחָד *'eḥad*, Syriac ܚܕ *ḥad* 'one'
- expansion: Hebrew צִפֹּרֶן *sippōren*, Syriac ܛܦܪܐ *ṭiprā* 'nail'
- morphological pattern: Hebrew קַל *qal* (**CaCC**), Syriac ܩܠܝܠ *qallīl* (**CaCCīC**) 'light'
- gender: Hebrew לַיְלָה *laylā* (**f.**), Syriac ܠܝܠܝܐ *līlyā* (**m.**) 'night'
- number: Hebrew שָׁמַיִם *šāmayim*, Syriac ܫܡܝܐ *šmayyā* 'sky'
- verb type: Hebrew הִשְׁתַּעֵל *hišta'ēl*, Syriac ܫܥܠ *š'al* 'cough'
- meaning: Hebrew נָחִיר *nāḥīr* '**nostril**', Syriac ܢܚܝܪܐ *nḥīrā* '**nose**'

There may be two or more types of skewing present, as in Syriac ܦܘܪܬܥܢܐ *purta'nā* / Arabic بُرْغُوث *burγūθ* 'flea', where we see irregular correspondence of *p : b*, differing vocalization, metathesis of the third and fourth consonants, and a suffix in the Syriac that is absent from the Arabic. It may be difficult to decide whether two items are skewed reflexes of a single source item or unrelated. For example, Ge'ez ዝእብ *zǝ'b* 'hyena' could easily be a multiply skewed reflex of the Proto-Semitic item that gives Arabic ضَبُع *ḍab'*. It would involve two consonantal skewings, a vocalic skewing, and a metathesis, all of which are plentifully attested. The only reason we can rule out such an interpretation is the existence of Ge'ez ፀብዕ *ḍǝb'* 'hyena' and Arabic ذِئْب *δi'b* 'wolf'. This allows us to sort out the pairs as Ge'ez ዝእብ *zǝ'b* 'hyena' : Arabic ذِئْب *δi'b* 'wolf', with semantic skewing but regular formal correspondence, and Ge'ez ፀብዕ *ḍǝb'* : Arabic ضَبُع *ḍab'* 'hyena', with identical meaning but skewing in vowel correspondence.

In some cases, a particular type of skewing may be so frequent that it could be treated as regular. For instance, as seen in Table 13, Syriac often has a reflex with *i* where one would expect *a*. There is no clear conditioning, but one is reluctant to expand the reconstructed inventory of vowels; despite the number of cases, this is still treated as skewing. It should be remembered that every case of a regular but nonidentical correspondence began as a skewing.

Lexical morphemes that are longer or shorter than average are particularly likely to show skewing. While skewed items are not as useful as items that show regular correspondences, they cannot be ignored without losing some important evidence for linguistic prehistory.

For example, although no two of the Akkadian, Hebrew, Syriac, and Arabic words for 'flea' correspond regularly, they are similar enough to rule out coincidence as an explanation. It is possible to compare them and reconstruct a Proto-Semitic shape. Given the data in Table 14, we reason thus:

Table 14. Skewed Correspondence

Akkadian	*paršuʾu*
Hebrew	*parʿōš*
Syriac	*purtaʿnā*
Arabic	*burɣūθ*

a. For the first consonant, *p : p : p : f* and *b : b : b : b* are regular correspondences in these languages. There is no phonological reason to assume the Arabic *b* or the *p* of the remaining languages to be original, so with the majority we reconstruct initial **p*, considering the Arabic initial skewed.

b. For the second consonant, *r : r : r : r* show regular correspondence and identity; we assume **r*.

c. The third and fourth consonants have apparently metathesized in some languages. The correspondences are regular: *š : š : t : θ* indicate **θ*, ∅ : ʿ : ʿ : ɣ indicate **ɣ*. Hebrew and Arabic agree on a consonant sequence **prɣθ*, Akkadian and Syriac show **prθɣ*. In the data available there is no reason to prefer one order to the other. We either choose randomly or present alternative reconstructions.

d. The *n* of Syriac is not attested in the other languages and is assumed to be a skewing. It will not be reflected in reconstruction.

e. Akkadian, Hebrew, and Arabic agree in showing a high back vowel in the second syllable. We take the Syriac vocalization to be skewed, representing either ***purtuʿnā* with the second vowel lowered by ʿ or ***partuʿnā* with metathesis of the voweling seen in Akkadian and Hebrew.

f. Akkadian, Hebrew, and Syriac agree in showing two originally short vowels (Hebrew *ō* is the normal reflex of **u* in this position). We take the long second vowel of Arabic to be skewed.

g. Akkadian, Hebrew, and (if we assume metathesis) Syriac agree on **a* in the first syllable. Arabic and Syriac show **u*; in addition, Akkadian has a variant, *puršuʾu*. This variant Akkadian form and the Arabic could readily be explained as the result of assimilation to the second vowel; the forms with first syllable **a* could not so easily be accounted for. We assume the first vowel to be **a*.

h. Accordingly, we reconstruct *parθuγ-* or *parγuθ-* as the most probable source for the forms attested.

Exercise 3. Determining Cognates and Skewed Reflexes

Use Wordlist A again, this time as data for an exercise in discriminating cognates and skewed reflexes. Use the same pair of languages and list of regular correspondences you used for the previous exercise.

In addition to the regularly corresponding cognates identified earlier, you will find different types and degrees of skewing. List skewed items, identifying the type of skewing. Can you be sure of the direction of skewing? Note the problems of determining cognacy when regular correspondences are somewhat doubtful. What does this imply for the construction of lists?

Part 4

Lexicostatistics: Some Alternatives

LEXICOSTATISTICS* involves judging degrees of linguistic relationship on the basis of the frequency of shared features. Any type of data (vocabulary, inflectional morphemes, syntactic patterns, and even cultural traits) may be used, but the most common type of data is lexical, because the number of data is critical. If the inventory of items compared is too small, the corpus will very likely not be representative and will give a false picture of relationships within the group. If the inventory is too large, however, relationships may also be obscured; the differences that always exist between two languages will outweigh the similarities. In counting vocabulary, it is normal to use lists of between 100 and 500 items per language. Counts of linguistic features other than lexicon are rare because there simply are not enough phonemes or verbal constructions.

Opinions differ on which items should be included in a lexicostatistical wordlist. It is generally preferable to include relatively culture-free vocabulary—body parts rather than iron-working terminology, numerals rather than color terms. Vocabulary with strong links to culture will bias the count. In some cases, wordlists with a high proportion of culture-bound vocabulary may seem quite similar, even where the languages are unrelated; cultural vocabulary is readily borrowed. On the other hand, otherwise very similar languages may be strongly differentiated by the inclusion of technical terms (compare British and American English). Culture-bound vocabulary also may limit the wordlist; we can be sure any language will have a word for 'eye', but we may not be able to elicit a term for 'mead' or 'grain offering' from all of the languages in our study.

Most lexicostatistical studies use variations on one of the wordlists devised by Morris Swadesh (see the 200-word list on page 40). However, it is often more convenient (especially when dealing with extinct languages for which many items on the Swadesh lists are not attested) to devise a list specific to the study. Almost any reasonably culture-free list will do. It is desirable, however, to include vocabulary from a variety of semantic domains (not focusing

---

* LEXICOSTATISTICS is frequently confused with GLOTTOCHRONOLOGY, which involves calculating dates for linguistic separation from the results of lexicostatistics. Many linguists are highly skeptical about the assumptions, procedures, and results of glottochronology, and are likely to reject lexicostatistical studies even when no conclusions are drawn concerning time scale. There are many scholars involved with the reconstruction of linguistic history, however, who consider lexicostatistics a valuable technique. There are also very serious investigators who are convinced of the validity of glottochronological dating. In this section, we will examine lexicostatistics but will not attempt to convert the results into dates.

Table 15. Semitic Number Words

	Proto-Semitic	Akkadian	Syriac	Geʿez	Soqoṭri
one	*ʾaḥad-	ištēn	ḥad	ʾaḥadū	ṭad
two	*θn-ā-	šena	treyn	kəlʾē	tróh
three	*śalāθ(-at)-	šalāšat	tlātā	šalāstū	śaʿtəh
four	*ʾarbaʿ(-at)-	erbet	ʾarbʿā	ʾarbāʿəttū	ʾerbáʿah
five	*xamš(-at)-	xamšat	ḥammšā	xamməstū	ḥámoh

on body parts or verbs of motion, for example). It is also important to include both nouns and verbs. In some studies, where nouns and verbs have been counted separately, they have been found to differ in retention rate (verb lists tend to be more conservative). Of course, in working with poorly attested ancient languages and modern languages for which full dictionaries do not exist, you may just have to "take what you can get." It is comforting to know that as long as we do not select our data with an eye to emphasizing similarity or dissimilarity, the overall pattern of relationships should not be seriously affected.

In every case, the contents of a pair of lists are compared and similar items identified. The degree and type of similarity required will vary with the nature and goals of the study. In PAIR-REFERENCED counts, the most common type, each list is compared with every other, to give a sense of the network of interrelationships within the group. In NORM-REFERENCED counts, one list (often a list of reconstructed protoforms) is treated as the norm with which the other lists are compared; the result is an estimate of degrees of conservatism, rather than a subgrouping.

Note also that the pair-referenced and norm-referenced counts are complementary. The former give a picture of how each language relates to every other; the latter indicate relationship to the group as a whole.

Both types of counts can be SIMPLE or, less commonly, WEIGHTED. In a simple count, judgments of relationship are made on a cognate/non-cognate basis. In a weighted count, regularly corresponding forms will be assessed differently from skewed items. A weighted count is useful in increasing the degree of differentiation when the languages are very similar or when the inventory is small. Simple counts are more common partly because they involve fewer judgments.

We can show how these types of count differ by presenting in Table 15 the first five number words in Akkadian, Syriac, Geʿez, and Soqoṭri. Ignoring weighting for the moment, we will recognize Syriac *ḥad* and Geʿez *ʾaḥadū* as cognate < *ʾaḥad-; Akkadian *šena*, Syriac *treyn*, Soqoṭri *tróh* as cognate < *θn-ā-; and all entries for 'three', 'four', and 'five' as cognate. The scores resulting from the four counts appear in Table 16.

A simple pair-referenced count, then, finds that Akkadian and Syriac have four out of five possible cognates ('two', 'three', 'four', 'five'), Akkadian and Geʿez three out of the five ('three', 'four', 'five'), Akkadian and Soqoṭri four ('two', 'three', 'four', 'five'), Syriac and Geʿez four ('one', 'three', 'four', 'five'), and Syriac and Soqoṭri four ('two', 'three', 'four', 'five'). These figures are turned into percentages (four of five = 80%, three of five = 60%).

The simple (unweighted) norm-referenced count tabulates retentions from the Proto-Semitic reconstructions: four ('two', 'three', 'four', 'five') in Akkadian, all five Syriac items, four ('one', 'three', 'four', 'five') in Geʿez, and four ('two', 'three', 'four', 'five') in Soqoṭri.

The weighted counts will give one point for regular correspondence, $\frac{2}{3}$ point for simple skewing, and $\frac{1}{3}$ point for multiple skewing. No point is given when the items compared are not

Table 16. Lexicostatistical Investigation of Number Words in Four Semitic Languages

	SIMPLE PAIR-REFERENCED				SIMPLE NORM-REFERENCED Retentions from Proto-Semitic	WEIGHTED PAIR-REFERENCED				WEIGHTED NORM-REFERENCED Retentions from Proto-Semitic
	Ak	Sy	Ge	So		Ak	Sy	Ge	So	
Ak		4	3	4	4		$3\frac{1}{3}$	2	$2\frac{2}{3}$	4
Sy	80%		4	4	5	67%		$2\frac{2}{3}$	$2\frac{2}{3}$	$3\frac{2}{3}$
Ge	60%	80%		3	4	40%	53%		$1\frac{1}{3}$	3
So	80%	80%	60%		4	53%	53%	27%		$2\frac{2}{3}$

seen as related. Using the same five number words as data, we will count as skewings the loss of initial **ʾa* in Syriac *ḥad*, the shift of **n* to *r* in Syriac *treyn* / Soqoṭri *tróh*, *t* for **ś* in Syriac *tlātā*, lengthening of the second vowel and gemination of **t* in Geʿez *ʾarbāʿəttū*, and gemination of **m* in Syriac *ḥammšā* / Geʿez *xamməstū*, and absence of **s* in Soqoṭri *ḥámoh*. Soqoṭri *śaʿtəh* is seen as multiply skewed (loss of **l*, loss of **ā*, insertion of ʿ).

The weighted count is as follows: Akkadian/Syriac: 0, $\frac{2}{3}$, 1, 1, $\frac{2}{3}$ (total $3\frac{1}{3}$ or 67%); Akkadian/Geʿez: 0, 0, 1, $\frac{1}{3}$, $\frac{2}{3}$ (total 2 or 40%); Akkadian/Soqoṭri: 0, $\frac{2}{3}$, $\frac{1}{3}$, 1, $\frac{2}{3}$ (total $2\frac{2}{3}$ or 53%); Syriac/Geʿez: $\frac{2}{3}$, 0, $\frac{2}{3}$, $\frac{1}{3}$, 1 (total $2\frac{2}{3}$ or 53%); Syriac/Soqoṭri: 0, 1, $\frac{1}{3}$, 1, $\frac{1}{3}$ (total $2\frac{2}{3}$ or 53%); and Geʿez/Soqoṭri: 0, 0, $\frac{1}{3}$, $\frac{1}{3}$, $\frac{2}{3}$ (total $1\frac{1}{3}$ or 27%).

Akkadian *šalāšat* / Syriac *tlātā* were counted as fully cognate because Akkadian *š* regularly corresponds to Syriac *t*; Syriac *ḥammšā* / Geʿez *xamməstū* and Syriac *treyn* / Soqoṭri *tróh* are fully cognate because they show the same skewings relative to Proto-Semitic.

The weighted norm-referenced count is made the same way. Akkadian retains *šena* 1, *šalāšat* 1, *erbet* 1, *xamšat* 1 (total 4); Syriac retains *ḥad* $\frac{2}{3}$, *treyn* $\frac{2}{3}$, *tlātā* $\frac{2}{3}$, *ʾarbʿā* 1, *ḥammšā* $\frac{2}{3}$ (total $3\frac{2}{3}$); Geʿez retains *ʾaḥadū* 1, *šalāstū* 1, *ʾarbāʿəttū* $\frac{1}{3}$, *xamməstū* $\frac{2}{3}$ (total 3); and Soqoṭri retains *tróh* $\frac{2}{3}$, *śaʿtəh* $\frac{1}{3}$, *ʾerbáʿah* 1, *ḥámoh* $\frac{2}{3}$ (total $2\frac{2}{3}$).

Note how weighting can affect the interpretation. In the simple pair-referenced count, Syriac appears to be equally close to Akkadian, Geʿez, and Soqoṭri. When skewing is considered in the weighted pair-referenced count, the figure for Syriac and Akkadian is seen to be well above the other two.

Interpretation, in fact, needs to be done cautiously. The figures in Table 16 do not give anything like a subgrouping. Going by the weighted pair-referenced count, one might see any of the following groupings, depending on one's cut-off figure for clusters:

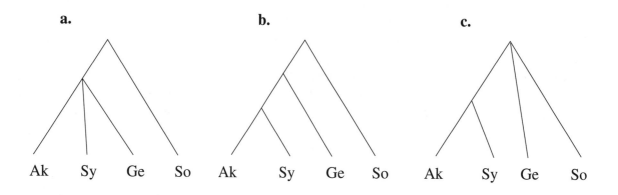

a. b. c.

Ak   Sy   Ge   So   Ak   Sy   Ge   So   Ak   Sy   Ge   So

In some cases, to be sure, the figures unambiguously support a specific grouping; a lexico-statistical survey of modern Semitic languages would clearly show the boundaries of Arabic, Aramaic, Ethiopic, and Modern South Arabian subgroups. But often one must appeal to other criteria before one can choose between alternative subgroupings.

In fact, here we have run up against another of the clashes between fact and fiction that make linguistics so interesting. Up to a point, in many language families it is possible to draw a neat tree diagram—the classic "Stammbaum"—representing linguistic relationships in terms of a hierarchy of simple splits. Thus diagram **b** above suggests that Soqotri split off from the main body of Semitic, followed sometime afterward by Geʿez, while Syriac and Akkadian remained a single language until much later. Simple and easy to grasp, the model is useful in formulating other hypotheses about linguistic prehistory. Unfortunately, this is not the way language relationships really work.

In reality, linguistic differentiation begins before there is a real separation of communities, and linguistic contact, with mutual influence, persists long after two languages are differentiated. Lexicostatistics necessarily reflects this reality. The vocabulary that we find shared by two languages derives in part from common inheritance, in part from borrowing between the two languages (in either direction), in part from borrowing (by both) from other languages, and we have no easy way to differentiate sources. In our sample calculation, the relatively high figure for Akkadian sharings with Syriac probably reflects their greater geographic proximity and the higher level of skewing in Geʿez and Soqotri.

In Semitic in general, for example, the figures do not clearly support any one subgrouping tree for the seven branches. In such cases, the best one can do is reflect the relationships spatially but nonhierarchically, as is done in figure **d** for our count of numerals:

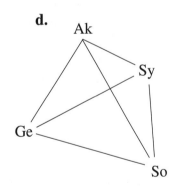

Exercise 4. Pair-Referenced Lexicostatistics (General Semitic)

This exercise in pair-referenced lexicostatistics involves Wordlist B. This is a relatively short list (100 items) with entries for 21 Semitic languages: **Ak**kadian (East Semitic); **Ug**aritic, **He**brew, **Ph**oenician (Canaanite); **A**chaemenid **A**ramaic, **Sy**riac, **Ma**ʿlula, **Ur**mi, **M**odern **M**andaic (Aramaic); Classical **Ar**abic, **Mo**roccan Arabic, **Eg**yptian Arabic, **Ir**aqi Arabic (Arabic); **Ge**ʿez, **Ti**grinya, **Am**haric, **Ha**rari (Ethiopic); **Sa**bean (Old South Arabian); **So**qoṭri, **Me**ḥri, **Ji**bbali (Modern South Arabian).

To what extent is the accepted subgrouping supported by lexicostatistics? The time depth and the short list present challenges. How much weight should we give to vocalization when we have no information on voweling for Phoenician and Sabean and incompletely voweled listings for Ugaritic and Achaemenid Aramaic?

Turn in a copy of the wordlist marking cognates. Include notes for difficult cases. Summarize your results in tabular form.

Exercise 5. Norm-Referenced Lexicostatistics

Your exercise in norm-referenced lexicostatistics is based on Wordlist C, a 275-item list with entries for 6 Ethiopic languages: **Ge**ʿez, **Ti**gre, **Ti**grinya, **Am**haric, **Ha**rari, and **Ch**aha. Multiple entries have been allowed. The sources are varied and it is not possible to guarantee synonymy. In cases like *moon/month*, where for many languages a single word is listed under two glosses, you will have to decide which data to admit. Particularly in the case of Chaha, you will need to be alert for cognates masquerading behind phonetic shifts.

Turn in a copy of the wordlist, marking the items you considered cognate with Geʿez. Include notes for difficult cases, explaining why you decided they were or were not cognates. Summarize your results in tabular form.

Exercise 6. Pair-Referenced Lexicostatistics (Ethiopic)

Again using Wordlist C, make a pair-referenced lexicostatistical count for Ethiopic. Summarize your findings in tabular form. How would you subgroup Ethiopic? How do these results compare with those of the norm-referenced exercise?

Worksheets for Exercises 4, 5, and 6 are given on the following page.

General Semitic Worksheet for Exercise 4

	Ak	Ug	He	Ph	AA	Sy	Ma	Ur	MM	Ar	Mo	Eg	Ir	Ge	Ti	Am	Ha	Sa	So	Me	Ji
Ak																					
Ug	%																				
He	%	%																			
Ph	%	%	%																		
AA	%	%	%	%																	
Sy	%	%	%	%	%																
Ma	%	%	%	%	%	%															
Ur	%	%	%	%	%	%	%														
MM	%	%	%	%	%	%	%	%													
Ar	%	%	%	%	%	%	%	%	%												
Mo	%	%	%	%	%	%	%	%	%	%											
Eg	%	%	%	%	%	%	%	%	%	%	%										
Ir	%	%	%	%	%	%	%	%	%	%	%	%									
Ge	%	%	%	%	%	%	%	%	%	%	%	%	%								
Ti	%	%	%	%	%	%	%	%	%	%	%	%	%	%							
Am	%	%	%	%	%	%	%	%	%	%	%	%	%	%	%						
Ha	%	%	%	%	%	%	%	%	%	%	%	%	%	%	%	%					
Sa	%	%	%	%	%	%	%	%	%	%	%	%	%	%	%	%	%				
So	%	%	%	%	%	%	%	%	%	%	%	%	%	%	%	%	%	%			
Me	%	%	%	%	%	%	%	%	%	%	%	%	%	%	%	%	%	%	%		
Ji	%	%	%	%	%	%	%	%	%	%	%	%	%	%	%	%	%	%	%	%	

Ethiopic Worksheet for Exercise 5

	Te	Ta	Am	Ha	Ch
Matches with Geʿez					

Ethiopic Worksheet for Exercise 6

	Ge	Te	Ta	Am	Ha	Ch
Ge						
Te	%					
Ta	%	%				
Am	%	%	%			
Ha	%	%	%	%		
Ch	%	%	%	%	%	

Appendix to Part 4
The Swadesh 200-Word Basic Vocabulary List

1. all	51. to float	101. narrow	151. to stand
2. and	52. to flow	102. near	152. star
3. animal	53. flower	103. neck	153. stick (of wood)
4. ashes	54. to fly	104. new	154. stone
5. at	55. fog	105. night	155. straight
6. back	56. foot	106. nose	156. to suck
7. bad	57. four	107. not	157. sun
8. bark (tree)	58. to freeze	108. old	158. to swell
9. because	59. fruit	109. one	159. to swim
10. belly	60. to give	110. other	160. tail
11. big	61. good	111. person	161. that
12. bird	62. grass	112. to play	162. there
13. to bite	63. green	113. to pull	163. they
14. black	64. guts	114. to push	164. thick
15. blood	65. hair	115. to rain	165. thin
16. to blow (wind)	66. hand	116. red	166. to think
17. bone	67. he	117. right (correct)	167. this
18. to breathe	68. head	118. right (hand)	168. thou
19. to burn (intrans.)	69. to hear	119. river	169. three
20. child (young)	70. heart	120. road	170. to throw
21. cloud	71. heavy	121. root	171. to tie
22. cold (weather)	72. here	122. rope	172. tongue
23. to come	73. to hit	123. rotten (log)	173. tooth (front)
24. to count	74. hold (in hand)	124. rub	174. tree
25. to cut (with knife)	75. how	125. salt	175. to turn (veer)
26. day (not night)	76. to hunt (game)	126. sand	176. two
27. to die	77. husband	127. to say	177. to vomit
28. to dig	78. I	128. scratch (itch)	178. to walk
29. dirty	79. ice	129. sea (ocean)	179. warm (weather)
30. dog	80. if	130. to see	180. to wash
31. to drink	81. in	131. seed	181. water
32. dry (substance)	82. to kill	132. to sew	182. we
33. dull (knife)	83. know (facts)	133. sharp (knife)	183. wet
34. dust	84. lake	134. short	184. what?
35. ear	85. to laugh	135. to sing	185. when?
36. earth (soil)	86. leaf	136. to sit	186. where?
37. to eat	87. left (hand)	137. skin (of person)	187. white
38. egg	88. leg	138. sky	188. who?
39. eye	89. to lie (on side)	139. to sleep	189. wide
40. to fall (drop)	90. to live	140. small	190. wife
41. far	91. liver	141. to smell (perceive)	191. wind (breeze)
42. fat (substance)	92. long	142. smoke	192. wing
43. father	93. louse	143. smooth	193. wipe
44. to fear	94. man (male)	144. snake	194. with (accompanying)
45. feather (large)	95. many	145. snow	195. woman
46. few	96. meat (flesh)	146. some	196. woods
47. to fight	97. mother	147. to spit	197. worm
48. fire	98. mountain	148. to split	198. ye
49. fish	99. mouth	149. to squeeze	199. year
50. five	100. name	150. to stab (or stick)	200. yellow

Part 5

Linguistic Reconstruction: Comparative and Internal

The most important thing to remember about reconstruction is that it is *not* the reconstruction of an ancestral language. The best we can do is to make inherently unverifiable deductions about structural features and morpheme shapes that may have been present. If one applies reconstructive techniques to Romance languages, one does not reconstruct Latin; reconstruction based on modern Arabic dialects fails to yield Classical Arabic. If a feature has been lost in most members of a group, it cannot be reconstructed.

A good way of thinking about it is to view *reconstruction* as basically a synchronic tabulation of what the languages have in common, followed by some (ideally cautious) speculation regarding origins. Thus in the reconstruction of the phonemic system of Proto-Semitic, we tabulate regular correspondences and then decide, for example, that a merger of θ and t in Aramaic is more probable than a splitting of t into two phonemes in Arabic.

Internal reconstruction differs from comparative reconstruction in its data—the morphophonemic processes of a single language, rather than correspondences across languages. It does not differ in its historicity. The assumption underlying it is that a single morpheme at one point had a single shape. This, however, is rarely true in living languages, and there is no reason to believe it was the case in their ancestors. Internal reconstruction based on Cairene Arabic will not yield Classical Arabic any more than comparative reconstruction from colloquial Arabic will.

Either type of reconstruction can be applied to most types of linguistic structure: phonemic systems, probable phonetic values, lexicon, and inflectional systems. Comparative reconstruction is more commonly applied to phonology and lexicon, internal reconstruction most often to inflectional morphology.

The results of either type of reconstruction can be applied in a variety of ways. Reconstructed lexicon or morphology may serve as the norm in a norm-referenced lexicostatistical study or serve as the basis for the techniques of geographic analysis and cultural reconstruction discussed in Part 6; reconstruction makes the identification of borrowed material more reliable. If reconstructions are made for different time depths, conclusions can then be drawn about the relative timing of linguistic changes. Finally, the results of a preliminary reconstruction can shed light on regular correspondences in order to correct and expand the reconstruction itself.

Table 17. Phonological Reconstructions

	Moroccan	Tigrinya	Jibbali	Maʕlula	Suggested
1	ʕ	ʕ	ʕ	ʕ	*ʕ
2	t	t	t	č	*t
3	γ	ʕ	γ	ʕ	*γ
4	q	ḳ	ḳ	q	*q

Table 18. Reconstructions of Dead Languages

	Akkadian	Arabic	Geʕez	Ugaritic	Suggested
1	ṣ	ṣ	ṣ	ṣ	*ṣ
2	∅	ʕ	ʕ	ʕ	*ʕ
3	ṣ	ḍ	ḍ	ṣ	*ḍ
4	p	f	f	p	*p

Comparative Reconstruction: Phonology

Let us begin with some exercises in the comparative reconstruction of phonology. The process seems at first to be simple enough. We have already practiced identifying cognates and regular correspondences. In its simplest form, phonological reconstruction takes a set of regular correspondences and gives it a label—a symbol preceded by an asterisk. We usually try to pick a symbol associated with what might have been the sound in the ancestral language. Consider the correspondences in Table 17.

In cases such as correspondence 1 where all languages agree, one can normally assume that the protolanguage also agreed. In correspondence 2, where most languages agree, it is generally acceptable to follow the majority, unless the majority show a merger. In 3 and 4 there is apparently no majority. Our reconstruction for 3 follows Moroccan and Jibbali because Tigrinya and Maʕlula show a merger with correspondence 1; in 4 there is no clear reason in the data to prefer one reconstruction to the other.

The reconstructions in Table 18 at first sight are exactly parallel to those above. There is, however, an important difference. Whereas we have modern, reliable phonetic descriptions of Moroccan Arabic, Tigrinya, Jibbali, and the Neo-Aramaic of Maʕlula, our transcriptions of Classical Arabic and Geʕez rest on traditional rather than living pronunciations, and much of our Akkadian and Ugaritic transcriptions rests on conjecture and extrapolation. These reconstructions should, therefore, wherever possible be confirmed by appealing to modern reflexes.

The exercises to follow will give you some practice with comparative reconstruction. In each case, identify regular correspondences among emphasized consonants and assign appropriate starred symbols. Note any skewings. In some cases, the data from one exercise may be relevant to another. You may need to reevaluate your conclusions as further data become available. For Exercises 7–10, "checklists" are provided so that you can check your results against a language that seems to have preserved the original set of contrasts.

Exercise 7. Phonological Reconstruction A

	Akkadian		Syriac		Arabic	
1	*šālu*	ask	*šil*	ask	*saʾala*	ask
2	*šumēlu*	left	*simmālā*	left	*šimāl*	left
3	*sikkānu*	rudder	*sukkānā*	rudder	*sukkān*	rudder
4	*asāru*	capture	*ʾisar*	tie	*ʾasara*	capture
5	*bašālu*	cook	*bšil*	be cooked	*basula*	be brave
6	*ešer*	ten	*ʾisar*	ten	*ʿašar*	ten
7	*karšu*	stomach	*karsā*	belly	*kirš*	stomach
8	*parāsu*	divide	*pras*	divide	*farasa*	devour
9	*simmu*	poison	*sammā*	drug	*summ*	poison
10	*xamiš*	five	*ḥammiš*	five	*xams*	five

Exercise 8. Phonological Reconstruction B

	Akkadian		Maʿlula		Urmi	
1	*ašru*	place	*bōθar*	after	*ətrə*	place
2	*ebēru*	cross	*eʿber*	enter	*vara*	cross
3	*ekallu*	palace	*haykla*	altar	*heklə*	temple
4	*eqlu*	field	*ḥaqla*	field	*xəqlə*	field
5	*malū*	fill	*iml*	fill	*mləjə*	fill
6	*nāru*	river	*nahra*	river	*nərə*	river
7	*naxīru*	nostril	*manxra*	nose	*nəxijrə*	nose
8	*petū*	open	*ifθaḥ*	open	*ptəxə*	open
9	*rāṣu*	run	*arḥeṭ*	run	*rxaṭa*	run
10	*ṣapū*	soak	*iṣbaʿ*	dye	*sbaja*	dye
11	*ṭēmu*	sense	*aṭʿmi*	feed	*ṭjama*	taste
12	*ṭēnu*	grind	*iṭḥan*	grind	*ṭxana*	grind
13	*warxu*	moon	*yarḥa*	month	*jərxə*	month
14	*xamšat*	five	*ḥammša*	five	*xəmšə*	five
15	*zēru*	seed	*zarʿa*	seed	*zarra*	seed

Exercise 9. Phonological Reconstruction C

	Akkadian		Syriac		Geʿez	
1	šalāšat	three	tlātā	three	šalāstū	three
2	šūru	bull	tawrā	bull	sōr	bull
3	axāzu	take	ʾiḥad	take	ʾaxaza	take
4	erēšu	sow	ḥrat	plow	ḥarasa	plow
5	mašālu	be like	matlā	parable	məsl	parable
6	našāku	bite	nkat	bite	nasaka	bite
7	naṣāru	guard	nṭar	guard	naṣṣara	look
8	nazāru	curse	ndar	vow	nāzara	be consecrated
9	ṣupru	nail	ṭiprā	nail	ṣəpr	nail
10	zakāru	mention	dkar	remember	zakara	remember

Exercise 10. Phonological Reconstruction D

	Hebrew		Syriac		Geʿez	
1	ʿāṣar	squeeze	ʿṣar	squeeze	ʿaṣara	squeeze
2	ʿśārā	ten	ʿisrā	ten	ʿaššartū	ten
3	bēyṣā	egg	bīʿtā	egg	bēṣa	be white
4	ḥōṣen	bosom	ḥanna	bosom	ḥəḍn	bosom
5	nāṣar	guard	nṭar	guard	naṣṣara	look
6	qāraṣ	slice	qraṣ	nip off	qaraṣa	incise
7	qāṭān	small	qaṭṭīnā	narrow	qaṭṭīn	fine, thin
8	rāʿā	graze	rʿā	graze	rəʿya	graze
9	ṣābōʿ	hyena	ʾapʿā	hyena	ḍəbʿ	hyena
10	ṣāmad	harness	ṣmad	bind up	ḍamada	yoke
11	ṣārā	co-wife	ʿarrtā	co-wife	ḍar	enemy
12	ṣēl	shadow	ṭillālā	shadow	ṣəlālōt	shadow
13	ṣillā	pray for	ṣallī	pray	ṣallaya	pray
14	ṣippōren	nail	ṭiprā	nail	ṣəfr	nail
15	ṭāḥan	grind	ṭḥin	grind	ṭaḥana	grind

Table 19. "Checklists" for Exercises 7–10

	Exercise 7 Jibbali	
1	*šɛ̄l*	demand pay
2	*śəmlí*	left
3	*skkun*	rudder
4	*ʾésɔ́r*	hobble
5	*béšəl*	be cooked
6	*ɔ́śər*	ten
7	*ŝirś*	belly
8	*fɔ́rɔ́s*	mash
9	*sɛhm*	poison
10	*xĩš*	five

	Exercise 9 Arabic	
1	*θalāθaᵗ*	three
2	*θawr*	bull
3	*ʾaxaδa*	take
4	*haraθa*	plow
5	*maθal*	parable
6	*nakaθa*	break off
7	*naẓara*	look
8	*naδara*	consecrate
9	*ẓifr*	nail
10	*δakara*	remember

	Exercise 8 Geʿez	
1	*ʾašar*	footprint
2	*ʿabara*	cross
3	*haykal*	temple
4	*ḥaql*	field
5	*malʾa*	fill
6	*nahār*	river
7	*mənxar*	bellows
8	*fatḥa*	open
9	*rōṣa*	run
10	*ṣabxa*	dip
11	*ṭəʿma*	taste
12	*ṭaḥana*	grind
13	*warx*	moon
14	*xamməstū*	five
15	*zaraʿa*	sow

	Exercise 10 Arabic	
1	*ʿaṣara*	squeeze
2	*ʿašaraᵗ*	ten
3	*bayḍaᵗ*	egg
4	*ḥiḍn*	bosom
5	*naẓara*	look
6	*qaraṣa*	gnaw
7	*ʾaqṭan*	stooped
8	*raʿā*	graze
9	*ḍabʿ*	hyena
10	*ḍamada*	bandage
11	*ḍarraᵗ*	co-wife
12	*ẓill*	shadow
13	*ṣallā*	pray
14	*ẓifr*	nail
15	*ṭaḥana*	grind

Exercise 11. Phonological Reconstruction E

The Syriac transcription is phonetic, not phonemic.

	Syriac	Jibbali		Syriac	Jibbali
approach	*qəriβ*	*qérəb*	graves	*qaβrín*	*qabrín*
bury	*qəβar*	*qɔ́r*	heart	*libbā*	*ub*
dress (imperf.)	*nilbaš*	*yɔ́lbəs*	honey	*diβšā*	*dɛbš*
dress (perf.)	*ləβiš*	*lɔ́s*	house	*baytā*	*bot*
drum (n.)	*ṭaβlā*	*ṭēl*	milk (n.)	*ḥalbā*	*ḥɔ́lɔ́b*
finger	*ṣiβˤəθā*	*ʾiṣbáˤ*	milk (v.)	*ḥəlaβ*	*ḥɔ́lɔ́b*
four	*ʾarbəˤā*	*ɛrbəˤɔ́t*	onion	*biṣlā*	*béṣál*
grave	*qaβrā*	*qɔ́r*	seven	*šaβˤā*	*šəbˤɔ́t*

Exercise 12. Phonological Reconstruction F

In light of your reconstructions for Exercise 7, provide explanations for the following sets of correspondences.

A	Akkadian		Syriac		Arabic	
	sebe	seven	*šbaˤ*	seven	*sabˤ*	seven
	sīqu	leg	*šāqā*	leg	*sāq*	leg
	suʾālu	cough	*šˤal*	cough	*saˤala*	cough

B	Akkadian		Syriac		Arabic	
	šammu	drug	*sammā*	medicine	*summ*	poison
	šipru	writing	*siprā*	book	*sifr*	book
	pāštu	axe	*pustā*	axe	*faʾs*	axe

C	Akkadian		Syriac		Arabic	
	šamšu	sun	*šimšā*	sun	*šams*	sun
	šuršu	root	*širšā*	root	*širš*	root

D	Syriac		Arabic		Jibbali	
	šabbtā	sabbath	*sabt*	Saturday	*sabt*	Saturday
	gušmā	body	*jism*	body	*gɛsm*	body
	lbiš	dress	*labisa*	dress	*lɔ́s*	wear
	dibšā	honey	*dibs*	syrup	*dɛbš*	honey
					dɛbs	date honey

Table 20. Modern Arabic Correspondence Sets

	Bear	Build	Calf	Cry	Die
Mo	*wled*	*bna*	*ʕžel*	*bka*	*mat*
Eg	*wilid*	*bana*	*ʕigl*	*baka*	*māt*
Ir	*wilad*	*bina*	*ʕijil*	*bica*	*māt*

	Door	Dream	Egg	Feather	Guest
Mo	*bab*	*ḥlem*	*biḍa*	*riša*	*ḍif*
Eg	*bāb*	*ḥilim*	*bēḍa*	*rīša*	*ḍēf*
Ir	*bāb*	*ḥilam*	*bēδa*	*rīša*	*ḍēf*

	Hear	Leg	Milk (v.)	Mountain	Oil
Mo	*smeʕ*	*ržel*	*ḥleb*	*žbel*	*zit*
Eg	*simiʕ*	*rigl*	*ḥalab*	*gabal*	*zēt*
Ir	*simaʕ*	*rijil*	*ḥilab*	*jibal*	*zēt*

	See	Shoulder	Wash	Well	Wind
Mo	*šaf*	*ktef*	*ɣsel*	*bir*	*riḥ*
Eg	*šāf*	*kitf*	*ɣasal*	*bīr*	*rīḥ*
Ir	*šāf*	*citif*	*ɣisal*	*bīr*	*rīḥ*

Table 21. Modern Arabic Phonological Reconstructions

Mo	Eg	Ir	PMA	Mo	Eg	Ir	PMA	Mo	Eg	Ir	PMA
a	*a*	*a*	**a*	*b*	*b*	*b*	**b*	*f*	*f*	*f*	**f*
e	*a*	*a*	**æ*	*d*	*d*	*d*	**d*	*s*	*s*	*s*	**s*
a	*ā*	*ā*	**ā*	*ž*	*g*	*j*	**g*	*š*	*š*	*š*	**š*
∅	*a*	*i*	**A*	*ḍ*	*ḍ*	*δ*	**ḍ*	*z*	*z*	*z*	**z*
e	*i*	*a*	**ä*	*t*	*t*	*t*	**t*	*l*	*l*	*l*	**l*
i	*ē*	*ē*	**ē*	*k*	*k*	*c*	**k*	*r*	*r*	*r*	**r*
∅	*i*	*i*	**I*	*m*	*m*	*m*	**m*	*ɣ*	*ɣ*	*ɣ*	**ɣ*
i	*ī*	*ī*	**ī*	*n*	*n*	*n*	**n*	*ʕ*	*ʕ*	*ʕ*	**ʕ*
e	*∅*	*i*	**∅*	*w*	*w*	*w*	**w*	*ḥ*	*ḥ*	*ḥ*	**ḥ*

Comparative Reconstruction: Lexicon

If you have reconstructed phonology, lexical reconstruction can be simple. Consider the data from Modern Arabic in Table 20. We assume that all correspondences are regular, even though not all of the consonant correspondences are attested three times. We find the correspondences in Table 21, for which I have suggested reconstructions. In these data, nine vowel correspondences are found, a fact that necessitates an arbitrary assignment of symbols. The correspondence *a/a/a* is simple, and is assigned the symbol **a.* In three cases (*a/ā/ā, i/ē/ē,* and *i/ī/ī*),

Table 22. Proto-Modern Arabic Reconstructions Compared with Classical Arabic

	Bear	Build	Calf	Cry	Die
PMA	*wIlläd	*bAna	*ʕIgl	*bAka	*māt
CA	walada	banā	ʕijl	bakā	māta

	Door	Dream	Egg	Feather	Guest
PMA	*bāb	*ḥIläm	*bēda	*rīš	*ḍēf
CA	bāb	ḥalama	bayḍaᵗ	rīš	ḍayf

	Hear	Leg	Milk (v.)	Mountain	Oil
PMA	*sImäʕ	*rIgl	*ḥAlæb	*gAbæl	*zēt
CA	samiʕa	rijl	ḥalaba	jabal	zayt

	See	Shoulder	Wash	Well	Wind
PMA	*šāf	*kItf	*ɣAsæl	*bīr	*rīḥ
CA	raʾā	katif	ɣasala	biʾr	rīḥ

Egyptian and Iraqi agree against Moroccan, and I have followed Egyptian and Iraqi. Three correspondences involve the absence of a vowel in one dialect. The correspondence e/∅/i consistently occurs between the second and third consonants. I have taken this to reflect epenthesis in Moroccan and Iraqi, and reconstruct *∅; no vowel is written in reconstructions.

The remaining two correspondences (∅/a/i, ∅/i/i) occur only after the initial consonant and are arbitrarily assigned *A and *I. They are differentiated only in Egyptian, as are the correspondences e/a/a and e/i/a (arbitrarily *æ and *ä), which occur only between the second and third consonants. It will be noted that these correspondences show conditioning in Egyptian. The correspondence *A (Egyptian a) is found if the second vowel in Egyptian is a. Otherwise, Egyptian has i, giving correspondence *I. Looked at from the other direction, *æ (Egyptian a) occurs only where the first syllable in Egyptian has a; otherwise Egyptian has i, representing *ä.

It would be possible to use this complementarity to eliminate one of the correspondences but not both. We could merge *A and *I to ∅/(a ~ i)/i, or *æ and *ä to e/(a ~ i)/a. There is no clear case in the data for preferring one solution over the other, so I have ignored the conditioning.

Using these reconstructions, we can reconstruct the list of items (Table 22). It is as well here to remind you that what is "reconstructed" is in fact a synchronic construct. Note the differences between the reconstructed "Proto–Modern Arabic" and Classical Arabic.

Exercise 13. Regular Correspondences and Reconstruction

This is another exercise using the Ethiopic data of Wordlist C. By now you should have all the cognates marked, though it is a good idea to review the lists; often one finds new cognates after putting the data aside for a while. Work out regular correspondences and reconstruct as many lexical morphemes as possible. You will need to decide how many cognates, with what distribution, justify making a reconstruction. Next use your list of reconstructions as the norm for a norm-referenced lexicostatistic count. Compare your results with the results from Exercise 5.

Table 23. Semantic Development

Akkadian	𒀸𒂖𒅗𒆠 *warāqu* 'be green, pale', 𒀸𒌝𒅗𒆠 *warqu* 'green', 𒀸𒌝𒅗𒆠𒅗 *warqū* (pl.) 'vegetables'
Ugaritic	𐎜𐎗𐎖 *yrq* 'gold'
Hebrew	יָרַק *yāraq* 'be green', יָרֹק *yārōq* 'green', יֶרֶק *yereq* 'green plant', יָרָק *yārāq* (coll.) 'vegetables', יֵרָקוֹן *yērāqōn* 'jaundice', יְרוֹקָה *yrōqā* 'moss'
Syriac	ܐܘܪܩ *'awriq* 'be green, pale', ܝܘܪܩܐ *yūrāqā* 'green, pale', ܝܪܩܐ *yarqā* 'vegetable', ܡܘܪܝܩܢܐ *mūrīqannā* 'jaundice'
Arabic	ورق *wariq* 'leafy', وَرَقَةّ *waraqa^t* 'leaf, paper', وَرَّاق *warrāq* 'stationer', وَرْق *warq* 'silver coin'
Geʿez	ወርቅ ፡ *warq* 'gold'
Sabean	𐩥𐩧𐩤 *wrq* (coll.) 'vegetables', *wrq* 'gold'
Jibbali	*érḳt* 'leaf, sheet of paper'

Comparative Reconstruction: Semantics

It is possible to reconstruct semantic as well as formal development. Consider the data in Table 23. We deduce that the basic reference is to a yellowish-green color. The items glossed 'green', 'yellow', and 'pale' may be derived directly. A further logical shift to objects of this color gives the items glossed 'leaf', 'vegetables', and 'gold'. The meaning '(sheet of) paper' is readily derived from 'leaf'; 'silver coin' probably is an extension from 'gold'. These deductions are in part confirmed by the evidence of Berber, where **wrɣ* is 'be yellow, be pale' and **urɣ* is 'gold'.

Exercise 14. Semantic Ranges

What can be deduced from the semantic ranges of the data sets in Table 24?

Internal Reconstruction

Internal reconstruction is primarily useful in phonology and morphology, though it may also be useful in semantics. Consider the Hebrew paradigms in Table 25. Each noun illustrated is typical of a larger set of nouns. We begin with the assumption that at some point in time there was a single shape for each noun stem, such as we see in nouns like סוס 'horse' (*sūs, sūs hāʾiš, sūsī*). We have postulated an underlying base form for each noun. None of these base forms contains any vowel other than (short) *a*. For brevity's sake we will not give all of the grounds for this assumption; let it suffice to say that the behavior of underlyingly long vowels is different. Given these data and this assumption, we may deduce:

a. In antepenultimate open syllables, **a* was eliminated: **zahab-ī > *zhabī*. This change also applied to constructs, since the phrase stress in the possessive construction falls on the following word: **zahab hāʾiš >* זְהַב הָאִישׁ *zhab hāʾiš*.

Table 24. Semantic Ranges

	A			B	
Akkadian	*šabāṭu*	smite	*bašālu*	cook
	šabbīṭu	scepter	*bašlu*	cooked, ripe
Hebrew	*šēbeṭ*	staff, tribe	*bāšal*	be cooked, ripe
Syriac	*šabṭā*	stick, tribe	*bšil*	be cooked, ripe
Arabic	*sibṭ*	tribe, grandchild	*basula*	be brave
	subāṭaᵗ	bunch		
Geʿez	*sabṭ*	pointed rod	*basala*	be cooked, ripe
Sabean	*šbṭ*	strike	*bšl*	sacrifice
Jibbali	*sɔ̄ṭ*	hit with stick	*béšəl*	be cooked, ready

	C			D	
Akkadian	*kabru*	fat	*qālu*	be silent
	kubāru	great	*qūlu*	silence
Hebrew	*kabbīr*	mighty	*qōl*	voice
	kbār	long ago		
Syriac	*kabbīr*	abundant	*qālā*	voice
	kbar	long ago		
Arabic	*kabara*	be older	*qāla*	say
	kabīr	big	*qawl*	saying
Geʿez	*kəbūr*	honored	*qāl*	voice, word
Sabean	*kbr*	great, many	*qwl*	chief
	kbr	chieftain		
Jibbali	*kēr*	elder (n.)	*qabl*	truce

Table 25. Hebrew Nominal Paradigms

	Absolute	The man's ___	My ___	Base form
slave	*ʿebed*	*ʿebed hāʾīš*	*ʿabdī*	**ʿabd*
gold	*zāhāb*	*zhab hāʾīš*	*zhābī*	**zahab*
carpet	*marbad*	*marbad hāʾīš*	*marbaddī*	**marbadd*
blood	*dām*	*dam hāʾīš*	*dāmī*	**dam*
lord	*rab*	*rab hāʾīš*	*rabbī*	**rabb*

b. In open syllables and in singly closed syllables bearing phrase stress, **a* became *ā*: **zahab* > זָהָב *zāhāb*.

c. Before word boundary, original geminate consonants were simplified: **rabb* > רַב *rab*.

d. Before word boundary, a consonant cluster was broken up by the insertion of *e*: **ʿabd* > **ʿabed*.

e. In words of shape *CaCeC*, **a* became *e*: **ʿabed* > עֶבֶד *ʿebed*.

This series of phonological changes gives us a clue to what changes occurred in the past, most of which can be confirmed by comparative evidence (for instance, Arabic has عَبْد *'abd*, دَم *dam*, ذَهَب *δahab*, and رَبّ *rabb* matching assumed Hebrew **'abd*, **dam*, **zahab*, and **rabb*). It also indicates a probable sequencing of these changes. For example, the vowel insertion of rule (d) very likely followed the deletion in rule (a), since the other order would incorrectly predict **'abd hā'iš > **'bad hā'iš*. Similarly, the reduction of geminate consonants in rule (c) has to follow the lengthening in rule (b); the other order predicts **rabb > *rab > **rāb*. While the ordering of changes arrived at through internal reconstruction is not perfect, it can be an important tool in reconstructing linguistic history.

A similar line of reasoning may be used in morphology. We will look at the Arabic case and number endings shown in Table 26.

Table 26. Arabic Case and Number Endings

Gender	Case	Singular	Dual	Plural
Masculine	Nominative	*-u-n*	*-ā-ni*	*-ū-na*
	Accusative	*-a-n*	*-ay-ni*	*-ī-na*
	Genitive	*-i-n*		
Feminine	Nominative	*-at-u-n*	*-at-ā-ni*	*-āt-u-n*
	Accusative	*-at-a-n*	*-at-ay-ni*	*-āt-i-n*
	Genitive	*-at-i-n*		

We note:

a. All endings include a morpheme with initial *n* which is omitted in some syntactic contexts (caution: the contexts for omission of *-na/-ni* differ from those for *-n*).
b. In dual and plural, the contrast between nominative and accusative/genitive is marked by a vowel shift, with accusative/genitive consistently front.
c. In singular and dual, the feminine is distinguished by a suffix *-at-*; in the feminine plural, we see *-āt-*.
d. All plural endings involve long vowels.

Table 27. Internal Reconstruction of Arabic Case and Number Endings

Gender	Case	Singular	Dual	Plural
Masculine	Nominative	*-u-n*	*-ay-u-n*	*-w-u-n*
	Accusative	*-a-n*	*-ay-i-n*	*-w-i-n*
	Genitive	*-i-n*		
Feminine	Nominative	*-at-u-n*	*-at-ay-u-n*	*-w-at-u-n*
	Accusative	*-at-a-n*	*-at-ay-i-n*	*-w-at-i-n*
	Genitive	*-at-i-n*		

From the data, we reconstruct the forms in Table 27. The phonetic shifts needed for changing, for example, **-ay-u-* to *-ā* are well documented within Arabic in verbal and derivational morphophonemics. The dual and plural endings **-ay-* and **-w-* are confirmed from Egyptian, where the feminine marker is followed by the dual suffix but preceded by the plural precisely as reconstructed here. We will need to add a vowel to the nasal suffix in dual and plural, including a dissimilation. While not all of the questions we might ask can be resolved internally, the process does help to understand the history of the paradigm.

Internal semantic reconstruction is also possible. The data in Table 28 are from Hebrew. I take the meaning 'large' to be primary. From 'large in size' to 'great in importance' or to 'large in number' is a short step. From 'great' to 'great one', then 'master' or 'lord', is natural. So is the link between 'master' and 'schoolmaster'. The gloss 'ten thousand' is an extension of 'many'; to 'boast' is to claim to be great.

Table 28. Semantic Internal Reconstruction

rab	'many, great'
rab	'master, teacher'
rābab	'be great, increase'
rbābā	'ten thousand'
ribbōn	'lord'
ribrēb	'boast'

Exercise 15. Reconstructing Morphology

Choose one of the languages treated in the appendixes and use as data the tables of subject and object marking on the verb (Paradigms B, pp. 77, 81, 83, 85, 87, 89). Determine as far as possible the underlying/probable original shapes of object markers and subject suffix markers. I do not recommend trying to determine a shape ancestral to both prefixed and suffixed subject markers or a common origin for subject and object markers. Not all the students in one class will use the same language for this exercise, which should be interesting as the resulting "original" shapes are compared.

Comparative/Internal Reconstruction

It is possible to combine the techniques of comparative and internal reconstruction. First compare languages to reconstruct the ancestral language, then carry out internal reconstruction techniques on the result. Alternatively, reconstruct a system internally in each of several languages, and compare the results. Often this can carry us a step further into prehistory.

While comparative/internal reconstruction may be used in the areas of phonology, morphology, lexicon, or semantics, it is perhaps most useful when applied to a coherent system within the language such as the verbal system, kinship terminology, or numerals. Typically, inflectional paradigms and coherent lexical subsets such as numerals and kinship terms show paradigmatic pressure—morphemes close to one another in the paradigm influence one another's development.

Though no two systems reconstruct in quite the same way, we will have an illustration. Consider the data on verbal derivation in Table 29. Very restricted forms, forms with primarily aspectual function, Arabic passives of all but G, and Geᶜez derivatives of all but G have been omitted. The "meanings" given are generalized, and individual derivations show much variation.

Reconstructing forms is relatively simple; meanings are more difficult. We will look at one stem at a time.

a. D-stems (with second radical geminated) are attested in Akkadian, Hebrew, Syriac, Arabic, and Geᶜez. The D-stem seems to have as primary meaning intensive or multiplicative action. It would be tempting to take the frequent transitivizing meaning as primary, but this meaning seems more appropriate for the forms discussed in (b) below.

b. Causative stems exist in Akkadian, Hebrew, Syriac, Arabic, Geᶜez, and Jibbali. These Š-, H-, and ʾ-stems seem to reflect an original causative with prefixed *ša-. This shape is inherited from Afroasiatic, as confirmed by, for example, Berber and Egyptian evidence. The correspondence pattern Akkadian š : West Semitic h is also found in 3d-person pronouns. The forms in ʾ reflect a further loss of initial *h in this prefix. Note that the *š is retained with reflexive *t in Arabic, Geᶜez, and Jibbali. The vocalization matches that of the D-stem in each language.

c. An L-stem, with a lengthened vowel in the first syllable of the stem, is found in Arabic, Geᶜez, and Jibbali. It is absent in Akkadian, Canaanite, and Aramaic. In Modern South Arabian, it seems to have absorbed the D-stem. Geᶜez shows both L- and D-stems but with no clear semantic pattern, and only in Arabic is the contrast between L and D clear. Nor is there clear evidence for an L-stem outside Semitic (though the D-stem is well attested in Berber). This is probably a recent innovation in the south of Semitic.

d. The reflexive/mediopassive stems in *t are clearly original, confirmed by Berber and Cushitic evidence. In this case, the shape is more obscure than the function. In Akkadian and Jibbali, t is consistently infixed after the first stem consonant; in Hebrew and Syriac, it is consistently prefixed except after sibilants. Geᶜez and Arabic show both *t and *ta; the other languages have vowelless forms. We may reconstruct vowelless *t-, prefixed rather than infixed. The infixation with initial sibilants is probably an early Semitic innovation.

e. The N-stem (Akkadian, Hebrew, Arabic) is similarly reconstructed as a vowelless prefix *n-. It is clearly a passive in Semitic, contrasting with the primarily reflexive *t-. Semantically it is an innovation; it continues the widespread Afroasiatic intransitive / reciprocal forms in *m. In Semitic it has become less and less distinct in meaning from the forms in *t-, which probably accounts for its absence from much of later Semitic.

f. The Hebrew Du and Hu are related to the Arabic Gu and unlisted passives of derived stems. Though the Jibbali passive εCCíC/əCCɔ́S, like surviving passives in many Arabic dialects, lacks the characteristic u, it probably belongs here. Nothing like these passives in *u is found in other branches of Afroasiatic. However, the attestation of such forms in Canaanite, Arabic, and Modern South Arabian makes it probable that these reflect an early Semitic innovation.

g. For most derived stems we can reconstruct an alternation in vocalization between *a and *i, though languages differ concerning which form shows which vowel. This alternation is identical to the normal vocalization of quadriliterals, which is reasonable, since most derivatives involve the addition of a consonant. Passives reverse the alternation. There is some evidence that *t- reflexives also reverse it or showed

Table 29. Basics of Semitic Verbal Derivation

Akkadian	G	*iCaCCVC*	*iCCVC*	base
	Gt	*iCtaCCiC*	*iCtaCiC*	reciprocal
	D	*uCaC:aC*	*uCaC:iC*	transitivizing, multiplicative
	Dt	*uCtaC:aC*	*uCtaC:iC*	passive of D
	Š	*ušaCCaC*	*ušaCCiC*	causative, transitivizing
	Št	*uštaCaC:aC*	*uštaCCiC*	reciprocal of Š
	Št	*uštaCCaC*	*uštaCCiC*	passive of Š (rare)
	N	*inCaCCiC*	*inCaCiC*	passive of G, reciprocal
Hebrew	G	*CāCVC*	*yiCCVC*	base
	D	*CiC:ēC*	*yCaC:ēC*	transitivizing, intensive
	Du	*CuC:aC*	*yCuC:aC*	passive of D
	tD	*hitCaC:ēC*	*yitCaC:ēC*	reflexive of D
	H	*hiCCīC*	*yaCCīC*	causative
	Hu	*hoCCaC*	*yoCCaC*	passive of H
	N	*niCCaC*	*yiC:āCēC*	passive/reflexive of G
Syriac	G	*CCVC*	*niCCVC*	base
	tG	*ʾitCCiC*	*nitCCiC*	passive/reflexive of G
	D	*CaC:iC*	*nCaC:iC*	transitivizing, causative
	tD	*ʾitCaC:aC*	*nitCaC:aC*	passive/reflexive of D
	ʾ	*ʾaCCiC*	*naCCiC*	causative
	tʾ	*ʾittaCCaC*	*nittaCCaC*	passive/reflexive of ʾ
Arabic	G	*CaCVCa*	*yaCCVCu*	base
	Gu	*CuCiCa*	*yuCCaCu*	passive of G
	Gt	*iCtaCaCa*	*yaCtaCiCu*	reflexive of G
	D	*CaC:aCa*	*yuCaC:iCu*	transitivizing, intensive
	tD	*taCaC:aCa*	*yataCaC:aCu*	reflexive of D
	L	*CāCaCa*	*yuCāCiCu*	associative
	tL	*taCāCaCa*	*yataCāCaCu*	reflexive of L
	ʾ	*ʾaCCaCa*	*yuCCiCu*	causative
	N	*inCaCaCa*	*yanCaCiCu*	passive, reflexive of G
	St	*istaCCaCa*	*yastaCCiCu*	reflexive of ʾ
Geʿez	G	*CaCVCa*	*yəCCVC*	base
	tG	*taCaCCa*	*yətCaCaC*	passive/reflexive of G
	ʾG	*ʾaCCaCa*	*yāCCəC*	transitivizing, causative of G
	stG	*ʾastaCCaCa*	*yāstaCCəC*	reflexive of ʾG, causative of tG
	D	*CaC:aCa*	*yəCaC:əC*	no consistent meaning
	L	*CāCaCa*	*yəCāCəC*	no consistent meaning
Jibbali	Ga	*Cɔ́Cɔ́C*	*yɔ́CCəC*	base a
	Gta	*Cɔ́tCəC*	*yəCtéCəC*	reflexive of Ga, L
	Ŝta	*ŝəCéCəC*	*yəŝCɛ́CəC*	reciprocal
	Gi	*CéCəC*	*yəCCɔ́C*	base b
	Gti	*əCtəCér*	*yəCtɔ́CuC*	reflexive of Gi
	Ŝti	*ŝəCCéC*	*yŝɛ́CCəC*	passive/reflexive of ʾ
	Gu	*CiCíC*	*əCCɔ́S*	passive of G
	L	*eCóCəC*	*yCɔ́CəC*	intensive, causative
	ʾ	*eCCéC*	*yɛ́CCəC*	causative

nonalternating *a, but this could easily be assimilation to the *u*-passive in vocalization as well as sense.

h. While the vocalization of prefixes is unclear, Akkadian and Arabic indicate *u as the vowel of the subject prefix in transitive derived stems. In Akkadian it is also found in the reciprocals of such stems.

i. Akkadian and Jibbali support an original contrast between *ša-t- as causative of the reflexive and *t-ša- as reflexive of the causative. The early shift of the latter to *š-t-a- and the relative infrequency of these combinations seem to have led to a formal and semantic merger.

Altogether, we reconstruct the forms in Table 30.

Table 30. Reconstructed Semitic Verbal Derivation

Semitic	G	*CaCVCa	*yVCCVCu	base
	Gu	*CuCiCa	*yuCCaCu	passive of G
	tG	*tCVCVCa	*yitCVCVCu	reflexive/mediopassive of G
	D	*CaC:aCa	*yuCaC:iCu	multiplicative, transitivizing
	Du	*CuC:iCa	*yuCuC:aCu	passive of D
	tD	*tCaC:VCa	*yitCaC:VCu	reflexive/mediopassive of D
	Š	*šaCCaCa	*yušaCCiCu	causative
	Šu	*šuCCiCa	*yušuCCaCu	passive of Š
	Št	*štaCCVCa	*yVštaCCVCu	reflexive/mediopassive of Š
	ŠtG	*šatCVCVCa	*yVšatCVCVCa	causative of tG
	N	*nCaCVCa	*yVnCaCiCu	reciprocal, passive of G

Exercise 16. Reconstructing Verbal Inflection

Use the tables of verbal inflection in Paradigms C, pp. 95, 98, 100, 101, 102, 104, 107, 109, 111, 113. Reconstruct as much as possible of the verbal inflection of Proto-Semitic. You should not at this point include the data from the Afroasiatic languages, but you may use the non-Semitic languages Coptic and Ghadamsi.

You will find that you need to take date of attestation into consideration—it is clear that the later stages of Semitic have lost original features. But you cannot concentrate alone on Akkadian, Ugaritic, Classical Arabic, and Geʿez, since other languages may preserve features that they have lost. Notice that in dealing with a restricted inventory like this, you have to make some hard and rather arbitrary decisions.

Part 6

Various Less-Common Techniques

The literature of diachronic linguistics includes a wide variety of techniques. Many are variations of lexicostatistics or reconstruction; many are ingenious experiments that can yield very interesting results. Only a few techniques other than lexicostatistics and reconstruction are practiced with any frequency. I will provide you with brief introductions to three of these.

Loan Analysis

Languages constantly affect one another through contact. All areas of language are involved. Phonology is affected as languages add or eliminate phonemic contrasts or go through sound changes together. Inflectional and derivational markers may be borrowed, and case or tense and aspect systems can be restructured on the model of an unrelated language.

There are also semantic and syntactic borrowings. The meaning of a native lexical item may change under the influence of a semantic shift in another language, or compounds may be translated literally into another language. The basic syntactic structures of one language may move in the direction of another language with which the first is in contact (as Ethiopian Semitic is assumed to have moved toward Cushitic syntactic structure). Languages like Urmi, Maltese, or Chaha, which are in contact with languages very different in structure, display a wide variety of such changes.

All of these effects can be used in the reconstruction of linguistic prehistory. We will consider here only the use of lexical borrowings—LOANWORDS. The term is of course a misnomer—languages do not return "borrowed" vocabulary. The first problem with loan analysis is recognizing the loanwords. It is hard enough when languages are unrelated or only very distantly related. Similar forms may arise in unrelated languages through coincidence or without borrowing (many resemblances in animal names can be explained by the cry of the animal, for instance).

Special problems arise when languages are closely related; it is always difficult to be sure whether similarities are due to borrowing, common inheritance, or (in the case of derivatives) parallel development. The most difficult situation is two related languages that are not merely in contact but in a diglossic relationship: that is, both languages are in daily use in the same community, one usually being a "high" language, used in the court, in liturgy, or by the educated. This is the case in most of the Arab world, for example, where "colloquial Arabic" dialects exist

Table 31. Loanwords in Egyptian Arabic

Loanword	Gloss	Source	Evidence of Borrowing
ba's	boxwood	English? but 'box' < Latin *buxus* < Greek *puxos*	no indication of borrowed status
bar'ū'	plum	Greek	unusual phonological structure
barγūt	flea	inherited Semitic, despite unusual phonological structure	
basmil	invoke God	innovation in Classical Arabic, from بِسْمِ اللّٰه *bi-sm-i l-lāhi* 'in God's name'	
basxa	plowshare	Coptic	no indication of borrowed status
bāša	pasha	Turkish	abnormal morphology, cultural innovation
baṭṭ	duck	Persian	an old loan into Semitic, no indication of borrowed status
bidingān	eggplant	Persian	unusual phonological structure
bujēh	spark plug	French	unusual phonological structure, abnormal morphology, cultural innovation
buks	boxing	English	cultural innovation
burg	tower	German	no indication of borrowed status
busṭa	mail	Italian	cultural innovation
busṭagi	mailman	Italian, with Turkish derivational suffix	unusual phonological structure, abnormal morphology

side by side with educated literary Arabic. Even uneducated speech will include words or forms belonging to the high language; even the language of the elite will include words and constructions of the low language. It is hard to disentangle the two languages.

There are clues, of course. Words that do not fit the regular phonological patterns of one language are often assumed to be borrowed (especially if they do match the regular correspondences in the putative source language). In some cases, items pertaining to an area of culture or technology known or assumed to be alien may be borrowed. Again, lexical derivatives that cannot be explained in terms of the language's native morphology may prove to be borrowed. However, any attempt to treat these as rigid criteria is doomed to failure; some borrowings do not show any such indications, and some items that do meet the criteria are not borrowed.

To illustrate some of the problems and possibilities, I give in Table 31 a small sample of Egyptian Arabic. As far as possible, the sources have been noted.

Geographic Analysis

Geographic analysis is much used in dialectology and is a technique that is especially useful in dealing with closely related languages. It involves first plotting and then analyzing the areal distribution of linguistic features, whether phonological developments, morphological patterns,

---

Exercise 17. Identifying Loanwords

Wordlist D provides 220-entry vocabularies of Classical **Ar**abic, **Mo**roccan Arabic, **Ma**ltese, and the Berber languages **Se**nhayi, **A**yt **S**eghrouchen, and **Gh**adamsi. The situation as we know it is this: through the diglossia common in Islamic Arabic-speaking areas, Classical Arabic continues to exert an influence on Moroccan Arabic that it does not have on Maltese. Maltese has had considerable influence from Italian; Moroccan, Ayt Seghrouchen, and Ghadamsi from French; and Senhayi from Spanish. Berber has been affected by and has influenced North African Arabic; Berber loanwords have been identified even in Maltese. Berber also has some older loanwords from Latin and Punic, but these may not be obvious to you. Look for evidence of contact, trying to identify probable direction of borrowing. Consider the possibility of common inheritance; Berber shares some cognates with Semitic inherited from their Afroasiatic ancestry. You may have to consult French, Italian, or Spanish dictionaries.

---

lexical items, or even cultural traits. The data may be entered either on a map or on a stylized chart like the one in Table 32.

One can then draw lines (ISOGLOSSES) on the map or chart to demarcate areas taken as sharing "the same" form. Different types of lines may serve to reflect a hierarchy of relationships. In our example, heavy lines set off areas with major differences. A narrower line separates Arabic from Syriac and Hebrew; the systems are essentially the same, but Syriac and Hebrew have lost the final vowels that differentiate the moods in Arabic.

Table 32. Semitic Verbal Patterns, Base Form: Perfect/Imperfect/Subjunctive

Before drawing isoglosses:

Syriac	Akkadian
$CCaC$	$iCCaC$
$niCCuC$	$iCaCCuC$

Hebrew	
$C\bar{a}CaC$	
$yiCC\bar{o}C$	

	Arabic
	$CaCaCa$
	$yaCCuCu$
	$yaCCVCa$

Ge͑ez	Jibbali
$CaCaCa$	$C\acute{ɔ}C\acute{ɔ}C$
$yəCaCCəC$	$yC\acute{ɔ}CəC$
$yəCCəC$	$y\acute{ɔ}CCəC$

Before drawing isoglosses

After drawing isoglosses:

Syriac		Akkadian
$CCaC$		$iCCaC$
$niCCuC$		$iCaCCuC$

Hebrew		
$C\bar{a}CaC$		
$yiCC\bar{o}C$		

	Arabic	
	$CaCaCa$	
	$yaCCuCu$	
	$yaCCVCa$	

Ge͑ez		Jibbali
$CaCaCa$		$C\acute{ɔ}C\acute{ɔ}C$
$yəCaCCəC$		$yC\acute{ɔ}CəC$
$yəCCəC$		$y\acute{ɔ}CCəC$

After drawing isoglosses

The preliminary processes—mapping forms and drawing isoglosses—are rather simple and to a degree mechanical. They can be done with a fairly simple computer program. As usual, the interpretation is the hard part. Let us suppose that Akkadian and Jibbali (greatly separated in time and space) are linked by a number of isoglosses and separated from the remainder of Semitic. Are we to conclude (a) that Akkadian and Jibbali are more closely related than one would expect; (b) that Akkadian and Jibbali, being on the periphery of the Semitic range, have failed to share in an innovation adopted elsewhere; or (c) that the particular isoglosses are without historical significance?

While a single isogloss may be very important, greater weight is usually put on bundles of isoglosses—a number of isoglosses that set off the same languages. The correlation between isogloss bundles and lexicostatistics is not perfect, but it exists, and isoglosses can be used for subgrouping in much the same way as lexicostatistics. Of course, isogloss bundles may not all point the same way. Some lexical isoglosses align Arabic with Canaanite and Aramaic; others link Arabic with Ethiopian Semitic and Old South Arabian. Again, isoglosses may reflect chance similarities or contact rather than common innovation. The similarity between Soqotri *trɔ* and Syriac ܬܪܝܢ *treyn* 'two', from Proto-Semitic *θn-ay-*, involves two isoglosses. Both Soqotri and Syriac regularly have stops as the reflexes of Semitic dental fricatives; both Soqotri and Syriac have *r* as the reflex of *n* in the originally vowelless stems for 'two' and 'son'. These reflexes are characteristic of Aramaic, but the isoglosses do not allow us to postulate any special relationship between Soqotri and Aramaic.

There is only one rule of interpretation that can be taken to be firm. When the isoglosses match with what one would expect, given our knowledge of geography, they should be assumed to reflect geography and not linguistic history. Similarities between adjacent languages, the existence of a core of similar languages in the center of a language group, and archaic items retained by peripheral languages are generally to be ignored. Note here that the distance that produces these effects need not be simply measurable in miles. A relatively impassable river or strip of forest, though narrow, can be more of a barrier than hundreds of miles of good road. Further, there is social distance—factors such as cultural differences or hostility—which can be a serious barrier to the daily intercourse that minimizes language differences.

Exercise 18. Drawing Isoglosses

Wordlist E contains 120 entries for Geʿez and 7 modern Ethiopian Semitic languages, 3 ancient and 5 modern Aramaic languages, and Classical Arabic and 7 forms of colloquial Arabic. The languages included have been chosen to include at least one language from the 2 major subdivisions of each group, and one pair of closely related languages separated by the religion of the speakers. In one case, this is all that separates them—the speakers of the modern Aramaic dialect labeled Azerbaijani Jewish are Jews who live among the Christian speakers of Urmi.

Pick one of the 3 groups and draw isoglosses. You can expect to find some interesting patterns of relationship. Look for effects of geographic and cultural separation and (especially if you choose to work on Aramaic) time depth. Note that, as with lexicostatistics, different parts of speech may pattern differently.

Cultural Reconstruction

Cultural reconstruction is a technique (also called *Wörter und Sachen* 'words and things', or "linguistic paleontology") that is often applied but that is low in reliability, largely because people who use it apply it in very different ways. The basic assumption is unexceptionable. Language is part of culture, and the vocabulary of a language reflects the material and conceptual culture of its speakers.

Cultural reconstruction makes claims such as the following: the fact that we may reconstruct Proto-Semitic *kalb-* 'dog' gives evidence that the speakers of Proto-Semitic had dogs living with them. One can, of course, make much more sophisticated claims, such as this: Ethiopic has reflexes of Proto-Semitic *δi'b-* 'wolf' but uses these words for 'hyena'; we may therefore assume that the ancestors of the Ethiopic-speakers left a region where wolves were common for a region where they were not.

Of course, there are many problems. As with geographic analysis, we have to weed out as useless all that is already obvious from other sources. For example, one very thoroughly researched study sought to identify the original homeland of a group of languages on the basis of reconstructible plant and animal terminology and the distribution of the plants and animals themselves. Since the meaning assigned to the reconstruction was the meaning most common in the languages, and since the majority of the languages were spoken in an area with fairly uniform flora and fauna, the assumed "homeland" proved to be in the geographical center of the group.

There will also be false predictions, especially where there has been semantic change during a period of continued intercourse among members of the group. In the case of Semitic, the early cultural influence of Akkadian and the later dominance of Arabic and Islam have made reconstruction of original cultural traits much more difficult in such areas as religious and legal vocabulary.

Exercise 19. Cultural Reconstruction

Use your reconstructions of Ethiopian Semitic based on Wordlist C as a basis for conclusions about culture and environment. How much of this could have been deduced from other sources?

Part 7

Onward and Beyond

This manual does not exhaust the inventory of techniques available for diachronic linguistics. Readers will find others described in the literature on a variety of language families and may well develop some innovative techniques themselves.

One obvious way to pass beyond the borders of what we have done is to get into the comparison of fine points, especially in the area of syntax (we have not included syntactic comparison in the examples and exercises, largely because the units are too large and flexible for really simple evaluation). Consider these entries rejected as too specialized from our bibliography:

Bravmann, Meir M. 1939–40. Some Aspects of the Development of Semitic Diphthongs. *Orientalia* 8: 244–60, 9: 45–60.

Cowan, William. 1960. Arabic Evidence for Proto-Semitic */awa/ and */ō/. *Language* 36: 60–62.

Eisler, Robert. 1939. Loan Words in Semitic Languages Meaning 'Town'. *Antiquity* 13: 449–55.

Eitan, I. 1928. Hebrew and Semitic Particles. *American Journal of Semitic Languages* 44: 177–205.

Goetze, Albrecht. 1942. The So-Called Intensive of Semitic Languages. *Journal of the American Oriental Society* 62: 1–8.

Kienast, Burkhart. 1957. Der Präfixvokal *u* im Kausative und im D-Stamm des Semitischen. *Münchener Studien zur Sprachwissenschaft* 11: 104–8.

Leslau, Wolf. 1953. The Imperfect in Southeast Semitic. *Journal of the American Oriental Society* 73: 164–66.

Poebel, Arno. 1932. *Das appositionell bestimmte Pronomen der 1 pers. sing. in den westsemitischen inschriften und im AT.* Chicago: The University of Chicago Press.

Rosen, Haiim B. 1959. Zur Vorgeschichte des Relativsatzes im Nordwestsemitischen. *Archiv Orientální* 27: 186–98.

Speiser, E. A. 1947. The Elative in West Semitic and Akkadian. *Journal of Cuneiform Studies* 6: 81–92.

Semitic and Afroasiatic

Another way to get beyond the borders of our study of Semitic is to apply precisely the same techniques to Afroasiatic. This is also a much-needed contribution. It is by no means true of everyone in the field, but too many scholars working in Semitic know little or nothing of other languages of Afroasiatic, and too many people contributing to Afroasiatic linguistics have hardly any Semitic expertise.

I have taken the reader a little beyond, by including Coptic and Ghadamsi in the appended paradigms, for example. But there remains much to do. As the student begins to do it, I want to urge him to keep his eyes open. If the basic methodology presented here is applied directly to reliable Afroasiatic language data, solid conclusions can be reached. If the student reads comparative work by others and looks for matches with Semitic as she knows it, these questions can be asked:

- Is a consistent standard of cognacy being applied?
- Is regular correspondence a criterion?
- How close a semantic match does the researcher require?
- Do the conclusions follow from the evidence presented?
- Is the method an adequate support for the types of conclusions drawn?
- Does the researcher in fact apply the criteria he or she presents?
- Are the languages or groups from which data are drawn appropriate?
- How well does the researcher know the languages or groups studied?

The answers to these questions should help the student to evaluate the validity of the researcher's conclusions.

Exercise 20. Critical Reading in Afroasiatic Studies

Read critically any three books or major articles dealing with Afroasiatic comparison. You may include one focused on the reconstruction of an Afroasiatic subgroup other than Semitic. Comment on the selection and use of data and on the conclusions. How might each be improved?

Evading the Triconsonantal Root

It is generally known that the Semitic languages are characterized by root morphemes consisting of three consonants. Of course, there are morphemes that seem to have just one consonant (*bi* 'in, with'), others with just two (*θn-* 'two'), and some with four or more (*parθuγ-* 'flea'). But triconsonantal roots predominate numerically. In addition, some quadriliteral roots seem to be secondary (reduplications like *šal-šal-at* 'chain', possible expansions of triliterals like *θaʕl-ab-* ~ *θaʕl-* 'fox', and cases like the Arabic denominative verb بَسْمَلَ *basmala* 'say bi-smi-llāhi'). When a denominative verb is based on a Semitic noun with two consonants, a radical is added (for example, the Arabic verb سَمَّى *sammā* 'name' with presumed Semitic root **šmy* from *ism* 'name' < *šm-*).

However, there have been attempts to show that the triconsonantal root is innovative in Semitic and that roots of two consonants underlie most if not all triliterals. It must be admitted that there is support for such a hypothesis:

- Many of the quadriliteral roots are clearly reduplications of two-consonant sequences (*kabkab-* 'star').

Exercise 21. Reconstructing Proto–Berber-Semitic

Wordlist F presents Berber and Semitic equivalents for 175 correspondence sets. The Berber languages are the ideal choice for a preliminary comparison between Semitic and other Afroasiatic languages. While clearly distinct from Semitic, they are closely enough related to allow us to find clear cognates and share some important similarities of structure. There is also enough variation within Berber to allow for a reconstruction with significant time depth. As type languages for Semitic, you are given **Ak**kadian, **Ug**aritic, **Sy**riac, Classical **Ar**abic, **Ge**ʿez, and **Ji**bbali. The Berber languages are **Je**bel **N**efusa, **Gh**adamsi, **W**argla, **A**yt **S**eghrouchen, **Ka**byle, and **Sh**ilḥa.

Note that in Berber transcriptions, the symbol : is used to mark geminate or fortis consonants; a sequence of two identical symbols indicates a syllable break. Berber nouns show either prefixal or both prefixal and suffixal markers of gender and number; thus in Ayt Seghrouchen we find *adbir* 'pigeon', feminine *tadbirt,* with plurals *idbirn* and *idbirin* respectively. The most common markings are: masculine-singular *a-,* masculine-plural *i-n,* feminine-singular *ta-t,* feminine-plural *ti-in.* In Berber base verbs, assume a triconsonantal root; there are some with four consonants, however. Vowels in the citation form of the verb in the modern languages should be assumed to reflect a semivowel in the protolanguage (much as in Semitic); otherwise postulate Ø for missing consonants.

Reconstruct Proto-Berber and Proto-Semitic forms. Now compare Proto-Berber and Proto-Semitic. You may reconstruct Proto–Berber-Semitic forms or try a lexicostatistical analysis.

- Verbs with semivowel radicals generally have at least some "biliteral" forms (*šin-at-* 'sleep' < *wašina* 'sleep', Hebrew וַיִּ֫בֶן *wayyiben* 'and he built' < *banaya* 'build', Arabic قم *qum* 'stand up!' < *qawama* 'stand').
- There is some tendency to move roots from one category to another, either shifting the position of the weak radical or moving to the final geminate category. This is most obvious in the modern languages, but consider 'spit': Hebrew יָרַק *yāraq*, Geʿez ⵡⵕⵉ: *waraqa* < *waraqa*; Hebrew רָקַק *rāqaq*, Syriac ܪܩ *raqq* < *raqaqa*; Arabic ريق *rīq* 'saliva' < **rayaqa*.
- There exist sets of roots of similar meaning but with differing final consonants, which could be suffixes: Arabic بَرِئَ *bariʾa* 'be free', بَرِحَ *bariḥa* 'leave', بَرَزَ *baraza* 'emerge', بَرَعَ *baraʿa* 'excel', بَرَى *barā* 'scrape off', all of which could be analyzed as involving outward motion (compare *barr-* 'outside, open country').
- There exist sets of roots of similar meaning sharing an initial consonant that could be a prefix: *qaṭaʿa* 'cut', *qaṣaṣa* 'chop', *qariḥa* 'cut off hair', *qarṭima* 'cut off', *qalapa* 'peel', *qadiḥa* 'drill', all sharing initial *q* and all referring to some type of cutting.

This evidence would not be very convincing, however, were it not that biliteral roots appear to predominate in Afroasiatic, and Proto-Indo-European (with which Semitic has often been compared) shows roots with two consonants. Even this support is not overwhelming. The relationship with Indo-European, while frequently suggested, has not been proven, and the predominance of biliteral roots in Afroasiatic may be only apparent. In Cushitic and Chadic verbs, to be sure, it seems likely that roots with two consonants predominate (though more complex structures are common in nouns in both groups). But in Egyptian and Berber verbs, it seems probable that the norm is the triliteral root, as in Semitic. Many Egyptian biliteral verbs whose history and conjugation are known reflect a defective writing system or the loss over time of various consonants. Many Berber biliteral verbs with cognates elsewhere in Afroasiatic also show consonant losses, like *ls* 'dress', cognate with Semitic **labiša*. In just the same way, Phoenician and other Semitic languages attested only in consonantal scripts, or Urmi and other phonetically much-altered languages, would appear to have many biliteral roots if we did not have other Semitic languages to alert us to their triconsonantal status.

Further, most of the interpretations of triliteral roots as augmented biliterals are not based on a reconstructed Proto-Semitic lexicon but on data from individual languages, such as Arabic, and lexicons incorporating much poetic and dialectal vocabulary. But I would prefer that the student drew conclusions from exercises such as the three that follow.

Exercise 22. Identifying a Prefix

Consider Table 33's set of Proto-Semitic verbs in initial **n*. Is there enough evidence to identify the initial as a prefix?

Table 33. Proto-Semitic Verbs with *n-*

*našiya	'forget'	**naqaba*	'pierce'
*nabaḥa	'bark'	**naqara*	'pick at'
*nakaθa ~ *naθaka	'bite'	**naṣaba*	'plant, set up'
*naẓara	'guard, watch'	**nawama*	'slumber'
*napala	'fall'	**naxara*	'snort'
*napaxa	'blow'	**naśiʾa*	'pick up'

Exercise 23. Identifying a Suffix

Consider Table 34's set of Proto-Semitic verbs in final **m*. Is there enough evidence to identify the final as a suffix?

Table 34. Proto-Semitic Verbs with *-m*

*gazama	'cut, trim'	**qawama*	'stand'
*ḥalama	'dream'	**ragama*	'stone'
*ḥamima	'be hot'	**raḥima*	'love, pity'
*ḥarima	'be forbidden'	**ṭaʿima*	'taste'
*nawama	'slumber'	**xatama*	'seal'
*qadama	'precede'	**śayama*	'set'

Exercise 24. Identifying Roots and Affixes

Consider Table 35's set of Proto-Semitic verbs relating to various kinds of cutting. Does the evidence support the hypothesis that triliteral roots are complex?

Table 35. Proto-Semitic Verbs Relating to 'cutting'

*gazama	'cut, trim'	*qalapa	'peel'
*gazaza	'shear, reap'	*qaraṣa	'nip'
*naqaba	'pierce'	*qariḥa	'cut off hair'
*naqara	'pick at'	*qaṣaṣa	'chop'
*paṭara	'split open'	*qaṣaya	'cut off'
*qadida	'cut open'	*qaṭapa	'pluck'

Ebla and What Next?

It is really not all that long ago—200 years or so—that the Semitic family consisted of Hebrew, Chaldee and Syriac, Arabic, and Geʿez (with Modern Aramaic unknown to the scholarly world and Modern Arabic and the contemporary languages of Ethiopia receiving little or no study). There has been a tremendous expansion in the study of the modern languages, but even the opening up of Modern South Arabian has not had as great an effect on our understanding of the Semitic family as the three more recent great recoveries of ancient Semitic.

First came Akkadian. We had, thanks to the record of the Old Testament, an awareness that Assyrian and Babylonian existed and even a small corpus of Akkadian words and names. Then the cuneiform writings were deciphered, and Akkadian proved to be unmistakably Semitic, though quite distinct from the rest of the family.

Next came Ugaritic. Ugarit and its language were a total surprise. Ras Shamra began to be dug in 1929, and its tablets in a cuneiform but alphabetic script added to our inventory of Semitic a language nearly as old and arguably quite as conservative as Akkadian but so close in language and even detail of poetic expression to Biblical Hebrew as to change drastically our view of Northwest Semitic.

And now Ebla. In the 1970s, newspaper articles appeared telling of the discovery of an amazing new, amazingly old Semitic language. This too promised to revolutionize Semitic studies—a language contemporary with Akkadian, whose linguistic structure included features much more like those of West Semitic—or so it seemed.

Fascinating and important as Eblaite is, it has not proven easy to extract and analyze Eblaite linguistic data, written as they are in a mix of Sumerograms, conventional Akkadian spellings, and phonetic signs that may be read in several different ways. Akkadian specialists have become adept at dealing with similar material, but the sheer volume and diversity of Akkadian texts and the maturity of Akkadian studies make for greater agreement on interpretation. At Ebla, the bulk of the usable evidence is Sumerian-Eblaite glossaries and personal names—names of persons who may not even have been from Ebla. We do not as yet have anything like the voluminous texts and phonetically based script of Ugarit. Perhaps not surprisingly, the immediate result has been considerable disagreement about the affinities and implications of Eblaite. For a time it seemed as if the subgrouping of Semitic would be seri-ously altered. Today we can relax—or so it seems. Eblaite now appears to be one more dialect of East Semitic. It is useful and interesting enough but does not force us to rework our picture of Semitic prehistory. In terms of our reconstruction of Proto-Semitic phonology and lexicon, Eblaite will not add a great deal. The volume of useful material—phonetically written and se-mantically clear—is just too small.

This is not to downplay the importance of Eblaite or other "new" Semitic languages (an-cient or modern) that may be discovered. New discoveries keep us from getting too set in our ways, too fixed on a particular view of earliest Semitic history or a particular set of features "defining" Semitic or one of its subgroups. They do add or modify reconstructions and can shed light on odd semantic shifts or on the original sense of Biblical Hebrew hapax legomena.

But permit me to sound a note of caution. Newly discovered Semitic languages, both an-cient and modern, need to be taken cautiously, and I would recommend becoming familiar with the material before being persuaded by the dicta of an enthusiastic specialist. Most of the newly discovered ancient languages give us very few, very short, very fragmentary documents. Scholars may quibble over the value of a sign but be willing to fill lacunae. When an inscrip-tion is transcribed, it often must be interpreted on the basis of other languages—we search the corners of Classical and dialectal Arabic vocabulary to find words whose root and meaning might fit the context of a Sabean inscription. We need to ask, Is there enough context, are there enough parallel texts to justify our identifications?

The modern discoveries are not much more help. Large parts of the Gurage, Modern Ara-maic, or Modern South Arabian material are very interesting, but compared to Akkadian, Clas-sical Arabic, Geʿez, Hebrew, and Syriac, these languages have been through centuries more erosion of phonology, reformation of grammatical structure, semantic shift, and borrowing—often borrowing from their better-known relatives.

So when the next language turns up, analysts must check it out carefully, using some of these techniques to do their own evaluation and examine what the discoverer is doing with the primary sources. For now, here is a final exercise, intended to give the reader an idea of how much difference it really makes to factor a new language into the calculations.

Exercise 25. Reconstructing Proto-Semitic with Classical, Ancient, and Modern Data

Using Wordlist G (a 200-entry list for Hebrew, Syriac, Arabic, and Geʿez), recon-struct vocabulary; call this Proto-Semitic A. As far as possible, reconstruct vocaliza-tion of nouns and base conjugation verbs. For most adjectives, vocalization probably cannot be reconstructed.

Now add the Akkadian and Ugaritic data of Wordlist H and reconstruct on the basis of the six languages; this you may call Proto-Semitic B. Note changes in the inventory of reconstructible items and in the shapes you reconstruct.

Finally, add the Maʿlula and Jibbali data from Wordlist I and reconstruct Proto-Semitic C using all eight languages. What is the contribution of these two modern languages to the overall picture?

Conclusion

I trust that by now it is clear, from occasional remarks in this text, from the instructors' comments, and from the students' practical experiences working through the exercises, that the techniques for reconstructing linguistic history are flawed. This does not mean we cannot or should not use them—a great many of us have been using them for a long time. But it does mean that we should always apply more than one of the available techniques and look for agreements between various techniques that do not simply tell us what we could guess from a look at the map.

If, as I hope, these manipulations, analyses, calculations, and extrapolations have been enjoyable, the reader may want to continue. Before attempting serious work in comparative Semitic linguistics, his knowledge of the languages and scripts of Semitic scholarship may need to be expanded.

It is also good to read fairly widely in comparative linguistics. One may not choose to focus on theory, but it is important to check out what has been done and what the trends are in linguistic reconstruction. While the student should focus on Semitic, she will also need to go beyond Semitic, at least into Afroasiatic. Such reading should be done with an open mind, but critically. One should not accept the conclusions of other comparative linguists until checking their facts and logic.

The student will probably find it necessary to specialize somewhat. The Semitic field is just too rich: a complete bibliography of Arabic (or Hebrew, or Aramaic, or Akkadian, or Ethiopic) linguistics would in itself be a weighty tome; there are subfields and sub-subfields. But even a specialist needs breadth of perspective. One is a better Hebraist for knowing some Geʿez, a better Semitist for having a sense of the rest of Afroasiatic.

At all times, keep in mind the truth about comparative linguistics, indeed about all of linguistics. Nothing is real except the raw facts of the language, the words people say, the scratchings on the rock. All linguistic analysis is fiction or educated guess; all linguistic description is a more-or-less simplified and distorted mapping of the complexities of speech on a sheet of paper. When drawing a conclusion that is elegant and innovative, one should not fall in love with it. Remember, with honesty and humility, that one new fact can reshuffle the cards and force a totally different (but equally elegant) analysis.

Paradigms A

Phonology

Proto-Semitic

The consonant system of Proto-Semitic is rather easy to reconstruct. It is less easy to be certain of the phonetic value of certain contrastive units. Some consonants pose no problem for reconstruction. The reflex of *b*, for example, is nearly always a voiced bilabial.

p	θ	t	s	ś	š	k	x	ḥ	h
b	δ	d	z	l		g	γ	ʿ	ʾ
	θ̣	ṭ	ṣ	ẓ́		q			
		r							
m		n							
			y	w					

The vowel system is also unambiguously reconstructable. There are three short vowels with three corresponding long vowels. The long vowels in some cases seem to be derived from sequences of vowels or from vowel plus semivowel but in other instances function as units. The diphthongs *aw* and *ay* have been added to the list; although in Proto-Semitic they generally function as sequences, in the daughter languages they are often realized as units comparable to the three original long vowels.

i	a	u	ī	ā	ū	aw	ay

Note the asymmetries of the system. There is no emphatic bilabial, though the evidence of Chadic makes it probable that one existed in Afroasiatic. The *š is much more common than *s; it seems likely that Afroasiatic *s became *š and that Semitic *s mostly derives from skewings and borrowings. It seems illogical to align the glottal stop * ʾ with the voiced consonants, when it is necessarily voiceless, but that is how it seems to pattern.

In the sketches below, I present the phonological inventory for each language twice. The table on the left shows the reflexes of the above Proto-Semitic phonemes. Where mergers have occurred, the same symbol may occur twice. Where there are splits, two units may appear

68

reflecting a single phoneme of the protolanguage. By contrast, the table to the right is arranged to show the pattern of phonemic contrasts within the daughter language. Some of the phonemes included may not have a Proto-Semitic source.

Old Babylonian

Though pharyngeals and glottals are not indicated in transcriptions and were mostly lost, some were still present in the earliest stages. In Old Babylonian and later Akkadian, *a* was replaced with *e* in syllables with original ʿ, ḥ, and γ.

p	š	t	s	š	š	k	x	Ø	Ø
b	z	d	z	l		g	Ø	Ø	Ø
		ṣ	ṭ	ṣ	ṣ		q		
		r							
m		n							
				y	w				

i	a, e	u	ī	ā, ē	ū	ī	ū

p	t	s	š	k	x
b	d	z		g	
ṭ	ṣ		q		
	r				
	l				
m	n				
		y	w		

i/ī	u/ū
e/ē	a/ā

Syriac

All nonemphatic stops have fricative allophones when postvocalic and not geminate.

p/f	t/θ	t/θ	s	s	š	k/x	ḥ	ḥ	h
b/β	d/δ	d/δ	z	l		g/γ	ʿ	ʿ	ʾ
	ṭ	ṭ	ṣ	ʿ		q			
		r							
m		n							
				y	w				

i	a	u	ī	ā	ū	ay	aw

p/f	t/θ	s	š	k/x	ḥ	h
b/β	d/δ	z		g/γ	ʿ	ʾ
ṭ	ṣ		q			
l						
r						
m	n					
		y	w			

i/ī		u/ū
	a/ā	

Urmi

The system found in Modern Aramaic dialects has been greatly altered by loanwords from Arabic, Turkish, Kurdish, Russian, and Farsi, as well as by significant levels of phonetic skewing. The transcription used, based on a Soviet romanization, treats emphasis as a feature of vowels (except for $ṭ$). Unfortunately, emphasis is not marked for *e*, *o*, or *u*. The asterisks in the consonant tables indicate that no special consonant symbol is used; instead, the word is pronounced with emphatic vowels. Other analyses would include at least ʿ and ṣ.

p	t	t	s	s	š	k/x	x	x	h
b/v	d	d	z	l		g	∅*	∅*	∅
	ṭ	ṭ	s*	∅*		q			
		r							
m		n							

		j	v		

p	t	č	k	x	h
b	d	ç	g	γ	∅
f	s	š			
v	z	ž			
	ṭ	ṣ	q		
	l		j		
	r				
m	n				

i, ï	ə, a	u	i, ï	ə, a	u	e	o

i		u
e		o
	ə	

ï		u
e		o
	a	

Ugaritic

Values for some Ugaritic consonants cannot be determined. Transcriptions in syllabic script are not precise. It seems that texts differ phonologically, reflecting different periods or dialects.

p	θ	t	s	š	š	k	x	ḥ	h
b	δ	d	z	l		g	γ	ʿ	ʾ
	ḍ	ṭ	ṣ	ṣ		q			
		r							
m		n							

		y	w		

p	θ	t	s	š	k	x	ḥ	h
b	δ	d	z		g	γ	ʿ	ʾ
		ṭ	ṣ		q			
	ḍ							
		l						
		r						
m		n						
			y	w				

i	a	u	ī	ā	ū	ē	ō

i/ī		u/ū
ē		ō
	a/ā	

Hebrew

All nonemphatic stops have fricative allophones when postvocalic and not geminate. The interpretation of the vowel system here is only one of the possible analyses. The reflex of a given reconstructed Semitic vowel is conditioned by syllable structure and stress.

p/f	š	t/θ	s	ś	š	k/x	ḥ	ḥ	h
b/β	z	d/δ	z	l		g/γ	ʿ	ʿ	ʾ
	ṣ	ṭ	ṣ	ṣ		q			
		r							
m		n							
				y	w				

p/f	t/θ	s	š	k/x	ḥ	h
b/β	d/δ	z		g/γ	ʿ	ʾ (aleph)
	ṭ	ṣ		q		
	l					
	r					
m	n					
		y	w			

i/ē	a, ā, e	u, ō, o	ī	ā/ō	ū	ayi, ē	awe, ō

i/ī		u/ū
ē		ō
	a/ā	

Classical Arabic

There is evidence that ḍ was once a lateral for some dialects, and ẓ is often realized as a dental.

f	θ	t	s	š	s	k	x	ḥ	h
b	δ	d	z	l		g	γ	ʿ	ʾ
	ẓ	ṭ	ṣ	ḍ		q			
		r							
m		n							
				y	w				

f	θ	t	s	š	k	x	ḥ	h
b	δ	d	z		g	γ	ʿ	ʾ
		ṭ	ṣ		q			
		ḍ	ẓ					
		l						
	r							
m		n						
				y	w			

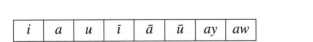

i	a	u	ī	ā	ū	ay	aw

i/ī		u/ū
	a/ā	

Egyptian Arabic

As in many dialects of Modern Arabic, emphasis is a "long component" only loosely associated with any particular consonants.

f	t	t	s	š	s	k	x	ḥ	h
b	d	d	z	l		g	γ	ʿ	ʾ
	ẓ	ṭ	ṣ	ḍ		ʾ			
		r/ṛ							
m		n							
				y	w				

f	t	s	š	k	x	ḥ	h
b	d	z		g	γ	ʿ	ʾ
	ṭ	ṣ					
	ḍ	ẓ					
	l						
	r						
	ṛ						
m	n						
		y	w				

i/ī		u/ū
ē		ō
	a/ā	

i	a	u	ī	ā	ū	ē	ō

Ge'ez

The labialized velars could be treated as part of vocalization. Note later mergers of ḍ (the reflex of *ẓ́) with ṣ and š (the reflex of *ś) with s; ḍ and š may still have been laterals.

f	s	t	s	š	s	k/kʷ	x	ḥ	h
b	z	d	z	l		g/gʷ	ʿ	ʿ	ʾ
	ṣ	ṭ	ṣ	ḍ		q/qʷ			
		r							
m		n							
				y	w				

f	t	s	š	k	kʷ	x	ḥ	h
b	d	z		g	gʷ		ʿ	ʾ
	ṭ	ṣ		q	qʷ			
	ḍ							
	l							
	r							
m	n							
		y		w				

ī	ə	ū
ē		ō
	a/ā	

ə	a	ə	ī	ā	ū	ē	ō

Tigre

The most noticeable change is the development of palatal consonants from the dentals.

f	s/š	t/č	s/š	s/š	s/š	k/kʷ	ḥ	ḥ	h
b	z/ž	d/j	z/ž	l		g/gʷ	ʕ	ʕ	ʔ
	ṣ/č̣	ṭ/č̣	ṣ/č̣	ṣ/č̣		q/qʷ			
		r							
m		n							
				y	w				

f	t	s	č	š	k	kʷ	ḥ	h
b	d	z	j	ž	g	gʷ	ʕ	ʔ
	ṭ	ṣ	č̣		q	qʷ		
	ḍ							
	l							
	r							
m	n							
			y		w			

i	ə	u
e	ä	o
a		

ə	ä	ə	i	a	u	e	o

Jibbali

The sounds *ź* and *ẓ́* are voiced lateral fricatives, the latter glottalized. The sounds *ŝ* and *ṣ̂* are dorsoalveolar fricatives with rounding but no contact between tongue and alveolum. The sounds *ṭ*, *ṣ*, *q*, and *ṣ̂* are ejective; *ḍ* and *ẓ́* are post-glottalized fricatives, often heard as ejective *θ* and *ṣ́*. The phoneme *ź* is often affricated. The acute accent marks prominence. The vowels of prominent syllables, according to T. M. Johnstone (*Jibbali Lexicon*, p. xv), are stressed and slightly longer than unstressed vowels. Though most languages do not allow sequences of stressed syllables, Jibbali often has two or more consecutive prominent syllables in a word, as in *kónús* 'sweep'. Nasal vowels, marked with the tilde ~, are long. The vocalic reflexes are affected by syllable structure, stress placement, and neighboring consonants. The charts here given are greatly simplified.

f	θ	t	s	ś	š	k/ŝ	x	ḥ	h
b/∅	δ	d	z	l/ź		g/ẑ	γ	ʕ~∅	ʔ
	δ̣	ṭ	ṣ	ẓ́		q/ṣ̂			
		r							
m/∅		n							
				y/∅	w/∅				

f	θ	t	ś	s	š	k	x	ḥ	h
b	δ	d	ź	z		g	γ	ʕ	ʔ
		ṭ		ṣ		q			
	δ̣	ḍ	ẓ́						
		r	l						
m		n							
				y	w				

i		u
e	ə	o
ε		ɔ
a		

ε/ə/i	a/ɔ/u	ε/ə/i	ε/ə/i	a/ɔ/u	ε/ə/i	o/u	o/u

Paradigms B

Morphology: Nouns and Pronouns

I do not include reconstructed Proto-Semitic nominal or pronominal systems in this section on the morphology of nouns and pronouns; the reader may be asked to construct them. I will provide the Coptic and Ghadamsi systems for comparison. I include markings of gender, number, case, and state for nouns; regrettably, the shapes of the so-called "broken plurals" are too various to be included. For pronouns I give personal pronouns, independent and affixed. Personal markers used in verbal inflection are included, demonstratives and interrogatives omitted. In most cases the interaction of subject and object markings has been indicated separately.

Old Babylonian

Nouns

		SINGULAR			MD	MP	MPl		MDPA	FDP
		masc.	fem.							
Absolute	N	-um	-(a)t-um	N	-ān	-ū	-ānū	N	-ūtum	-ātum
	A	-am	-(a)t-am	AG	-īn	-ī	-ānī	AG	-ūtim	-ātim
	G	-im	-(a)t-im							
Construct	NAG	-(i)	-(a)t(i)	NA	-ā	-ū	-ānū	NAG	-ūt	-āt
				G	-ī	-ī	-ānī			
Possessed	NA	-(a)	-(a)t(a)	NA	-ā	-ū	-ānū	NA	-ūtū	-ātū
	G	-ī	-(a)tī	G	-ī	-ī	-ānī	G	-ūtī	-ātī

The plurals in *-ānū* refer to groups of individuals rather than aggregates. The suffix *-ūtum* is used with adjectives. In the masculine of adjectives and in the feminines, dual and plural are not distinguished.*

Pronouns

	INDEPENDENT			SUFFIX			VERBAL SUBJECT	
	Nom.	Obl.	Dat.	Poss.	Obj.	Dat.	Pref. Conj.	Stative
1s	anāku	yāti	yāšim	-ī/-(y)a	-ni		a-	-āku
2ms	attā	kāta	kāšim	-ka		-kum	ta-	-āta
2fs	attī	kāti	kāšim	-ki		-kim	ta--ī	-āti
3ms	šū	šuāti	šuāsim	-šu		-šum	i-	Ø
3fs	šī	šiāti	šiāšim	-ši		-šim	i-	-at
3md							i--ā	-ā
1p	nīnu	niāti	niāšim	-ni	-niāti	-niāšim	ni-	-ānu
2mp	attunu	kunūti	kunūšim	-kunu	-kunūti	-kunūšim	ta--ā	-ātunu
2fp	attina	kināti	kināšim	-kina	-kināti	-kināšim	ta--ā	-ātina
3mp	šunu	šunūti	šunūšim	-šunu	-šunūti	-šunūšim	i--ū	-ū
3fp	šina	šināti	šināšim	-šina	-šināti	-šināšim	i--ā	-ā

Subject and object markers do not interact.

* Due to lack of space in some of the paradigm charts, I am using the abbreviations MD for masculine dual, MP for masculine plural, MPl for masculine plural individual, MDPA for masculine dual/plural adjective, and FDP for feminine dual/plural. N, A, and G, of course, stand for nominative, accusative, and genitive.

Syriac

Nouns

	SINGULAR		PLURAL	
	masc.	fem.	masc.	fem.
Absolute	*Stem 1*	*Stem 2 -ā*	*Stem 2 -īn*	*Stem 2 -ān*
Construct	*Stem 1*	*Stem 2 -at*	*Stem 2 -ay*	*Stem 2 -āt*
Possessed	*Stem 2-*	*Stem 2 -(a)t*	*Stem 2 -ay*	*Stem 2 -āt*
Definite	*Stem 2 -ā*	*Stem 2 -tā*	*Stem 2 -ē*	*Stem 2 -ātā*

Many nominals have two shapes, one used without suffixes (in the masculine-singular absolute and contruct) and one used with suffixes (all other forms). Note the paradigm below for *mlik/ malk* 'king/queen':

	SINGULAR		PLURAL	
	masc.	fem.	masc.	fem.
Absolute	*mlik*	*malkā*	*malkīn*	*malkān*
Construct	*mlik*	*malkat*	*malkay*	*malkāt*
'my ...'	*malk^y*	*malkat^y*	*malkay*	*malkāt^y*
'his ...'	*malkih*	*malktih*	*malkaw*	*malkātih*
'your ...'	*malkkunn*	*malkatkunn*	*malkaykunn*	*malkātkunn*
Definite	*malkā*	*malktā*	*malkē*	*malkātā*

Pronouns

	Indep.	Clitic	Possessive	Object	Pref. Conj.	Perfect
1s	*ʾinā*	*nā*	*-^{y}*	*-n^y*	*ʾi-*	*-it*
2ms	*ʾatt*	*att*		*-(ā)k*	*ti-*	*-t*
2fs	*ʾatt^y*	*att^y*		*-(i)k^y*	*ti--īn*	*-t^y*
3ms	*hū*	*ū*		*-ih ~ -w*	*ni-*	*-Ø*
3fs	*hī*	*ī*		*-(ā)h*	*ti-*	*-at*
1p	*(ʾina)ḥnan*	*nan*		*-(a)n*	*ni-*	*-n*
2mp	*ʾattunn*	*tunn*		*-kunn*	*ti--ūn*	*-tunn*
2fp	*ʾattinn*	*tinn*		*-kinn*	*ti--ān*	*-tinn*
3mp	*hinnunn*	*innunn*	*-hunn*	CLITIC	*ni--ūn*	*-^{w}*
3fp	*hinninn*	*inninn*	*-hinn*	CLITIC	*ni--ān*	*-^{y}*

Subject and Object Markers

	No Obj.	1s	2ms	3ms	3fs	2mp
			Perfective			
1s	qiṭlit		qṭaltāk	qṭaltih	qṭaltāh	qṭaltkunn
2ms	qṭal	qṭaltān^y		qṭaltāy	qṭaltāh	
2fs	qṭalt^y	qṭaltīn^y		qṭaltīw	qṭaltīh	
3ms	qṭal	qaṭlan^y	qaṭlāk	qaṭlih	qaṭlāh	qaṭlkunn
3fs	qiṭlat	qṭaltan^y	qṭaltāk	qṭaltih	qṭaltāh	qiṭlatkunn
1p	qṭaln		qṭalnāk	qṭalnāy	qṭalnāh	qṭalnākunn
2mp	qṭaltunn	qṭaltunnān^y		qṭaltunnāy	qṭaltunnāh	
2fp	qṭaltinn	qṭaltinnān^y		qṭaltinnāy	qṭaltinnāh	
3mp	qṭal^w	qaṭlūn^y	qaṭlūk	qaṭlūy	qaṭlūh	qaṭlūkunn
3fp	qṭal^y	qaṭlān^y	qaṭlāk	qaṭlāy	qaṭlāh	qṭalinnākunn
			Imperfective			
1s	ʾiqṭul		ʾiqṭlāk	ʾiqṭlīw	ʾiqṭlīh	ʾiqṭulkunn
2ms	tiqṭul	tiqṭlan^y		tiqṭlīw	tiqṭlīh	
2fs	tiqṭlīn	tiqṭlīnān^y		tiqṭlīnāy	tiqṭlīnāh	
3ms	niqṭul	niqṭlan^y	niqṭlāk	niqṭlīw	niqṭlīh	niqṭulkunn
3fs	tiqṭul	tiqṭlan^y	tiqṭlāk	tiqṭlīw	tiqṭlīh	tiqṭulkunn
1p	niqṭul		niqṭlāk	niqṭlīw	niqṭlīh	niqṭulkunn
2mp	tiqṭlūn	tiqṭlūnān^y		tiqṭlūnāy	tiqṭlūnāh	
2fp	tiqṭlān	tiqṭlānān^y		tiqṭlānāy	tiqṭlānāh	
3mp	niqṭlūn	niqṭlūnān^y	niqṭlūnāk	niqṭlūnāy	niqṭlūnāh	niqṭlūnākunn
3fp	niqṭlān	niqṭlānān^y	niqṭlānāk	niqṭlānāy	niqṭlānāh	niqṭlānākunn
			Imperative			
2ms	qṭul	qṭulayn^y		qṭulāy	qṭuleyh	
2fs	qṭul^y	qṭulīn^y		qṭulīw	qṭulīh	
2mp	qṭul^w	quṭlūn^y		quṭlūy	quṭlūh	
2fp	qṭul^y	qṭulān^y		qṭulāy	qṭulāh	

The type verb is *qṭal* 'kill'. 1p object forms are identical with 1s except that the suffix is *-n* instead of *-n^y*. 2fs and 2fp objects are identical to 2ms and 2mp respectively, but with *-(i)k^y* and *-kinn* instead of *-(ā)k* and *-kunn*. There are no 3p suffixes.

Urmi

Nouns

	SINGULAR		PLURAL	
	masc.	fem.	masc.	fem.
Absolute	*-ə*	*-tə*	*-i*	*-ətə*
Possessed	*-∅-*	*-t-*	*-∅-*	*-ət-*

Plural formation is somewhat irregular. Many nouns have more than one plural form. The construct survives only in a small number of compound nouns; nominal possession is marked with the preposition *d-*.

Pronouns

	Indep.	Subject	Poss.	Object
1ms	*ənə*	*-in*	*-i*	*-li*
1fs	*ənə*	*-an*	*-i*	*-li*
2ms	*ət*	*-it*	*-ux*	*-lux*
2fs	*ət*	*-ət*	*-əx*	*-ləx*
3ms	*o*	*∅*	*-o*	*-li*
3fs	*e*	*-ə*	*-ə*	*-lə*
1p	*əxnə(n)*	*-əx*	*-ən*	*-lun*
2p	*əxt(ox)un*	*-itun*	*-oxun*	*-loxun*
3p	*ənni*	*-i*	*-e*	*-li*

All suffixes are subject to vowel harmony rules. Those in *ə* and *i* will alternate with *a* and *ï* respectively; the variation in the other vowels is not reflected in this transcription. If an object marker follows a subject marker ending in *n* (1ms, 1fs, 2p), the initial *l* is assimilated to *n*: *ki axlïnnï < axl-in-li* 'I am eating it'.

Ugaritic

Most of the extant Ugaritic material is written in a script that marks vowel quality only after ʾ and then fails to differentiate between *i*, *ī*, and *ē*, for example. From Ugaritic documents in Akkadian script we can glean more information on voweling, but quantity remains unclear. In the tables that follow, known vowels are inserted in small capitals. Quantity is conjectural. *V* is used for vowel-initial suffixes of unknown quality.

Nouns

		SINGULAR			DUAL			PLURAL	
		masc.	fem.		masc.	fem.		masc.	fem.
Absolute	N	-U	-(A)tU	N	-ĀmA ~ -ĀmI	-(A)tĀmA ~ -(A)tĀmI		-ŪmA	-ĀtU
	A	-A	-(A)tA	AG	-ĒmA ~ -ĒmI	-(A)tĒmA ~ -(A)tĒmI		-ĪmA	-AtI
	G	-I	-(A)tI						
Construct	N	-U	-(A)tU	N	-Ā	-(A)tĀ		-Ū	-ĀtU
	A	-A	-(A)tA	AG	-Ē	-(A)tĒ		-Ī	-ĀtI
	G	-I	-(A)tI						

Many personal names and a few other nouns use *-a* for both accusative and genitive. Predicate nominals use *-m*, which seems to play no part in determination.

Pronouns

	Independent	Poss.	Obj.	Imperfect	Perfect
1s	ʾAn ~ ʾAnĀkU	-ī/-y	-n	ʾA- ~ ʾI- ~ ʾU-	-t
2ms	ʾAttA		-k	tA- ~ tI-	-t
2fs	ʾAt		-k	t--n	-t
3ms	N: hUwA AG: hwt		-hU	yA-	-A
3fs	N: hy AG: hyt		-h	t-	-At
1d			-ny	n--n	-ny
2d			-km	t--n	-tm
3md	N: hm AG: hmt		-hm	t- ~ y--Ā(n)	-V
3fd				t--n	-t
1p			-n	n-	
2mp	ȧtm		-km	t--Ūn	-tm
2fp			-kn	t--n	-tn
3mp	N: hm AG: hmt		-hm	t- ~ y/yA--Ū(n)	-Ū
3fp			-hn	t--n	-V

The vowel of the imperfect prefix is *u* for hollow verbs, *i* for verbs with imperfect vowel *a*, otherwise *a*. Imperfect suffixes of the dual, plural, and 2sf appear without the nasal-initial syllable in subjunctive and jussive, and occasionally in the indicative.

Hebrew

Nouns

	SINGULAR		DUAL		PLURAL	
	masc.	fem.	masc.	fem.	masc.	fem.
Absolute	*Stem 1*	-ā ~ -et	-ayim	-ātayim	-īm	-ōt
Construct	*Stem 2*	-at	-ē	-ātē	-ē	-ōt
Possessed	*Stem 3*	-at-	-ē-	-ātē-	-ē-	-ōtē-

Masculine-singular forms have no suffix marking gender and number, but some nouns require three different stems. For both masculine and feminine plurals yet another stem may be used. Construct and possessed forms of the masculine dual are identical to the masculine plural. Note the paradigm below for *melek/malk-/mlâk-* 'king/queen':

	SINGULAR		DUAL		PLURAL	
	masc.	fem.	masc.	fem.	masc.	fem.
Absolute	*melek*	*malkā*	*malkayim*	*malkātayim*	*mlākīm*	*mlākōt*
Construct	*melek*	*malkat*	*malkē*	*malkātē*	*malkē*	*mlākōt*
'my ...'	*malkī*	*malkātī*	*mlākay*	*malkātay*	*mlākay*	*mlākōtay*
'his ...'	*malkō*	*malkātō*	*mlākāw*	*malkātāw*	*mlākāw*	*mlākōtāw*
'their ...'	*malkəkem*	*malkatkem*	*malkēkem*	*malkātēkem*	*malkēkem*	*malkōtēkem*

Pronouns

	Indep.	Poss.	Obj.	Pref. Conj.	Perfect
1s	*ʾān(ōk)ī*	-ī	-nī	*ʾe-*	-tī
2ms	*ʾattā*	-kā		ti-	-tā
2fs	*ʾatt*	-k		ti--ī	-t
3ms	*hū*	-ō ~ -w	-hū ~ -ō	yi-	-∅
3fs	*hī*	-hā		ti-	-ā
1p	*(ʾa)naḥnū*	-ēnū	-nū	ni-	-nū
2mp	*ʾattem*	-kem		ti--ū	-tem
2fp	*ʾattēn(ā)*	-ken		ti--nā	-ten
3mp	*hēm(mā)*	-ām ~ -hem	-(ā)m	yi--ū	-ū
3fp	*hēn(nā)*	-ān ~ -hen	-(ā)n	ti--nā	-ū

Subject and Object Markers

	No Obj.	1s	2ms	2fs	3ms	3fs	1p	3mp
Perfect								
1s	*qāṭaltī*		*qāṭaltīkā*	*qāṭaltīk*	*qṭaltīhū*	*qṭaltīhā*		*qṭaltīm*
2ms	*qāṭaltā*	*qṭaltanī*			*qṭaltō*	*qṭaltāh*	*qṭaltānū*	*qṭaltām*
2fs	*qāṭalt*	*qṭaltīnī*			*qṭaltīhū*	*qṭaltīhā*	*qṭaltīnū*	*qṭaltīm*
3ms	*qāṭal*	*qṭālanī*	*qṭālkā*	*qṭālēk*	*qṭālō*	*qṭālāh*	*qṭālānū*	*qṭālām*
3fs	*qāṭlā*	*qṭālatnī*	*qṭālatkā*	*qṭālātek*	*qṭālattū*	*qṭālattāh*	*qṭālatnū*	*qṭālātam*
1p	*qāṭalnū*		*qṭalnūkā*	*qṭalnūk*	*qṭalnūhū*	*qṭalnūhā*	*qṭalnūm*	
2mp	*qṭaltem*	*qṭaltūnī*			*qṭaltūhū*	*qṭaltūhā*	*qṭaltūnū*	*qṭaltūm*
2fp	*qṭalten*							
3p	*qāṭlū*	*qṭālūnī*	*qṭālūkā*	*qṭālūk*	*qṭālūhū*	*qṭālūhā*	*qṭālūnū*	*qṭālūm*
Imperfect								
1s	*ʾeqtōl*		*ʾeqtōlkā*	*ʾeqtəlēk*	*ʾeqtəlēhū*	*ʾeqtəlehā*		*ʾeqtəlēm*
2ms	*tiqtōl*	*tiqtəlēnī*			*tiqtəlēhū*	*tiqtəlehā*	*tiqtəlēnū*	*tiqtəlēm*
2fs	*tiqtəlī*	*tiqtəlīnī*			*tiqtəlīhū*	*tiqtəlīhā*	*tiqtəlīnū*	*tiqtəlīm*
3ms	*yiqtōl*	*yiqtəlēnī*	*yiqtōlkā*	*yiqtəlēk*	*yiqtəlēhū*	*yiqtəlehā*	*yiqtəlēnū*	*yiqtəlēm*
3fs	*tiqtōl*	*tiqtəlēnī*	*tiqtōlkā*	*tiqtəlēk*	*tiqtəlēhū*	*tiqtəlehā*	*tiqtəlēnū*	*tiqtəlēm*
1p	*niqtōl*		*niqtōlkā*	*niqtəlēk*	*niqtəlēhū*	*niqtəlehā*		*niqtəlēm*
2mp	*tiqtəlū*	*tiqtəlūnī*			*tiqtəlūhū*	*tiqtəlūhā*	*tiqtəlūnū*	*tiqtəlūm*
2fp	*tiqtōlnā*							
3mp	*yiqtəlū*	*yiqtəlūnī*	*yiqtəlūkā*	*yiqtəlūk*	*yiqtəlūhū*	*yiqtəlūhā*	*yiqtəlūnū*	*yiqtəlūm*
3fp	*tiqtōlnā*	*tiqtəlūnī*	*tiqtəlūkā*	*tiqtəlūk*	*tiqtəlūhū*	*tiqtəlūhā*	*tiqtəlūnū*	*tiqtəlūm*
Imperative								
2ms	*qṭōl*	*qoṭlēnī*			*qoṭlēhū*	*qoṭlehā*	*qoṭlēnū*	*qoṭlēm*
2fs	*qiṭlī*	*qiṭlīnī*			*qiṭlīhū*	*qiṭlīhā*	*qiṭlīnū*	*qiṭlīm*
2mp	*qiṭlū*	*qiṭlūnī*			*qiṭlūhū*	*qiṭlūhā*	*qiṭlūnū*	*qiṭlūm*
2fp	*qṭōlnā*							

The type verb is *qāṭal* 'kill'. There is no m/f distinction in 2p forms with object. 2mp object suffixes are rare; 2fp object suffixes are not found. Forms with 3fp object replace the final *m* of the 3mp suffix with *n*.

Classical Arabic

Nouns

		SINGULAR			DUAL			PLURAL	
		masc.	fem.		masc.	fem.		masc.	fem.
Indefinite	N	-un	-atun	N	-āni	-atāni		-ūna	-ātun
	A	-an	-atan	AG	-ayni	-atayni		-īna	-ātin
	G	-in	-atin						
Definite	N	al--u	al--atu	N	al--āni	al--atāni		al--ūna	al--ātu
	A	al--a	al--ata	AG	al--ayni	al--atayni		al--īna	al--āti
	G	al--i	al--ati						
Construct	N	-u	-atu	N	-ā	-atā		-ū	-ātu
	A	-a	-ata	AG	-ay	-atay		-ī	-āti
	G	-i	-ati						

Broken plurals are frequent. One class of nominals does not take final *n* in the indefinite singular and uses *-a* for both accusative and genitive; these show the regular endings in the definite and construct.

Pronouns

		Indep.	Poss.	Obj.	Pref. Conj.	Perfect
1s		ʾanā	-ī/-ya	-nī	ʾa-	-tu
2ms		ʾanta		-ka	ta-	-ta
2fs		ʾanti		-ki	ti--ī(na)	-ti
3ms		huwa		-hu/-hi	ya-	-a
3fs		hiya		-hā	ta-	-at
2d		ʾantumā		-kumā	ta--ā(ni)	-tumā
3md		humā		-humā/-himā	ya--ā(ni)	-ā
3fd		humā		-humā/-himā	ta--ā(ni)	-atā
1p		naḥnu		-nā	na-	-nā
2mp		ʾantum		-kum	ta--ū(na)	-tum
2fp		ʾantunna		-kin	ta--na	-tunna
3mp		hum		-hum/-him	ya--ū(na)	-ū
3fp		hunna		-hunna/-hinna	ya--na	-na

The *-nV* suffixes of the prefix conjugation (except for those of the 2fp and 3fp) are omitted in the subjunctive and jussive.

Subject and Object Markers

	No Object	1s	2ms	3ms	3fs
Perfect					
1s	*qataltu*		*qataltuka*	*qataltuhu*	*qataltuhā*
2ms	*qatalta*	*qataltanī*		*qataltahu*	*qataltahā*
2fs	*qatalti*	*qataltinī*		*qataltihi*	*qataltihā*
3ms	*qatala*	*qatalanī*	*qatalaka*	*qatalahu*	*qatalahā*
3fs	*qatalat*	*qatalatnī*	*qatalatka*	*qatalathu*	*qatalathā*
3fd	*qatalatā*	*qatalatānī*	*qatalatāka*	*qatalatāhu*	*qatalatāhā*
3md	*qatalā*	*qatalānī*	*qatalāka*	*qatalāhu*	*qatalāhā*
2mp	*qataltum*	*qataltumūnī*		*qataltumūhu*	*qataltumūhā*
3mp	*qatalū*	*qatalūnī*	*qatalūka*	*qatalūhu*	*qatalūhā*
3fp	*qatalna*	*qatalnanī*	*qatalnaka*	*qatalnahu*	*qatalnahā*
Imperfect					
1s	*ʾaqtulu*		*ʾaqtuluka*	*ʾaqtuluhu*	*ʾaqtuluhā*
2ms	*taqtulu*	*taqtulunī*		*taqtuluhu*	*taqtuluhā*
2fs	*taqtulīna*	*taqtulīnanī*		*taqtulīnahu*	*taqtulīnahā*
3ms	*yaqtulu*	*yaqtulunī*	*yaqtuluka*	*yaqtuluhu*	*yaqtuluhā*
3fs	*taqtulu*	*taqtulunī*	*taqtuluka*	*taqtuluhu*	*taqtuluhā*
3md	*yaqtulāni*	*yaqtulāninī*	*yaqtulānika*	*yaqtulānihi*	*yaqtulānihā*
3fd	*taqtulāni*	*taqtulāninī*	*taqtulānika*	*taqtulānihi*	*taqtulānihā*
1p	*naqtulu*		*naqtuluka*	*naqtuluhu*	*naqtuluhā*
2mp	*taqtulūna*	*taqtulūnānī*		*taqtulūnahu*	*taqtulūnahā*
2fp	*taqtulna*	*taqtulnanī*		*taqtulnahu*	*taqtulnahā*
3mp	*yaqtulūna*	*yaqtulūnanī*	*yaqtulūnaka*	*yaqtulūnahu*	*yaqtulūnahā*
3fp	*yaqtulna*	*yaqtulnanī*	*yaqtulnaka*	*yaqtulnahu*	*yaqtulnahā*
Imperative					
2ms	*uqtul*	*uqtulnī*		*uqtulhu*	*uqtulhā*
2fs	*uqtulī*	*uqtulīnī*		*uqtulīhi*	*uqtulīhā*
2d	*uqtulā*	*uqtulānī*		*uqtulāhu*	*uqtulāhā*
3mp	*uqtulū*	*uqtulūnī*		*uqtulūhu*	*uqtulūhā*
3fp	*uqtulna*	*uqtulnanī*		*uqtulnahu*	*uqtulnahā*

The type verb is *qatala* 'kill'. Forms with 1p object are identical to 1s but with suffix *-nā* instead of *-nī*. 2fs, 2d, 2mp, and 2fp objects replace *-ka* of the 2ms with *-ki*, *-kumā*, *-kum*, *-kunna*, respectively. 3d, 3mp, and 3fp substitute *-humā*, *-hum*, and *-hunna*, respectively, for *-hu* of the 3ms; all of these forms in *hu* shift to *hi* after *i*.

Egyptian Arabic

Nouns

	SINGULAR		DUAL		PLURAL	
	masc.	fem.	masc.	fem.	masc.	fem.
Absolute	-∅	-a	-ēn	-(i)tēn	-īn	-āt
Definite	ʾil--∅	ʾil--a	ʾil--ēn	ʾil--(i)tēn	ʾil--īn	ʾil--āt
Construct	-∅	-(i)t	-ēn	-(i)tēn	-īn	-āt

Broken plurals are frequent. The dual takes plural concord. With possessive suffixes, the final *n* of the dual drops.

Pronouns

	Indep.	Poss.	Obj.	Pref. Conj.	Perfect
1s	ʾana	-i/-ya	-ni	ʾa-	-t
2ms	ʾinta	-ak/-k		ti-	-t
2fs	ʾinti	-ik/-ki		ti--i	-ti
3ms	huwwa	-u(h)/-h		yi-	-∅
3fs	hiyya	-ha		ti-	-it
1p	ʾiḥna	-na		ni-	-na
2p	ʾintu	-ku(m)		ti--u	-tu
3p	humma	-hum		yi--u	-u

Subject and Object Markers

	No Obj.	1s	2ms	3ms	3fs	2p
			Perfect			
1s	ʾatalt		ʾataltak	ʾataltuh	ʾataltiha	ʾataltukum
2ms	ʾatalt	ʾataltini		ʾataltuh	ʾataltiha	
2fs	ʾatalti	ʾataltīni		ʾataltīh	ʾataltīha	
3ms	ʾatal	ʾatalni	ʾatalak	ʾataluh	ʾatalha	ʾatalkum
3fs	ʾatalit	ʾatalitni	ʾatalitak	ʾatalituh	ʾataliha	ʾatalitkum
1p	ʾatalna		ʾatalnak	ʾatalnah	ʾatalnaha	ʾatalnakum
2mp	ʾataltu	ʾataltūni		ʾataltūh	ʾataltūha	
3mp	ʾatalu	ʾatalūni	ʾatalūk	ʾatalūh	ʾatalūha	ʾatalūkum
			Imperfect			
1s	ʾaʾtil		ʾaʾtilak	ʾaʾtiluh	ʾaʾtilha	ʾaʾtilkum
2ms	tiʾtil	tiʾtilni		tiʾtiluh	tiʾtilha	
2fs	tiʾtilī	tiʾtilīni		tiʾtilīh	tiʾtilīha	
3ms	yiʾtil	yiʾtilunī	yiʾtilak	yiʾtiluh	yiʾtilha	yiʾtilkum
3fs	tiʾtil	tiʾtilni	tiʾtilak	tiʾtiluh	tiʾtilha	tiʾtilkum
1p	niʾtil		niʾtilak	niʾtiluh	niʾtilha	niʾtilkum
2p	tiʾtilu	tiʾtilūni		tiʾtilūh	tiʾtilūha	
3p	yiʾtilu	yiʾtilūni	yiʾtilūk	yiʾtilūh	yiʾtilūha	yiʾtilūkum

The type verb is *ʾatal* 'kill'. Forms with 1p object are identical to 1s but with suffix *-na* instead of *-ni*. 2fs, 2d, 2mp, 2fp objects replace *-ak/-k* of the 2ms with *-ik/-ki*. 3p substitutes *-(u)hum* for *-(u)kum* of the 3p.

Ge'ez

Nouns

		SINGULAR		PLURAL	
		masc.	fem.	masc.	fem.
Absolute	NG	-∅	-t	-ān	-āt
	A	-a	-ta	-āna	-āta
Construct	NAG	-a	-ta	-āna	-āta
Possessed	NG	-(ə)	-t(ə)	-ān(ə)	-āt(ə)
	A	-a	-ta	-āna	-āta

Broken plurals are frequent, and there is no consistent relationship between the form of the noun and gender.

Pronouns

	Indep.	Poss.	Obj.	Vb. Pref.	Vb. Suff.
1s	ʾana	-ya	-nī	ʾə-	-kū
2ms	ʾanta		-ka	tə-	-ka
2fs	ʾantī		-kī	tə--ī	-kī
3ms	wəʾətū	-(h)ū	-hū ~ -ō	yə-	-a
3fs	yəʾətī		-(h)ā	tə-	-at
1p	nəḥna		-na	nə-	-na
2mp	ʾantəmū		-kəmū	tə--ū	-kəmū
2fp	ʾantən		-kən	tə--ā	-kən
3mp	ʾəmūntū		-(h)ōmū	yə--ū	-ū
3fp	ʾəmāntū		-(h)ōn	yə--ā	-ā

Subject and Object Markers

	No Obj.	1s	2ms	3ms	3fs
		Perfect			
1s	qatalkū		qatalkūka	qatalkəwwō	qatalkəwwā
2ms	qatalka	qatalkanī		qatalkō	qatalkā
2fs	qatalkī	qatalkənī		qatalkəyyō	qatalkəyyā
3ms	qatala	qatalanī	qatalaka	qatalō	qatalā
3fs	qatalat	qatalatanī	qatalataka	qatalatō	qatalatā
1p	qatalna		qatalnāka	qatalnāhū	qatalnāha
2mp	qatalkəmū	qatalkəmūnī		qatalkəməwwō	qatalkəməwwā
2fp	qatalkən	qatalk(ən)ānī		qatalk(ən)āhū	qatalk(ən)āhā
3mp	qatalū	qatalūnī	qatalūka	qataləwwō	qataləwwā
3fp	qatalā	qatalānī	qatalāka	qatalāhū	qatalāhā
		Subjunctive			
1s	ʾəqtəl		ʾəqtəlka	ʾəqtəlō	ʾəqtəlā
2ms	təqtəl	təqtəlanī		təqtəlō	təqtəlā
2fs	təqtəlī	təqtəlīnī		təqtələyyō	təqtələyyā
3fs	təqtəl	təqtəlanī	təqtəlka	təqtəlō	təqtəlā
3ms	yəqtəl	yəqtəlanī	yəqtəlka	yəqtəlō	yəqtəlā
1p	nəqtəl		nəqtəlka	nəqtəlō	nəqtəlā
2mp	təqtəlū	təqtəlūnī		təqtələwwō	təqtələwwā
2fp	təqtəlā	təqtəlānī		təqtəlāhū	təqtəlāhā
3mp	yəqtəlū	yəqtəlūnī	yəqtəlūka	yəqtələwwō	yəqtələwwā
3fp	yəqtəlā	yəqtəlānī	yəqtəlāka	yəqtəlāhū	yəqtəlāhā

The type verb is *qatala* 'kill'. Forms with 1p object have *-na* instead of 1s *-nī*. 2fs, 2mp, 2fp objects replace 2ms *-ka* with *-kī*, *-kəmū*, *-kən* respectively.

Tigre

Nouns

	SINGULAR		PLURAL	
	masc.	fem.	masc.	fem.
	-∅	-t	-ām	-āt

Although the above gender markings continue the general Semitic distinctions, there is no consistent relationship between the form of the noun and its gender or number, except in diminutives that are marked for gender. Animate nouns will take agreements appropriate to the sex of the referent regardless of form, and inanimates may take either gender. Broken plurals are frequent. Animate plurals take plural concord and follow the gender of the singular, while inanimate plurals usually take ms agreements. The construct has not survived, but some nouns have a special stem used with possessive suffixes. The shape of these possessive stems is not predictable.

Pronouns

	Indep.	Poss.	Obj.	Vb. Pref.	Vb. Suff.
1s	ʾana	-ye	-ni	ʾə-	-ko
2ms	ʾənta		-ka	tə-	-ka
2fs	ʾənti		-kī	tə--i	-ki
3ms	hətu	-(h)u	-(h)u ~ o	lə-	-a
3fs	həta		-(h)a	tə-	-at
1p	ḥəna		-na	nə-	-na
2mp	ʾəntum		-kum	tə--o	-kum
2fp	ʾəntən		-kən	tə--a	-kən
3mp	hətom		-(h)om	lə--o	-aw
3fp	hətan		-(h)an	lə--a	-aya

Subject and Object Markers

	No Obj.	1s	2ms	3ms	3fs
			Perfect		
1s	qatalko		qatalkoka	qatalkwo	qatalkwa
2ms	qatalka	qatalkanni		qatalkahu	qatalkaha
2fs	qatalki	qatalkini		qatalkəyo	qatalkəya
3ms	qatla	qatlenni	qatlekka	qatlayu	qatlaya
3fs	qatlat	qatlattani	qatlattakka	qatlatto	qatlatta
1p	qatalna		qatalnaka	qatalnahu	qatalnaha
2mp	qatalkum	qatalkuni		qatalkumo	qatalkuma
2fp	qatalkən	qatalkənani		qatalkənahu	qatalkənaha
3mp	qatlaw	qatlawni	qatlawka	qatlawo	qatlawa
3fp	qatlaya	qatlayani	qatlayaka	qatlayahu	qatlayaha
			Imperfect		
1s	ʾəqattəl		ʾəqatlakka	ʾəqattəllo	ʾəqattəlla
2ms	təqattəl	təqatlanni		təqattəllo	təqattəlla
2fs	təqatli	təqatlini		təqattilo	təqattila
3ms	ləqattəl	ləqatlanni	ləqatlakka	ləqattəllo	ləqattəlla
3fs	təqattəl	təqatlanni	təqatlakka	təqattəllo	təqattəlla
1p	nəqattəl		nəqatlakka	nəqattəllo	nəqattəlla
2mp	təqatlo	təqatluni		təqattulo	təqattula
2fp	təqatla	təqatlani		təqatlahu	təqatlaha
3mp	ləqatlo	ləqatluni	ləqatluka	ləqattulo	ləqattula
3fp	ləqatla	ləqatlani	ləqatlaka	ləqatlahu	ləqatlaha
			Jussive		
1s	ʾəqtal		ʾəqtalakka	ʾəqtallo	ʾəqtalla
2ms	təqtal	təqtalanni		təqtallo	təqtalla
2fs	təqtali	təqtalini		təqtelo	təqtela
3ms	ləqtal	ləqtalanni	ləqtalakka	ləqtallo	ləqtalla
3fs	təqtal	təqtalanni	təqtalakka	təqtallo	təqtalla
1p	nəqtal		nəqtalakka	nəqtallo	nəqtalla
2mp	təqtalo	təqtaluni		təqtolo	təqtola
2fp	təqtala	təqtalani		təqtalahu	təqtalaha
3mp	ləqtalo	ləqtaluni	ləqtaluka	ləqtolo	ləqtola
3fp	ləqtala	ləqtalani	ləqtalaka	ləqtalahu	ləqtalaha

The type verb is *qatla* 'kill'. Forms with 1p object are identical to 1s but with suffix *-na* instead of *-ni*. 2fs, 2mp, 2fp objects replace *-ka* of the 2ms with *-ki*, *-kum*, *-kən* respectively. 3mp and 3fp substitute *-om* and *-an* respectively for *-a* of the 3fs.

Jibbali

Nouns

	SINGULAR	PLURAL
masc.	fem.	common
-∅	-V*t*	-(V)*tə*

Broken plurals are frequent; there does not seem to be a specifically masculine sound plural marker. There is a prefixal definite marker *e-*.

Pronouns

	Indep.	Poss./Obj.	Prefix Conjugation	Perfect
1s	*hé*	-*i*	*ə-*	-*k*
2ms	*hɛt*	-*k*	*t-*	-*k*
2fs	*hit*	-*ŝ*	*t-* with vowel change	-*ŝ*
3ms	*šɛh*	-*š*	*y-*	-∅
3fs	*sɛh*	-*s*	*t-*	-*ɔ́t*
1d	*ʾətí*	-*ŝi*	*n--ɔ́*	-*ŝi*
2d	*tí*	-*ki* ~ -*ŝi*	*t--ɔ́*	-*ŝi*
3md	*ši*	-*ši*	*y--ɔ́*	-*ɔ*
3fd	*ši*	-*ši*	*t--ɔ́*	-*tɔ*
1p	*nḥán*	-*ən*	*n-*	-*ən*
2mp	*tum*	-*kum*	*t--ən*	-*kum*
2fp	*tɛn*	-*kən*	*t--ən*	-*kən*
3mp	*šuhm*	-*hum*	*y-*	-∅
3fp	*sɛhn*	-*sən*	*t--ən*	-∅

There is not enough information to permit discussion of combinations of subject and object markings.

Coptic

Nouns

By the time of Coptic, the Egyptian nominal system had been greatly "simplified," for which read, it had become chaotic. Number and gender distinctions remained: three concord sets, masculine singular, feminine singular, and plural. There was no longer any distinction in agreement between masculine plural and feminine plural; and the dual, still alive in Egyptian, was lost. In a few cases we can see reflexes of the original gender/number markings.

Plural formation is irregular enough to remind one of the so-called "broken" plurals. However, in most cases our knowledge of earlier forms of Egyptian/Coptic allows us to see that the "sound" plural marker of Egyptian, -*w*, is involved.

Many nouns have construct forms, but the construct is mainly used either in verbs (earlier verbal nouns) with nominal objects or in compounding. Construct forms are not predictable. A few nouns are used with possessive suffixes; in most cases the suffixed noun is not in regular use; for example, *βal* 'eye', *yat-əf* 'his eye'.

Clitic demonstrative pronouns and possessives may be preposed to nouns (independent forms of all of these exist). There is also a system of "articles":

| | SINGULAR | | PLURAL | |
| | masc. | fem. | masc. | fem. |
	'brother'	'sister'	'brothers'	'sisters'
	son	*sōne*	*snēw*	*sōnēwe*
my	*pason*	*tasōne*	*nasnēw*	*nasōnēwe*
this	*peyson*	*teysōne*	*neysnēw*	*neysōnēwe*
the	*pson*	*tsōne*	*nesnēw*	*nsōnēwe*
a/some	*uson*	*usōne*	*hensnēw*	*hensōnēwe*

Pronouns

| | INDEPENDENT | | SUFFIX | | VERBAL SUBJECT | |
	Absolute	Construct	Poss./Obj.	Clitic Poss.	Initial	Post Aux.
1s	*anok*	*anək*	-*t*/-*y*/-∅-*ni*	-*a*-	*ti*-	-*y*-/-*i*-
2ms	*ntok*	*ntək*	-*k*	-*k*-	*k*-	-*k*-/-*ek*-
2fs	*nto*	*nte*	-*e*/-∅	-*u*-	*te*-	-*re*-/-*e*-
3ms	*ntof*		-*f*	-*f*-	*f*-	-*f*-/-*ef*-
3fs	*ntos*		-*s*	-*s*-	*s*-	-*s*-/-*es*-
1p	*anon*	*an*	-*n*	-*n*-	*tn*-	-*n*-/-*en*-
2p	*ntōtn*	*ntetn*	-*tēwtn*/-*tn*	-*tn*-	*tetn*-	-*tetn*-/-*etn*-
3p	*ntos*		-*u*/-*w*	-*ew*-	*se*-	-*w*-/-*u*-

Ghadamsi

Nouns

In Ghadamsi, nouns fall into one of four concord sets: masculine singular—/aḷæmm/ 'camel'; feminine singular—/taḷamt/ 'she-camel'; masculine plural—/ḷammaan/ 'camels'; feminine plural—/təḷammæn/ 'she-camels'. Pluralization is highly irregular. The initial syllable of all but the masculine plural is normally a fossilized prefix, which is no longer important in inflection, though it can be isolated in analyzing derivation. Most plurals end in suffixed /-n/; most feminines are marked with prefixed /t-/. In the feminine singular the suffixed /-t / may or may not be present.

Other forms of Berber have a construct form that is unusual in Afroasiatic in involving a change in the prefix syllable. This is lacking in Ghadamsi. In possessive constructions, the order is possessed-possessor, with a preposition /n/ preposed to the possessor. As in most of Afroasiatic, nouns do take pronominal possessive suffixes, but except with a few kinship terms the noun stem is not modified.

While most case relations are expressed by word order or prepositions, there is a locative form for nouns, marked by a suffix or infix; it is not clear what determines when the locative is infixed, and there are two different treatments when the suffix occurs with final vowels:

	Noun		Locative	
masc.	*dāž*	house	*dāži*	in the house
	γazær	ditch	*γazēr*	in the ditch
	almūdu	mosque	*almudū*	in the mosque
	ōfa	fire	*ōfayi*	in the fire
fem.	*tašæd:ūt*	pot	*tašæd:ūti*	in the pot
	tāli	room	*talī*	in the room
	tamada	garden	*tamadā*	in the garden
	tōlifsa	viper	*tōlifsayi*	to a viper
pl.	*al:ūnæn*	holes	*al:ūnēn*	in the holes
	āmān	water	*āmēn*	in the water

Clitic demonstrative pronouns and possessives may be postposed to nouns (independent forms of all of these exist):

	SINGULAR		PLURAL	
	masc.	fem.	masc.	fem.
	'boy'	'girl'	'boys'	'girls'
	antʃāl	*tawažet:*	*əd:rari*	*twažatēn*
this here	*antʃālodæt*	*tawažet:odæt*	*əd:rariyidæt*	*twažatēnīdæt*
this	*antʃālo*	*tawažet:o*	*əd:rariyi*	*twažatēni*
that	*antʃāle*	*tawažet:e*	*əd:rariyīd*	*twažatēnīd*
that yonder	*antʃālæn:*	*tawažet:æn:*	*əd:rariyin:*	*twažatēnin:*

Pronouns

	INDEPENDENT	SUFFIX Dir. Obj.	Ind. Obj.	Prep. Obj.	Poss.	VERBAL SUBJECT
1s	*næš:*	*-i*	*-i*	*-i*	*-ən:ūk*	*æ--æ ʿ/ə-(-æ ʿ)*
2ms	*šæg:*	*-šək*	*-āk*	*-ək*	*-ən:æk*	*tæ--ət/tə-(-ət)*
2fs	*šæm:*	*-kæm*	*-ām*	*-əm*	*-ən:æm*	*tæ--ət/tə-(-ət)*
3ms	*nit:o*	*-t*	*-ās*	*-əs*	*-ən:æs*	*yæ-/i-*
3fs	*nit:āt*	*-tæt*	*-ās*	*-əs*	*-ən:æs*	*tæ-/tə-*
1p	*næk:ænēn*	*-ānæʿ*	*-ānæʿ*	*-næʿ*	*-ən:anæʿ*	*næ-/nə- (excl.)*
						næ--æt/nə--æt (incl. masc.)
						næ--mæt/nə--mæt (incl. fem.)
2mp	*šəkwēn*	*-kum*	*-āwən*	*-wən*	*-ən:awən*	*tæ--æm/tə--æm*
2fp	*šəkmatēn*	*-kmæt*	*-ākmæt*	*-əkmæt*	*-ən:ækmæt*	*tæ--mæt/tə--mæt*
3mp	*əntænēn*	*-tæn*	*-āsæn*	*-sæn*	*-ən:asæn*	*æ--æn/ə--æn*
3p	*əntnatēn*	*-tənæt*	*-āsnæt*	*-əsnæt*	*-ən:asnæt*	*æ--næt/ə--næt*

Paradigms C

Morphology: Verbs

For each of the type languages I present information on verbal derivation. For the Semitic languages (other than Ugaritic), I also include examples of base conjugation verbs of a variety of shapes, especially to illustrate the variant shapes found where the root contains semivowels or other consonants that condition morphophonemic changes. Most paradigms are abridged; fuller subject and object tables are found in Paradigms B.

Old Babylonian

Base	Stem	Stem + -t-	Stem + -tan-
Present	$iC_1aC_2C_2VC_3$	$iC_1taC_2C_2VC_3$	$iC_1tanaC_2C_2VC_3$
Perfect	$iC_1taC_2VC_3$	$iC_1tatC_2VC_3$	$iC_1tataC_2C_2VC_3$
Preterite	$iC_1C_2VC_3$	$iC_1taC_2VC_3$	$iC_1taC_2C_2VC_3$
Imperative	$C_1VC_2VC_3$	$C_1itC_2VC_3$	$C_1itaC_2C_2VC_3$
Participle	$C_1aC_2iC_3um$	$muC_1taC_2C_3um$	$muC_1taC_2C_2VC_3um$
Infinitive	$C_1aC_2aC_3um$	$C_1itC_2uC_3um$	$C_1itaC_2C_2uC_3um$
Verbal adj.	$C_1aC_2C_3um$		
Stative	$C_1aC_2iC_3$	$C_1itC_2uC_3$	$C_1itaC_2C_2uC_3$

Geminate			
Present	$uC_1aC_2C_2aC_3$	$uC_1taC_2C_2aC_3$	$uC_1tanaC_2C_2aC_3$
Perfect	$uC_1taC_2C_2iC_3$	$uC_1tataC_2C_2iC_3$	$uC_1tataC_2C_2iC_3$
Preterite	$uC_1uC_2C_2iC_3$	$uC_1taC_2C_2iC_3$	$uC_1taC_2C_2iC_3$
Imperative	$C_1uC_2C_2iC_3$	$C_1utaC_2C_2iC_3$	$C_1utaC_2C_2iC_3$
Participle	$muC_1aC_2C_2iC_3um$	$muC_1taC_2C_2iC_3um$	$muC_1taC_2C_2iC_3um$
Infinitive	$C_1uC_2C_2uC_3um$	$C_1utaC_2C_2uC_3um$	$C_1utaC_2C_2uC_3um$
Verbal adj.	$C_1uC_2C_2uC_3um$		
Stative	$C_1uC_2C_2uC_3$		$C_1utaC_2C_2uC_3$

Š-prefix			
Present	$ušaC_1C_2aC_3$	$uštaC_1aC_2C_2aC_3$	$uštanaC_1C_2aC_3$
Perfect	$uštaC_1C_2iC_3$	$uštataC_1C_2iC_3$	$uštataC_1C_2iC_3$
Preterite	$ušaC_1C_2iC_3$	$uštaC_1C_2iC_3$	$uštaC_1C_2iC_3$
Imperative	$šuC_1C_2iC_3$	$šutaC_1C_2iC_3$	$šutaC_1C_2iC_3$
Participle	$mušaC_1C_2iC_3um$	$muštaC_1C_2iC_3um$	$muštaC_1C_2iC_3um$
Infinitive	$šuC_1C_2uC_3um$	$šutaC_1C_2uC_3um$	$šutaC_1C_2uC_3um$
Verbal adj.	$šuC_1C_2uC_3um$		
Stative	$šuC_1C_2uC_3$		

N-prefix			
Present	$iC_1C_1aC_2C_2VC_3$		$ittanaC_1C_2VC_3$
Perfect	$ittaC_1C_2VC_3$		
Preterite	$iC_1C_1aC_2iC_3$		$ittaC_1C_2VC_3$
Imperative	$naC_1C_2iC_3$		$itaC_1C_2VC_3$
Participle	$muC_1C_1aC_2C_3um$		$muttaC_1C_2iC_3um$
Infinitive	$naC_1C_2uC_3um$		$itaC_1C_2uC_3um$
Verbal adj.	$naC_1C_2uC_3um$		
Stative	$naC_1C_2uC_3$		$itaC_1C_2uC_3$

The base conjugation has four variants, distinguished by voweling of present and preterite: *a*, *i*, *u*, and *a/u*; the last shows *u* in preterite and imperative and *a* in present and perfect. Verbs in *a* and *a/u* are generally transitive. Those in *u* are usually intransitive, often expressing motion or process, while verbs in *i* are either transitive or stative.

The conjugation with medial gemination forms transitives from intransitive verbs; it may also be used as a multiplicative. The conjugation with prefixed *š-* is causative or transitivizing. The conjugation with prefixed *n-* is passive or reciprocal when used with a transitive verb; with an intransitive it is inchoative.

The base form with infixed *-t-* is reciprocal or durative. The geminate stem with infixed *-t-*, however, is passive. Prefixed *š-* with infixed *-t-* forms causative reciprocals. There is a rare formation with prefixed *š-* and infixed *-t-* that is a passive of the causative; this differs from the causative reciprocal only in the present, where it shows $uštaC_1C_2aC_3$. The forms with infixed *-tan-* are iterative or habitual.

The present is used for future as well as present. The preterite is the form normally used for the past. The perfect is used as a present perfect, of action just completed, and is also used as the second in a series of past actions; it later became the normal form for past action. The stative is atemporal and may be active or passive.

In the paradigms below, illustrating variants of the base form, the 3fs is rare and identical to the 2ms; the 2p substitutes *-ā* for the *-ī* of the 2fs; the 3d is identical to the 3fp, which substitutes *-ā* for the *-ū* of the 3mp.

	Beat	Trust	Put	Fall	Approach	Eat	Enter	Ask	Rule
Preterite									
1s	amxaṣ	apqid	aškun	amqut	eqrib	ākul	ērub	ašāl	ebēl
2m	tamxaṣ	tapqid	taškun	tamqut	teqrib	tākul	tērub	tašāl	tebēl
2fs	tamxaṣī	tapaqqidī	taškunī	tamqutī	teqribī	tākulī	tērubī	tašālī	tebēlī
3ms	imxaṣ	ipaqqid	iškun	imqut	iqrib	īkul	īrub	išāl	ibēl
1p	nimxaṣ	nipaqqid	niškun	nimqut	niqrib	nīkul	nīrub	nišāl	nibēl
3mp	imxaṣū	ipaqqidū	iškunū	imqutū	iqribū	īkulū	īrubū	išālu	ibēlu
Present									
1s	amaxxaṣ	apaqqid	ašakkan	amaqqut	eqerrib	akkal	errub	ašāl	ebēl
2ms	tamaxxaṣ	tapaqqid	tašakkan	tamaqqut	teqerrib	takkal	terrub	tašāl	tebēl
2fs	tamaxxaṣī	tapaqqidī	tašakkanī	tamaqqutī	teqerribī	takkalī	terrubī	tašallī	tebellī
3ms	imaxxaṣ	ipaqqid	išakkan	imaqqut	iqerrib	ikkal	irrub	išāl	ibēl
1p	nimaxxaṣ	nipaqqid	nišakkan	nimaqqut	niqerrib	nikkal	nirrub	nišāl	nibēl
3mp	imaxxaṣū	ipaqqidū	išakkanū	imaqqutū	iqerribū	ikkalū	irrubū	išallū	ibellū
Imperative									
2ms	maxaṣ	piqid	šukun	muqut	qirib	akal	erub	šāl	bēl
2fs	maxṣī	piqdī	šuknī	muqtī	qirbī	aklī	erbī	šālī	bēlī
2p	maxṣā	piqdā	šuknā	muqtā	qirbā	aklā	erbā	šālā	bēlā

	Give	Sit	Be	Decide	Build	Be High	Fill	Open	Go
Preterite									
1s	addin	ūšib	akūn	ašīm	abni	ašqu	amla	epte	allik
2m	taddin	tūšib	takūn	tašīm	tabni	tašqu	tamla	tapte	tallik
2fs	taddinī	tušbī	takūnī	tašīmī	tabnī	tašqī	tamlī	taptī	tallikī
3ms	iddin	ūšib	ikūn	išīm	ibni	išqu	imla	ipte	illik
1p	niddin	nūšib	nikūn	nišīm	nibni	nišqu	nimla	nipte	nillik
3mp	iddinū	ušbū	ikūnū	išīmū	ibnū	išqū	imlū	iptū	illikū
Present									
1s	anaddin	uššab	akān	ašiam	abanni	ašaqqu	amalla	epette	allak
2ms	tanaddin	tuššab	takān	tašiam	tabanni	tašaqqu	tamalla	tepette	tallak
2fs	tanaddinī	tuššabī	takunnī	tašimmī	tabannī	tašaqqī	tamallī	tepettī	tallakī
3ms	inaddin	uššab	ikān	išiam	ibanni	išaqqu	imalla	ipette	illak
1p	ninaddin	nuššab	nikān	nišiam	nibanni	nišaqqu	nimalla	nipette	nillak
3mp	inaddinū	uššabū	ikunnū	išimmū	ibannū	išaqqū	imallū	ipettū	illakū
Imperative									
2ms	idin	šib	kūn	šīm	bini	šuqu	mala	pete	illik
2fs	idnī	šibī	kūnī	šīmī	binī	šuqī	malī	petī	illikī
2p	idnā	šibā	kūnā	šīmā	biniā	šuqā	malā	peteā	illikā

Syriac

	Base	Geminate	Prefixed
Perfect	$C_1C_2VC_3$	$C_1aC_2C_2iC_3$	$\text{ʾ}aC_1C_2iC_3$
Imperfect	$niC_1C_2VC_3$	$nC_1aC_2C_2iC_3$	$naC_1C_2iC_3$
Imperative	$C_1C_2VC_3$	$C_1aC_2C_2iC_3$	$\text{ʾ}aC_1C_2iC_3$
Infinitive	$miC_1C_2aC_3$	$mC_1aC_2C_2\bar{a}C_3\bar{u}$	$maC_1C_2\bar{a}C_3\bar{u}$
Active part.	$C_1\bar{a}C_2iC_3$	$mC_1aC_2C_2iC_3$	$maC_1C_2iC_3$
Passive part.	$C_1C_2\bar{i}C_3$	$mC_1aC_2C_2aC_3$	$maC_1C_2aC_3$

	Base Reflexive	Gem. Reflexive	Pref. Reflexive
Perfect	$\text{ʾ}itC_1C_2iC_3$	$\text{ʾ}itC_1aC_2C_2aC_3$	$\text{ʾ}ittaC_1C_2aC_3$
Imperfect	$nitC_1C_2iC_3$	$nitC_1aC_2C_2aC_3$	$nittaC_1C_2aC_3$
Imperative	$\text{ʾ}itC_1aC_2C_3$	$\text{ʾ}itC_1aC_2C_2aC_3$	$\text{ʾ}ittaC_1C_2aC_3$
Infinitive	$mitC_1C_2\bar{a}C_3\bar{u}$	$mitC_1aC_2C_2\bar{a}C_3\bar{u}$	$mittaC_1C_2\bar{a}C_3\bar{u}$
Participle	$mitC_1C_2iC_3$	$mitC_1aC_2C_2aC_3$	$mittaC_1C_2aC_3$

The base conjugation has variants distinguished by voweling of perfect and imperfect: $C_1C_2aC_3$, $C_1C_2iC_3$, or rarely $C_1C_2uC_3$ / $niC_1C_2uC_3$, $niC_1C_2aC_3$, or rarely $niC_1C_2iC_3$. The vowel of the imperfect is not totally predictable from the vowel of the perfect or vice versa, though *a/u* (often active) and *i/a* (often intransitive) are the most common patterns.

The geminate conjugation is usually transitive, sometimes causative, and often denominative. The conjugation with prefixed *ʾa-* is generally causative or inchoative. The reflexives may operate as passives or reflexives.

The perfect is past or present perfective. The imperfect is generally future. Constructions based on the participles are used to express present and past continuous.

	Kill	Fear	Leave	Eat	Stand	Raid	Reveal	Sit
				Perfective				
1s	*qiṭlit*	*diḥlit*	*nipqit*	*ʾiklit*	*qāmit*	*bizzit*	*glīt*	*yitbit*
2ms	*qṭalt*	*dḥilt*	*npaqt*	*ʾəkalt*	*qāmt*	*bazzt*	*glayt*	*ītibt*
3ms	*qṭal*	*dḥil*	*npaq*	*ʾəkal*	*qām*	*bazz*	*glā*	*ītib*
3fs	*qiṭlat*	*diḥlat*	*nipqat*	*ʾiklat*	*qāmat*	*bizzat*	*glāt*	*yitbat*
3mp	*qṭal^w*	*dḥil^w*	*npaq^w*	*ʾəkal^w*	*qām^w*	*bazz^w*	*glaw*	*ītib^w*
3fp	*qṭal^y*	*dḥil^y*	*npaq^y*	*ʾəkal^y*	*qām^y*	*bazz^y*	*glay*	*ītib^y*
				Imperfective				
1s	*ʾiqṭul*	*ʾidḥal*	*ʾippuq*	*ʾikul*	*ʾəqūm*	*ʾibbuz*	*ʾigle*	*ʾittib*
2ms	*tiqṭul*	*tidḥal*	*tippuq*	*tikul*	*tqūm*	*tibbuz*	*tigle*	*tittib*
2fs	*tiqṭlīn*	*tidḥlīn*	*tippqīn*	*tiklīn*	*tqūmīn*	*tibbzīn*	*tigleyn*	*tittbīn*
2mp	*tiqṭlūn*	*tidḥlūn*	*tippqūn*	*tiklūn*	*tqūmūn*	*tibbzūn*	*tiglōn*	*tittbūn*
2fp	*tiqṭlān*	*tidḥlān*	*tippqān*	*tiklān*	*tqūmān*	*tibbzān*	*tiglyān*	*tittbān*
				Imperative				
2ms	*qṭul*	*dḥal*	*puq*	*ʾakul*	*qūm*	*buzz*	*glī*	*tib*
2fs	*qṭul^y*	*dḥal^y*	*puq^y*	*ʾakul^y*	*qūm^y*	*buzz^y*	*glāy*	*tib^y*
2mp	*qṭul^w*	*dḥal^w*	*puq^w*	*ʾakul^w*	*qūm^w*	*buzz^w*	*glaw*	*tib^w*
2fp	*qṭul^y*	*dḥal^y*	*puq^y*	*ʾakul^y*	*qūm^y*	*buzz^y*	*glāyen*	*tib^y*

The perfective 2fs, 1p, 2mp and 3mp are identical to the 2ms, except that the suffixes are *-t^y*, *-n*, *-tunn*, and *-tinn*, respectively. The imperfect 3fs is identical to the 2ms; the 3ms and 1p are identical to the 2ms except for the prefix *n(i)-*. The imperfect 3mp and 3fp are identical to the 2mp and 2fp, respectively, except for the prefix *n(i)-*.

Urmi

	Base	Factitive A	Factitive B
Active base	$C_1 \partial C_2 i C_3$	$C_1 \partial C_2 i C_3$	$m\partial C_1 C_2 i C_3$
Perfective	$C_1 C_2 i C_3 li$	$C_1 u C_2 i C_3 li$	$mu C_1 C_2 i C_3 li$
Passive base	$C_1 C_2 ij C_3$	$C_1 u C_2 i C_3$	$mu C_1 C_2 i C_3$
Imperative	$C_1 C_2 u C_3$	$C_1 \partial C_2 i C_3$	$m\partial C_1 C_2 i C_3$
Infinitive	$C_1 C_2 \partial C_3 \partial$	$C_1 \partial C_2 u C_3 i$	$m\partial C_1 C_2 u C_3 i$

The two factitives are not semantically distinct; a given base will form only one, the choice of pattern being unpredictable. Except for the base form imperative, none of these continues older Semitic finite verb forms. Conjugation of present and past uses the clitic pronouns; the perfective uses possessive suffixes. Since the perfective and imperfective forms are based on the older participles, distinct feminine forms exist for all persons, agreeing with the object in the perfective; otherwise with the subject.

    These basic forms are combined with various particles to mark a complex system of tense, aspect, and mood. There is a past tense marker *və* used with perfective and imperfect forms. Other forms are marked by prefixes to the imperfect: the continuous with *ki*, the future with *bit*, and so forth. The infinitive is also used as a base for verbal constructions.

	ACTIVE		PASSIVE			
	masc.	fem.	masc.	fem.	IMPERATIVE	INFINITIVE
Comb	*səriq*	*sərqə*	*srijqə*	*sriqtə*	*sruq*	*srəqə*
Say	*əmir*	*əmirə*	*mijrə*	*mirtə*	*mur*	*mərə*
Learn	*jəlip*	*jəlpə*	*lijpə*	*liptə*	*lup*	*ljəpə*
Insult	*ləjim*	*lemə*	*lijmə*	*limtə*	*lum*	*ljəmə*
Buy	*zəvin*	*zonə*	*zvijnə*	*zvintə*	*zun*	*zvənə*
Explain	*gəli*	*gəljə*	*giljə*	*glijtə*	*glij*	*gləjə*
Live	*xəjji*	*xəjjə*	*xijə*	*xijtə*	*xij*	*xəjə*
Beg	*gəvi*	*gojə*	*gujə*	*gvijtə*	*gvij*	*gvəjə*
Mourn	*jəli*	*jəljə*	*jiljə*	*ljijtə*	*ljij*	*ljəjə*
Worry	*əjiq*	*eqə*	*ijqə*	*iqtə*	*uq*	*jəqə*
Make	*əvid*	*odə*	*vijdə*	*vidtə*	*vud*	*vədə*
Come	*əti*	*ətjə*	*tijə*	*tijtə*	*tə*	*təjə*

Ugaritic

	Base	Geminate	Causative 1	Causative 2
Perfect	$C_1 A C_2 V C_3 A$	$C_1 A C_2 C_2 I C_3 A$		$\check{s} C_1 C_2 C_3$
Imperfect	$y V C_1 C_2 V C_3 U$	$y A C_1 A C_2 C_2 V C_3 U$	$y A C_1 C_2 I C_3 U$	$y A \check{s} C_1 C_2 I C_3$
Jussive	$y V C_1 C_2 V C_3$			
Imperative	$C_1 C_2 V C_3$	$C_1 A C_2 C_2 V C_3$		$\check{s} C_1 C_2 C_3$
Active part.	$C_1 \bar{A} C_2 I C_3 U$	$m u C_1 A C_2 C_2 I C_3 U$		$m \check{s} C_1 C_2 C_3$
Passive perf.	$C_1 C_2 C_3$			
Passive impf.	$y u C_1 C_2 C_3$	$C_1 C_2 C_2 C_3$		$y \check{s} C_1 C_2 C_3$
Passive part.	$C_1 A C_2 \bar{I} C_3 U$	$m C_1 C_2 C_2 C_3$		
Infinitive	$C_1 A C_2 \bar{A} C_3 U$	$C_1 U C_2 C_2 A C_3 U$		
Inf. Construct	$C_1 C_2 C_3$-			

	Base Reflexive	Gem. Reflexive	Caus. Reflexive	Nasal
Perfect		$t C_1 C_2 C_2 C_3$		$n A C_1 C_2 A C_3 A$
Imperfect	$y I C t_1 V C_2 I C_3 U$		$y \check{s} t C_1 C_2 C_3$	$y C_1 C_1 A C_2 C_3$
Jussive				
Imperative	$ʾ I C_1 t C_2 C_3$			
Active Part.				$n A C_1 C_2 A C_3 U$
Passive Perf.				
Passive Impf.				
Passive Part.				
Infinitive				
Inf. Construct	$ʾ I C_1 t A C_2 C_3$-			

Vowels that can be identified from syllabic or alphabetic transcriptions are inserted in small capitals. V is used where vocalization varies. In all cases, vowel quantity is conjectural.

The base conjugation has variants, distinguished by voweling of perfect and imperfect: $C_1 A C_2 A C_3 A$, $C_1 A C_2 I C_3 A$ / $y A C_1 C_2 V C_3 U$, $y I C_1 C_2 A C_3 U$. The vowel of the imperfect is in most cases predictable from the vowel of the perfect, though with a guttural in second or third position $y I C_1 C_2 A C_3 U$ is found where $y A C_1 C_2 U C_3 U$ would be expected.

The geminate conjugation is usually transitive, sometimes intensive; since neither alphabetic nor syllabic transcription marks gemination consistently, it is usually difficult to identify with certainty. Causatives with prefixed *ʾa-* are found only in the imperfect, where they are often not distinguishable in alphabetic texts. The difference in meaning from the causatives in *š-* cannot be determined. The form with prefixed *n-* is passive; the difference from the internal passive is not clear.

In prose texts the perfect is past or present perfective; the imperfect is present or future. In poetry the imperfect is also found as a consecutive. There may have existed a subjunctive in final *-a*, as in Arabic. The jussive is used to express a wish or command.

Hebrew

	Base	Geminate	Causative
Perfect	$C_1aC_2VC_3$	$C_1iC_2C_2\bar{e}C_3$	$hiC_1C_2\bar{i}C_3$
Imperfect	$yiC_1C_2VC_3$	$yC_1aC_2C_2\bar{e}C_3$	$yaC_1C_2\bar{i}C_3$
Imperative	$C_1C_2VC_3$	$C_1aC_2C_2\bar{e}C_3$	$haC_1C_2\bar{e}C_3$
Infinitive	$C_1aC_2\bar{o}C_3$	$C_1aC_2C_2\bar{o}C_3$	$haC_1C_2\bar{e}C_3$
Inf. constr.	$C_1C_2\bar{o}C_3$	$C_1aC_2C_2\bar{e}C_3$	$haC_1C_2\bar{i}C_3$
Active part.	$C_1aC_2\bar{e}C_3$	$mC_1aC_2C_2\bar{e}C_3$	$maC_1C_2\bar{i}C_3$
Passive part.	$C_1aC_2\bar{u}C_3$		

	Nasal	Geminate Passive	Caus. Passive
Perfect	$niC_1C_2aC_3$	$C_1uC_2C_2aC_3$	$hoC_1C_2aC_3$
Imperfect	$yiC_1C_1aC_2\bar{e}C_3$	$yC_1uC_2C_2aC_3$	$yoC_1C_2aC_3$
Imperative	$hiC_1C_1aC_2\bar{e}C_3$		
Infinitive	$hiC_1C_1aC_2\bar{o}C_3$	$C_1uC_2C_2\bar{o}C_3$	$hoC_1C_2\bar{e}C_3$
Inf. constr.	$hiC_1C_1aC_2\bar{e}C_3$	?	?
Participle	$niC_1C_2aC_3$	$mC_1uC_2C_2aC_3$	$moC_1C_2aC_3$

	Gem. Reflexive	
Perfect	$hitC_1aC_2C_2\bar{e}C_3$	The geminate conjugation is usually transitive, sometimes intensive, and often denominative. The nasal conjugation serves as passive and reflexive for the base conjugation.
Imperfect	$yitC_1aC_2C_2\bar{e}C_3$	
Imperative	$hitC_1aC_2C_2\bar{e}C_3$	
Infinitive	$hitC_1aC_2C_2\bar{o}C_3$	
Inf. constr.	$hitC_1aC_2C_2\bar{e}C_3$	
Participle	$mitC_1aC_2C_2\bar{e}C_3$	

The base conjugation has variants, distinguished by voweling of perfect and imperfect: $C_1aC_2aC_3$, $C_1aC_2\bar{e}C_3$, $C_1aC_2\bar{o}C_3$ / $yiC_1C_2\bar{o}C_3$, or $yiC_1C_2aC_3$. The vowel of the imperfect is not totally predictable from the vowel of the perfect or vice versa, though $a/\bar{o}$ (often active), $\bar{e}/a$ (often intransitive), and u/a (often stative) are common.

The perfect is past or present perfective. The imperfect is present or future. There is a jussive that is close to the imperfect in shape (see the following table). The perfect is used as consecutive to an imperfect, the imperfect as consecutive, to a perfect. In each case there is an accentual shift: in the perfect as consecutive, the accent is moved toward the end of the verb; with the imperfect the accent is pulled back.

Note the vowel changes in some patterns in the jussive and imperfect consecutive.

	Kill	Be Heavy	Be Small	Fall	Stand	Surround	Reveal	Sit
Perfective								
1s	*qāṭaltī*	*kābadtī*	*qāṭōntī*	*nāpaltī*	*qamtī*	*sabbōtī*	*gālītī*	*yāšabtī*
2ms	*qāṭaltā*	*kābadtā*	*qāṭōntā*	*nāpaltā*	*qamtā*	*sabbōtā*	*gālītā*	*yāšabtā*
2fs	*qāṭalt*	*kābadt*	*qāṭōnt*	*nāpalt*	*qamt*	*sabbōt*	*gālīt*	*yāšabt*
3ms	*qāṭal*	*kābēd*	*qāṭōn*	*nāpal*	*qām*	*sābab*	*gālāh*	*yāšab*
3fs	*qāṭlāh*	*kābdāh*	*qāṭnāh*	*nāplāh*	*qāmāh*	*sābäbāh*	*gāltāh*	*yāšabāh*
1p	*qāṭalnū*	*kābadnū*	*qāṭōnnū*	*nāpalnū*	*qamnū*	*sabbōnū*	*gālīnū*	*yāšabnū*
2mp	*qṭaltem*	*kbadtem*	*qṭontem*	*npaltem*	*qamtem*	*sabbōtem*	*glītem*	*yšabtem*
2fp	*qṭalten*	*kbadten*	*qṭonten*	*npalten*	*qamten*	*sabbōten*	*glīten*	*yšabten*
3p	*qāṭlū*	*kābdū*	*qāṭnū*	*nāpalū*	*qāmū*	*sābäbū*	*gālū*	*yāšbū*
Imperfective								
1s	*ʾeqṭōl*	*ʾekbad*	*ʾeqṭan*	*ʾeppōl*	*ʾāqūm*	*ʾāsōb*	*ʾegleh*	*ʾēšēb*
2ms	*tiqṭōl*	*tikbad*	*tiqṭan*	*tippōl*	*tāqūm*	*tāsōb*	*tigleh*	*tēšēb*
2fs	*tiqṭlī*	*tikbdī*	*tiqṭnī*	*tipplī*	*tāqūmī*	*tāsōbbī*	*tiglī*	*tēšbī*
3ms	*yiqṭōl*	*yikbad*	*yiqṭan*	*yippōl*	*yāqūm*	*yāsōb*	*yigleh*	*yēšēb*
3fs	*tiqṭōl*	*tikbad*	*tiqṭan*	*tippōl*	*tāqūm*	*tāsōb*	*tigleh*	*tēšēb*
1p	*niqṭōl*	*nikbad*	*niqṭan*	*nippōl*	*nāqūm*	*nāsōb*	*nigleh*	*nēšēb*
2mp	*tiqṭlū*	*tikbdū*	*tiqṭnū*	*tipplū*	*tāqūmū*	*tāsōbbū*	*tiglū*	*tēšbū*
2fp	*tiqṭōlnāh*	*tikbadnāh*	*tiqṭannāh*	*tippōlnāh*	*tqūmeynāh*	*tsubbeynāh*	*tigleynāh*	*tēšabnāh*
3mp	*yiqṭlū*	*yikbdū*	*yiqṭnū*	*yipplū*	*yāqūmū*	*yāsōbbū*	*yiglū*	*yēšbū*
3fp	*tiqṭōlnāh*	*tikbadnāh*	*tiqṭannāh*	*tippōlnāh*	*tqūmeynāh*	*tsubbeynāh*	*tigleynāh*	*tēšabnāh*
Jussive								
3ms	*yiqṭōl*	*yikbad*	*yiqṭan*	*yippōl*	*yāqōm*	*yāsōb*	*yigel*	*yēšēb*
Imperfect Consecutive								
3ms	*wayyiqṭōl*	*wayyikbad*	*wayyiqṭan*	*wayyippōl*	*wayyāqom*	*wayyāsob*	*wayyigel*	*wayyēšeb*
Imperative								
2ms	*qṭōl*	*kbad*	*qṭan*	*npōl*	*qūm*	*sōb*	*glēh*	*šēb*
2fs	*qiṭlī*	*kibdī*	*qiṭnī*	*niplī*	*qūmī*	*sōbbī*	*glī*	*šbī*
2mp	*qiṭlū*	*kibdū*	*qiṭnū*	*niplū*	*qūmū*	*sōbbū*	*glū*	*šbū*
2fp	*qṭōlnāh*	*kbadnāh*	*qṭannāh*	*npōlnāh*	*qōmnāh*	*subbeynāh*	*gleynāh*	*šēbnāh*

Classical Arabic

	Base	Geminate	Lengthened	Causative
Perfect	$C_1aC_2VC_3a$	$C_1aC_2C_2aC_3a$	$C_1aC_2aC_3a$	$ʾaC_1C_2aC_3a$
Imperfect	$yaC_1C_2VC_3u$	$yuC_1aC_2C_2iC_3u$	$yuC_1aC_2iC_3u$	$yuC_1C_2iC_3u$
Subjunctive	$yaC_1C_2VC_3a$	$yuC_1aC_2C_2iC_3a$	$yuC_1aC_2iC_3a$	$yuC_1C_2iC_3a$
Jussive	$yaC_1C_2VC_3$	$yuC_1aC_2C_2iC_3$	$yuC_1aC_2iC_3$	$yuC_1C_2iC_3$
Imperative	$VC_1C_2VC_3$	$C_1aC_2C_2iC_3$	$C_1aC_2iC_3$	$ʾaC_1C_2iC_3$
Active part.	$C_1aC_2iC_3^{un}$	$muC_1aC_2C_2iC_3^{un}$	$muC_1aC_2iC_3^{un}$	$muC_1C_2iC_3^{un}$
Passive perf.	$C_1uC_2iC_3a$	$C_1uC_2C_2iC_3a$	$C_1\bar{u}C_2iC_3a$	$ʾuC_1C_2iC_3a$
Passive impf.	$yuC_1C_2aC_3u$	$yuC_1aC_2C_2aC_3u$	$yuC_1aC_2aC_3u$	$yuC_1C_2aC_3u$
Passive part.	$maC_1C_2\bar{u}C_3^{un}$	$muC_1aC_2C_2aC_3^{un}$	$muC_1aC_2aC_3^{un}$	$muC_1C_2aC_3^{un}$
Verbal noun	VARIOUS	$taC_1C_2\bar{i}C_3^{un}$	$C_1iC_2aC_3^{un}$	$ʾiC_1C_2aC_3^{un}$

	Base Reflexive	Gem. Reflexive	Lnth. Reflexive	Caus. Reflexive
Perfect	$iC_1taC_2aC_3a$	$taC_1aC_2C_2aC_3a$	$taC_1aC_2aC_3a$	$istaC_1C_2aC_3a$
Imperfect	$yaC_1taC_2iC_3u$	$yataC_1aC_2C_2aC_3u$	$yataC_1aC_2aC_3u$	$yastaC_1C_2iC_3u$
Subjunctive	$yaC_1taC_2iC_3a$	$yataC_1aC_2C_2aC_3a$	$yataC_1aC_2aC_3a$	$yastaC_1C_2iC_3a$
Jussive	$yaC_1taC_2iC_3$	$yataC_1aC_2C_2aC_3$	$yataC_1aC_2aC_3$	$yastaC_1C_2iC_3$
Imperative	$iC_1taC_2iC_3$	$taC_1aC_2C_2aC_3$	$taC_1aC_2aC_3$	$istaC_1C_2iC_3$
Active part.	$muC_1taC_2iC_3^{un}$	$mutaC_1aC_2C_2iC_3^{un}$	$mutaC_1aC_2iC_3^{un}$	$mustaC_1C_2iC_3^{un}$
Passive perf.	$uC_1tuC_2iC_3a$	$tuC_1uC_2C_2iC_3a$	$tuC_1\bar{u}C_2iC_3a$	$ʾustaC_1C_2iC_3a$
Passive impf.	$yuC_1tuC_2aC_3u$	$yutaC_1aC_2C_2aC_3u$	$yutaC_1aC_2aC_3u$	$yustaC_1C_2aC_3u$
Passive part.	$muC_1taC_2aC_3^{un}$	$mutaC_1aC_2C_2aC_3^{un}$	$mutaC_1aC_2aC_3^{un}$	$mustaC_1C_2aC_3^{un}$
Verbal noun	$iC_1tiC_2aC_3^{un}$	$taC_1aC_2C_2uC_3^{un}$	$taC_1aC_2uC_3^{un}$	$ʾistiC_1C_2aC_3^{un}$

	Nasal	
Perfect	$inC_1aC_2aC_3a$	Omitted are forms with geminate third radical, which are almost exclusively denominatives from adjectives.
Imperfect	$yanC_1aC_2iC_3u$	
Subjunctive	$yanC_1aC_2iC_3a$	
Jussive	$yanC_1aC_2iC_3$	
Imperative	$inC_1aC_2iC_3$	
Active part.	$munC_1aC_2iC_3^{un}$	
Passive perf.	$ʾunC_1uC_2iC_3a$	
Passive impf.	$yunC_1aC_2aC_3u$	
Passive part.	$munC_1aC_2aC_3^{un}$	
Verbal noun	$ʾinC_1iC_2aC_3^{un}$	

The base conjugation has variants, distinguished by voweling of perfect and imperfect: $C_1aC_2aC_3a$, $C_1aC_2iC_3a$, or $C_1aC_2uC_3a$ / $yaC_1C_2aC_3u$, $yaC_1C_2iC_3u$, or $yaC_1C_2uC_3u$. The vowel of the imperfect is not predictable from the vowel of the perfect or vice versa, though *a/u* (often active), *i/a* (often intransitive), and *u/u* (often stative) are common.

The geminate conjugation is usually transitive, sometimes intensive, and often denominative. The geminate conjugation with lengthened first syllable is often associative. Causatives are formed with prefixed *'a-*, though geminate stems may have similar meaning. The forms with prefixed *ta-* or infixed *t-* are generally reflexives (with lengthened vowel reciprocal), and the forms with prefixed *n-* reflexive or passive. But all derived forms show much semantic inconsistency, so that even transitivity is not predictable.

The perfect is past or present perfective. The imperfect is present or (often with preposed *sa(wfa)*) future; in subordinate clauses it may also be used as a past continuous. The subjunctive is used in clauses of purpose or consequence; the jussive is used in commands and (with *lam*) as a past negative.

	Write	Wear	Be Good	Return	Stand	Sleep	Throw	Call
Perfective								
1s	*katabtu*	*labistu*	*ḥasuntu*	*radadtu*	*qumtu*	*nimtu*	*ramaytu*	*daʿawtu*
2ms	*katabta*	*labista*	*ḥasunta*	*radadta*	*qumta*	*nimta*	*ramayta*	*daʿawta*
2fs	*katabti*	*labisti*	*ḥasunti*	*radadti*	*qumti*	*nimti*	*ramayti*	*daʿawti*
3ms	*kataba*	*labisa*	*ḥasuna*	*radda*	*qāma*	*nāma*	*ramā*	*daʿā*
3fs	*katabat*	*labisat*	*ḥasunat*	*raddat*	*qāmat*	*nāmat*	*ramat*	*daʿat*
2d	*katabtumā*	*labistumā*	*ḥasuntumā*	*radadtumā*	*qumtumā*	*nimtumā*	*ramaytumā*	*daʿawtumā*
3md	*katabā*	*labisā*	*ḥasunā*	*raddā*	*qāmā*	*nāmā*	*ramayā*	*daʿawā*
3fd	*katabatā*	*labisatā*	*ḥasunatā*	*raddatā*	*qāmatā*	*nāmatā*	*ramātā*	*daʿātā*
1p	*katabnā*	*labisnā*	*ḥasunnā*	*radadnā*	*qumnā*	*nimnā*	*ramaynā*	*daʿawnā*
2mp	*katabtum*	*labistum*	*ḥasuntum*	*radadtum*	*qumtum*	*nimtum*	*ramaytum*	*daʿawtum*
2fp	*katabtunna*	*labistunna*	*ḥasuntunna*	*radadtunna*	*qumtunna*	*nimtunna*	*ramaytunna*	*daʿawtunna*
3mp	*katabū*	*labisū*	*ḥasunū*	*raddū*	*qāmū*	*nāmū*	*ramaw*	*daʿaw*
3fp	*katabna*	*labisna*	*ḥasunna*	*radadna*	*qumna*	*nimna*	*ramayna*	*daʿawna*
Imperfective								
1s	*ʾaktubu*	*ʾalbasu*	*ʾaḥsunu*	*ʾaruddu*	*ʾaqūmu*	*ʾanāmu*	*ʾarmī*	*ʾadʿū*
2ms	*taktubu*	*talbasu*	*taḥsunu*	*taruddu*	*taqūmu*	*tanāmu*	*tarmī*	*tadʿū*
2fs	*taktubīna*	*talbasīna*	*taḥsunīna*	*taruddīna*	*taqūmīna*	*tanāmīna*	*tarmīna*	*tadʿīna*
3ms	*yaktubu*	*yalbasu*	*yaḥsunu*	*yaruddu*	*yaqūmu*	*yanāmu*	*yarmī*	*yadʿū*
3fs	*taktubu*	*talbasu*	*taḥsunu*	*taruddu*	*taqūmu*	*tanāmu*	*tarmī*	*tadʿū*
2d	*taktubāni*	*talbasāni*	*taḥsunāni*	*taruddāni*	*taqūmāni*	*tanāmāni*	*tarmiyāni*	*tadʿuwāni*
3md	*yaktubāni*	*yalbasāni*	*yaḥsunāni*	*yaruddāni*	*yaqūmāni*	*yanāmāni*	*yarmiyāni*	*yadʿuwāni*
3fd	*taktubāni*	*talbasāni*	*taḥsunāni*	*taruddāni*	*taqūmāni*	*tanāmāni*	*tarmiyāni*	*tadʿuwāni*
1p	*naktubu*	*nalbasu*	*naḥsunu*	*naruddu*	*naqūmu*	*nanāmu*	*narmī*	*nadʿū*
2mp	*taktubūna*	*talbasūna*	*taḥsunūna*	*taruddūna*	*taqūmūna*	*tanāmūna*	*tarmūna*	*tadʿūna*
2fp	*taktubna*	*talbasna*	*taḥsunna*	*tardudna*	*taqumna*	*tanamna*	*tarmīna*	*tadʿūna*
3mp	*yaktubūna*	*yalbasūna*	*yaḥsunūna*	*yaruddūna*	*yaqūmūna*	*yanāmūna*	*yarmūna*	*yadʿūna*
3fp	*yaktubna*	*yalbasna*	*yaḥsunna*	*yardudna*	*yaqumna*	*yanamna*	*yarmīna*	*yadʿūna*
Imperative								
2ms	*uktub*	*ilbas*	*uḥsun*	*urdud*	*qum*	*nam*	*irmi*	*udʿu*
2fs	*uktubī*	*ilbasī*	*uḥsunī*	*ruddī*	*qūmī*	*nāmī*	*irmī*	*udʿī*
2d	*uktubā*	*ilbasā*	*uḥsunā*	*ruddā*	*qūmā*	*nāmā*	*irmiyā*	*udʿuwā*
2mp	*uktubū*	*ilbasū*	*uḥsunū*	*ruddū*	*qūmū*	*nāmū*	*irmū*	*udʿū*
2fp	*uktubna*	*ilbasna*	*uḥsunna*	*urdudna*	*qumna*	*namna*	*irmīna*	*udʿūna*

Egyptian Arabic

	Base	Geminate	Lengthened
Perfect	$C_1VC_2VC_3$	$C_1aC_2C_2iC_3$	$C_1aC_2iC_3$
Imperfect	$yVC_1C_2VC_3$	$yiC_1aC_2C_2iC_3$	$yiC_1aC_2iC_3$
Imperative	$'VC_1C_2VC_3$	$C_1aC_2C_2iC_3$	$C_1aC_2iC_3$
Active participle	$C_1aC_2iC_3$	$miC_1aC_2C_2iC_3$	$miC_1aC_2iC_3$
Passive part.	$maC_1C_2\bar{u}C_3$		
Verbal noun	VARIOUS	$taC_1C_2iC_3$	$miC_1aC_2C_3a$

	Base Reflexive A	Gem. Reflexive	Lnth. Reflexive
Perfect	$'itC_1aC_2aC_3$	$'itC_1aC_2C_2iC_3$	$'itC_1aC_2iC_3$
Imperfect	$yitC_1iC_2iC_3$	$yitC_1aC_2C_2iC_3$	$yitC_1aC_2iC_3$
Imperative	$'itC_1aC_2iC_3$	$'itC_1aC_2C_2iC_3$	$'itC_1aC_2iC_3$
Active participle	$miC_1tiC_2iC_3$	$mitC_1aC_2C_2iC_3$	$mitC_1aC_2iC_3$
Passive part.			
Verbal noun		$taC_1aC_2C_2uC_3$	$taC_1aC_2uC_3$

	Caus. Reflexive	Nasal	Base Reflexive B
Perfect	$'istaC_1C_2iC_3$	$'inC_1aC_2aC_3$	$'iC_1taC_2aC_3$
Imperfect	$yistaC_1C_2iC_3$	$yinC_1iC_2iC_3$	$yiC_1tiC_2iC_3$
Imperative	$'istaC_1C_2iC_3$	$'inC_1aC_2iC_3$	$'iC_1taC_2iC_3$
Active participle	$mistaC_1C_2iC_3$	$minC_1iC_2iC_3$	$miC_1tiC_2iC_3$
Passive part.			
Verbal noun	$'istiC_1C_2aC_3^{un}$	$'inC_1iC_2aC_3$	$'iC_1tiC_2aC_3$

Omitted are forms with geminate third radical, which are almost exclusively denominatives from adjectives. The base conjugation has variants, distinguished by voweling of perfect and imperfect: $C_1aC_2aC_3/yiC_1C_2iC_3 \sim yuC_1C_2uC_3$ and $C_1iC_2iC_3/yiC_1C_2iC_3$. In all conjugations, i in the last syllable is replaced by a in certain consonantal environments. The vowel of the imperfect is not predictable from the vowel of the perfect or vice versa.

The geminate and lengthened conjugations are probably not derivationally productive; there is little semantic predictability. The forms labeled reflexive are intransitive or passive; the base reflexive B and causative reflexive seem to include only fixed forms, while the ones with prefixed *'it-* are productively related to the transitive conjugations. The form with prefixed *n-* is equivalent to the base reflexive A; verbs select one or the other as the preferred reflexive. But all derived forms show much semantic inconsistency. There are inconsistencies of shape, in part owing to the influence of Classical Arabic patterns.

The perfect is past or present perfective. The imperfect with prefixed *bi-* is present; with prefixed *ha-* it is future. The same form without prefixed tense marking is used as a complement of other verbs, as a jussive or in a series of imperfects. A variety of tense/aspect combinations can be formed with auxiliary verbs.

	Write	Drink	Be Silent	Put	Get Up	Sell	Throw	Find	Fall
Perfective
1s	katabt	širibt	sikitt	ḥattēt	ʾumt	biʿt	ramēt	liʾēt	wiʾiʿt
2ms	katabt	širibt	sikitt	ḥattēt	ʾimt	biʿt	ramēt	liʾēt	wiʾiʿt
2fs	katabti	širibti	sikitti	ḥattēti	ʾimti	biʿti	ramēti	liʾēti	wiʾiʿti
3ms	katab	širib	sikit	ḥatt	ʾām	bāʿ	rama	liʾi	wiʾiʿ
3fs	katabit	širibit	sikitit	ḥattit	ʾāmit	bāʿit	ramit	liʾyit	wiʾiʿit
1p	katabna	širibna	sikitna	ḥattēna	ʾimna	biʿna	ramēna	liʾēna	wiʾiʿna
2p	katabtu	širibtu	sikittu	ḥattētu	ʾimtu	biʿtu	ramētu	liʾētu	wiʾiʿtu
3p	katabu	širibu	sikitu	ḥattu	ʾāmu	bāʿu	ramu	liʾu	wiʾiʿu
Imperfective
1s	ʾaktib	ʾašrab	ʾaskut	ʾaḥutt	ʾaʾūm	ʾabīʿ	ʾarmi	ʾalʾa	ʾawʾaʿ
2ms	tiktib	tišrab	tuskut	tiḥutt	tiʾūm	tibīʿ	tirmi	tilʾa	tuʾaʿ
2fs	tiktibi	tišrabi	tuskuti	tiḥutti	tiʾūmi	tibīʿi	tirmi	tilʾi	tuʾaʿi
3ms	yiktib	yišrab	yiskut	yiḥutt	yiʾūm	yibīʿ	yirmi	yilʾa	yuʾaʿ
3fs	tiktib	tišrab	tiskut	tiḥutt	tiʾūm	tibīʿ	tirmi	tilʾa	tuʾaʿ
1p	niktib	nišrab	niskut	niḥutt	niʾūm	nibīʿ	nirmi	nilʾa	nuʾaʿ
2p	tiktibu	tišrabu	tiskutu	tiḥuttu	tiʾūmu	tibīʿu	tirmu	tilʾu	tuʾaʿu
3p	yiktibu	yišrabu	yiskutu	yiḥuttu	yiʾūmu	yibīʿu	yirmu	yilʾu	yuʾaʿu
Imperative
2ms	ʾiktib	ʾišrab	ʾuskut	ḥutt	ʾūm	bīʿ	ʾirmi	ʾilʾa	ʾuʾaʿ
2fs	ʾiktibi	ʾišrabi	ʾuskuti	ḥutti	ʾūmi	bīʿi	ʾirmi	ʾilʾi	ʾuʾaʿi
2p	ʾiktibu	ʾišrabu	ʾuskutu	ḥuttu	ʾūmu	bīʿu	ʾirmu	ʾilʾu	ʾuʾaʿu

Ge'ez

	Base	Mediopassive	Causative	Caus/Reflexive
Perfect	$C_1aC_2(a)C_3a$	$taC_1aC_2C_3a$	$ʾaC_1C_2aC_3a$	$ʾastaC_1C_2aC_3a$
Imperfect	$yəC_1aC_2C_{2ə}C_3$	$yətCaC_2C_{2ə}C_3$	$yāC_1aC_2C_{2ə}C_3$	$yāstaC_1aC_2C_{2ə}C_3$
Subjunctive	$yəC_1C_2VC_3$	$yətC_1aC_2aC_3$	$yāC_1C_{2ə}C_3$	$yāstaC_1C_{2ə}C_3$
Imperative	$C_{1ə}C_2VC_3$	$taC_1aC_2aC_3$	$ʾaC_1C_{2ə}C_3$	$ʾastaC_1C_{2ə}C_3$
Agent Noun	$C_1aC_2āC_3ī$	$taC_1aC_2aC_3ī$	$maC_1C_{2ə}C_3$	$mastaC_1C_{2ə}C_3$
Infinitive	$C_1aC_2īC_3$	$taC_1aC_2C_3ō$	$ʾaC_1C_{2ə}C_3ō$	$ʾastaC_1aC_2C_{2ə}C_3ō$
Absolute	$C_1aC_2īC_3a$	$taC_1aC_2īC_3a$	$ʾaC_1C_2īC_3a$	$ʾastaC_1aC_2īC_3a$

	Geminate	Mediopassive	Causative	Caus/Reflexive
Perfect	$C_1aC_2C_2aC_3a$	$taC_1aC_2C_2aC_3a$	$ʾaC_1aC_2C_2aC_3a$	$ʾastaC_1aC_2C_2aC_3a$
Imperfect	$yəC_1ēC_2C_{2ə}C_3$	$yətC_1ēC_2C_{2ə}C_3$	$yāC_1ēC_2C_{2ə}C_3$	$yāstaC_1ēC_2C_{2ə}C_3$
Subjunctive	$yəC_1aC_2C_{2ə}C_3$	$yətC_1aC_2C_{2ə}C_3$	$yāC_1aC_2C_{2ə}C_3$	$yāstaC_1aC_2C_{2ə}C_3$
Imperative	$C_1aC_2C_{2ə}C_3$	$taC_1aC_2C_{2ə}C_3$	$ʾaC_1aC_2C_{2ə}C_3$	$ʾastaC_1aC_2C_{2ə}C_3$
Agent Noun	$maC_1aC_2C_{2ə}C_3$	$mastaC_1aC_2C_{2ə}C_3$		
Infinitive	$C_1aC_2C_{2ə}C_3ō$	$taC_1aC_2C_{2ə}C_3ō$	$ʾaC_1aC_2C_{2ə}C_3ō$	$ʾastaC_1aC_2C_{2ə}C_3ō$
Absolute	$C_1aC_2C_2īC_3a$	$taC_1aC_2C_2īC_3a$	$ʾaC_1aC_2C_2īC_3a$	$ʾastaC_1aC_2C_2īC_3a$

	Lengthened	Mediopassive	Causative	Caus/Reflexive
Perfect	$C_1āC_2aC_3a$	$taC_1āC_2aC_3a$	$ʾaC_1āC_2aC_3a$	$ʾastaC_1āC_2aC_3a$
Imperfect	$yəC_1āC_{2ə}C_3$	$yətC_1āC_2C_3$	$yaC_1āC_{2ə}C_3$	$yāstaC_1āC_{2ə}C_3$
Subjunctive	$yəC_1āC_{2ə}C_3$	$yətC_1āC_2C_3$	$yaC_1āC_{2ə}C_3$	$yāstaC_1āC_{2ə}C_3$
Imperative	$C_1āC_{2ə}C_3$	$taC_1āC_2C_3$	$ʾaC_1āC_{2ə}C_3$	$ʾastaC_1āC_{2ə}C_3$
Agent Noun	$maC_1āC_{2ə}C_3$	$taC_1āC_2aC_3ī$	$mastāC_1aC_{2ə}C_3$	
Infinitive	$C_1āC_{2ə}C_3ō$	$taC_1āC_{2ə}C_3ō$	$ʾaC_1āC_{2ə}C_3ō$	$ʾastaC_1āC_{2ə}C_3ō$
Absolute	$C_1āC_2īC_3a$	$taC_1āC_2īC_3a$	$ʾaC_1āC_2īC_3a$	$ʾastaC_1āC_2īC_3a$

The base conjugation has variants, distinguished by voweling of perfect and subjunctive: $C_1aC_2aC_3a$ or $C_1aC_2C_3a$ / $yəC_1C_{2ə}C_3$ or $yəC_1C_2aC_3$. The vowel of the subjunctive is not predictable from the vowel of the perfect or vice versa, though $a/ə$ (often active) and $\emptyset/a$ (often stative) are common.

The conjugations with medial gemination and long first vowel do not show any regular semantic patterning, though there are relics of productive derivational relationships.

The medio-passives (usually used without agent) may also be reflexive. The causatives form transitives from intransitive verbs and causatives (doubly transitive) from transitives. The forms with prefixed *ʾasta-* are often either causatives of medio-passives or reflexives of causatives. Forms also exist with prefixed *ta-* and lengthened vowel identical in shape to the mediopassive of the lengthened conjugation, with corresponding causative/reflexive in *ʾasta-* with lengthened vowel. These express reciprocal, joint, or iterative action. All derived forms show a considerable amount of semantic unpredictability.

The imperfect is used of past and future continuous and habitual as well as present. The perfect is for the past and for present perfect. The absolute, which is formally a nominal in the accusative (subject is marked with the suffixed possessive pronouns), is used in subordinate clauses of actions prior to the action of the main clause.

	Kill	Work	Believe	Ask	Be Rich	Fear	Bear	Die	Appoint	Cry
					Perfective					
1s	qatalkū	gabarkū	ʾamankū	saʾalkū	bəʿəlkū	farāhkū	waladkū	mōtkū	šēmkū	bakaykū
2ms	qatalka	gabarka	ʾamanka	saʾalka	bəʿəlka	farāhka	waladka	mōtka	šēmka	bakayka
2fs	qatalkī	gabarkī	ʾamankī	saʾalkī	bəʿəlkī	farāhkī	waladkī	mōtkī	šēmkī	bakaykī
3ms	qatala	gabra	ʾamna	saʾala	bəʿla	farha	walada	mōta	šēma	bakaya
3fs	qatalat	gabrat	ʾamnat	saʾalat	bəʿlat	farhat	waladat	mōtat	šēmat	bakayat
1p	qatalna	gabarna	ʾamanna	saʾalna	bəʿəlna	farāhna	waladna	mōtna	šēmna	bakayna
2mp	-alkəmū	-arkəmū	-ankəmū	-alkəmū	-əlkəmū	-āhkəmū	-adkəmū	-ōtkəmū	-ēmkəmū	-aykəmū
2fp	qatalkən	gabarkən	ʾamankən	saʾalkən	bəʿəlkən	farāhkən	waladkən	mōtkən	šēmkən	bakaykən
3mp	qatalū	gabrū	ʾamnū	saʾalū	bəʿlū	farhū	waladū	mōtū	šēmū	bakayū
3fp	qatalā	gabrā	ʾamnā	saʾalā	bəʿlā	farhā	waladā	mōtā	šēmā	bakayā
					Imperfective					
3ms	yəqattəl	yəgabbər	yaʾammən	yəsaʾʾəl	yəbaʿʿəl	yəfarrəh	yəwalləd	yəmawwət	yəšayyəm	yəbakkī
					Subjunctive					
1s	ʾəqtəl	ʾəgbar	ʾəʾman	ʾəsʾal	ʾəbʿal	ʾəfrāh	ʾəlad	ʾəmūt	ʾəšīm	ʾəbkī
2ms	təqtəl	təgbar	təʾman	təsʾal	təbʿal	təfrāh	təlad	təmūt	təšīm	təbkī
2fs	təqtəlī	təgbarī	təʾmanī	təsʾalī	təbʿalī	təfrəhī	təladī	təmūtī	təšīmī	təbkayī
3ms	yəqtəl	yəgbar	yəʾman	yəsʾal	yəbʿal	yəfrāh	yəlad	yəmūt	yəšīm	yəbkī
3fs	təqtəl	təgbar	təʾman	təsʾal	təbʿal	təfrāh	təlad	təmūt	təšīm	təbkī
1p	nəqtəl	nəgbar	nəʾman	nəsʾal	nəbʿal	nəfrāh	nəlad	nəmūt	nəšīm	nəbkī
2mp	təqtəlū	təgbarū	təʾmanū	təsʾalū	təbʿalū	təfrəhū	təladū	təmūtū	təšīmū	təbkayū
2fp	təqtəlā	təgbarā	təʾmanā	təsʾalā	təbʿalā	təfrəhā	təladā	təmūtā	təšīmā	təbkayā
3mp	yəqtəlū	yəgbarū	yəʾmanū	yəsʾalū	yəbʿalū	yəfrəhū	yəladū	yəmūtū	yəšīmū	yəbkayū
3fp	yəqtəlā	yəgbarā	yəʾmanā	yəsʾalā	yəbʿalā	yəfrəhā	yəladā	yəmūtā	yəšīmā	yəbkayā
					Imperative					
2ms	qətəl	gəbar	ʾəman	saʾal	baʿal	firāh	lad	mūt	šīm	bəkī
2fs	qətəlī	gəbarī	ʾəmanī	saʾalī	baʿalī	firəhī	ladī	mūtī	šīmī	bəkayī
2mp	qətəlū	gəbarū	ʾəmanū	saʾalū	baʿalū	firəhū	ladū	mūtū	šīmū	bəkayū
2fp	qətəlā	gəbarā	ʾəmanā	saʾalā	baʿalā	firəhā	ladā	mūtā	šīmā	bəkayā

The imperfect is not given in full; its markings are identical with the markings of the subjunctive; only the vocalization of the root differs.

Tigre

	Base	Mediopassive	Causative	Caus/Reflexive
Perfect	$C_1aC_2C_3a$	The geminate mediopassive is used here.	$'aC_1C_2aC_3a$	$'attaC_1C_2aC_3a$
Imperfect	$ləC_1aC_2C_2əC_3$		$laC_1aC_2C_2əC_3$	$lattaC_1aC_2əC_3$
Jussive	$ləC_1C_2aC_3$		$laC_1C_2əC_3$	$lattaC_1C_2əC_3$
Imperative	$C_1əC_2aC_3$		$'aC_1C_2əC_3$	$'attaC_1C_2əC_3$
Active part.	$C_1\bar{a}C_2əC_3$		$maC_1C_2əC_3\bar{a}y$	
Passive part.	$C_1əC_2uC_3$		$'əC_1C_2uC_3$	$'əttəC_1C_2uC_3$
Infinitive	VARIOUS		$'aC_1C_2aC_3ot$	$'attaC_1C_2aC_3ot$

	Geminate	Mediopassive	Causative	Caus/Reflexive
Perfect	$C_1aC_2C_2aC_3a$	$taC_1aC_2C_2aC_3a$	$'aC_1aC_2C_2aC_3a$	$'atC_1aC_2C_2aC_3a$
Imperfect	$ləC_1aC_2C_2əC_3$	$lətC_1aC_2C_2aC_3$	$laC_1aC_2C_2əC_3$	$latC_1aC_2C_2əC_3$
Subjunctive	$ləC_1aC_2C_2əC_3$	$lətC_1aC_2C_2aC_3$	$laC_1aC_2C_2əC_3$	$latC_1aC_2C_2əC_3$
Imperative	$C_1aC_2C_2əC_3$	$təC_1aC_2C_2aC_3$	$'aC_1aC_2C_2əC_3$	$'atC_1aC_2C_2əC_3$
Active part.	$maC_1aC_2C_3\bar{a}y$	$matC_1aC_2C_2əC_3\bar{a}y$	$maC_1aC_2C_3\bar{a}y$	
Passive part.	$C_1əC_2C_2uC_3$	$C_1əC_2C_2uC_3$	$C_1əC_2C_2uC_3$	
Infinitive	$C_1aC_2C_2aC_3ot$	$matC_1aC_2C_2\bar{a}C_3$	$'aC_1aC_2C_2aC_3ot$	

	Lengthened	Mediopassive	Causative	Caus/Reflexive
Perfect	$C_1aC_2aC_3a$	$təC_1\bar{a}C_2aC_3a$	$'aC_1\bar{a}C_2aC_3a$	$'at(ta)C_1\bar{a}C_2aC_3a$
Imperfect	$ləC_1\bar{a}C_2əC_3$	$lətC_1\bar{a}C_2aC_3$	$laC_1\bar{a}C_2əC_3$	$lat(ta)C_1\bar{a}C_2əC_3$
Subjunctive	$ləC_1\bar{a}C_2əC_3$	$lətC_1\bar{a}C_2aC_3$	$laC_1\bar{a}C_2əC_3$	$lat(ta)C_1\bar{a}C_2əC_3$
Imperative	$C_1\bar{a}C_2əC_3$	$təC_1\bar{a}C_2aC_3$	$'aC_1\bar{a}C_2əC_3$	$'at(ta)C_1\bar{a}C_2əC_3$
Active part.	$maC_1\bar{a}C_2C_3\bar{a}y$	$matC_1\bar{a}C_2C_3\bar{a}y$	$maC_1\bar{a}C_2C_3\bar{a}y$	$matC_1\bar{a}C_2C_3\bar{a}y$
Passive part.	$C_1uC_2uC_3$	$C_1uC_2uC_3$		$'ətC_1uC_2uC_3$
Infinitive	$C_1\bar{a}C_2aC_3ot$			

The conjugations with medial gemination and long first vowel do not show any regular semantic patterning, though there are relics of productive derivational relationships. Not shown is a pattern with reduplicated second radical ($C_1aC_2\bar{a}C_2aC_3a$), which is frequentive, intensive, or attenuative.

The mediopassives (usually used without agent) may also be interpreted as reflexive. The causatives form transitives from intransitive verbs and causatives (doubly transitive) from transitives. The forms with prefixed *'at(ta)*- are often either causatives of mediopassives or reflexives of causatives. The two forms seem to be not quite in complementary distribution. All derived forms show a considerable amount of semantic unpredictability.

The imperfect is used of present and future. The perfect is used for the past, as a present perfect and in unreal conditions. The jussive is used in commands, purpose clauses, and as a verbal complement. All three of these, plus the participles, are used with auxiliaries to yield a fairly complex system of tense/aspect marking. Infinitives are used as complements with some verbs.

	Kill	Dry	Bear	Wash	Load	Eat	Work	Go	Die
Perfective									
1s	qätälko	yäbäsko	wälädko	ḥäṣabko	ṣäʿänko	bälʿäko	šäqeko	gəsko	mətko
2ms	qätälka	yäbäska	wälädka	ḥäṣäbka	ṣäʿänka	bälʿäka	šäqeka	gəska	mətka
2fs	qätälki	yäbäski	wälädki	ḥäṣäbki	ṣäʿänki	bälʿäki	šäqeki	gəski	mətki
3ms	qätla	yäbsa	wälda	ḥäṣba	ṣäʿäna	bälʿa	šäqa	gesä	motä
3fs	qätlät	yäbsät	wäldät	ḥäṣbät	ṣäʿänät	bälʿät	šäqet	gesät	motät
1p	qätälna	yäbäsna	wälädna	ḥäṣäbna	ṣäʿänna	bälʿäna	šäqena	gəsna	mətna
2mp	qätälkum	yäbäskum	wälädkum	ḥäṣäbkum	ṣäʿänkum	bälʿäkum	šäqekum	gəskum	mətkum
2fp	qätälkən	yäbäskən	wälädkən	ḥäṣäbkən	ṣäʿänkən	bälʿäkən	šäqekən	gəskən	mətkən
3mp	qätläw	yäbsäw	wäldäw	ḥäṣbäw	ṣäʿänäw	bälʿäw	šäqäw	gesäw	motäw
3fp	qätläya	yäbsäya	wäldäya	ḥäṣbäya	ṣäʿänäya	bälʿäya	šäqäya	gesäya	motäya
Imperfective									
1s	ʾəqättəl	ʾəyäbbəs	ʾəwälləd	ḥässəb	ʾəṣʿən	ʾəbälləʿ	ʾəšäqqe	ʾəgäyəs	ʾəmäwət
2ms	təqättəl	təyäbbəs	təwälləd	tähässəb	təṣʿən	təbälläʿ	təšäqqe	təgäyəs	təmäwət
2fs	təqätli	təyäbsi	təwäldi	tähäṣbi	təṣʿəni	təbälləʿi	təšäqqi	təgäysi	təmäwti
3ms	ləqättəl	ləyäbbəs	ləwälləd	lähässəb	ləṣʿən	ləbälläʿ	ləšäqqe	ləgäyəs	ləmäwət
3fs	təqättəl	təyäbbəs	təwälləd	tähässəb	təṣʿən	təbälläʿ	təšäqqe	təgäyəs	təmäwət
1p	ʾənqättəl	ʾənyäbbəs	ʾənwälləd	nähässəb	nəṣʿən	ʾənbälläʿ	ʾənšäqqe	ʾəngäyəs	ʾənmäwət
2mp	təqätlo	təyäbso	təwäldo	tähäṣbo	təṣʿäno	təbälləʿu	təšäqqu	təgäyso	təmäwto
2fp	təqätla	təyäbsa	təwälda	tähäṣba	təṣʿäna	təbälləʿa	təšäqya	təgäysa	təmäwta
3mp	ləqätlo	ləyäbso	ləwäldo	lähäṣbo	ləṣʿäno	ləbälləʿu	ləšäqqu	ləgäyso	ləmäwto
3fp	ləqätla	ləyäbsa	ləwälda	lähäṣba	ləṣʿäna	ləbälləʿa	ləšäqya	ləgäysa	ləmäwta
Subjunctive									
1s	ʾəqtäl	ʾibäs	ʾiläd	ḥisäb	ʾəṣʿän	ʾəbläʿ	ʾəšqe	ʾigis	ʾimut
2ms	təqtäl	tibäs	tiläd	təhäsäb	təṣʿän	təbläʿ	təšqe	tigis	timut
2fs	təqtäli	tibäsi	tilädi	təhäsäbi	təṣʿäni	təbləʿi	təšqäy	tigisi	timuti
3ms	ləqtäl	libäs	liläd	ləhäsäb	ləṣʿän	ləbläʿ	ləšqe	ligis	limut
3fs	təqtäl	tibäs	tiläd	təhäsäb	təṣʿän	təbläʿ	təšqe	tigis	timut
1p	nəqtäl	nibäs	niläd	nəhäsäb	nəṣʿän	nəbläʿ	nəšqe	nigis	nimut
2mp	təqtälo	tibäso	tilädo	təhäsäbo	təṣʿäno	təbləʿu	təšqäw	tigiso	timuto
2fp	təqtäla	tibäsa	tilädа	təhäsäba	təṣʿäna	təbləʿa	təšqäya	tigisa	timuta
3mp	ləqtälo	libäso	lilädo	ləhäsäbo	ləṣʿäno	ləbləʿu	ləšqäw	ligiso	limuto
3fp	ləqtäla	libäsa	liläda	ləhäsäba	ləṣʿäna	ləbləʿa	ləšqäya	ligisa	limuta
Imperative									
2ms	qətäl	yəbäs	läd	ḥəṣäb	ṣäʿän	bäläʿ	šəqe	gis	mut
2fs	qətäli	yəbäsi	lädi	ḥəṣäbi	ṣäʿäni	bälʿi	šəqay	gisi	muti
2mp	qətälo	yəbäso	lädo	ḥəṣäbo	ṣäʿäno	bälʿu	šəqäw	giso	muto
2fp	qətäla	yəbäsa	läda	ḥəṣäba	ṣäʿäna	bälʿa	šəqäya	gisa	timuta

Jibbali

	Base A	Base B	Passive	Base Reflex. A	Base Reflex. B
Perfect	C_1ɔ́C_2ɔ́C_3	C_1ēC_2əC_3	ɛC_1C_2íC_3	C_1ɔ́tC_2əC_3	əC_1təC_2éC_3
Imperfect	yC_1ɔ́C_2əC_3	yC_1éC_2ɔ́C_3	iCeC_2ɔ́C_3	yəC_1téC_2ɔ́C_3	yəC_1təC_2éC_3ən
Subjunctive	yɔ́C_1C_2əC_3	yəC_1C_2ɔ́C_3	əC_1C_2ɔ́C_3	yəC_1téC_2əC_3	yəC_1tɔ́C_2uC_3
Conditional	yəC_1C_2íC_3ən	yəC_1C_2íC_3ən		yəC_1tíC_2əC_3ən	yəC_1tíC_2əC_3ən
Imperative	C_1C_2éC_3	C_1C_2ɔ́C_3			

	Causative	Intens./Conative	Caus. Reflex. A	Caus. Reflex. B
Perfect	eC_1C_2éC_3	eC_1ɔ́C_2əC_3	ŝəC_1éC_2əC_3	ŝəC_1C_2éC_3
Imperfect	íC_1C_1éC_2ɔ́C_3	iC_1ɔ́C_2əC_3ən	yəŝC_1éC_2əC_3ən	yəŝC_1éC_2ɔ́C_3
Subjunctive	yéC_1C_2əC_3	yC_1ɔ́C_2əC_3	yəŝC_1éC_2əC_3	yəŝC_1éC_2əC_3
Subjunctive	yēC_1əC_2C_3ən	yC_1úC_2əC_3ən	yəŝC_1íC_2əC_3ən	yŝíC_1C_2əC_3ən

The two types of Jibbali base conjugation (and reflexives), like the three base conjugation variants in Arabic, correlate to some degree with an active/stative distinction. No geminate conjugation is distinguished. The initial *e-* of the intensive/conative perfect is used where the initial consonant is voiced or glottalized.

The table below presents full conjugations for only one verb from base A and one from base B. For other types only principal parts are given, in the absence of complete paradigms and because of the complexity of Jibbali morphophonemics. Some verbs may be assigned to the wrong base.

	Perf.	Imperf.	Subj.	Cond.	Imv.		Perf.	Imperf.	Subj.
		Lie						**Base A**	
1s	fɔ́gɔ́rk	əfɔ́gər	l-ɔ́fgər	l-əfgírən		Cross	ʕɔr	yʕɔr	yʕēr
2ms	fɔ́gɔ́rk	tfɔ́gər	tɔ́fgər	təfgírən	fgér	Say	ʕɔ̃r	yʕɔ̃r	yáʕmɛr
2fs	fɔ́gɔ́rŝ	tfígər	tífgir	təfgírən	fgír	Dam	ʕerr	yʕarér	yáʕʕar
3ms	fɔ́gɔ́r	yfɔ́gər	yɔ́fgər	yəfgírən		Separate	bedd	yebdéd	yɔ́bbəd
3fs	fɔ́gɔ́rɔ́t	tfɔ́gər	tɔ́fgər	təfgírən		Compose	bédaʕ	yɔ̄daʕ	yɔ́bdaʕ
1d	fɔ́gɔ́rŝi	nfəgérɔ́	l-fɔ́grɔ́	nəfgɔ́rɔ́n		Wander	dɛ̄r	ydír	yédər
2d	fɔ́gɔ́rŝi	tfəgérɔ́	təfgɔ́rɔ́	təfgɔ́rɔ́n	fəgrɔ́	Uncover	nkɔ́ŝ	ynúkŝ	yúnkəŝ
3md	fɔ́gɔ́rɔ́	yfɔ́gɔ́rɔ́	yəfgɔ́rɔ́	təfgɔ́rɔ́n		Steal	šɛ́rɔ́q	yšɔ́rq	yɔ́šrəq
3fd	fɔ́gɔ́rtɔ́	tfɔ́gɔ́rɔ́	təfgɔ́rɔ́	yəfgɔ́rɔ́n		Wet	θéré	íθɔ́r	yéθər
1p	fɔ́gɔ́rən	nfɔ́gər	nəfgér	nəfgérən		Lend	ezúm	yézúm	yzɛ́m
2mp	fɔ́gɔ́rkum	tfɔ́gər	təfgɔ́r	təfgérən	fgɔ́r	Tread	ɛrfɔ́ṣ	yrɔ́fṣ	yɔ́rfəṣ
2fp	fɔ́gɔ́rkən	tfɔ́gərən	təfgérən	təfgérən	fgérən	Dig	ħfɔr	yħéfər	yħéfər
3mp	fɔ́gɔ́r	yfɔ́gər	yəfgɔ́r	yəfgɔ́rɔ́n		Bend	ɣónúṣ	yɣénṣ	yɣénṣ
3fp	fɔ́gɔ́r	yfɔ́gərən	təfgérən	təfgérən		Come	níkaʕ	ynúkaʕ	yənkáʕ
		Be Near						**Base B**	
1s	qérəbək	əqérɔ́b	l-əqrɔ́b	l-əqríbən		Follow	ʔéθəl	yéθɔ́l	yθɔ́l
2ms	qérəbək	tqérɔ́b	təqrɔ́b	təqríbən	qrɔ́b	Be Dumb	ʕégəm	yʕágúm	yáʕgum
2fs	qérəbəŝ	tqiríb	təqríb	təqríbən	qríb	Outrun	bédər	yēdɔ́r	yəbdɔ́r
3ms	qérəb	yqérɔ́b	yəqrɔ́b	yəqríbən		Be Wet	θíri	yθɔ́r	yəθré
3fs	qiribɔ́t	tqérɔ́b	təqrɔ́b	təqríbən		Chase	naʕáf	ynoʕɔ́f	yənʕúf
1d	qérəbŝi	nqərébɔ́	l-qərəbɔ́	nəqrɔ́bɔ́n		Melt	ðɛb	yðɔ̄b	yðɔ́b
2d	qérəbŝi	tqərébɔ́	təqrəbɔ́	təqrɔ́bɔ́n	qərəbɔ́	Hear	šĩʕ	yšũʕ	yəšmáʕ
3md	qérébɔ́	yqərébɔ́	yəqrəbɔ́	yəqrɔ́bɔ́n		Know	édaʕ	yɔ́daʕ	ydáʕ
3fd	qérébtɔ́	tqərébɔ́	təqrəbɔ́	təqrɔ́bɔ́n		Understand	fhɛm	yəfhúm	yəfhúm
1p	qérəbən	nqérɔ́b	nəqrɔ́b	nəqrébən		Promise	daxál	ydɔxɔ́l	yədxɔ́l
2mp	qérəbkum	tqéréb	təqréb	təqrɔ́bɔ́n	qréb	Bleed	ðéréʔ	íðɔ́r	yəðré
2fp	qérəbkən	tqérɔ́bən	təqrɔ́bən	təqrébən	qrɔ́bən	Lessen	xeff	yəxféf	yxíf
3mp	qérəb	yqéréb	yəqréb	yəqrɔ́bɔ́n		Be Bent	ɣénəṣ	yɣánúṣ	yaɣnúṣ
3fp	qérəb	tqérɔ́bən	təqrɔ́bən	təqrɔ́bɔ́n		Able	himm	yəhmím	yhím

Coptic

The Coptic verbal system contains very little of relevance to the Semitist—it is an extreme departure from the older Egyptian system, which was already tremendously modified from what we must postulate as common Afroasiatic. The Coptic verb comes in two types, infinitive and qualitative, which are both marked for tense/aspect/clause type, and so on, by means of auxiliary verbs.

The Infinitive conjugation is based on a verbal noun; the stem of the verb is treated as a masculine-singular noun (although some were originally feminine nouns). Being nouns, they occur in absolute (e.g., 'hear' *sōtəm*), construct (*setəm*), and pronominal (*sotm=*) forms. The qualitative is descended from a masculine or feminine form of the so-called old perfective/pseudo-participle/stative of Egyptian. Most, but not all, verbs have both infinitive and qualitative.

Coptic verbal constructions divide into two groups, durative and limitative. The distinction is in part semantic—durative indicates state or continued action, while limitative indicates that the action is punctual (neutral, completive, or habitual aspects). The distinction is syntactically important as well; qualitative verbs are restricted to durative constructions, and transitive verbs in durative constructions may not take a direct object. Instead objects may be expressed by the preposition *ən*, pronominal *əmo=* 'in': *tisōtəm əmos* 'I hear it'. The future (a limitative construction) uses the pronominal stem with suffixed pronoun: *tinasotməs* 'I shall hear it'.

Independent durative constructions include present (present continuous/habitual) and imperfect (past continuous/habitual). The independent limitative constructions are the perfect (past neutral/present perfect) and pluperfect (past perfect), future (future neutral) and future imperfect (past projected), and habitual (present habitual) and past habitual.

Also found in main clauses are a series of jussive constructions. For most verbs the imperative is simply the infinitive. A few verbs retain an old imperative form (*ačō < čō* 'say'). In addition to the imperative, there is the so-called third future. This is an emphatic future or a strong wish: *efesōtəm* 'he shall hear/may he hear'. The optative expresses a slightly weaker wish.

There is also a set of consecutives (my term, not a Coptic grammarian's) that are not subordinate but are also not found in independent clauses. The so-called fourth future is frequent after a question or an imperative. The conjunctive is common with imperative and future but rare after the perfect; it is also used with conjunctions in purpose clauses.

The system found in independent clauses is paralleled by a set of forms specialized for placing focus on an adverbial element. Such forms exist for the present, perfect, habitual, and future.

I would add constructions restricted to subordinate clauses to the above. The circumstantial (one of the durative constructions) is used in temporal clauses of simultaneous action or state, as is the contemporaneous temporal. The future circumstantial and prospective temporal are used in temporal clauses with projected aspect. The perfect with preposed *e-* is similarly used with perfective aspect, as is the so-called past temporal. It is not clear to me how the circumstantial and temporal constructions differ in usage. We may add to this the "tense of unfulfilled action," which translates as 'until'.

The negation of verb forms is not predictable.

Relative clauses are also marked by what could be considered special verb forms. Three situations need to be considered for present and future:

a. Antecedent indefinite: *e-* prefixed to the verbal auxiliary.

b. Antecedent definite, same as subject: *et-* prefixed to the verb or the future auxiliary *na-*, no subject marker.

c. Antecedent definite, not same as subject: *et-* prefixed to the subject marker (*etere-* prefixed to noun subject).

Otherwise, we have relative markers *ent-* before the perfect, *ete-* before a negative, and *e-* elsewhere.

The Egyptian verbal derivation system continued the system reconstructible to Afroasiatic. There were two derivational prefixes. Transitive/causatives were formed with *s-* and intransitive/reciprocals with *m-*. There seems to have been no reflex of the intransitive/reflexive *t-*. Some Egyptian derived verbs have survived into Coptic, but these formations are not at all productive. However, Coptic has a fairly productive transitive/causative formation marked with a prefixed *t-* (a contraction of *ti* 'give'): *tanho* 'bring to life' < *ōnəh* 'live' (compare *saʾnəš* 'cause to live', an old causative in *s-*).

Ghadamsi

The verb in Ghadamsi, as in the rest of Berber, does not differentiate a suffix conjugation and a prefix conjugation, except with the qualitative verbs. The personal markers have already been listed in the table of pronouns (but there are no suffixes in the future singular). In order to show the presence or absence of the suffix, 1s, not 3ms, forms are used below:

	Affirmative	Negative
Base		
Aorist	$æC_1C_2əC_3æ^ʕ$	$ak\ C_1əC_2C_2əC_3æ^ʕ$
Preterite	$əC_1C_2æC_3æ^ʕ$	$ak\ əC_1C_2ēC_3æ^ʕ$
Future	$d\text{-}əC_1C_2æC_3$	$ak\ da\ C_1C_2æC_3$
Optative	$æC_1C_2əC_3nētæ^ʕ$	$wæl\ æC_1C_2əC_3æ^ʕ$
Imperative	$æC_1C_2əC_3$	$wæl\ C_1əC_2C_2əC_3$
Pret. part.	$iC_1C_2æC_3æn$	$wælæn\ iC_1C_2eeC_3$
Fut. part.	$iC_1æC_2C_2æC_3æn$	$wælæn\ iC_1æC_2C_2æC_3$
Infinitive	$aC_1əC_2C_2əC_3$	
Intensive		
Aorist	$C_1æC_2C_2æC_3æ^ʕ$	$ak\ C_1əC_2C_2əC_3æ^ʕ$
Preterite	$al\ C_1æC_2C_2æC_3æ^ʕ$	$al\ C_1æC_2C_2æC_3æ^ʕ\ ənte$
Future		$ad\ C_1əC_2C_2əC_3æ^ʕ$
Optative		
Imperative	$C_1əC_2C_2əC_3$	
Pret. part.		
Fut. part.		
Infinitive		

The preterite is past and present perfective; the aorist is present continuous and is used in narration as a consecutive. The future is used of future time. The optative (expressing a wish) adds -*nēt* to the stem of the aorist; all personal suffixes other than the 1s -*æ*ʕ are dropped. There are no second-person optative forms; the imperative, based on the aorist, is used instead.

There is a separate habitual/continuous conjugation, the so-called intensive forms. These are based on a distinct stem, usually marked by gemination of the medial consonant. In many verbs, especially the verbs where gemination would not be distinctive, a prefix *t-* (which, like the derivational markers discussed below, is geminated in finite forms) is used instead. Both formations are found in other Berber languages, where the derivation of the intensive stem is highly unpredictable.

The so-called "participles" of Ghadamsi, except possibly the participles from qualitative verbs, are relative verbs rather than adjectives. They are marked for tense and may be negated. Only third-person forms are found; qualitative forms are similar but lack the prefix. In most but not all cases, the infinitive is related in shape to the intensive stem, so that *ækrəz* 'cultivate' has intensive *kær:æzæ*ʕ, infinitive *ak*ʕ*ər:əz*, with the *a-* prefix typical of masculine nouns.

The other paradigm to be illustrated is the qualitative verb, exemplified with 'be small'. These verbs are varied as to shape but agree in the irregular inflection of the preterite. No personal distinctions are given for the plural preterite. Note that the qualitative preterite is similar in form to the Semitic suffix conjugation (and functionally close to the Akkadian suffix conjugation), while the nonqualitative future closely resembles the Semitic prefix conjugation.

		Aorist	Preterite	Future
sing.	1c	*əmti:tæ*ᶜ	*mæt:ītæ*ᶜ	*d-æmtīt*
	2c	*təmtītət*	*mæt:ītət*	*ət-təmtīt*
	3m	*imtīt*	*mæt:īt*	*əd-imtīt*
	3f	*təmtīt*	*mæt:ītæt*	*ət-təmtīt*
pl.	1c	*nəmtīt*	*mæt:ītit*	*ən-nəmtīt*
	1–2m	*nəmtītæt*	*mæt:ītit*	*ən-nəmtītæt*
	1–2f	*nəmtitmæt*	*mæt:ītit*	*ən-nəmtitmæt*
	2m	*təmtītæm*	*mæt:ītit*	*ət-təmtītæm*
	2f	*təmtitmæt*	*mæt:ītit*	*ət-təmtitmæt*
	3m	*mtītæn*	*mæt:ītit*	*d-əmtītæn*
	3f	*mtitnæt*	*mæt:ītit*	*d-əmtitnæt*

The Ghadamsi verbal derivation system continues the system reconstructible to Afroasiatic and is relatively productive, though of course there are many fossilized stems. There are two derivational prefixes. Transitive/causatives are formed with *s-*. Intransitive/passives are formed with *m-*. Both prefixes are geminated in finite forms of the verb. The two combine to give a passive of the causative (without gemination).

The third of the common Afroasiatic derivational markers, the intransitive/reflexive **t-*, is perhaps continued in the alternative marker of the intensive, discussed above. The semantic connection is unclear, but the formal identity is striking.

Bibliography

This bibliography does not purport to be complete. There are bibliographies for individual Semitic languages that outweigh this manual. I have tried to include the most important references for Afroasiatic, Semitic, the Semitic subgroups, and some individual languages, written in the most well-known languages (concentrating on English, though again I urge the serious student to prepare to read other languages). Except in the case of Modern South Arabian, works dealing with modern languages are generally omitted unless they have been used in compiling the paradigms. Text collections (unless they also constitute a major lexical resource) and works on writing systems are also excluded. For further references, check the bibliographies of the works listed.

General Semitic and Afroasiatic

Bergsträsser, Gotthelf. 1983. *Introduction to the Semitic Languages: Text Specimens and Grammatical Sketches.* Translated with notes, bibliography, and an appendix on the scripts by Peter T. Daniels. Repr. 1995. Winona Lake, Indiana: Eisenbrauns. [Translation of *Einführung in die semitischen Sprachen: Sprachproben und grammatische Skizzen.* Munich: Max Hueber, 1928]

Botterweck, G. J. 1952. *Der Triliterismus im Semitischen.* Bonn: Hunstein.

Brockelmann, Carl. 1908–13. *Grundriss der vergleichenden Grammatik der semitischen Sprachen.* Berlin: Reuther & Reichard. Repr. Hildesheim: Olms, 1961.

Castellino, G. R. 1962. *The Akkadian Personal Pronouns and Verbal System in the Light of Semitic and Hamitic.* Leiden: Brill.

Cohen, Marcel. 1947. *Essai comparatif sur le vocabulaire et la phonétique du chamito-sémitique.* Paris: Honoré Champion.

Dalman, Gustav. 1938. *Aramäisch-neuhebräisches Handwörterbuch zum Targum, Talmud und Midrasch.* 3d ed. Göttingen: Pfeiffer. Repr. Hildesheim: Olms, 1967.

Diakonoff, I. M. 1988. *Afrasian Languages.* Moscow: Nauka.

Ehret, Christopher. 1995. *Reconstructing Proto-Afroasiatic (Proto-Afrasian).* Berkeley and Los Angeles: University of California Press.

Fronzaroli, Pelio. 1964–71. "Studi sul lessico comune semitico." *Accademia Nazionale dei Lincei. Rendiconti della classe di scienze morale, storiche e filologiche,* ser. 8, 19: 155–72, 243–80; 20: 135–50, 246–69; 23: 267–303; 24: 285–320; 26: 603–43.

Garr, W. Randall. 1985. *Dialect Geography of Syria-Palestine, 1000–586 B.C.E.* Philadelphia: University of Pennsylvania Press.

[Gesenius, W.] Buhl, Frants. 1921. *Wilhelm Gesenius' Handwörterbuch über das Alte Testament,* 17th ed. Leipzig: Vogel. Repr. Berlin: Springer, 1949.

Greenberg, Joseph H. 1950a. "Studies in African Language Classification IV: Hamito-Semitic." *Southwestern Journal of Anthropology* 6/1: 47–63.

_____ . 1950b. "The Patterning of Root Morphemes in Semitic." *Word* 6: 162–81.

_____ . 1970. *The Languages of Africa*. 3d ed. Bloomington: Indiana University Press / The Hague: Mouton.

Hetzron, Robert. 1987. "Afroasiatic Languages." Pp. 645–53 in *The World's Major Languages*, ed. Bernard Comrie. London: Croom Helm / New York: Oxford University Press.

_____ . 1987. "Semitic Languages." Pp. 654–63 in *The World's Major Languages*, ed. Bernard Comrie. London: Croom Helm / New York: Oxford University Press.

_____ (ed.). 1997. *The Semitic Languages*. London: Routledge.

Hodge, Carleton T. (ed.). 1971. *Afroasiatic: A Survey*. The Hague: Mouton. [Repr. from *Current Trends in Linguistics*, ed. Thomas A. Sebeok, vols. 6–7]

Hoftijzer, J., and Jongeling, K. 1995. *Dictionary of the North-West Semitic Inscriptions*. 2 vols. Leiden: Brill.

Hospers, J. H. (ed.). 1973. *A Basic Bibliography for the Study of the Semitic Languages*. 2 vols. Leiden: Brill.

Jean, Charles F., and Hoftijzer, J. 1960. *Dictionnaire des inscriptions sémitiques de l'Ouest*. Leiden: Brill.

Kuryłowicz, Jerzy. 1961. *L'Apophonie en sémitique*. Prace Językoznawcze 24. Krakow: Jagiellonian University Press

_____ . 1973. *Studies in Semitic Grammar and Metrics*. Prace Językoznawcze 67. Krakow: Jagiellonian University Press

Lambdin, Thomas O. 1983. *Introduction to Sahidic Coptic*. Macon, Georgia: Mercer University Press.

Lanfry, J. 1968–73. *Ghadamès: Étude linguistique et ethnographique*. Fort-National: Fichier de documentation berbere.

Lipiński, Edouard. 1997. *Semitic Languages: Outline of a Comparative Grammar*. Leuven: Peeters.

Morag, Shlomo. 1961. *The Vocalization Systems of Arabic, Hebrew, and Aramaic*. Janua Linguarum, Series minor 13. The Hague: Mouton.

Moscati, Sabatino, Anton Spitaler, Edward Ullendorff, and Wolfram Von Soden. 1964. *An Introduction to the Comparative Grammar of the Semitic Languages: Phonology and Morphology*. Wiesbaden: Harrassowitz.

Noville, E. H. 1920. *L'Évolution de la langue égyptienne et les langues sémitiques*. Paris: Geuthner.

Orel, Vladimir E., and Stolbova, Olga V. 1995. *Hamito-Semitic Etymological Dictionary: Materials for a Reconstruction*. Handbuch der Orientalistik, division 1, vol. 18. Leiden: Brill.

Petrácek, Karel. 1960–64. "Die innere Flexion in den semitischen Sprachen." *Archiv Orientální* 28: 547–606, 29: 513–45, 30: 361–408, 31: 577–624, 32: 185–222.

Rabin, Chaim. 1963. "The Origins of the Subdivisions of Semitic." Pp. 104–15 in *Hebrew and Semitic Studies Presented to Godfrey Rolles Driver*, ed. D. Winton Thomas and W. D. McHardy. Oxford: Clarendon.

Rundgren, Frithiof. 1955. *Über Bildungen mit (ä) und n-t- Demonstrativen in Semit*. Uppsala: Almqvist & Wiksell.

_____ . 1959. *Intensiv und Aspekt-Korrelation: Studien zur äthiopischen und akkadischen Verbalstammbildung*. Uppsala Universitets Årsskrift 1959/5.

Růžička, R. 1909. *Konsonantische Dissimulation in den semitischen Sprachen*. Leipzig: Hinrichs.

Sola-Solé, J. M. 1961. *L'infinitif sémitique*. Paris: Champion.

Spuler, Berthold (ed.). 1953–54. *Semitistik*. Handbuch der Orientalistik, division 1, vol. 3. Leiden: Brill.

Thacker, T. W. 1954. *The Relationship of the Semitic and Egyptian Verbal Systems*. Oxford: Clarendon.

Thomas, D. Winton, and McHardy, W. D. 1964. *Hebrew and Semitic Studies Presented to Godfrey Rolles Driver in Celebration of His Seventieth Birthday.* Oxford: Clarendon.

Tsereteli, George V. 1967. "The Problem of the Identification of Semitic Languages." *27th International Congress of Orientalists: Papers Presented by the USSR Delegation.* Moscow.

Ullendorff, Edward. 1958. "What Is a Semitic Language?" *Orientalia* 27: 66–75.

Akkadian

Gelb, I. J. 1961. *Old Akkadian Writing and Grammar.* 2d ed. Materials for the Assyrian Dictionary 2. Chicago: Oriental Institute.

Gelb, I. J., et al. (eds.). 1956–. *The Assyrian Dictionary of the Oriental Institute of the University of Chicago.* Chicago: Oriental Institute.

Heidel, Anton. 1940. *The System of the Quadriliteral Verb in Akkadian.* Assyriological Studies 13. Chicago: University of Chicago Press.

Huehnergard, John. 1997. *A Grammar of Akkadian.* Harvard Semitic Museum Studies 45. Atlanta: Scholars Press.

Reiner, Erica. 1966. *A Linguistic Analysis of Akkadian.* Janua Linguarum, Series Practica 21. The Hague: Mouton.

Riemschneider, Kaspar K. 1977. *An Akkadian Grammar.* Trans. Thomas A. Caldwell, John N. Oswalt, and John F. X. Sheehan. Milwaukee: Marquette University. [Orig. *Lehrbuch des akkadischen.* Leipzig: Verlag Enzyklopädie, 1969]

Soden, Wolfram von. 1959–81. *Akkadisches Handwörterbuch.* Wiesbaden: Harrassowitz.

_____. 1995. *Grundriss der akkadischen Grammatik.* 3d ed. Analecta Orientalia 33/47. Rome: Pontifical Biblical Institute.

Arabic

Aboul-Fetouh, Hilmi M. 1969. *A Morphological Study of Egyptian Colloquial Arabic.* The Hague: Mouton.

Bakalla, M. H. 1983. *Arabic Linguistics: Introduction and Bibliography.* London: Mansell.

Badawi, El-Said, and Hinds, Martin. 1986. *A Dictionary of Egyptian Arabic.* Beirut: Librairie du Liban.

Birkeland, Harris. 1954. *Stress Patterns in Arabic.* Oslo: Norske Videnskabs-Akademi.

Brockelmann, Carl. 1960. *Arabische Grammatik,* 14th ed. Leipzig: Harrassowitz.

Cantineau, Jean. 1960. *Cours de phonétique arabe.* Paris: Klincksieck.

Fischer, Wolfdietrich. 1987. *Grammatik des Klassischen Arabisch.* 2d ed. Porta Linguarum Orientalum 11. Wiesbaden: Harrassowitz.

Rabin, Chaim. 1951. *Ancient Westarabian.* London: Taylor.

Wehr, Hans. 1961. *A Dictionary of Modern Written Arabic.* Trans. J. Milton Cowan. Wiesbaden: Harrassowitz. 4th ed., Ithaca, New York: Spoken Language Services, 1997.

Wright, William. 1896–98. *A Grammar of the Arabic Language.* 3d ed. Cambridge: Cambridge University Press.

Aramaic

Altheim, Franz, and Stiehl, Ruth. 1960. *Die aramäische Sprache unter den Achaimeniden.* Frankfurt: Klostermann.

Beyer, K. 1986. *The Aramaic Language.* Trans. J. F. Healey. Göttingen: Vandenhoeck & Ruprecht.

Brockelmann, Carl. 1955. *Syrische Grammatik*. 7th ed. Leipzig: Verlag Enzyklopädie.

Cantineau, Jean. 1930–32. *Le nabatéen*. 2 vols. Paris: Leroux.

_____ . 1935. *Grammaire du palmyrénien épigraphique*. Cairo: Institut français d'archéologie orientale.

Drower, E. S., and Macuch, Rudolf. 1963. *A Mandaic Dictionary*. Oxford: Clarendon.

Epstein, J. N. 1960. *A Grammar of Babylonian Aramaic*. Jerusalem: Magnes.

Fitzmyer, Joseph A., and Kaufman, Stephen A. 1992. Part 1 of *An Aramaic Bibliography*. Baltimore: The Johns Hopkins University Press.

Ginsberg, H. L. 1942. "Aramaic Studies Today." *Journal of the American Oriental Society* 62: 229–38.

Macuch, Rudolf. 1965. *Handbook of Classical and Modern Mandaic*. Berlin: de Gruyter.

_____ . 1982. *Grammatik des samaritanischen Aramäisch*. Berlin: de Gruyter.

Marcus, David. 1981. *A Manual of Babylonian Jewish Aramaic*. Washington: University Press of America.

Margolis, H. L. 1910. *Lehrbuch der aramäischen Sprache des babylonischen Talmuds*. Munich: Beck.

Marogulov, Q. I. 1976. *Grammaire néo-syriaque pour écoles d'adultes (dialecte d'Urmia)*. Trans. Olga Kapeliuk. Groupe Linguistique d'Études Chamito-Sémitiques, Comptes-rendues, Supplément. Paris: Geuthner.

Müller-Kessler, Christa. 1991. *Grammatik des Christlich-Palästinisch-Aramäischen*. Hildesheim: Olms.

Muraoka, Takamitsu. 1987. *Classical Syriac for Hebraists*. Wiesbaden: Harrassowitz.

Nöldeke, Theodor. 1904. *A Compendious Syriac Grammar*. Trans. James A. Crichton. London: Williams & Norgate. [Orig. *Kurzgefasste syrische Grammatik*. 2d ed. Leipzig: Weigel, 1898. Repr. Darmstadt: Wissenschaftliche, 1966, with transcription of the annotations in Nöldeke's own copy and addenda by Anton Schall]

Payne Smith, J. 1903. *A Compendious Syriac Dictionary*. Oxford: Clarendon.

Payne Smith, R. 1868–97. *Thesaurus Syriacus*. Oxford: Clarendon.

Rosenthal, Franz. 1939. *Die aramäistische Forschungen seit Th. Nöldeke's Veröffentlichungen*. Leiden: Brill.

_____ . 1963. *A Grammar of Biblical Aramaic*. Wiesbaden: Harrassowitz.

Schulthess, F. 1903. *Lexicon Syropalästinum*. Berlin: Reimer.

_____ . 1924. *Grammatik des christlich-palästinischen Aramäisch*. Tübingen: Mohr. Repr. Hildesheim: Olms, 1965.

Sokoloff, Michael. 1990. *A Dictionary of Jewish Palestinian Aramaic*. Ramat-Gan: Bar-Ilan University Press.

Stevenson, William B. 1962. *Grammar of Palestinian Jewish Aramaic*. Oxford: Clarendon.

Canaanite

Aistleitner, Joseph. 1974. *Wörterbuch der ugaritischen Sprache*. 4th ed. Berlin: Akademie.

Bauer, Hans, and Leander, Pontus. 1918–22. *Historische Grammatik der hebräischen Sprache des Alten Testamentes*. Halle: Niemeyer. Repr. Hildesheim: Olms, 1962.

Blake, F. R. 1951. *A Resurvey of Hebrew Tenses*. Rome: Pontifical Biblical Institute.

Blau, Joshua. 1976. *A Grammar of Biblical Hebrew*. Wiesbaden: Harrassowitz.

Brown, F.; Driver, S. R.; and Briggs, C. A. 1906. *A Hebrew and English Lexicon of the Old Testament*. Oxford: Clarendon.

Clines, D. J. A. (ed.). 1993–. *The Dictionary of Classical Hebrew*. Sheffield: Sheffield Academic Press.

Friedrich, Johannes, and Röllig, Wolfgang. 1970. *Phönizisch-punische Grammatik*. 2d ed. Analecta Orientalia 46. Rome: Pontifical Biblical Institute.

Goetze, Albrecht. 1941. "Is Ugaritic a Canaanite Dialect?" *Language* 17: 127–38.

Gordon, Cyrus H. 1967. *Ugaritic Textbook*. 2d ed. Analecta Orientalia 38. Rome: Pontifical Biblical Institute.

Goshen-Gottstein, Moshe H. 1958. "Linguistic Structure and Tradition in the Qumran Documents." *Scripta Hierosolymitana* 4: 101–37.

Harris, Zellig S. 1936. *Grammar of the Phoenician Language*. American Oriental Series 8. New Haven, Connecticut: American Oriental Society.

_____. 1939. *Development of the Canaanite Dialects*. American Oriental Series 16. New Haven, Connecticut: American Oriental Society.

_____. 1941. "Linguistic Structure of Hebrew." *Journal of the American Oriental Society* 61: 143–67.

Huehnergard, John. 1987. *Ugaritic Vocabulary in Syllabic Transcription*. Harvard Semitic Studies 32. Atlanta: Scholars Press.

Klein, Ernest. 1987. *A Comprehensive Etymological Dictionary of the Hebrew Language for Readers of English*. New York: Macmillan.

Koehler, Ludwig, and Baumgartner, W. 1953. *Lexicon in Veteris Testamenti libros*. Leiden: Brill.

_____. 1958. *Supplementum ad lexicon in Veteris Testamenti libros*. Leiden: Brill.

Malone, Joseph C. 1993. *Tiberian Hebrew Phonology*. Winona Lake, Indiana: Eisenbrauns.

Segal, M. H. 1958. *A Grammar of Mishnaic Hebrew*. 2d ed. Oxford: Clarendon.

Segert, Stanislav. 1976. *A Grammar of Phoenician and Punic*. Munich: Beck.

_____. 1984. *A Basic Grammar of the Ugaritic Language*. Berkeley and Los Angeles: University of California Press.

Speiser, E. A. 1926–34. "The Pronunciation of Hebrew according to the Transliterations of the Hexapla." *Jewish Quarterly Review* 16: 343–82; 23: 233–65; 24: 9–46.

Tomback, R. S. 1978. *A Comparative Semitic Lexicon of the Phoenician and Punic Languages*. Missoula, Montana: Scholars Press.

Waldman, Nahum M. 1989. *The Recent Study of Hebrew*. Cincinnati: Hebrew Union College Press / Winona Lake, Indiana: Eisenbrauns.

Waltke, Bruce K., and O'Connor, M. 1990. *An Introduction to Biblical Hebrew Syntax*. Winona Lake, Indiana: Eisenbrauns.

Ethiopic

Dillmann, A. 1907. *Ethiopic Grammar*. Trans. James A. Crichton. London: Williams & Norgate. [Orig. *Grammatik der äthiopischen Sprache*. 2d ed. Rev. Carl Bezold. Leipzig: Tauchitz, 1899]

Hetzron, Robert. 1972. *Ethiopian Semitic: Studies in Classification*. Journal of Semitic Studies Monograph 2. Manchester: Manchester University Press.

Lambdin, Thomas O. 1978. *Introduction to Classical Ethiopic (Ge ʿez)*. Harvard Semitic Studies 24. Missoula, Montana: Scholars Press.

Leslau, Wolf. 1956. *The Scientific Investigation of the Ethiopic Languages*. Leiden: Brill.

_____ . 1965. *An Annotated Bibliography of the Semitic Languages of Ethiopia.* The Hague: Mouton.

_____ . 1987. *Comparative Dictionary of Ge'ez.* Wiesbaden: Harrassowitz.

_____ . 1995. *Reference Grammar of Amharic.* Wiesbaden: Harrassowitz.

_____ . 1996. *Concise Amharic Dictionary.* Wiesbaden: Harrassowitz.

Raz, Shlomo. 1983. *Tigre Grammar and Texts.* Malibu: Undena.

Ullendorff, Edward. 1955. *The Semitic Languages of Ethiopia: A Comparative Phonology.* London: Taylor.

Modern South Arabian

Johnstone, T. M. 1975. "The Modern South Arabian Languages." *Afroasiatic Linguistics* 1/5 = 1: 93–121.

_____ . 1977. *Ḥarsūsi Lexicon and English-Ḥarsūsi Word-List.* London: Oxford University Press.

_____ . 1981. *Jibbāli Lexicon.* Oxford: Oxford University Press.

_____ . 1987. *Mehri Lexicon and English-Mehri Word-List.* London: School of Oriental and African Studies.

Leslau, Wolf. 1938. *Lexique soqoṭri (sudarabique moderne).* Paris: Klincksieck.

_____ . 1946. *Modern South Arabic Languages: A Bibliography.* New York: New York Public Library.

Nakano, Aki'o. 1986. *Comparative Vocabulary of Southern Arabic: Mahri, Gibbali, and Soqotri.* Tokyo: Institute for the Study of Languages and Cultures of Asia and Africa.

Old South Arabian

Beeston, A. F. L. 1962. *A Descriptive Grammar of Epigraphic South Arabian.* London: Luzac.

_____ . 1984. *Sabaic Grammar.* Manchester: University of Manchester Press.

Beeston, A. F. L., M. A. Ghul, W. W. Müller, and J. Ryckmans. 1982. *Sabaic Dictionary (English-French-Arabic).* Louvain: Peeters.

Biella, Joan Copeland. 1982. *Dictionary of Old South Arabic, Sabaean Dialect.* Harvard Semitic Studies 25. Chico, California: Scholars Press.

Conti Rossini, Carlo. 1931. *Chrestomathia arabica meridionalis epigraphica.* Rome: Istituto per l'Oriente.

Writing

Daniels, Peter T. 1997. "Scripts of Semitic Languages." Pp. 16–45 in *The Semitic Languages,* ed. Robert Hetzron. London: Routledge.

Daniels, Peter T., and William Bright (eds.). 1996. *The World's Writing Systems.* New York: Oxford University Press.

Driver, G. R. 1976. *Semitic Writing.* 3d ed. completed by Simon Hopkins. London: Oxford University Press.

Naveh, Joseph. 1987. *Early History of the Alphabet.* 2d ed. Jerusalem: Magnes.

Table 36. Some Periodicals to Check Through (with recognized abbreviations)

AAWL	*Abhandlungen der Akademie der Wissenschaften unter der Literature in Mainz, Geistes-und Sozialwissenschaftliche Klasse (Wiesbaden)*
ACIO	*Actes du Congrès International des Orientalists*
AfO	*Archiv für Orientforschung*
AJA	*American Journal of Archaeology*
AJP	*American Journal of Philology*
AJSL	*American Journal of Semitic Languages and Literature (Hebraica)*
ANLM	*Atti della Accademia nazionale dei Lincei. Memorie*
ArOr	*Archiv Orientální (Prague)*
AS	*Archiv für Schriftkunde*
Bib	*Biblica*
BA	*Biblical Archaeologist*
BASOR	*Bulletin of the American Schools of Oriental Research*
BIES	*Bulletin of the Israel Exploration Society*
BiOr	*Bibliotheca Orientalis (Leiden)*
BJRL	*Bulletin of the John Rylands Library*
BT	*Bible Translator*
CBQ	*Catholic Biblical Quarterly*
CILP	*Conférences de l'Institut de Linguistique de Paris*
CRAI	*Comptes Rendus de Séances de l'Academie des Inscriptions et Belles-Lettres*
DLZ	*Deutsche Literaturzeitung*
ET	*Expository Times*
FF	*Forschungen und Fortschritte*
HTR	*Harvard Theological Review*
HUCA	*Hebrew Union College Annual*
IEJ	*Israel Exploration Journal*
IF	*Indogermanische Forschung*
JA	*Journal Asiatique*
JAI	*Journal of the Anthropological Institute of Great Britain and Ireland*
JAOS	*Journal of the American Oriental Society*
JBL	*Journal of Biblical Literature*
JCS	*Journal of Cuneiform Studies*
JEA	*Journal of Egyptian Archaeology*
JNES	*Journal of Near Eastern Studies*
JPOS	*Journal of the Palestine Oriental Society*
JQR	*Jewish Quarterly Review*
JRAS	*Journal of the Royal Asiatic Society of Great Britain and Ireland*

Table 36. Some Periodicals to Check Through (with recognized abbreviations)

JSOR	*Journal of the Society of Oriental Research*
JSS	*Journal of Semitic Studies*
MAOG	*Mitteilungen der Altorientalischen Gesellschaft (Leipzig)*
MPAW	*Monatsberichte der königlichen preussischen Akademie der Wissenschaften*
MPIE	*Mémoires présentés a l'Institut de l'Égypte*
Or	*Orientalia*
OIP	*Oriental Institute Publications (Chicago)*
OLZ	*Orientalistische Literaturzeitung*
PEF	*Quarterly Statement of the Palestine Exploration Fund*
PEQ	*Palestine Exploration Quarterly*
QDA	*Quarterly of the Department of Antiquities (Jerusalem)*
RA	*Revue Archaeologique*
RB	*Revue Biblique*
RESem	*Revue des Études Sémitiques*
RQ	*Revue de Qumran*
RS	*Revue Sémitique d'Épigraphie et d'Histoire Ancienne*
RT	*Recueil de Travaux Relatif à la Philologie et à l'Archéologie Égyptiennes et Assyriennes*
Syria	*Syria (French journal from 1929 on)*
SBO	*Studia Biblica et Orientalia*
WZKM	*Wiener Zeitschrift für die Kunde des Morgenlandes*
ZAS	*Zeitschrift für Ägyptische Sprache*
ZAW	*Zeitschrift für die alttestamentliche Wissenschaft*
ZDMG	*Zeitschrift der deutschen morgenländischen Gesellschaft*
ZDPV	*Zeitschrift des deutschen Palestina Vereins*

Wordlist A

Cognates and Skewed Reflexes
Exercises 2 and 3

Arabic
- Ar Classical Arabic
- Eg Egyptian Arabic
- Su Sudanese Arabic

Ethiopic
- Ge Geʿez
- Ta Tigrinya
- Te Tigre

	1. Bee		2. Bird		3. Book		4. Breast	
Ar	naḥlaᵗ	naḥl	ṭayr	ṭuyūr	kitāb	kutub	θady	ʾaθdāʾ
Eg	naḥla	naḥl	ṭēr	ṭuyūr	kitāb	kutub	ṣidr	ṣudūr
Su	naḥla	naḥal	ṭayra	ṭayr	kitāb	kutub	ṣadr	ṣudūr
Ge	nəhb	ʾanhāb	ʿōf	ʾaʿwāf	maṣḥaf	maṣāḥəft	ṭəb	ʾaṭbāt
Ta	nəhbi	ʾanahib	ʿif	ʾaʿwaf	mäṣḥaf	mäṣaḥəfti	ṭub	ʾaṭwab
Te	nəhbät	nəhəb	särerät	säräyər	kətab	ʾäkətbät	ṭəb	ʾäṭbay

	5. Brother		6. Bull		7. Calf		8. Camel	
Ar	ʾax	ʾixwa	θawr	θīrān	ʿijl	ʿujūl	jamal	jimāl
Eg	ʾaxx	ʾixwāt	ṭōr	tīrān	ʿigl	ʿigūl	gamal	gimāl
Su	ʾaxu	ʾuxwān	ṭōr	ṭērān	ʿijil	ʿijūl	jamal	jumāl
Ge	ʾəxw	ʾaxaw	sōr	ʾaswār	ʾəgʷalt	ʾəgʷal	gamal	gamalāt
Ta	ḥaw	ʾaḥat	bəʿray	ʾabaʿur	mərax	ʾamraxut	gämäl	ʾagmal
Te	ḥu	ḥäw	wəhər	ʾäwhərät	ʾəgal	ʾəgəl	gämäl	ʾägmal

	9. Chair		10. Chicken		11. Cow		12. Daughter	
Ar	kursīy	karāsīy	dajājaᵗ	dajāj	baqaraᵗ	baqar	bint	banāt
Eg	kursi	karāsi	farxa	firāx	baʾara	baʿar	bint	banāt
Su	kursī	karāsī	jadāda	jadād	bagara	bagar	bitt	banāt
Ge	manbar	manābərt	dōrhō	dawārəh	lāhm	ʾalhəmt	walatt	ʾawāləd
Ta	mänbär	mänabərti	därho	därahu	lahmi	ʾalahəm	gʷal	ʾagʷalat
Te	mämbär	mänabər	derho	däräwəh	wəʾät	ʾäha	wälätt	ʾawaləd

	13. Day		14. Dog		15. Donkey		16. Ear	
Ar	yawm	ʾayyām	kalb	kilāb	ḥimār	ḥamīr	ʾuðun	ʾāðān
Eg	yōm	ʾayyām	kalb	kilāb	ḥumāṛ	ḥimīr	widn	widān
Su	yōm	ʾayyām	kalib	kilāb	ḥumār	ḥamīr	ʾadān	ʾiḍnēn
Ge	maʿālt	mawāʿəl	kalb	kalabāt	ʾadg	ʾadəgt	ʾəzn	ʾəzan
Ta	maʿalti	mäwaʿəl	kälbi	ʾaxlabat	ʾadgi	ʾaʾdug	ʾəzni	ʾaʾzan
Te	məʿəl	ʾämʾəlotat	käləb	ʾäklub	ʾädəg	ʾädug	ʾəzən	ʾəzän

	17. Elephant		18. Eye		19. Foot		20. Friend	
Ar	fīl	fiyalaᵗ	ʿayn	ʿuyūn	rijl	ʾarjul	ṣadīq	ʾaṣdiqāʾ
Eg	fīl	ʾafyāl	ʿēn	ʿiyūn	ʾadam	ʾiʾdām	ṣāḥib	ʾaṣḥāb
Su	fīl	ʾafyāl	ʿēn	ʿiyūn	rijil	rijlēn	ṣāḥib	ʾaṣḥāb
Ge	ḥarmaz	harāməz	ʿayn	ʾaʿəyyənt	ʾəgr	ʾəgar	ʿark	ʿarkān
Ta	ḥarmaz	harraməz	ʿāyni	ʾaʿinti	ʾəgri	ʾaʾgar	fätawi	-ti
Te	ḥärmaz	härämməz	ʿən	ʿəntat	ʾəgər	ʾəgär	mäsni	mäsanit

	21. Goat		22. Grave		23. Hand		24. Head	
Ar	ʿanzaᵗ	ʿanzāt	qabr	qubūr	yad	ʾaydi	raʾs	ruʾūs
Eg	miʿza	miʿīz	ʾabr	ʾubūr	ʾīd	ʾayādi	ṛāṣ	rūs
Su	γanamāyya	-āt	gabur	gubūr	ʾīd	ʾīdēn	rās	rīsēn
Ge	ṭalīt	ʾaṭālī	maqbar	maqābər	ʾəd	ʾədaw	rəʾs	ʾarʾəst
Ta	ṭäl	ʾaṭal	mäqabər	-ti	ʾid	ʾaʾdaw	rəʾsi	ʾaraʾəs
Te	ṭälit	ʿaṭal	qäbər	ʾäqbər	ʾəde	ʾəday	rəʾäs	ʾärʾəs

	25. Horn		26. Horse		27. House		28. King	
Ar	qarn	qurūn	ḥiṣān	ḥuṣun	bayt	buyūt	malik	mulūk
Eg	ʾarn	ʾurūn	ḥuṣān	ḥiṣina	bēt	biyūt	malik	mulūk
Su	garin	gurūn	ḥaṣān	ḥaṣīn	bēt	biyūt	malik	mulūk
Ge	qarn	ʾaqrənt	faras	ʾafrās	bēt	ʾabyāt	nəgūš	nagašt
Ta	qärni	ʾaqrənti	färäs	ʾafras	bet	bäyayiti	nəgus	nägästi
Te	qärr	ʾäqərnät	färäs	ʾäfräs	bet	ʾäbyat	nəgus	näggäs

	29. Knee		30. Leaf		31. Leg		32. Leopard	
Ar	rukbaᵗ	rukab	waraqaᵗ	waraq	rijl	ʾarjul	namir	numur
Eg	rukba	rukab	waraʾa	waraʾ	rigl	-ēn	fahd	fihūd
Su	rukba	rukab	ṣafaga	ṣafag	sāg	sēgān	nimir	numūr
Ge	bərk	bərak	qʷaṣl	qʷaṣlāt	qʷə(y)ṣ	qʷəyaṣ	namr	ʾanāmərt
Ta	bərki	ʾabrax	qʷäṣli	ʾaqʷṣälti	ʾəgri	ʾaʾgar	näbri	ʾanabər
Te	bərək	ʾäbrak	qätfät	qätäf	ʾəqb	ʿaqab	ḥəmmäm	ḥämämmit

	33. Lion		34. Man		35. Month		36. Mountain	
Ar	ʾasad	ʾusud	rajul	rijāl	šahr	ʾašhur	jabal	jibāl
Eg	ʾasad	ʾusūd	ṛāgil	riggāla	šahṛ	šuhūr	gabal	gibāl
Su	ʾasad	ʾusūd	rājil	rujāl	šahar	šuhūr	jabal	jibāl
Ge	ʿanbasā	ʿanābəst	ʿəd	ʿədaw	warx	ʾawrāx	dabr	ʾadbār
Ta	ʾanbäsa	ʾanabəs	säbʾay	säbaʾut	wärḥi	ʾawarəḥ	däbri	ʾadbar
Te	ḥäyät	ḥayut	ʾənas	säb	wärəḥ	ʾäwärrəḥat	däbər	ʾädbər

	37. Nail		38. Needle		39. Person		40. Rib	
Ar	ẓifr	ʾazfār	ʾibraᵗ	ʾibar	ʾinsān	nās	ḍilʿ	ḍulūʿ
Eg	ḍāfir	dawāfir	ʾibra	ʾibar	ʾinsān	nās	ḍalʿ	ḍilūʿ
Su	ḍufur	ḍufūr	ʾibra	ʾibar	ʾinsān	nās	ḍuluʿ	ḍulaʿ
Ge	ṣəfr	ṣəfar	marfiʾ	marāfiʾ(t)	bəʾsī	sabʾ	gabō	gabawāt
Ta	ṣəfri	ʾaṣafər	märfəʾ	märafəʾ	säb	säbʾat	gʷädni	ʾagʷdənti
Te	ṣəfər	ʾäsfar	ʾəbrät	ʾəbär	ʾäddam	-at	sətet	säytat

	41. Root		42. Sheep		43. Sister		44. Slave	
Ar	ʾaṣl	ʿuṣūl	šāᵗ	šāʾ	ʾuxt	ʾaxawāt	ʿabd	ʿabīd
Eg	gidr	gidūr	naʿga	naʿgāt	ʾuxt	ʾixwāt	ʿabd	ʿabīd
Su	ʿirig	ʿirūg	ḍān	ḍān	ʾuxut	ʾuxwāt	ʿabd	ʿabīd
Ge	šərw	šəraw	baggəʿ	ʾabāgəʿ	ʾəxt	ʾaxāt	gabr	ʾagbərt
Ta	sur	ʾaswar	bäggiʿ	ʾabaggiʿ	ḥafti	ʾaḥat	barya	barot
Te	qərəd	ʿäqrud	bägguʿ	ʾäbagəʿ	ḥət	ḥäwat	gäbər	ʾägbər

	45. Snake		46. Son		47. Star		48. Stone	
Ar	ḥayyaᵗ	ḥayyāt	ibn	ʾabnāʾ	kawkab	kawākib	ḥajar	ʾaḥjār
Eg	tiʿbān	taʿābīn	ʾibn	ʾabnāʾ	nigma	nugūm	ḥagaṛa	ḥagaṛ
Su	dabīb	dabāyib	walad	ʾawlād	najma	nijūm	ḥajar	ḥujār
Ge	ʾarwē	ʾarāwīt	wald	wəlūd	kōkab	kawākəbt	ʾəbn	ʾəban
Ta	tämän	ʾatman	wäldi	däqqi	koxob	käwaxəb	ʾəmni	ʾaʾman
Te	ʾärwe	ʾärawit	wädd	wəlad	kokäb	käwakəb	ʾəbbänät	ʾəbən

	49. Sword		50. Tooth		51. Tree		52. Woman	
Ar	sayf	suyūf	sinn	ʾasnān	šajaraᵗ	šajar	imraʾa	niswān
Eg	sēf	siyūf	sinn	ʾasnān	šagaṛa	šagaṛ	sitt	sittāt
Su	sēf	siyūf	sinn	sunūn	šajara	šajar	mara	nuswān
Ge	sayf	ʾasyāf	sənn	sənan	ʿōm	ʿōmāt	ʾanəst	ʾaʾnūs
Ta	säyfi	ʾasifti	sənni	ʾasnan	ʾom	ʾaʾwam	säbäti	ʾanəsti
Te	säyəf	ʾäsäyəf	ʾänjebät	ʾänjab	ʾəçyät	ʾəçäy	ʾəssit	ʾänəs

Wordlist B

Pair-Referenced Lexicostatistics and Subgrouping
Exercise 4

East Semitic
  Ak Akkadian
Canaanite
  Ug Ugaritic
  He Hebrew
  Ph Phoenician
Aramaic
  AA Achaemenid Aramaic

Sy Syriac
Ma Maʿlula
Ur Urmi
MM Modern Mandaic
Arabic
Ar Classical Arabic

Mo Moroccan Arabic
Eg Egyptian Arabic
Ir Iraqi Arabic
Ethiopic
Ge Geʿez
Ta Tigrinya

Am Amharic
Ha Harari
Old South Arabian
Sa Sabean
Modern South Arabian
So Soqotri
Me Mehri
Ji Jibbali

	1. After	2. All	3. Ask	4. Be
Ak	*warki*	*kalū*	*šālu*	*ewū*
Ug	*áxr, áθr*	*kl*	*šảl*	*kn*
He	*ʾaḥar*	*kōl*	*šāʾal*	*hāyā*
Ph	*ʾḥr*	*kl*	*šʾl*	*kn*
AA	*ʾaḥrēy*	*kol*	*šʾl*	*hwy*
Sy	*bātar*	*kull*	*šʾil*	*hwā*
Ma	*bōθar*	*uxxul*	*šaʿel*	*wōb*
Ur	*bar*	*kul*	*baqurï*	*vəjə*
MM	*bāθer, xelef*	*kol*	*šiyyel*	*howā*
Ar	*baʿda*	*kull*	*saʾala*	*kāna*
Mo	*men beʿd*	*koll*	*ṣeqṣa*	*kan*
Eg	*baʿd*	*kull*	*saʾal*	*kān*
Ir	*baʿad*	*kull*	*siʾal*	*cān*
Ge	*dəxra*	*kʷəllū*	*saʾala*	*kōna, hallawa*
Ta	*daḥar*	*kʷïllew*	*ṭäyyäqä*	*konä, näbärä*
Am	*kä bähʷala*	*hullu*	*ṭäyyäqä*	*honä*
Ha	*bäḥär*	*kullu-, qiṭṭe*	*(at)ḥēbära*	*xāna*
Sa	*bʾθr*	*kl*	*šʾl*	*k(w)n~kyn*
So	*baʿd*	*kɔl*	*réʾiš*	*kɔn*
Me	*bād*	*kal*	*šəxbōr*	*wēqa*
Ji	*baʿd, mən ðér*	*kɔl*	*ŝxəbér*	*kun*

130

	5. Bear (a child)	6. Big	7. Bless	8. Brother
Ak	*walādu*	*rabū*	*karābu*	*axu*
Ug	*yld*	*gdl, rabbu*	*brk*	*ȧx*
He	*yālad*	*gādōl*	*bērak*	*ʾāḥ*
Ph	*yld*	*rb*	*brk*	*ʾḥ*
AA	*yld*	*rabb*	*bārik*	*ʾaḥ*
Sy	*īlid*	*rab*	*barrik*	*ʾaḥā*
Ma	*nacjaθ* (fem.sg.)	*rappa*	*bōrex*	*ḥōna*
Ur	*lədə*	*gura, raba*	*baruxï*	*əxunə*
MM	*yedlat* (fem.sg.)	*rab*	*barrex*	*ahā*
Ar	*walada*	*kabīr*	*bāraka*	*ʾax*
Mo	*wled*	*kbir*	*barek*	*ax*
Eg	*wilid*	*kibīr*	*bārik*	*ʾaxx*
Ir	*wilad*	*cbīr*	*bārak*	*ʾax*
Ge	*walada*	*ʿabīy*	*bāraka*	*ʾəxw*
Ta	*wälädä*	*ʿabiy*	*baräkä*	*ḥaw*
Am	*wällädä*	*təlləq*	*barräkä*	*wändəmm*
Ha	*wåläda*	*gidīr*	*duwā āša*	*əḥ*
Sa	*wld*	*kbr*	*brk*	*ʾx*
So	*bére*	*ʾəʾəb, ʿéqer*	*bōrik*	*qáqa, ʾəʿhi*
Me	*bərō*	*śōx*	*abōrək*	*γā*
Ji	*bíri*	*ʾéb*	*ōrək*	*ʾaγá*

	9. Build	10. Call	11. City	12. Come
Ak	*banū*	*šasū*	*ālu*	*kašādu*
Ug	*bny*	*qrȧ*	*qarītu, mdnt, ʿr*	*ȧtw, bȧ*
He	*bānā*	*qārāʾ*	*ʿīr, qiryā*	*ʾātā, bāʾ*
Ph	*bny*	*qrʾ*	*qrt*	*bʾ*
AA	*bny*	*qrʾ*	*mdīnā, qiryā*	*ʾty, mty*
Sy	*bnā*	*qrā*	*mdittā*	*ʾitā, mṭā*
Ma	*aʿmar*	*iqr*	*mδīnca*	*θōlē*
Ur	*bnəjə*	*qraja*	*mdijtə*	*təjə*
MM	*benā*	*qarrī*	*māθa*	*aθā*
Ar	*banā*	*daʿā*	*madīnaᵗ*	*jāʾa, ʾatā*
Mo	*bna*	*ʿeyyeṭ*	*mdina*	*ža*
Eg	*bana*	*nāda*	*madīna*	*ga*
Ir	*bina*	*ṣāḥ*	*madīna, wlāya*	*jā ~ ija*
Ge	*ḥanaṣa, nadaqa*	*bəhla*	*hagar*	*maṣʾa, ʾatawa*
Ta	*särḥe*	*ṣäwwäʿe*	*kätäma*	*mäṣʾe*
Am	*särra*	*ṭärra*	*kätäma*	*mäṭṭa*
Ha	*cēxäla*	*kälaḥa*	*bandar, gē*	*dīja*
Sa	*bny, brʿ*	*qrʾ*	*hgr*	*ʾtw, mẓʾ*
So	*béne*	*ṣaʿaq*	*madīna*	*gédaḥ*
Me	*bənō*	*ṣāq*	*rəḥbēt*	*nōka*
Ji	*ební*	*ṣaʿáq*	*ḥallét, məndə́r*	*zaḥám*

	13. Daughter	14. Day	15. Die	16. Door
Ak	*mārtu*	*ūmu*	*mātu*	*daltu, bābu*
Ug	*bt*	*ym*	*mt*	*ptḥ, dlt*
He	*bat*	*yōm*	*māt*	*delet, peteḥ*
Ph	*bt*	*ym*	*mt*	*dl*
AA	*brh*	*yōm*	*myt*	*traʿ*
Sy	*bartā*	*yawmā*	*mīt*	*tarʿā*
Ma	*berca*	*yōma*	*ameθ*	*θarʿa*
Ur	*brətə*	*jumə*	*mjətə*	*tarra*
MM	*baratta*	*yūma ~ yōma*	*mēθ*	*βāβa*
Ar	*bint*	*yawm*	*māta*	*bāb*
Mo	*bent*	*yōm*	*mat*	*bab*
Eg	*bint*	*yōm*	*māt*	*bāb*
Ir	*bitt*	*yōm*	*māt*	*bāb*
Ge	*walatt*	*maʿālt*	*mōta*	*xōxt, ʾanqaṣ*
Ta	*gʷal*	*maʿalti*	*motā*	*maʿṣo*
Am	*set ləj*	*qän*	*motā*	*bärr, mäzgiya*
Ha	*qaḥat*	*ayām, mōy*	*mōta*	*bäri, gäbti*
Sa	*b(n)t*	*y(w)m*	*m(w)t ~ myt*	*xlf, br, xw*
So	*fírhem, ʿəwgínoh*	*yóm, šam*	*ṣáme*	*ther ~ tár, mélfoh*
Me	*ḥə-brēt*	*nəhōr*	*mōt*	*bōb*
Ji	*brit*	*yum*	*xárɔ́g*	*ʾɔb, sīdet*

	17. Earth	18. Eight	19. Enter	20. Exit
Ak	*erṣetu*	*samānat*	*erēbu*	*waṣū*
Ug	*ʾarṣu*	*θmn*	*bả, ʿrb*	*yṣả*
He	*ʾereṣ*	*šmōnā*	*bāʾ*	*yāṣāʾ*
Ph	*ʾrṣ*	*šmnh*	*bʾ*	*yṣʾ*
AA	*ʾraʿ ~ ʾraq*	*tmnyh*	*ʿal*	*yʿ◌*
Sy	*ʾarʿā, midrā*	*tmānyā*	*ʿal*	*npaq*
Ma	*arʿa*	*θmōnya*	*eʿber*	*infeq*
Ur	*arra*	*tmənjə*	*vara*	*npəqə*
MM	*artīβel, deštā*	*təmānī*	*dāš*	*nefaq*
Ar	*ʾarḍ*	*θamāniyaᵗ*	*daxala*	*xaraja*
Mo	*ḷerḍ*	*tmenya*	*dxel*	*xrež*
Eg	*ʾarḍ*	*tamanya*	*daxal*	*xaṛag*
Ir	*ʾariδ*	*θmānya*	*xašš*	*ṭilaʿ*
Ge	*mədr*	*samānītū*	*bōʾa*	*waḍʾa*
Ta	*mədri*	*sommontä*	*ʾatäwä*	*wäṣʾe*
Am	*mədər, märet*	*səmmənt*	*gäbba*	*wäṭṭä*
Ha	*afär*	*sūt*	*bōʾa*	*wåṭaʾa*
Sa	*ʾrḍ, mdr*	*θmn(y)t*	*bwʾ, bhʾ, ʿdw*	*wṣʾ*
So	*ʾárḷ, fíẑeher*	*tǝ́mənəh*	*ʾékob*	*šérqaḥ*
Me	*ʾárẓ́*	*θəmənyēt*	*wəkōb*	*bərōz, fətōk*
Ji	*ʾɛrẓ́*	*θĩnát*	*égaḥ*	*ŝxəníṭ*

	21. Eye	22. Father	23. Field	24. Fill
Ak	*īnu*	*abu*	*eqlu*	*malū*
Ug	*ʿn*	*ȧb, ʾadānu*	*šadū*	*mlȧ*
He	*ʿayin*	*ʾāb*	*śāδe*	*mālēʾ*
Ph	*ʿn*	*ʾb*	*šd*	*mlʾ*
AA	*ʿayin*	*ʾab*	*bar*	*mlāʾ*
Sy	*ʿaynā*	*ʾabā*	*ḥaqlā*	*mlā*
Ma	*ʿayna*	*ōb*	*ḥaqla, ṣaḥrθa*	*iml*
Ur	*ajna*	*bəbə*	*xəqlə*	*mləjə*
MM	*īna*	*bāβa*	*ṣahrā*	*məlā*
Ar	*ʿayn*	*ʾab*	*ḥaql*	*malaʾa*
Mo	*ʿeyn*	*ḅḅa, bu*	*feddan*	*ʿemmer*
Eg	*ʿēn*	*ʾabb*	*γēṭ*	*mala*
Ir	*ʿēn*	*ʾab*	*ḥaqil*	*mila*
Ge	*ʿayn*	*ʾab*	*ḥaql, gadām, garāht*	*malʾa*
Ta	*ʿayni*	*ʾabbo*	*gərat*	*mälʾe*
Am	*ayn*	*abbat*	*mäsk, masa, meda*	*molla*
Ha	*īn*	*āw*	*ḥarši*	*mälaʾa*
Sa	*ʿyn*	*ʾb*	*ḥql, ḥbl, mśm*	*mlʾ*
So	*ʿáyn*	*bébe, ʾiif-*	*báqʿa, digdégeh*	*míleʾ*
Me	*ʾāyn*	*ḥayb*	*rīdēt*	*mīləʾ*
Ji	*ʿíhn*	*ʾiy*	*məšnúʾ*	*míźi*

	25. Five	26. Foot	27. Four	28. Friend
Ak	*xamšat*	*šēpu*	*erbet*	*ibru, ruʾu*
Ug	*xmš*	*riglu, ʾšd, pʿn*	*ȧrbʿ*	*rʿ*
He	*ḥmiššā*	*regel, paʿam*	*ʾarbāʿā*	*yādīd, ḥābēr, rēʿ*
Ph	*ḥmšt*	*pʿm*	*ʾrbʿt*	*ḥbr*
AA	*ḥmšh*	*rgl*	*ʾarbʿāh*	*ḥᵃbar*
Sy	*ḥammšā*	*riglā*	*ʾarbʿā*	*rāḥmā, ḥabrā*
Ma	*ḥamša*	*reγra*	*arpʿa*	*ṣtīqa, rfīqa*
Ur	*xəmšə*	*əqlə*	*arpa*	*dost*
MM	*hamša*	*kerāya*	*ārba*	*rafīq, dūs*
Ar	*xamsaᵗ*	*rijl*	*ʾarbaʿaᵗ*	*ṣadīq*
Mo	*xemsa*	*ržel*	*ṛebʿa*	*ṣaḥeb, ṣadiq*
Eg	*xamsa*	*ʾadam*	*ʾaṛbaʿa*	*ṣāḥib, ṣadīʾ*
Ir	*xamsa*	*rijil*	*ʾarbaʿa*	*ṣadīg*
Ge	*xamməstū*	*ʾəgr*	*ʾarbāʿəttū*	*ʿark*
Ta	*ḥamuštä*	*ʾəgri*	*ʾarbaʿtä*	*fätawi*
Am	*amməst*	*əgər*	*aratt*	*wädaj*
Ha	*ḥammisti*	*i(n)gir*	*ḥarat*	*mariň*
Sa	*xmšt*	*rgl*	*ʾrbʿt*	*ṣḥb, mwd*
So	*ḥámoh*	*śab ~ śaf*	*ʾerbáʿah*	*ʿaś*
Me	*xəmmōh*	*fām*	*ərbōt*	*ʾāśər*
Ji	*xõš*	*faʿm, śɛf*	*ɛrbəʿɔ́t*	*ʿáśər, sudq*

	29. From	30. Give	31. Go	32. Goat
Ak	*ištu*	*nadānu*	*alāku*	*enzu*
Ug	*l*	*ytn*	*hlk*	*ʕz*
He	*min*	*nātan, yāhab*	*hālak*	*ʕēz*
Ph	*mn*	*ytn*	*(y)lk*	*ʕz*
AA	*min*	*yhb, ntn*	*ʾzl, hwk*	*ʕēz*
Sy	*min*	*yab*	*ʾizal*	*ʕizzā, gadyā*
Ma	*m(n)*	*app*	*zalle, allex*	*ʕezza*
Ur	*min*	*jəvuli*	*zələ*	*ïzza*
MM	*men*	*ehaß*	*ezgā*	*enzā*
Ar	*min*	*wahaba, ʾaʕṭā*	*ðahaba*	*ʕanzaᵗ, maʕzaᵗ*
Mo	*men*	*ʕṭa*	*mša*	*meʕza*
Eg	*min*	*ʾidda*	*miši, rāḥ*	*miʕza*
Ir	*min*	*niṭa*	*rāḥ*	*ṣaxḷa*
Ge	*ʾəm*	*wahaba*	*ḥōra*	*ṭalīt*
Ta	*nay*	*habä*	*kedä*	*ṭäl*
Am	*kä*	*säṭṭä*	*hedä*	*fəyyal*
Ha	*-be*	*säṭa*	*ḥāra*	*dåw*
Sa	*bn*	*whb, wṣf, gdy*	*mśw ~ mśy*	*ʕnz*
So	*min*	*śe, ṭéf, índaq*	*ṭáher*	*ʾóz*
Me	*mən*	*wəzōm*	*səyōr*	*wōz*
Ji	*m(ən)*	*ezúm*	*aɣád*	*ʾɔz*

	33. God	34. Gold	35. Good	36. Hand
Ak	*ilu*	*xurāṣu*	*ṭābu, damqu*	*qātu*
Ug	*ʾilu*	*xrṣ*	*ṭābu, nʕm*	*yd*
He	*ʾlōhīm*	*zāhāb*	*ṭōb*	*yād*
Ph	*ʾl, ʾln*	*ḥrṣ*	*yʾ*	*yd*
AA	*ʾlāh*	*dhab*	*ṭāb*	*yad*
Sy	*ʾalāhā*	*dahəbā*	*ṭāb*	*īdā*
Ma	*alo*	*ðahba*	*ṭōb*	*īða*
Ur	*ələhə*	*dəvə*	*ṭava, spaj*	*ijdə*
MM	*māra*	*dahßa*	*šßīr, ṭāß*	*īda*
Ar	*aḷḷāh*	*ðahab*	*ṭayyib*	*yad*
Mo	*ḷḷāh*	*dheb*	*mezyan*	*idd*
Eg	*ʾaḷḷāh*	*dahab*	*kuwayyis, ṭayyib*	*ʾīd ~ yadd*
Ir	*ʾalḷa*	*ðahab*	*zēn, xōš, xēr*	*ʾīd*
Ge	*ʾəgzīʾa-bəḥēr*	*warq*	*šannəy, xēr*	*ʾəd*
Ta	*räbbi*	*wårqi*	*ṣəbbuq*	*ʾid*
Am	*əgzər*	*wärq*	*ṭəru, dähna*	*əjj*
Ha	*alla*	*zəqēḥ*	*qōrrām, ṭōňňam*	*iji*
Sa	*ʾl, ʾlh*	*ðhb, wrq*	*ṭyb*	*yd ~ ʾd*
So	*ʾallāh*	*deheb*	*díye, súwa, škár*	*ɛʾəd*
Me	*abāli*	*ðehēb*	*gīd*	*ḥayd*
Ji	*ʾɔẑ, ʾallāh*	*ṭíb*	*xár, ɛrḥím*	*éd*

	37. Head	38. Hear	39. Heart	40. Horse
Ak	*rēšu*	*šemū*	*libbu*	*sisū*
Ug	*rìš*	*šmˤ*	*lb*	*ssw*
He	*rōš*	*šāmaˤ*	*lēb*	*sūs*
Ph	*rˀš*	*šmˤ*	*lb*	*ss*
AA	*rēˀš*	*šmˤ*	*lēbb, lbab*	*sws*
Sy	*rìšā*	*šmaˤ*	*libbā*	*susyā*
Ma	*rayša*	*išmeˤ*	*leppa*	*ḥṣōna*
Ur	*rišǝ*	*šmaja*	*libbǝ*	*susi*
MM	*rīša*	*ṣāt*	*lebba*	*sosyā*
Ar	*raˀs*	*samiˤa*	*qalb*	*ḥiṣān*
Mo	*ṛaṣ*	*smeˤ*	*qelb*	*ˤewd*
Eg	*ṛās*	*simiˤ*	*ˀalb*	*ḥuṣān*
Ir	*rās*	*simaˤ*	*galub*	*ḥṣān*
Ge	*rǝˀs*	*samˤa*	*lǝbb*	*faras*
Ta	*rǝˀsi*	*sämˤe*	*lǝbbi*	*färäs*
Am	*ras*	*sämma*	*lǝbb*	*färäs*
Ha	*urūs*	*sämaˀa*	*qälbi*	*färäz*
Sa	*rˀš*	*šmˤ*	*lb*	*frš*
So	*réy*	*hyemáˤ*	*ˀílbib*	*ḥuṣun*
Me	*ḥǝ-roh*	*hēma*	*ḥǝ-wbēb*	*fǝrháyn*
Ji	*réš̃*	*š̃iˤ*	*ub, qɛlb*	*ḥáṣún*

	41. House	42. Hundred	43. Iron	44. King
Ak	*bītu*	*meˀat*	*parzillu*	*šarru*
Ug	*bt, dr*	*miˀtu*	*brðl*	*malku*
He	*bayit*	*mēˀā*	*barzel*	*melek*
Ph	*bt*	*mˀt*	*brzl*	*mlk*
AA	*bayit*	*mˀāh*	*przl*	*melek*
Sy	*baytā*	*māˀ*	*parzlā*	*malkā*
Ma	*payθa*	*emˤa*	*ḥatīta*	*malka*
Ur	*betǝ*	*immǝ*	*prizlǝ*	*mǝlkǝ*
MM	*bēθa*	*emma*	*parzǝlā*	*šihyāna*
Ar	*bayt*	*miˀaᵗ*	*ḥadīd*	*malik*
Mo	*ḍaṛ*	*mya*	*ḥdid*	*malik*
Eg	*bēt, dāṛ*	*miyya*	*ḥadīd*	*malik*
Ir	*bēt, ḥōš*	*miyya*	*ḥadīd*	*malik*
Ge	*bēt*	*mǝˀt*	*xaṣin*	*nǝgūš*
Ta	*bet*	*miˀti*	*ḥaṣṣin, bǝrät*	*nǝgus*
Am	*bet*	*mäto*	*brät*	*nǝgus*
Ha	*gār*	*bäqlä*	*brät*	*nägāši*
Sa	*b(y)t*	*mˀt*	*frzn*	*mlk*
So	*beyt, qáˤar*	*miˀe*	*ḥáshin*	*ṣáṭehan*
Me	*bayt*	*mǝyēt*	*ḥǝdáyd*	*mǝlēk*
Ji	*bot*	*mút*	*ḥádíd*	*mélík*

	45. Know	46. Lamb	47. Leg	48. Live
Ak	edū	kalūmu, puxādu	išdu	balāṭu
Ug	yd ʿ	ỉmr, kr	ʾišdu	ḥwy
He	yāda ʿ	kebeš, ṭāle	šōq	ḥāyā
Ph	yd ʿ	ʾmr, gdʾ	p ʿm	ḥyy
AA	yd ʿ	ʾimmar	šāq	ḥayāh
Sy	īda ʿ	ʾimrā, parrā	šāqā	ḥyā
Ma	iδa ʿ	qarqōra	siqanō	eḥi
Ur	daja	pirə	šəqə	xəjə
MM	qyādī	embara	šāqa	šboroxta eβad
Ar	ʿarifa	xarūf, ḥamal	sāq, rijl	ḥayiya, ʿāša
Mo	ʿref	xṛuf	ržel	ʿaš
Eg	ʿirif	xaṛūf ʾūzi	rigl	ḥiyi
Ir	ʿuraf	xārūf	rijil	ʿāš
Ge	ʾaʾmara, ʿōqa	māḥsəʿ	qʷə(y)ṣ	ḥaywa
Ta	mähärä, fäläṭä	rema	danga	ḥaywä
Am	awwäqä	ṭäbbot	əgər	norä
Ha	āqa	ṭāy wåldi	qulṭum	näbära
Sa	ś ʿr, γrb	ṭly	rgl	ḥyw
So	ɛda ʿ, ʿɛrɔb	kubś	śaf ~ śab	ʿāš
Me	wēda, γərōb	kabś	śəráyn	ʿāyōś
Ji	éda ʿ, γárɔ́b	kɔbś	fa ʿm	ʿɛ́ś

	49. Lord	50. Love	51. Make	52. Man
Ak	bēlu	rāmu	epēšu	zikāru
Ug	b ʿl, ảdn	ảhb	ʿšy	mt
He	ʾādōn, ba ʿal	ʾāhēb	ʿāśā	ʾīš, geber
Ph	ʾdn, b ʿl	ḥb	p ʿl	ʾ(y)š, gbr
AA	b ʿl, mrʾ	rḥm	ʿbad, p ʿl	gbar, ʾyš
Sy	ba ʿlā, mārā	ʾaḥibb	ʿbad	gabrā
Ma	mōra	irḥam	išwi	γabrōna, zalmθa
Ur	mərə, aγa	məxubi	vədə	gora, nəšə
MM	māra	rehem	eβad	gaβrā
Ar	sayyid, ba ʿl	ʾaḥabb	ʿamila, fa ʿala	rajul
Mo	sid	ḥabb	ʿmel	ražel
Eg	sayyid	ḥabb	ʿamal	rāgil
Ir	sayyid	ḥabb	sawwa	rijjāl ~ rajul
Ge	ʾəgzīʾ	ʾafqara	gabra	ʿəd, bəʾsī
Ta	gʷåyta	fätäwä	gäbärä	säbʾay
Am	geta	wäddädä	särra	wänd, säw
Ha	gōyta	wådäda	āňa, āša	usuʾ
Sa	b ʿl, mrʾ	wdd, ḥbb	f ʿl, ʿšy	ʾnš, ʾyš
So	bá ʿal	ʿéδan	ʿémor	ʿáj
Me	bāl	ʾáygəb, ḥəb	ʾáyməl	γayg
Ji	bá ʿal	ʿágəb, ḥebb	ʿɔl	γég

	53. Many	54. Meat	55. Month	56. Mother
Ak	mādu	šīru	warxu	ummu
Ug	mἰd, ʿẓm	bšr, šiʾru	yrx	ủm
He	rabbīm	bāśār	ḥōdeš	ʾēm
Ph	rbm	bšr, šʾr	yrḥ	ʾm
AA	śaggīʾ	bśar	yraḥ	ʾm
Sy	rabbā, saggīʾā	bisrā	yarḥā	ʾimmā
Ma	summar, baḥar	besra	yarḥa	emma
Ur	raba	bïsra	jərxə	jimmə
MM	genzā	besrā	yæhrā	emma
Ar	kaθīr	laḥm	šahr	ʾumm
Mo	bezzaf	lḥem	šher	ʾomm
Eg	kitīr	laḥm	šahr	ʾumm
Ir	hwāya	laḥam	šahar	ʾumm
Ge	bəzūx	šəgā	warx	ʾəmm
Ta	bəzuḥ	səga	wärḥi	ʾənno
Am	bəzu	səga	wär	ənnat
Ha	bäjīḥ	bäsär	wå̤ḥri	āy, abbāy
Sa	ʾxnh	bśr	wrx	ʾm
So	kin	téh ~ táh	śéhər	bíyo(h), ʾəm-
Me	mēkən	táywi	warx	ḥām
Ji	mɛ́kən	téʾ	ɔ́rx	ʾɛ́m

	57. Mountain	58. Mouth	59. Name	60. Night
Ak	šadū	pū	šumu	mūšu, līliātu
Ug	gbl, γr, δd	p	šm	ll
He	har	pe	šēm	laylā
Ph	hr	p	šm	ll
AA	ṭūr	pm	šum	lēylē
Sy	ṭūrā	pummā	šmā	līlyā ~ laylē
Ma	ṭūra	θemma	ešma	lēlya
Ur	ṭura	pummə	šimmə	leli
MM	ṭōra, aγma	pomma	ešma ~ ošma	lilyā
Ar	jabal	fam	ism	layl
Mo	žbel	fomm	sem	lila
Eg	gabal	fumm	ʾism	lēl(a)
Ir	jibal	ḥalig	ʾisim	lēla
Ge	dabr	ʾaf	səm	lēlīt
Ta	ʾəmba, kuma	ʾaf	səm	läyti
Am	gara, tärara	af	səm	lelit
Ha	säri	af	sum	ōrti, läyli
Sa	ʿr	f	šm	lyl ~ ll(y)
So	galas, fɛdhɔn	ḥáh	š(h)em	lílhe, ḥte
Me	kərmáym, gəbēl	xā	ham	láylət
Ji	giɛ́l, ḥɛ̄r	xɔh	šum	ʿáṣər

	61. On	62. One	63. Or	64. Peace
Ak	*eli*	*ištēnu*	*ū*	*šalāmu*
Ug	*ʿl*	*åḥd*	*ů*	*šlm*
He	*ʿal*	*ʾeḥād*	*ʾō*	*šālōm*
Ph	*ʿl*	*ʾḥd*	*ʾš*	*nḥt, šlm*
AA	*ʿal*	*ḥd*	*ʾw*	*šlām*
Sy	*ʿal*	*ḥad*	*ʾaw*	*šlāmā*
Ma	*ʿal*	*aḥḥaδ*	*yā*	*slōma*
Ur	*al*	*xə*	*jən*	*šləmə, šenə*
MM	*elle*	*ehdā ~ hedā*	*lo*	*salāmat*
Ar	*ʿalā*	*ʾaḥad*	*ʾaw*	*salām, ʾamān*
Mo	*ʿla*	*waḥed*	*wella*	*salam*
Eg	*ʿala*	*wāḥid*	*walla*	*salām*
Ir	*ʿala*	*wāḥid*	*lō*	*salām*
Ge	*lāʿla*	*ʾaḥadū*	*ʾaw*	*salām, sənʾ*
Ta	*ləʿli*	*ḥadä*	*wäy*	*ʿərqi*
Am	*lay*	*and*	*wäy*	*sälam*
Ha	*läʾay*	*aḥad*	*immā*	*amān*
Sa	*ʿl*	*wḥd*	*ʾw*	*šlm*
So	*thar*	*ṭad*	*ʾám*	*ʿafīya*
Me	* δār*	*ṭād*	*ʾaw*	*səlōm*
Ji	*δér*	*ṭad*	*mən*	*sélúm*

	65. Person	66. Road	67. Root	68. Sea
Ak	*awīlu*	*padānu*	*šuršu*	*tāmtu*
Ug	*ådm, npš, bunušu*	*ntb*	*šrš*	*ym*
He	*ʾādām*	*derek, šbīl*	*šōreš*	*yām*
Ph	*ʾdm*	*drk*	*šrš*	*ym*
AA	*ʾənāš*	*ʾorah*	*šrš*	*yamm*
Sy	*nāšā*	*ʾurḥā*	*širšā, ʿiqqārā*	*yammā*
Ma	*barnāš*	*tarba*	*šerša*	*baḥra, yamm*
Ur	*nəšə*	*urxə*	*ïqra*	*jəmə*
MM	*barnāša*	*ohrā*	*šerša*	*dæryā*
Ar	*ʾinsān*	*ṭarīq*	*ʾaṣl, ʿirq, širš*	*baḥr*
Mo	*ʾinsan, siyed*	*ṭriq*	*žder*	*bḥar*
Eg	*ʾinsān, šaxṣ*	*sikka, ṭarīʾ*	*gidr*	*baḥr*
Ir	*šaxiṣ*	*darub, ṭarīq*	*ʿirig, jaδir*	*bahar*
Ge	*bəʾsī*	*finōt, mangad*	*šərw*	*bāḥr*
Ta	*säb*	*mängäddi*	*sur*	*baḥəri*
Am	*säw*	*mängäd, gʷädana*	*sər*	*bahər*
Ha	*usuʾ*	*ūga, kara*	*sər*	*bäḥar*
Sa	*ʾ(n)š, mrʾ, rgl, grb*	*fnw(t), ʾrx, mšbl*	*śrs*	*bḥr*
So	*ḥoriš*	*fáne, ʾóʾorəm*	*šeríḥoh*	*rɛnhəm*
Me	*nófar*	*ḥ-ōrəm*	*ʾārq*	*ráwrəm*
Ji	*bírdɛ́m*	*ʾɔrm*	*śírɔ́x, ʿarq*	*rémnɛm*

	69. See	70. Send	71. Seven	72. Sheep
Ak	amāru	šapāru, ṭarādu	sebet	immeru, šu
Ug	ảmr, ḥdy, ʿn	lỉk, šlḥ	šbʿ	š, θảt
He	rāʾā	šālaḥ	šibʿā	śe
Ph	ḥzy	šlḥ	šbʿ	š
AA	ḥzy	šlḥ	šibʿāh	ʾmr
Sy	ḥzā	šlaḥ	šabʿā	niqyā
Ma	eḥmi	šattar	šobʿa	xarōfa
Ur	xzəjə	šadurï	šavva	vana
MM	hezā	šadder, waddī	šoββa	tattā, naʿja
Ar	raʾā	ʾarsala	sabʿaᵗ	šā, γanam
Mo	šaf	ṣifeṭ	sebʿa	kebš, neʿža, ḥawli
Eg	šāf	baʿat	sabʿa	naʿga, γanama
Ir	šāf	dazz	sabʿa	γanam (coll.)
Ge	rəʾya	laʾaka, fannawa	sabʿattū	baggəʿ
Ta	raʾayä ~ räʾayä	sädädä, lälaxä	šäwʿätä	bäggiʿə
Am	ayyä	lakä	säbatt	bäg
Ha	riʾa	laʾaxa ~ lāxa, gäfära	sātti	ṭāy
Sa	rʾy	ʾšy, ysr, blt, δky, nbl	šbʿt	xrf, hwr, śh, ḍʾn
So	śíni, ʾéqdom	bélog, ʾédʾe, ʾéṭbeg	hyəbʿah	téʾəh, laḥ
Me	śēni	xṣawb	yəbáyt	θīwēt
Ji	śíní	ebláγ	šəbʿə́t	θēt

	73. Silver	74. Sister	75. Sit	76. Six
Ak	kaspu	axātu	wašābu	šeššet
Ug	ksp	ʾaxātu	yθb	θθ
He	kesep	ʾāḥōt	yāšab	šiššā
Ph	ksp	ʾḥt	yšb	ššt
AA	ksap	ʾḥh	ytb	šittāh
Sy	kispā	ḥātā	ītib	štā
Ma	xesfa	ḥōθa	qʿōle	šecca
Ur	kispə, simə	xətə	tjəvə	ištə
MM	kaspa	hāθa	yehem	šitta
Ar	fiḍḍaᵗ	ʾuxt	qaʿada	sittaᵗ
Mo	feḍḍa	oxt ~ xet	gles	setta
Eg	faḍḍa	ʾuxt	ʾaʿad	sitta
Ir	fuδδa	ʾuxut	giʿad	sitta
Ge	bərūr	ʾəxt	nabara	səddəstū
Ta	bərri	ḥafti	täqämmäṭä	šädduštä
Am	bərr	əhət	täqämmäṭä	səddəst
Ha	mäʾet	əhit	tägēb(äl)a	siddisti
Sa	ṣrf	ʾxt	wθb	š(d)θt
So	fóδδa	ʾénneh, ʾé ʿḥet	ízʿem	híteh
Me	fəźźāt	γayt	śxəwəlōl	yətēt
Ji	fíźźát	γit	skɔf	štət

	77. Sky	78. Small	79. Son	80. Soul
Ak	šamū	ṣexru	māru	napištu
Ug	šamūma	ṣγr ~ ṣγr, dq, θrr	bn	npš
He	šāmayim	qāṭān, ṣāʿir	bēn	nepeš
Ph	šmm	qṭn	bn	npš
AA	šmīn	zʿīr, qṭyn	bar	npš
Sy	šmayyā	zʿūrā, daqdqā	brā	napšā
Ma	šmoya	izʿur, əzʿūṭ	ebra	nefša
Ur	šməjjə	surə, basura	brunə	nošə
MM	erqīha	honīn	ebrā	nešma
Ar	samāʾ	ṣaγīr	ibn	nafs
Mo	sma	ṣγiṛ	weld	nefs
Eg	sama	ṣuγayyaṛ	ʾibn, walad	nafs
Ir	sama	ẓγayyir	ʾibin	rūḥ
Ge	samāy	nəʾūs, ḥaṣūṣ	wald	nafs
Ta	sämay	nəʾuštäy	wäldi, wäddi	näfsi
Am	sämay	tənnəš	ləj	näfs
Ha	sämi	ṭənnäyyo	liji, wåldi	näfsi
Sa	šmy	ṣγr, qṭn	bn, wld	nfš
So	sáma	qéyhen	mógšam	ʿedd
Me	háytəm, səmāʿ	qənnáwn	bər	nafs, nəfəsēt
Ji	siɛ̃h	níṣán	bɛr	rəqbét, nəfsét

	81. Stone	82. Sun	83. Take	84. Ten
Ak	abnu	šamšu	axāzu, leqū	ešeret
Ug	ȧbn	šapšu	ȧxδ, lqḥ	ʿšr
He	ʾeben	šemeš	lāqaḥ	ʿśārā
Ph	ʾbn	šmš	lqḥ, nšʾ	ʿšrt
AA	ʾeben	šmš	ʾḥd, lqḥ	ʿaśrāh
Sy	kīpā, ʾabnā	šimšā	ʾiḥad	ʿisrā
Ma	xēfa	šimša	aḥaδ	ʿasra
Ur	kipə	šimšə	dvəqə	ïsra
MM	gelālta	šamšā	lexaṭ	asrā
Ar	ḥajar	šams	ʾaxaδa	ʿašaraᵗ
Mo	ḥežṛa	šemš	xda	ʿešṛa
Eg	ḥagaṛa	šams	ʾaxad	ʿašaṛa
Ir	ḥjāra	šamis	ʾaxaδ	ʿašra
Ge	ʾəbn	ḍaḥāy, ʾamīr	ʾaxaza, našʾa	ʿaššartū
Ta	ʾəmni	ṣähay	ḥazä	ʿasärtä
Am	dängiya	ṣähay	yazä	assər
Ha	ūn	īr	lähada	assir
Sa	ʾbn, ḥgr	śmš	ʾxδ, lqḥ	ʿśrt
So	ʾóben	šhom ~ šám	zé ʿe	ʿešéreh
Me	ṣāwər	hə-yám	lēqəf	ʾāśərēt
Ji	fúdún	yum	ḥōl	ʿəśírét

	85. Thousand	86. Three	87. Tie	88. Tongue
Ak	*līmu*	*šalāšat*	*kaṣāru, rakāsu*	*lišānu*
Ug	*ảlp*	*θlθ*	*rks, ảsr*	*lašānu*
He	*ʾelep*	*šlōšā*	*ʾāsar, qāšar*	*lāšōn*
Ph	*ʾlp*	*šlšt*	*ktr*	*lšn*
AA	*ʾlap*	*tlātāh*	*kpt*	*liššān*
Sy	*ʾalpā*	*tlātā*	*ʾisar, qṭar*	*liššānā*
Ma	*ōlef*	*θlōθa*	*iqṭar*	*liššōna*
Ur	*əlpə*	*ṭla*	*sara*	*lišənə*
MM	*alfa*	*klāθa*	*rāf, ṭərā, gəṭar*	*lišāna*
Ar	*ʾalf*	*θalāθaᵗ*	*rabaṭa*	*lisān*
Mo	*ʾalef*	*tlata*	*ʿqed*	*lsan*
Eg	*ʾalf*	*talāta*	*rabaṭ*	*lisān*
Ir	*ʾalif*	*θlāθa ~ tlāθa*	*rubaṭ*	*lisān*
Ge	*ʾəlf*	*šalastū*	*ʾasara, qʷaṣara*	*ləssān*
Ta	*šəḥ*	*sälästä*	*ʾasärä*	*mälḥās*
Am	*ši*	*sost*	*assärä, qäyyädä*	*məlas*
Ha	*alfi, kum*	*šiʾišti ~ šišti*	*agäda, qāṭära*	*arrāt*
Sa	*ʾlf*	*šlθt ~ θlθt*	*ʾsr*	*lšn*
So	*ʾalf*	*śáʿtɛh*	*ʿéṣem, kɛtɔf*	*léšin*
Me	*ʾāf*	*śāθáyt*	*ʾāṣáwb*	*əwšēn*
Ji	*ʾɔf*	*śɔθét*	*ʿɔ́ṣɔ́b, rɔ́ṭ*	*ɛlśɛ́n*

	89. Two	90. Under	91. Water (n.)	92. Well
Ak	*šina*	*šaplānu*	*mū*	*būru*
Ug	*θn*	*tḥt*	*my*	*nabku ~ napku*
He	*šnayim*	*taḥtī*	*mayim*	*bʾēr*
Ph	*šnm*	*tḥt*	*mym*	*bʾr*
AA	*trēyn*	*tḥot*	*myn*	*bʾr*
Sy	*treyn*	*tḥēt*	*mayyā*	*bīrā*
Ma	*iθr*	*cuḥc*	*mōya*	*bīra*
Ur	*tre*	*xut*	*mijjə*	*birə*
MM	*trēn*	*denβe*	*mēna*	*īna*
Ar	*iθnāni*	*taḥt*	*māʾ*	*biʾr*
Mo	*žuž*	*teḥt*	*ma*	*bir*
Eg	*ʾitnēn*	*taḥt*	*mayya*	*bīr*
Ir	*(ʾi)θnēn*	*jawwa, taḥat*	*māy*	*bīr*
Ge	*kəlʾē*	*tāḥta*	*māy*	*ʿazaqt*
Ta	*kələtä*	*taḥti*	*may*	*ʿelā*
Am	*hulätt*	*tac*	*wəha*	*gudgwad*
Ha	*koʾot ~ kōt*	*taḥay*	*mī(y)*	*mī gädu*
Sa	*kl(ʾ)y, θny*	*tḥt*	*mw*	*bʾr*
So	*trɔ*	*náḥaṭ*	*mérod, rího*	*ʿébhɔr*
Me	*əθrō*	*ənxāli*	*ḥə-mō*	*bayr*
Ji	*θroh*	*lxin*	*míh*	*ɣɔ̄r*

	93. West	94. What	95. Who	96. With
Ak	erbu	mīnū	mannu	itti
Ug	ʕrb	mn	my	ʕm
He	maʕrāb	mah	mī	ʕim
Ph	mʕrb	m	my	ʾt
AA	mʕrb	māh	man	ʕim
Sy	maʕrbā	mā	man	ʕam
Ma	maʕrba	mō	mōn	ʕemm
Ur	maarva	mudij	mənij	am
MM	ɣarb, maɣrib	mo	man	orke
Ar	ɣarb, maɣrib	mā	man	maʕa
Mo	ɣeṛb	aš	škun	mʕa
Eg	ɣaṛb, maɣrib	ʾēh	mīn	maʕa
Ir	ɣarb	šinu	minū	wiyya, maʕa
Ge	ʕarab, məʕrāb	mī, mənt	mannū	məsla
Ta	məʕrab	məntay	män	məs
Am	məʾərab	mən	man	kä gara
Ha	īr kiltəbūʕ	min	mān	-be
Sa	mʕrb	mhn	mn	ʕm
So	ɣárb	ʾinɛ́m	mán	ka
Me	məɣrāb	h-ɛ̄śən	mōn	bə-, kə-
Ji	múɣrub, qəblɛ́t	ʾínɛ́	mun	k-

	97. Woman	98. Wood	99. Write	100. Year
Ak	sinništu, iššu	iṣu	šaṭāru	šattu
Ug	ȧθt	ʕṣ	ktb, spr	šnt
He	ʾiššā	ʕēṣ	kātab	šānā
Ph	ʾšt	yʕr	ktb	št
AA	ʾantāh	ʕq	ktab	šnāh
Sy	ʾattətā	qaysā	ktab	šattā
Ma	eccθa, šunīθa	qīsa	ixθab	ešna
Ur	bəxtə	qesə	ktəvə	šitə
MM	eθθa	selwa, gowāza	kedaß	šettā
Ar	imraʾat	xašab	kataba	ʕām, sanat
Mo	mṛa	ʕud, xšeb (coll.)	kteb	ʕam
Eg	sitt, maṛa	xašab	katab	sana, ʕām
Ir	mara	xišab	kitab	sana, ʕām
Ge	bəʾsīt, ʾanəst	ʕəḍ	ṣaḥafa	ʕām(at)
Ta	säbäti	ʾənçäyti	ṣaḥafä	ʕamät
Am	set	ənçät	ṣafä	amät
Ha	i(n)dōc	inçi	kätäba	amät
Sa	ʾθt, mrʾt	ʕṣ́	štr, ṣhf	xrf, ʕwm
So	ʕáje(h)	ṭarb	ktōb	ʕénuh, sána
Me	tēθ	ðarb	kətōb	sənēt, ḥawl
Ji	teθ	ðarb	ktɔb	ʕɔ́nút, ḥabl

Wordlist C

Norm-Referenced and Pair-Referenced Lexicostatistics
Exercises 5, 6, 13, and 19

Ethiopic
Ge Ge'ez
Te Tigre
Ta Tigrinya
Am Amharic
Ha Harari
Ch Chaha

	1. Above	2. All	3. Anoint	4. Answer	5. Arm
Ge	lāʿla	kʷəllū	qabʾa	ʾawšəʾa	mazrāʿt
Te	läʿal	kəl	qäbʾa	bälsä	qəlčəm, ʾəde
Ta	ləʿli	kʷəllew	qäbʾe	mäläsä	qəlṣəm, wärci
Am	lay	hullu	qäbba	mälläsä	kənd
Ha	läʾay	kullu-, qiṭṭe	qābaʾa	argägäba	kuruʾ
Ch	nän	ənnəm	qäpa	žäpärä	xənä

	6. Arrive	7. Arrow	8. Ash	9. Ask	10. Axe
Ge	baṣha	ḥaṣṣ	ḥamad	saʾala	maḥṣē
Te	bäṣhä	mänṭig	ḥamäd	rämqä	mäsar, fas
Ta	bäṣhe	mantäg	ḥamäd	ṭäyyäqä	məsar, fas
Am	därräsä	fəlaṭṭa	amäd	ṭäyyäqä	fas, mäṭräbiya
Ha	bōräda	ḥināč, ṭiyya	ḥamäd	(at)ḥēbära	kalka
Ch	säna	adäbärä	amäd	(tä)sara	wesä, genzo

	11. Back	12. Bad	13. Barley	14. Be	15. Bear (child)
Ge	zabān	ʾəkūy, ḥəšūm	sagam	kōna, hallawa	walada
Te	ʿesat	kəfuʾ	səgäm	halla	wäldä
Ta	ʾəngədaʿ	kəfuʾ	səgäm	konä, näbärä	wälädä
Am	järba	kəfu	gäbs	honä	wällädä
Ha	ḥaci	yägässi	gūs	xāna	wåläda
Ch	gʾišä	buše	äkər	xärä, näpärä	čänä

	16. Beard	17. Bee	18. Belch	19. Bell	20. Big
Ge	ṣəhm	nəhb	gʷašʿa	dawal	ʿabīy
Te	šäkäm	nəhbät	gäsʿa	däwäl	ʿäbi
Ta	c̣əḥmi	nəhbi	gʷäš ʿe	däwäl	ʿabi
Am	ṭim	nəb	agässa	däwäl	tälləq
Ha	däbän	nijāt	giziʾ āša	däwwäl	gidīr
Ch	kʷəncəf	nəb	agäsa	däwäl	nəq

	21. Bird	22. Bite	23. Black	24. Blind	25. Blood
Ge	ʿōf	nasaka	ṣalīm	ʿəwwər	dam
Te	ʿof	näkša	ṣällim	ʿəwwur	däm
Ta	ʿuf	näxäsä	ṣällim	ʿəwwur	däm
Am	wäf	näkkäsä	ṭəqur	əwwər	däm
Ha	ūf	näxäsa	ṭäy	īn zälēla	däm
Ch	ãfʷ	näkäsä	ṭəqur	furṭ	däm

	26. Blow	27. Body	28. Bone	29. Bow	30. Break
Ge	nafxa	ʾakāl	ʿaḍm	qast	sabara
Te	näfḥa	ʾakal, gärob	ʿaṣəm	qärs	säbra
Ta	näfḥe	kärsi	ʿaṣmi	qästi	säbärä
Am	näffa	gäla	aṭənt	qäst	säbbärä
Ha	näfaha	qām	āṭ	lāwa	wåqäṭa
Ch	näfa	gäg	aṭəm	qäst	säpärä

	31. Breast	32. Brother	33. Build	34. Bull	35. Buy
Ge	ṭəb	ʾəxʷ	ḥanaṣa, nadaqa	sōr, bəʿr	zabbaya
Te	ṭəb	ḥu	nädqä	wəhər, tästay	zabe
Ta	ṭub	ḥaw	särḥe	bəʿray	ʿaddägä
Am	ṭut	wändəmm	särra	bäre, korma	gäzza
Ha	ṭōt	əḥ	cēxäla	baʾara	wåxäba
Ch	ṭu, data	gʷäpäya	aräšä	wur	səyä

	36. Calf	37. Call	38. Camel	39. Capture	40. Cave
Ge	ʾəgʷalt	bəhla	gamal	ḍēwawa	nədlat, gəbb
Te	ʾəgal, fəluy	särḥa	gämäl	maräka	bəʿät
Ta	märax	ṣäwwäʿe	gämäl	märäkä	bäʿatti
Am	ṭəjja, gidär	ṭärra	gəmäl	marräkä	wašša
Ha	ṭəja	kälaha	gāmäla	märäxa	gäb
Ch	däk	ṭäna	gamera	manäxä	wärä

	41. Chair	42. Cheek	43. Chew	44. Chicken	45. Child
Ge	manbar	maltāḥt	ḥēka, maṣara	dōrhō	wald, ʾəgʷāl
Te	mämbär	mäšdəg	mäc̣rä	derho	ʾələj
Ta	mänbär	gunc̣i	ḥayyäxä	därho	wäldi, ḥəṣan
Am	sänsälät	gunc̣	aňňäkä	doro	ləj
Ha	kursi	gumc̣i	ḥēka	atäwāq	wåldi, wīj
Ch	bwärc̣əma	gʷinc̣ä, danga	mesäxä	kutara	təkä

	46. City	47. Cloud	48. Coagulate	49. Come	50. Cough
Ge	*hagar*	*gīmē*	*ragꜤa*	*maṣʾa, ʾatawa*	*saꜤala*
Te	*dəgge*	*däbna*	*rägʾa*	*mäṣʾa*	*säꜤala*
Ta	*kätäma*	*dämmäna*	*rägʾe*	*mäṣʾe*	*saꜤalä*
Am	*kätäma*	*dämmäna*	*rägga*	*mätta*	*salä*
Ha	*bandar, gē*	*dānā*	*rägaʾa*	*dīja*	*oḥoʾ bāya*
Ch	*kätäma*	*dabära*	*näkä*	*cänä*	*dänägä*

	51. Cow	52. Cry	53. Dance (v.)	54. Daughter	55. Day
Ge	*lāhm*	*bakaya*	*zafana*	*walatt*	*maꜤālt*
Te	*wəʾät*	*bäka*	*gola*	*wälät(t)*	*məʾəl*
Ta	*lahmi*	*bäxäyä*	*tälähayä*	*gʷal*	*maꜤalti*
Am	*lam*	*aläqqäsä*	*čäffärä*	*set ləj*	*qän*
Ha	*lāṃ*	*bäka*	*säläḥa*	*qahat*	*ayām, mōy*
Ch	*äram*	*bäkʾä*	*dänäsä*	*gäräd*	*kärä*

	56. Die	57. Dog	58. Donkey	59. Door	60. Dove
Ge	*mōta*	*kalb*	*ʾadg*	*xōxt, ʾanqaṣ*	*rəgb*
Te	*motä*	*käləb*	*ʾadəg*	*bab*	*katra*
Ta	*motä*	*kälbi*	*ʾadgi*	*maꜤṣo*	*rəgbit*
Am	*motä*	*wəšša*	*ahəyya*	*bärr, mäzgiya*	*rəgəb*
Ha	*mōta*	*buci*	*wåčära*	*bäri, gäbti*	*ḥamīmi*
Ch	*motä*	*gəyä*	*əmar*	*wåfänca*	*bunyät*

	61. Dream (v.)	62. Drink	63. Ear	64. Earth	65. Eat
Ge	*ḥalama*	*satya*	*ʾəzn*	*mədr*	*balꜤa*
Te	*ḥalma*	*säta*	*ʾəzən*	*mədər*	*bälꜤa*
Ta	*ḥalämä*	*sätäyä*	*ʾəzni*	*mədri*	*bälꜤe*
Am	*allämä*	*ṭätta*	*joro*	*mədər, märet*	*bälla*
Ha	*bərzāz* (n.)	*säca*	*uzun*	*afär*	*bälaʾa*
Ch	*näzäzä*	*säčä*	*ənzər*	*afär*	*bäna*

	66. Egg	67. Eight	68. Elbow	69. Embrace	70. Enter
Ge	*ʾanqōqəhō*	*səmantū*	*kʷərnāꜤ*	*ḥaqafa*	*bōʾa*
Te	*ʾənqoqho*	*säman*	*ḥog*	*ḥaqfa*	*bäʾa*
Ta	*ʾənqulalih*	*sommontä*	*kʷärnaꜤ*	*ḥaqʷäfä*	*ʾatäwä*
Am	*ənqulal*	*səmmənt*	*kärən*	*aqqäfä*	*gäbba*
Ha	*aquḥ*	*sūt*	*kurumbāy*	*ḥafäqa*	*bōʾa*
Ch	*ənqura*	*səmwət*	*xuma*	*anqʾäfä*	*gäpa*

	71. Evening	72. Exit	73. Eye	74. Face	75. Fall
Ge	*məsēt*	*waḍʾa*	*Ꜥayn*	*gaṣṣ*	*wadqa*
Te	*məset*	*fägrä*	*Ꜥayn*	*gäṣ*	*wädqa*
Ta	*məsät*	*wäṣʾe*	*Ꜥāyni*	*gäṣ*	*wädäqä*
Am	*məšät*	*wätta*	*ayn*	*fit*	*wäddäqä*
Ha	*məšēt*	*wåṭaʾa*	*īn*	*fit*	*wådäqa*
Ch	*məsätä*	*wåṭa*	*en*	*yift*	*wåṭäqä*

	76. Fat	77. Father	78. Feather	79. Feces	80. Fill
Ge	šəbḥ	ʾab	ṣagʷr	ḍafʿ, zəbl	malʾa
Te	šəbaḥ	ʾäb	zoya	härəʾ	mälʾa
Ta	səbḥi	ʾabbo	kəntit	harʾi	mälʾe
Am	mora, səb	abbat	laba	ar	molla
Ha	säbaḥ	āw	kät, bālli	gäf	mälaʾa
Ch	manze, suwä	ab	qetuf	arä	mäna

	81. Finger	82. Fire	83. Firstborn	84. Fish	85. Five
Ge	ʾaṣbāʿt	ʾəsāt	bakʷr	ʿāšā	xamməstū
Te	çəbʿit	ʾəsat	bäkär	ʿasa	ḥaməs
Ta	ʾaṣabəʿti	ḥawi	bäkʷri	ʿasa	ḥamuštä
Am	ṭat	əsat	bäkʷər	asa	amməst
Ha	aṭābiňňa	əsāt	zugma	tuläm	ḥammisti
Ch	atebä	əsat	bäxər	asa	aməst

	86. Flea	87. Flee	88. Flour	89. Fly (n.)	90. Fly (v.)
Ge	qʷīnṣ	sakaya	harīḍ	ṣənṣənyā	sarara
Te	qaṣ	säka	häriç	çənçay	bärra
Ta	qunçi	ḥadämä	hərus	ṣənṣiya	näfärä
Am	qunəçça	šäššä	duqet	zəmb	bärrärä
Ha	qunāç	säka	fiça	zəmbi	bärära
Ch	qəraç	säkʾä	qämä	zəmb	bänärä

	91. Foot	92. Forget	93. Four	94. Friend	95. Give
Ge	ʾəgr	rasʿa	ʾarbāʿttū	ʿark	wahaba
Te	ʾəgär	tərässeʿa	ʾarbaʿ	fätay	habä
Ta	ʾəgri	rässəʿe	ʾarbaʿtä	fätawi	habä
Am	əgär	rässa	aratt	wädaj	sättä
Ha	igir	räsaʾa	harat	mariň	säṭa
Ch	ägər	täräsa	arbät	abägʷåda	abä

	96. Go	97. Goat	98. God	99. Gold	100. Good
Ge	ḥōra	ṭalīt	ʾəgzīʾa-bəḥēr	warq	šannəy, xēr
Te	gesä	ṭälit	räbbi	wärq	sänni
Ta	kedä	ṭäl	räbbi	wårqi	ṣəbbuq
Am	hedä	fəyyal	əgzər	wärq	ṭəru, dähna
Ha	ḥārǝ	dåw	alla	zəqēḥ	qōrrām
Ch	wärä	feq	əgzär	wärq	wäxe

	101. Grass	102. Grind	103. Grindstone	104. Guest	105. Hair
Ge	šāʿr	haraḍa, ṭahana	maḍḥē	nagd	šəʿərt, ṣagʷr
Te	säʿar	ṭähana	məddät	ʾəngəda	çägər
Ta	saʿəri	ṭahanä	mädid	gaša	çäguri
Am	sar	fäççä	mäj	əngəda	ṭägur
Ha	säʾar	fäça	mäjji	nugda	çigär
Ch	sär	fäçä	mäjä	bazära	dəgär

	106. Hammer	107. Hand	108. Hang	109. Hare	110. Hate
Ge	safēlyā	ʾid	saqala	ʾarnab	ṣalʾa
Te	modošša	ʾəd	säqla	mäntälle	ṣälʾa
Ta	mädoša	ʾid	säqälä	mantəlle	ṣälʾe
Am	mädoša	əjj	säqqälä	ṭəncäl	ṭälla
Ha	mädoša	iji	säqälä	ḥarbāňňō	ṭalaʾa
Ch	wädrägya	äj	säqärä	cəta	ṭäna

	111. Head	112. Hear	113. Heart	114. Honey	115. Horn
Ge	rəʾs	samʿa	ləbb	maʿār, dəbs	qarn
Te	rəʾäs	sämʿa	ləbb	mäʿar	qar
Ta	rəʾsi	sämʿe	ləbbi	maʿar	qärni
Am	ras	sämma	ləbb	mar	qänd
Ha	urūs	sämaʾa	qälbi	dūs	qär
Ch	gunär	säma	xʾən	wiyä	qän

	116. Horse	117. House	118. How Many	119. Hundred	120. Hunger
Ge	faras	bēt	ʾəsfintī	məʾt	raxab
Te	färäs	bet	käm	məʾət	räḥab
Ta	färäs	bet	kəndäy	miʾti	ṭəmet, räḥab
Am	färäs	bet	sənt	mäto	r(äḥ)ab
Ha	färäz	gār	misti	bäqlä	raḥab
Ch	färäz	bet	məraxər	bäqər	gajä

	121. Hunt	122. Hyena	123. Inherit	124. Iron	125. Kick
Ge	naʿawa	zəʾb, ṣəʿb	warasa	xaṣīn	ragaṣa
Te	näʿa	käray	wärsa	ḥasin	räqṣa
Ta	hädänä	zəbʾi	wäräsä	ḥaṣṣin, bərät	rägäṣä
Am	addänä	jəb	wärräsä	brät	räggäṭä
Ha	qasqāsa āša	wårāba	wåräsa	brät	rägäṭa
Ch	yäbädada wärä	gʷäncä	därät täšadä	brät	näqäṭä

	126. Kidney	127. Kill	128. King	129. Knee	130. Knife
Ge	kʷəlīt	qatala	nəgūš	bərk	maṭbāḥt
Te	kəlkəlʾot	qätlä	nəgus	bərək	mälaṣe
Ta	kulit	qätälä	nəgus	bərki	karra
Am	kulalit	gäddälä	nəgus	gulbät	billa, karra
Ha	kulāy	gädäla	nägāši	gəlib	mäšaḥ
Ch	əndäxräca	qyäṭärä	nəgʷs	gʷürbät	sända

	131. Know	132. Lamb	133. Laugh	134. Leaf	135. Learn
Ge	ʿōqa, ʾaʾmara	māḥsəʿ	šahaqa	qʷaṣl	tamhəra
Te	ʾamärä	ʿəyot	sähaqa	qäṭəl	ṣäbṭä
Ta	mähärä, fäläṭä	rema	sähaqä	qʷäṣli	tämahrä
Am	awwäqä	ṭäbbot	saqä	qäṭäl	tämarä
Ha	āqa	ṭāy wåldi	sēḥaqa	quṭṭi	lämäda
Ch	xarä	grangər	daqä	qəṭär	tämarä

	136. Leech	137. Left	138. Leg	139. Leopard	140. Lightning
Ge	ʿalaqt	ḍagām	qʷə(y)ṣ	namr	mabraq
Te	ʿaläq	gäläb	ʿəgəb	həmmäm	bärəq
Ta	ʿaläqti	ṣägamay	danga	näbri	nägʷäda
Am	aləqt	gra	əgər	näbər	mäbräq
Ha	ēqti	bito	qulṭum	gärgōra	bərāq
Ch	aräqəṭ	gəra	wä(də)r	zägʷara	božä

	141. Lion	142. Lip	143. Liver	144. Load	145. Locust
Ge	ʿanbasā	kanfar	kabd	ṣaʿana	ʾanbaṭā
Te	ḥäyät	kämfär	käbəd	ʾaṣʿana	ʿambäṭetay
Ta	ʾanbäsa	känfär	käbdi	ṣäʿanä	ʾambäṭa
Am	anbässa	känfär	gubbät	čanä	anbäṭa
Ha	wånag	läfläf	kūd	ṭaʾana	käfčōr
Ch	žäp	känfär	xäpt	čarä	fənṭa

	146. Long	147. Lot	148. Louse	149. Love	150. Lung
Ge	nawwīx	ʿədā	qʷīmāl	ʾafqara	sanbūʾ
Te	räyam	ʿəṣ	qəmäl	fäte	sämbuʾ
Ta	näwiḥ	ʿəṣa	qumal	fätäwä	sanbuʾ
Am	räjjim	əta	qəmal	wäddädä	samba
Ha	gudōr	ḥəṭa	qumāy	wådäda	kūf
Ch	gef, faṭura	ärṭ	qəmar	nämädä	sambwa

	151. Man	152. Many	153. Mare	154. Meat	155. Milk (n.)
Ge	ʿəd, bəʾsī	bəzūx	bāzrā	šägā	ḥalīb
Te	ʾənas	bəzuḥ	bazra	səga	ḥalib
Ta	säbʾay	bəzuḥ	bazra	səga	ṣäba
Am	wänd, säw	bəzu	bazra	səga	wätät
Ha	usuʾ	bäjīḥ	ənəsti färäz	bäsär	ḥay
Ch	säb	bəzä	wänad	bäsär	eb

	156. Milk (v.)	157. Month	158. Moon	159. Mosquito	160. Mother
Ge	ḥalaba	warx	warx	ṣāḍōt	ʾəmm
Te	ḥalbä	wärəh	wärəh	ṣasot	ʾəm
Ta	ḥaläbä	wärhi	wärhi	tənəniya	ʾənno
Am	alläbä	wär	čäräqa	tənəňň	ənnat
Ha	ḥaläba	wärhi	wåhri	bīmbe	āy, abbāy
Ch	anäbä	bänä	bänä	qəmčəna	adot

	161. M.-in-Law	162. Mountain	163. Mouth	164. Mule	165. Nail
Ge	ḥamāt	dabr	ʾaf	baql	ṣəfr
Te	ḥamat	däbər	ʾaf	bäqal	ṣəfər
Ta	ḥamat	ʾəmba, kuma	ʾaf	bäqli	ṣəfri
Am	amat	gara, tärara	af	bäqlo	ṭəfər
Ha	ḥamat	säri	af	bäqäl	ṭifir
Ch	amat	qʷäto	ãf	buqʷrä	ṭəfər

	166. Name	167. Narrow	168. Navel	169. Neck	170. Needle
Ge	səm	ṣabīb	ḥənbərt	kəsād	marfiʾ
Te	səm	ṣäbib	ḥəmbər	ʾangät	ʾəbrät
Ta	səm	ṣäbib	ḥəmbərti	kəsad	märfəʾ
Am	səm	ṭäbbab	əmbərt	angät	märfe
Ha	sum	ṭäbābu, ṭäbīb	ḥambūrṭi	angät	märfi
Ch	šəm	ṭäbəb	qʷårä	angät	märf

	171. New	172. Night	173. Nine	174. Nose	175. Oil
Ge	ḥaddīs	lēlīt	təsʿattū	ʾanf	qəbʾ
Te	ḥadis	lali	səʿ	ʾanəf	zet
Ta	ḥaddis	läyti	təšʿattä	ʾafənça, ʾanfi	zäyti
Am	addis	lelit	zäṭäňň	afənça	zäyt
Ha	ḥajīs	läyli, ōrti	zəḥṭäňň	ūf	zäyt
Ch	gädär	məsarä	žäṭäň	āfuna	zäyt

	176. One	177. Onion	178. Pass	179. Person	180. Pus
Ge	ʾaḥadū	baṣal	ʿadawa, xalafa	bəʾsī	məgl
Te	worot	bäslät	ḥalfa	säb	mägəl
Ta	ḥadä	šəggurti	ḥaläfä	säb	mägli
Am	and	šənkʷurt	alläfä	säw	mägəl
Ha	aḥad	šənkurta	ada	usuʾ	mägi
Ch	at	šənkʷərt	wärä	säb	məgər

	181. Rain	182. Rat	183. Red	184. Resemble	185. Return
Ge	zənām	ʾanṣawā	qayīḥ	masala	gabʾa
Te	zəlam	ʿänṣay	qäyəḥ	mäsla	ʾaqbälä
Ta	zənam	ʾançowa	qäy(y)əḥ	mäsälä	tämälsä
Am	zənab	ayṭ	qäyy	mässälä	tämälläsä
Ha	zənāb	fuʾur	qēḥ	mäsala	girägäba
Ch	zərab	fur	bəša	mäsärä	täžäpärä

	186. Rib	187. Right	188. River	189. Roast	190. Root
Ge	gabō	yamān	falag, wəḥīz	qalawa	šərw
Te	sətet	man	məʿṭən	qäla	sər
Ta	gʷädni	yäman	ruba	qäläwä	sur
Am	gʷädən	qäň	wänz	qʷälla	sər
Ha	miḥāṭ āṭ	qaňīt	zär	qala	sər
Ch	meyä	känä	bär, əxa	qʷänä	äsər

	191. Rope	192. Rub	193. Run	194. Saliva	195. Salt
Ge	ḥabl	ḥasaya	rōṣa	mərāq	ṣēw
Te	ḥäbəl	ḥasa	roṣä	mərraq	ṣewa
Ta	gämäd	ḥasäsä	gʷäyäyä	mərraq	çäw
Am	gämäd	aššä	roṭä	məraq	çäw
Ha	fätīt	ḥaša	rōta	mərāq	ṭirässu
Ch	gaja	äšäšä	noṭä	əmbaqʿä	aso

	196. Sand	197. Say	198. Scratch	199. Sea	200. See
Ge	xōṣā	bəhla	ḥakaka	bāḥr	rəʾya
Te	ḥoṣa	bela	ḥakka	bähar	raʾa
Ta	ḥaṣäwa	bälä	ḥakäkä	baḥəri	raʾayä
Am	aṣäwa	alä	akkäkä	bahər	ayyä
Ha	sēlāt, šiḥšēra	bāya	ḥakäka	bäḥar	riʾa
Ch	aṣäwa	barä	akäkä	bar	aṣä

	201. Seed	202. Seize	203. Seven	204. Sew	205. Shadow
Ge	zarʾ, bəzr	ʾaxaza, našʾa	sabʿattū	safaya	ṣəlālōt
Te	zärəʾ	ṣäbṭa	säbuʿ	säfa	ṣəlal
Ta	zärʾi	ḥazä	šäwʿatä	säfäyä	ṣəlal
Am	zär	yazä	säbatt	säffa	ṭəla
Ha	säňi	läḥada	sātti	säfa	çāya
Ch	zär	ṭäbäṭa	säbat	sefä	ṭərar

	206. Sheep	207. Short	208. Shoulder	209. Skin (n.)	210. Skin (v.)
Ge	baggəʿ	xaṣīr	matkaf(t)	māʾs	ṭabaḥa
Te	bəgguʿ	ḥaçir	mənkəb	qərab	ṭäbḥa
Ta	bäggiʿə	ḥaṣir	maʾgär	qʷärbät	ṭäbḥe
Am	bäg	aççər	täkäšša	qoda	ṭäbba
Ha	ṭāy	ḥaçīr	märmär	gōga	ṭäbäḥa
Ch	ṭä	açər	agat	goga	ṭäpa

	211. Sky	212. Slander	213. Slave	214. Sleep	215. Smoke
Ge	samāy	ḥamaya	bāryā, gabr	nōma	ṭīs, tann
Te	ʿästär	ḥama	gäbər	säkbä	tänan
Ta	sämay	ḥamäyä	barya	däqqäsä	ṭis, təkki
Am	sämay	amma	barya	täňňa	ṭis, çəs
Ha	sämi	ḥēma(ʾa)	gāfa, ḥawāz	ňēʾa	tän
Ch	säme	ama	barya, wäz	nəyä	tän

	216. Snake	217. Sneeze	218. Son	219. Soot	220. Sow
Ge	ʾarwē	ʿaṭasa	wald	ṭaqar	zarʾa
Te	ʾarwe	ḥaṭṭäša	wäd	ṭäqäro	zärʾa
Ta	tämän	hanṭäsä	wäldi, wäddi	ṭäqär	zärʾe
Am	əbab	anäṭṭäsä	ləj	ṭəqərša	zärra
Ha	ḥubāb	ḥaṭṭiš bāya	liji, wåldi	ṭiqär	zäraʾa
Ch	cərä	atreṭäsä	ärc	ṭäqär	zäna

	221. Speak	222. Spear	223. Spider	224. Spit	225. Splinter
Ge	nagara	ramḥ, kʷīnāt	šārēt	tafʾa, waraqa	šəṣār
Te	tähaqe	konat	saret	täfʾa	säṭṭar
Ta	tänagärä	kʷinat	saret	ʾəntəf bälä	sənçar
Am	näggärä	ṭor	šärärit	täffa	səntər
Ha	asēnāna	wåräm	ašširāraḥti	tuf bāya	säçīr
Ch	odä	çäxʷa	šet	täfa	səntər

	226. Star	227. Steal	228. Stick	229. Stomach	230. Stone
Ge	*kōkab*	*saraqa*	*batr*	*karš, kabd*	*ʾəbn*
Te	*kokäb*	*särqä*	*ḥəräṣ*	*käršät*	*ʾəbən*
Ta	*koxob*	*säräqä*	*bätri*	*kärši*	*ʾəmni*
Am	*kokäb*	*särräqä*	*bättər*	*hod*	*dängiya*
Ha	*ṭūy*	*rōja*	*bärti*	*kärsi, anqär*	*ūn*
Ch	*xoxäb*	*sänäqä*	*ənṭär*	*dän*	*əmər*

	231. Strangle	232. Suck	233. Sun	234. Swallow	235. Sweat
Ge	*xanaqa*	*ṭabawa*	*ḍahāy, ʾamīr*	*wəxta*	*haf*
Te	*ḥanqa*	*ṭäba*	*ṣäḥay*	*(wä)ḥata*	*lähabät*
Ta	*ḥanäqä*	*ṭäbäwä*	*ṣäḥay*	*waḥaṭä*	*rəḥaṣ*
Am	*annäqä*	*ṭäbba*	*ṣäḥay*	*waṭä*	*lab, wäz*
Ha	*ḥanäqa*	*ṭäba*	*īr*	*wäḥata*	*wüziʾ*
Ch	*anäqä*	*ṭäpwä*	*eyat, čet*	*waṭä*	*wəzat*

	236. Tail	237. Taste	238. Tear	239. Ten	240. Think
Ge	*zanab*	*ṭəʿma*	*ʾanbəʿ*	*ʿaššartū*	*ḥasaba*
Te	*zänäb*	*ṭäʿama*	*ʾənbəʿ*	*ʿassər*	*ḥasba*
Ta	*zänäb*	*ṭäʿamä*	*nəbʿat*	*ʿasärtä*	*ḥasäbä*
Am	*jərat*	*ṭamä*	*ənba*	*assər*	*assäbä*
Ha	*qänāwa*	*ṭāma*	*əbiʾ*	*assir*	*ḥēsäba*
Ch	*juwä*	*tamä*	*əmba*	*asər*	*asäbä*

	241. Thorn	242. Thousand	243. Three	244. Throw	245. Tomorrow
Ge	*šōk*	*ʾəlf*	*šalastū*	*ramaya*	*gēšam*
Te	*šokät*	*šäḥ*	*säläs*	*läkfä*	*gesäm*
Ta	*ʾəšoxʷ*	*šäḥ*	*sälästä*	*därbäyä*	*ṣəbaḥ*
Am	*šoh*	*ši*	*sost*	*ṭalä*	*nägä*
Ha	*usux*	*alfi, kum*	*šiʾišti*	*gäňa*	*gīš*
Ch	*sox*	*xʷəm*	*sost*	*adägä*	*nägä*

	246. Tongue	247. Tooth	248. Tree	249. Twin	250. Two
Ge	*ləssān*	*sənn*	*ʿəḍ, ʿōm*	*mantā*	*kəlʾē*
Te	*nəssal*	*ʾänjebät*	*ʿəčyät*	*mänta(y)*	*kəlʾot*
Ta	*mälḥās*	*sənni*	*ʾom*	*mänta*	*kələtä*
Am	*məlas*	*ṭərs*	*zaf*	*mänta*	*hulätt*
Ha	*arrāt*	*sən*	*läfu*	*mālta*	*koʾot*
Ch	*anäbät*	*sən*	*äčä*	*lämca*	*xʷet*

	251. Under	252. Urine	253. Village	254. Vomit	255. Want
Ge	*tāḥta*	*šənt*	*hagar*	*qēʾa*	*faqada*
Te	*tähat*	*šən*	*zäga*	*qäʾa*	*tämna*
Ta	*taḥti*	*šənti*	*ʿaddi*	*täfʾe*	*däläyä*
Am	*tac*	*šənt*	*mändär*	*qärräšä*	*ša*
Ha	*taḥay*	*šāḥat*	*gända*	*qäräša*	*xaša*
Ch	*täte*	*səmat*	*jäfwårä*	*änäqä*	*šä*

	256. War	257. Wash	258. Water	259. Week	260. What
Ge	ṣabʾa, kʷīnāt	xaḍaba, rəḥḍa	māy	sabūʿ	mī, mənt
Te	ḥarəb	ḥaṣba	may	samin	mi
Ta	kʷinat, wəggəʾ	ḥaṣabä	may	sämun	məntay
Am	ṭor	aṭṭäbä	wəha	sammənt	mən
Ha	ḥarbi	ḥaṭäba	mī	sātti	min
Ch	arəb	aṭäbä	əxa	samt	mər

	261. Wheat	262. When	263. Where	264. Which	265. White
Ge	šərnāy	māʾzē	ʾaytē	ʾay	ṣəʿdəw
Te	šənray	mäʾaze	ʾəttaya	ʾayi	ləṣuḥ
Ta	sərnay	maʾäze	ʾabay	ʾayän	ṣaʿda, nəṣuḥ
Am	sənde	mäce	yät	yätəññaw	näčč
Ha	qamädi	mäci	āyde	āy	näčīḥ
Ch	sənä	mäcä	ete	etätaw	näčä, gʷad

	266. Who	267. Widow	268. Wind (n.)	269. Wing	270. Wish
Ge	mannū	maballat	nafās	kənf	tamannaya
Te	män	mäbäl	wälwäl	mämfär, kənf	təmänna
Ta	män	maʾmän	näfas	kənfi	tämännäyä
Am	man	baltet	näfas	kənf	tämäññä
Ha	mān	armalla	dūf	ḥaräkkät	tämänni āša
Ch	mwan	wäbit	əmfas	qʷansa	mena

	271. Woman	272. Wood	273. Write	274. Year	275. Yesterday
Ge	bəʾsīt, ʾanəst	ʿəḍ	ṣahafa	ʿām(at)	təmaləm
Te	ʾəssit	ʿəččay	ṣäḥfa	ʿamät	təmale
Ta	säbäti	ʾənčäyti	ṣahafä	ʿamät	təmmali
Am	set	ənčät	ṣafä	amät	təlant
Ha	i(n)dōc	inči	kätäba	amät	tāčəna, tāʾina
Ch	məšt	äčä	ṭafä	xərəm	tənant, tərama

Wordlist D

Diglossia and Language Contact
Exercise 17

Arabic
   Ar   Classical Arabic
   Mo Moroccan Arabic
   Ma Maltese

Berber
   Se Senhayi
   AS Ayt Seghrouchen
   Gh Ghadamsi

	1. All	2. Answer	3. Ant	4. Arm	5. Arrive
Ar	*kull*	*ʾajāba*	*namlaᵗ*	*ðirāʕ*	*waṣala*
Mo	*koll*	*jāweb*	*nmel*	*draʕ*	*wṣel*
Ma	*kolloš*	*wiejeb*	*nemla*	*drieḥ*	*wasal*
Se	*kul*	*wažb*	*θafuzarθ*	*d:raʕ*	*awḍ*
AS	*q:aḥ*	*wajb*	*ašṭ:uf*	*aɣil*	*awḍ*
Gh	*kūl:u*	*s:ədmər*	*takətfet*	*āɣil*	*awəḍ*

	6. Ash	7. Ask	8. Axe	9. Back	10. Barley
Ar	*ramād*	*saʾala*	*faʾs, balṭaᵗ*	*ḍahr*	*šaʕir*
Mo	*ṛmaḍ*	*ṣeqṣa*	*qadum*	*ḍhaṛ*	*šʕir*
Ma	*rmied*	*staʾsa*	*mannara*	*dar*	*šīr*
Se	*iɣd*	*t:r*	*aylzim*	*aʕror*	*imndi*
AS	*iɣd*	*sal*	*ayz:im*	*tiwa*	*timzt:*
Gh	*ēšəd*	*æθ:ər*	*agʾælzim*	*akorm*	*təmzet*

	11. Be	12. Bear (child)	13. Beard	14. Beat	15. Big
Ar	*kāna*	*walada*	*liḥya, ðaqn*	*ḍaraba*	*kabīr*
Mo	*kan*	*wled*	*leḥya*	*ḍreb*	*kbir*
Ma	*kien*	*wildet* (fem. sg.)	*leḥya*	*ḥabbat*	*kbir*
Se	*ili*	*aru*	*θamarθ*	*uwθ*	*mq:or*
AS	*ili*	*aṛw*	*tmart*	*w:t*	*amq:ṛan*
Gh	*ili*	*ārəw*	*tōmært*	*æwət*	*mæq:or* (v.)

153

	16. Bird	17. Bite	18. Black	19. Blind	20. Blood
Ar	ṭayr, ʿuṣfūr	ʿaḍḍa	ʾaswad	ʾaʿmā	dam
Mo	ṭir	ʿeḍḍ	khel	ʿma	demm
Ma	āsfur	gidem	iswed	ʿama	demm
Se	afrux	ʿaṭš	abrçan	aδryal	d:m
AS	ajḍiḍ	qr:š	abr:an	aḍryal	idam:n
Gh	agʿaḍiḍ	æmbər	æzḏəf (v.)	d:əryəl (qual.)	dæm:æn

	21. Bone	22. Bread	23. Breast	24. Brother	25. Build
Ar	ʿaẓm	xubz	ṣadr, θady	ʾax	banā
Mo	ʿḍem	xobz	bezzula	ax	bna
Ma	āḍma	ḥobz	zeyza, bizzula	ḥu	bena
Se	iɣs	aɣrom	ab:iš	ašqiq	bnu
AS	iɣs:	aɣrum	if:	uma	bna
Gh	ɣæs:	tawagʿe	admār	aruma	ōsək

	26. Bull	27. Buy	28. Call	29. Camel	30. Cheek
Ar	θawr	ištarā	daʿā	jamal	xadd
Mo	tur	šra	ʿeyyeṭ	žmel	xedd
Ma	fart	štara	seyyaḥ	jemel	ḥadd
Se	azgar	saɣ	ɣr	alɣum	amg:iz
As	afunas	sɣ	ɣr	alɣm	madl, anbuz
Gh	afunas	æsæʿ	s:lil	āḷæm	agʿæẓ:

	31. Chew	32. Chicken	33. Child	34. Cloud	35. Cow
Ar	ʿalaka, maḍaya	dajājaᵗ	walad	saḥābaᵗ, ɣaymaᵗ	baqara
Mo	mḍeɣ	džaža	derri, ṭfel	shaba, ɣmama	begra
Ma	māad	tijieja	tifel	shaba	baʾra
Se	faz:	θayaẓiṭ:	arba	isgnu	θafunasθ
AS	fẓ:	tyaẓiṭ:	aslmya	isinw	tafunast
Gh	æf:əz	taẓiṭ	ara	tižnewt	tafunast

	36. Cry	37. Dance	38. Date	39. Daughter	40. Day
Ar	bakā	raqaṣa	balaḥ (coll.)	bint	yawm
Mo	bka	šṭeḥ	temṛa	bent	yōm
Ma	beka	zifen	tamra	bint	yum
Se	ru	šṭaḥ	t:mar	θarbaθ	nhar
AS	ru	šṭ:ḥ	tini	taslmyat, il:i	as:
Gh	æẓ:əf	dīz	aβēna	alæt	āsæf

	41. Die	42. Dig	43. Dog	44. Donkey	45. Door
Ar	māta	ḥafara	kalb	ḥimār	bāb
Mo	mat	ḥfer	kelb	ḥmaṛ	bab
Ma	miet	ḥafer	kelb	ḥmar	bieb
Se	m:θ	ḥfar	aharδan	aɣyul	θaw:rθ
AS	m:t	ɣz	aydi	aɣyul	lbab
Gh	əm:ət	æβrək	ēde	azēḍ	taβ:urt

	46. Dove	47. Dream	48. Dress	49. Drink	50. Ear
Ar	*ḥamāmaᵗ*	*ḥalima*	*labisa*	*šariba*	*ʾuðun*
Mo	*ḥmam*	*ḥlem*	*lbes*	*šṛeb*	*wden*
Ma	*ḥamiema*	*ḥolom*	*libes*	*šorob*	*widna*
Se	*θaḥmamt*	*warg*	*ls*	*su*	*amẓ:uγ*
AS	*adbir*	*irjit*	*iṛd*	*sw*	*amẓ:uγ*
Gh	*adaber*	*βərgʾ*	*æls*	*æsw*	*ēsəm*

	51. Earth	52. Eat	53. Egg	54. Eight	55. Enter
Ar	*ʾarḍ*	*ʾakala*	*bayḍaᵗ*	*θamāniyaᵗ*	*daxala*
Mo	*ḷerḍ*	*kla*	*biḍa*	*tmenya*	*dxel*
Ma	*art*	*kiel*	*bayda*	*tmienya*	*daḥal*
Se	*θamazirθ, açal*	*tš*	*θagfilθ*	*θmnya*	*çšm*
AS	*tamurt, šal*	*tš*	*taml:alt*	*tmnya*	*adf*
Gh	*tam:urt, ōkæl*	*æš:*	*tasadəlt*	*tām*	*ātəf*

	56. Exit	57. Eye	58. Face	59. Fall	60. Fat
Ar	*xaraja*	*ʿayn*	*wajh*	*saqaṭa, waqaʿa*	*šaḥm, duhn*
Mo	*xrež*	*ʿeyn*	*wžeh*	*ṭaḥ*	*šḥem*
Ma	*ḥarej*	*āyn*	*wicc*	*waʾa*	*šaḥam*
Se	*f:γ*	*θiṭ:*	*lužah*	*bḍu*	*θaδunt*
AS	*f:γ*	*tiṭ:*	*udm*	*uḍa*	*tadun*
Gh	*æf:əʿ*	*awæl:*	*ælwəž:*	*ūḍu*	*tas:əmt*

	61. Father	62. Feather	63. Feces	64. Fill	65. Fire
Ar	*ʾab*	*rīšaᵗ*	*rawθ, farθ*	*malaʾa*	*nār*
Mo	*ḅḅa, bu*	*riša*	*xṛa*	*ʿemmeṛ*	*ʿafya, naṛ*
Ma	*missier*	*riša*	*ḥara*	*melaʾ*	*nar*
Se	*baba*	*r:iša*	*ixran*	*δkar, tšur*	*θims:i*
AS	*ib:a*	*r:iš (coll.)*	*ix:an*	*ʿm:ṛ*	*tims:i*
Gh	*dæd:a*	*taržalt*	*iẓ:an*	*əṭkur*	*ofa*

	66. Finger	67. Fish	68. Five	69. Flour	70. Fly (n.)
Ar	*ʾuṣbaʿ*	*samak, nūn*	*xamsaᵗ*	*ṭaḥīn, daqīq*	*dubābaᵗ*
Mo	*ṣbeʿ*	*ḥuta*	*xemsa*	*ṭḥin*	*debbana*
Ma	*sabā*	*ḥuta*	*ḥamsa*	*dʾieʾ*	*dubbiena*
Se	*aḍaḍ*	*aslm*	*xamsa*	*t:ḥin, ibryn*	*izi*
AS	*ḍaḍ*	*aslm*	*xmsa*	*arn, ibrayn*	*izi*
Gh	*aḍək:əd*	*olisma*	*səm:əs*	*aβærn*	*izi*

	71. Fly (v.)	72. Foot	73. Forget	74. Four	75. Friend
Ar	*ṭāra*	*rijl*	*nasiya*	*ʾarbaʿaᵗ*	*ṣadīq*
Mo	*ṭaṛ*	*ṛžel*	*nsa*	*ṛebʿa*	*ṣaḥeb, ṣadiq*
Ma	*tar*	*sieʾ*	*nesa*	*erbā*	*ḥabib*
Se	*frfr*	*aḍar*	*t:u*	*arbʿa*	*amd:akʷl*
AS	*afrw*	*ḍaṛ*	*t:u*	*ṛbʿa*	*amd:akʷ:l*
Gh	*æk:əd*	*aḍar*	*ət:u*	*aq:oz*	*akawat*

	76. Frog	77. Give	78. Go	79. Goat	80. God
Ar	ḍifdaʿᵃᵗ	wahaba, ʾaʿṭā	ðahaba	ʿanzaᵗ, maʿzaᵗ	aḷḷāh
Mo	žṛana	ʿṭa	mša	meʿza	ḷḷāh
Ma	zrinj	ta	mar	mōza	alla
Se	aqarqur	k:	agul, ad:u, k:	θaɣaṭ	rb:i, al:ah
AS	ajru, aqrqra	uš	ṛaḥ	tɣaṭ:	ḷ:ah, ṛb:i
Gh	aʿæg':ur	ækf	ās, rar	tēʿaṭ	alla

	81. Gold	82. Good	83. Grass	84. Grind	85. Hair
Ar	ðahab	ṭayyib	ʿušb, ḥašīš	ṭahana	šaʿrᵃᵗ
Mo	dheb	mezyan	ṛbiʿ	ṭhen	šeʿra
Ma	deeb	tayyeb	ḥašiš	tahan	šāra
Se	ðhb	iṣbaḥ	r:biʿ	ẓḍ	inẓḍ
AS	uṛɣ	awḥdi	tuja	ẓḍ	anẓḍ, az:ar
Gh	oræɣ	ʿažib (qual.)	aš:əß	æẓəd	azaw

	86. Hand	87. Hare	88. Head	89. Hear	90. Heart
Ar	yad	ʾarnab	raʾs	samiʿa	qalb
Mo	idd	qniya	ṛaṣ	smeʿ	qelb
Ma	id	liebru	rās	smā	ʾalb
Se	afus	açbun	azj:if	sl	ul
AS	fus	awtul	ixf, azl:if	sl:	ul
Gh	ōfəs:	tag'ærẓiẓt	ēɣæf	æsl	ōg'əm

	91. He-Goat	92. Help	93. Hide	94. Honey	95. Horn
Ar	tays	sāʿada	satara, ʾaxfā	ʿasal	qarn
Mo	ʿetrus	ʿawwen, saʿed	xebbeʿ	ʿsel	qeṛn
Ma	bodbod	ān	satar, ḥeba	āsel	ʾarn
Se	aʿtrus	aʿwn	f:r	θam:nt	isk
AS	amyan	ʿawn	f:r	tamnt	iš:
Gh	ag'ur	āwəs	ækīf	taməmt	aškaw

	96. Horse	97. House	98. Hunger	99. Iron	100. Kid
Ar	ḥiṣān	bayt	jūʿ	ḥadīd	jady
Mo	ʿewd	ḍaṛ	žuʿ	ḥdid	ždi
Ma	ziemel	dar	juḥ	ḥadid	gidi
Se	agmar	ax:iam	j:oʿ	lḥðið	iɣyḍ
AS	yis	taxant, tad:art	ḷaẓ	uz:al, lḥdid	iɣid
Gh	ag'mar	daž	lāẓ	wəz:āl	aʿid

	101. Kidney	102. Kill	103. King	104. Knee	105. Knife
Ar	kulyaᵗ	qatala	malik	rukbaᵗ	sikkīn
Mo	kelwa	qtel	malik	rokba	mus
Ma	kilwa	ʾatel	sultan, re	rkobba	sikkina
Se	θigz:alt	nɣ	azžɩð	afuð	uz:al
AS	tiɣzlt	nɣ	ažl:id	fud	ažnwi
Gh	tag'æẓ:ult	æn:	ašæl:id	ōfəd	taßæṣ:

	106. Know	107. Lamb	108. Laugh	109. Left	110. Leg
Ar	ʿarifa	xarūf, ḥamal	ḍaḥika	šimāl, yasār	sāq, riǰl
Mo	ʿref	xṛuf	ḍḥek	iṣeṛ	ržel
Ma	āraf	ḥaruf	daḥak	šellug	rijel
Se	s(:)n	izim:ar	ḍsa	azlmaḍ	aḍar
AS	isin	aʿl:uš	ṭs	azlmaḍ	ḍaṛ, ilγ
Gh	æs:ən	ælxəruf	æḍs	azəlmaḍ	aḍar

	111. Lie	112. Lion	113. Lip	114. Live	115. Liver
Ar	kaδiba	ʾasad, sabʿ	šifaᵗ	ḥayiya, ʿāša	kabid
Mo	kdeb	sbeʿ	šarib	ʿāš	kebda
Ma	gideb	lyun	šoffa	ḥay	fwied
Se	skarks	izm	ašndur	d:r	θasa
AS	s:ḥil:l	izm	ahnfif	d:r	t:sa
Gh	ṣnīwət	aβōr	aḍalis	æd:ər	tōsa

	116. Long	117. Love	118. Lung	119. Make	120. Male
Ar	ṭawīl	ʾaḥabb	riʾaᵗ	ʿamila, faʿala	δakar
Mo	ṭwil	ḥabb	riya	ʿmel	dkeṛ
Ma	twil	ḥabb	pulmun	āmel	rajel
Se	ṭwil	ara	θurin (pl.)	g(:)	awθm
AS	azirar	ʿšq	turin (pl.)	ij	awtm
Gh	zəgʿrət (v.)	əβr	ṭōra	ægʿ	ōtəm

	121. Man	122. Many	123. Mare	124. Meat	125. Milk (n.)
Ar	raǰul	kaθīr	faras, ḥuǰraᵗ	laḥm	laban, ḥalīb
Mo	ražel	bezzaf	ʿewda	lḥem	ḥlib
Ma	rajel	bosta	debba	laḥam	halib
Se	aryaz	bz:af	θagmarθ	açsum	θaziçθ
AS	aryaz	ktir, bz:af	tajmart	aysum	aγi
Gh	wügʿ:id	ḥāl	tagʿmart	aksəm	yæf:, ælḥalib

	126. Milk (v.)	127. Month	128. Morning	129. Mother	130. Mouth
Ar	ḥalaba	šahr	ṣabāḥ	ʾumm	fam
Mo	ḥleb	šheṛ	ṣbaḥ	ʾomm	fomm
Ma	ḥaleb	šaar	ōdu	omm	fomm
Se	ẓ:g	š:har, ayur	ṣbah	im:a	imi
AS	ẓ:y	šhṛ	ṣ:baḥ	im:a	imi, aq:mu
Gh	æẓ:əgʿ	ōyær	əṣ:āla	mā	ame

	131. Nail	132. Name	133. Navel	134. Neck	135. Nine
Ar	ẓifr	ism	surraᵗ	ʿunq, raqabaᵗ	tisʿaᵗ
Mo	ḍfer	sem	ṣorṛa	ʿenq	tesʿud
Ma	difer	isem	zokra	ōnʾ	disā
Se	aškruḍ	ism	θimiṭṭ	lʿonq	tsʿud
AS	baš:r	ism	tmiṭ:	iri	tsʿa, tsʿud
Gh	aškar	ism	tameṭ	takorəmt	təṣō

	136. Nose	137. Oil	138. One	139. Onion	140. Pass
Ar	ʾanf	zayt	ʾaḥad	baṣalaᵗ	marra
Mo	nif, menxaṛ	zit	waḥed	beṣla	daz
Ma	mnieḥer	zeyt	wieḥed	basla	ādda
Se	θinzarθ	z:iθ	iwn	θibṣlθ	k:
AS	tinzar	z:it	idj	lbṣl (coll.)	k:
Gh	tənzart	ude	yōn	aflēlo	æxṭəm

	141. Person	142. Rain	143. Ram	144. Rat	145. Red
Ar	ʾinsān	maṭar	kabš	faʾr, jurδ	ʾaḥmar
Mo	ʾinsan, siyed	šta	kebš	ṭobba, faṛ	ḥmer
Ma	bniedem	šita	muntun, kibš	far	aḥmar
Se	bnaδm	anzar	içr:i	θaɣrδayθ	azugʷ:aɣ
AS	bnadm	anzaṛ	udad	aɣṛda	azgʷ:aɣ
Gh	awādəm	anaẓar	azōmær	oββg':an	azəg:aɣ

	146. Return	147. Ride	148. Right	149. River	150. Road
Ar	rajaʿa, θāba	rakiba	yamīn	nahr	ṭarīq
Mo	ṛžeʿ	rkeb	imin	wad	ṭriq
Ma	rejā	rikeb	lemin	šmara	triʾ
Se	aɣul	ani	afusi	iɣzar	izrf
AS	ʿid	ny	lymn:	iɣzr	abrid
Gh	ækri	æni	anfūs	ēββer	abrīd, aʿlad

	151. Root	152. Rope	153. Run	154. Salt	155. Say
Ar	ʾaṣl, ʿirq, širš	ḥabl	jarā, rakaḍa	milḥ	qāla
Mo	žder	ṭwal, ḥbel	žra	mleḥ ~ melḥ	gal
Ma	ērʾ	ḥabel	jera	melḥ	ʾal
Se	azwar	asɣun, iziçr	az:l	θisnt	ini
AS	aẓuṛ	asɣun, izišr	az:l	tisnt	ini
Gh	azur	tazara	æz:əl	tēsənt	æn

	156. Sea	157. See	158. Send	159. Seven	160. Shadow
Ar	baḥr	raʾā	ʾarsala	sabʿa	ẓill
Mo	bḥar	šaf	ṣifeṭ	sebʿa	ḍell
Ma	baḥar	ra	bāat	sebā	dell
Se	lbḥr	ẓar	gawz	sbʿa	θili
AS	lbḥṛ	ẓr	azn	sbʿa	tili
Gh	ælbəḥər	æl:əm	āzən	sā	tēle

	161. Shoulder	162. Sheep	163. Silver	164. Sing	165. Sister
Ar	katif, minkab	šā, ɣanam	fiḍḍaᵗ	ɣannā	ʾuxt
Mo	ktef	neʿža, ḥawli	feḍḍa	ɣenna	oxt ~ xet
Ma	spalla	nāja	fiḍḍa	ānna, kanta	oḥt
Se	θaɣaruṭ	θiçr:it	n:uqra	ɣn:a	θašqiqθ
AS	aɣiṛ	lksb, lisb	n:qrt	nš:d	ultma
Gh	taɣurəṭ	taββale	ælfiṭ:æt	ɣən:u	alætma

	166. Sit	167. Six	168. Sky	169. Sleep (v.)	170. Small
Ar	qaʕada	sitta¹	samāʾ	wasina, nāma	ṣaɣīr
Mo	gles	setta	sma	nʕes	ṣɣiṛ
Ma	ʾāad	sitta	sema	raʾad	zīr
Se	qim	st:a	ign:a	ṭ:as	imẓi
AS	q:im	st:a	ajn:a	jn	amz:yan
Gh	qēm	ṣuẓ	ažən:a	nəd:əm	əmtit (qual.)

	171. Smell	172. Smoke	173. Snake	174. Soul	175. Speak
Ar	šamma	duxān	ḥayya¹	nafs	takallama
Mo	šemm	doxxan	ḥenš	nefs, ṛuḥ	tkellem
Ma	xamm	duḥḥan	lifā	ruḥ	tkellem
Se	fuḥ	d:ux:an	ifiɣar, θalfsa	r:oḥ, iman, n:fs	siwl
AS	šḏ:u	d:x:an	ifiɣṛ, alfsa	ṛ:uḥ, n:fs	s:iwl
Gh	æk:	oβu	tolifsa	iman	sməg':i

	176. Spider	177. Spit	178. Star	179. Steal	180. Stick
Ar	ʕankabūt	tafala, baṣaqa	kawkab, najm	saraqa	ʕaṣā
Mo	rtila	bzeq, dfel	nežma	ṣṛeq	ʕṣa
Ma	brimba	bezaʾ	kewkba, stilla	seraʾ	āsluj
Se	saʕiδ lbn:ay	stutf, susf	iθri	açr	akš:uḍ
AS	awll:i	s:ufs	itri	ašr	aɣz:al, taɣṛiyt
Gh	sæd:ænkaya	sūfəs	iri	ōkər	taboret

	181. Stomach	182. Stone	183. Summer	184. Sun	185. Swallow
Ar	miʕda¹, kirš	ḥajar	ṣayf	šams	balaʕa
Mo	kerš	ḥeẓra	ṣif	šemš	bleʕ
Ma	zaʾʾ	ḥajra	ṣayf	šemš	balā
Se	θaʕd:isθ	azru	anbδu	θafuçθ	sɣli
AS	lmʕda, tadist	aẓṛu	anbdu	tafuyt	ṣṛḍ, lbʕ
Gh	tadist	ērəg'	anæβdu	tōfət	ælməẓ

	186. Sweat	187. Tail	188. Take	189. Tear	190. Ten
Ar	ʕaraq	δanab	ʾaxada	damʕa¹	ʕašara¹
Mo	ʕṛeq	šuwwal	xda	demʕa	ʕešṛa
Ma	āraʾ	denb	ḥa	demā	āšra
Se	θidi	azafal, ašwal	ṭ:f	amṭ:a(w)	ʕašra
AS	tidi	ajlal	asy	imṭ:awn (pl.)	ʕšṛa
Gh	tidi	tabaḥṣuṣ:	āβæʕ	amət:a	maraw

	191. Thigh	192. Thorn	193. Three	194. Throw	195. Tie
Ar	wark, faxδ	šawk, ḥasak	θalāθa¹	ramā	rabaṭa
Mo	fxed	šuka	tlata	ṛma	ʕqed
Ma	wirk, koššа	šewka	tlieta	terā	rabat
Se	θaɣma	asn:an	θlaθa	siyb	q:n, çrf
AS	tamṣ:aṭ:	asn:an	tlata	jr	q:n, šrf
Gh	taɣma	tədra	kāræd	æg'ər	ækrəd

	196. Tomorrow	197. Tongue	198. Tooth	199. Tree	200. Two
Ar	ɣad*an*	lisān	sinn	šajara*ᵗ*	iθnāni
Mo	ɣedda	lsan	senna	šeẓṛa	žuž
Ma	āda	ilsien	sinna	sijra	tneyn
Se	azk:a	ils	θiɣmsθ	s:žra	žuž
AS	dutša	ils	tiɣmst	s:jṛt	snat
Gh	azak:a	ēləs	asēn	tæmdikt	sən

	201. Uncle (mat.)	202. Uncle (pat.)	203. Urine	204. Village	205. Want
Ar	xāl	ʿamm	bawl	qarya	ʾarāda
Mo	xal	ʿemm	bul	qeṛya, ḍuwwaṛ	bɣa
Ma	barba	tsiyu	bewl, urina	raḥal	ried
Se	xali	ʿam:i	ibš:išn	d:šar	ura
AS	xali	ʿm:i	ibš:išn	aṛm, lfilaj	bɣa, štha
Gh	xāli	ʿam:i	alwāgʾæn	amæzdæʿ	əβr

	206. War	207. Wash	208. Water (n.)	209. Well	210. What
Ar	ḥarb	ɣasala	mā ʾ	bi ʾr	mā
Mo	ḥeṛb	ṣebben, ɣsel	ma	bir	aš
Ma	gwerra	ḥasel	ilma	bir	ši
Se	š:ar:, lbaruḍ	sird	aman	anu	ay
AS	lḥṛb, lbaṛuḍ	s:ird	aman	anu	ma(y), mi
Gh	ælfitnæt	sīrəd	āman	ānu	me

	211. Wheat	212. Where	213. White	214. Who	215. Wind (n.)
Ar	qamḥ, ḥinṭa*ᵗ*	ʾayna	ʾabyaḍ	man	rīḥ
Mo	gemḥ	fayn	byeḍ	škun	riḥ
Ma	ʾamḥ	feyn	abyad	min	riḥ
Se	irðn	ani	amj:ul	škun	asm:iḍ
AS	imndi	mani	aml:al	mi, may	aḍu
Gh	ayærd	din	mləl (qual.)	an:o	aḍo

	216. Wing	217. Woman	218. Wood	219. Write	220. Year
Ar	kanaf, janāḥ	imraʾa*ᵗ*	xašab	kataba	ʿām, sana*ᵗ*
Mo	ženḥ	mra	ʿud, xšeb	kteb	ʿam
Ma	jewnaḥ	mara	inyam, ūda	kiteb	sena
Se	afar	θamɣarθ	akš:uḍ	ari	lʿam
AS	afr	tamṭ:uṭ:	asɣaṛ, ayš:uḍ	ari	ʿam, asgʷ:as
Gh	afraw	talta	asɣēr	ōrəβ	aẓæg:as

Wordlist E

Isoglosses
Exercise 18

The classical languages are shown in *ordinary* type, the modern languages in *modern* type.

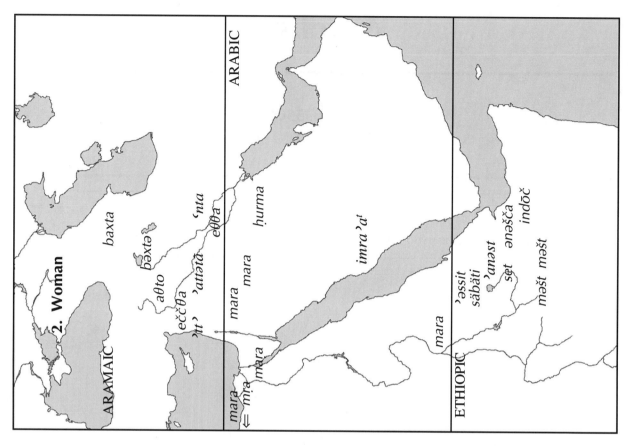

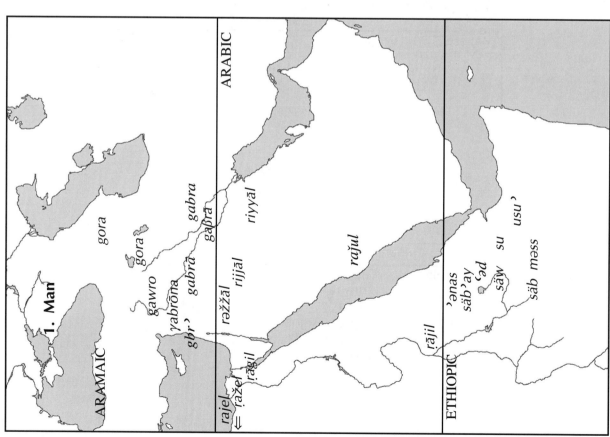

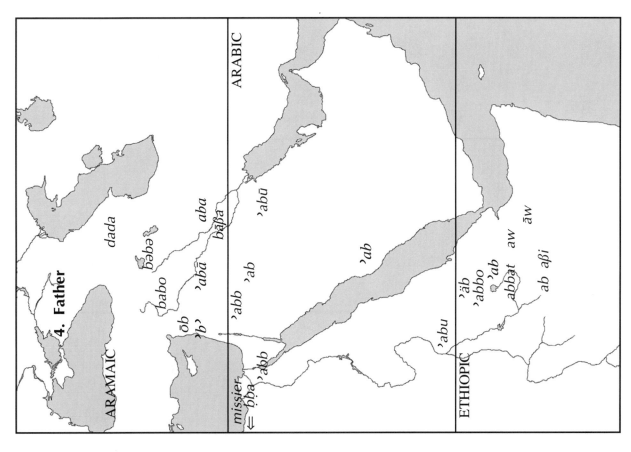

4. Father

ARAMAIC

ARABIC

ETHIOPIC

dada

babo

bebe

aba

ʾabā

bāβa

ōb

ʾbʾ

missier
⟸ bba

ʾabb

ʾabb

ʾab

ʾabū

ʾab

ʾabu

ʾib

ʾabbo

ʾab

abbat

aw

āw

ab aβi

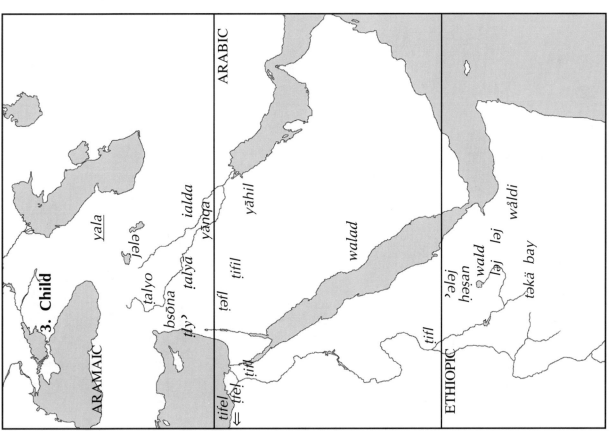

3. Child

ARAMAIC

ARABIC

ETHIOPIC

yala

ʤeʤe

talyo

bsōna

tly ʾ

talyā

ialda

yānqa

tifel
⟸ ṭfeʤi

ṭəʤi

ṭfil

ṭəfl

tifil

yāhil

walad

tifl

 waʤdi
ʾeseʤi
ʤeʤe

ʤeʤ

ʤeʤ

wāldi

təkä bay

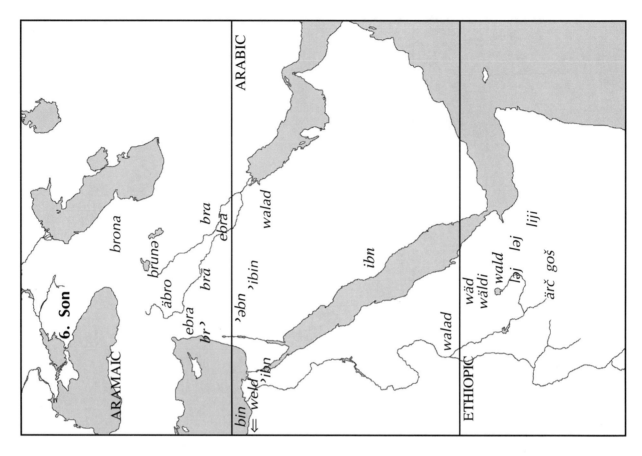

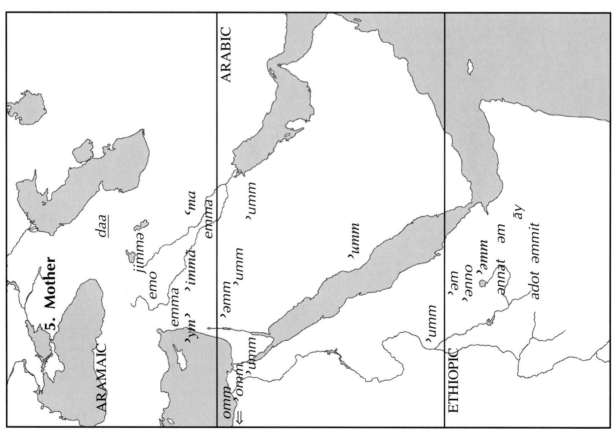

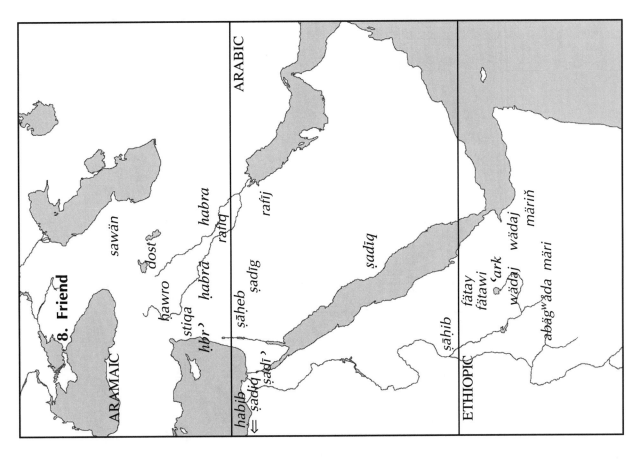

8. Friend

ARAMAIC

sawān

dost

ḥawro

stiqa

ḥbrʾ

ḥabrā

ḥabra

ḥabrā

rafīq

sāḥeb

ṣadīg

ḥabib ⇐

ṣadīq ⇐

ARABIC

rafīj

ṣadīq

sāhib

ETHIOPIC

fätay

fätawi

ʿark

wädaj

wädaj

märiñ

abägʷäda märi

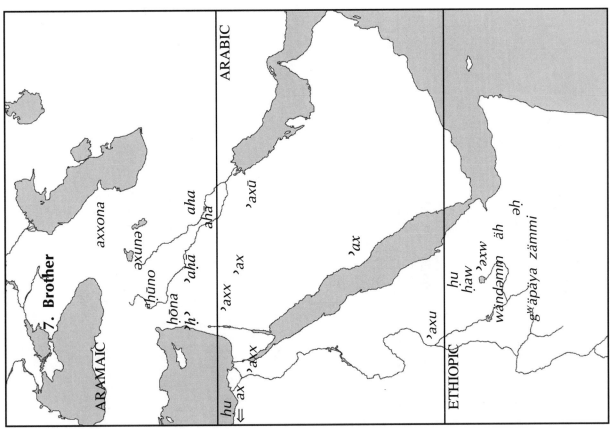

7. Brother

ARAMAIC

axxona

eunxe

ḥūno

ḥōna

ʾh̬

ʾi

ʾaḥā

ʾaḥā

aha

aha

ʾax

ʾaxx

hu ⇐

ax ⇐

ʾaxx

ARABIC

ʾaxū

ʾax

ʾax

ʾaxu

ETHIOPIC

ḥu

ḥaw

ʾaxw

wändämm

äh

əh

gʷäpäya zämmi

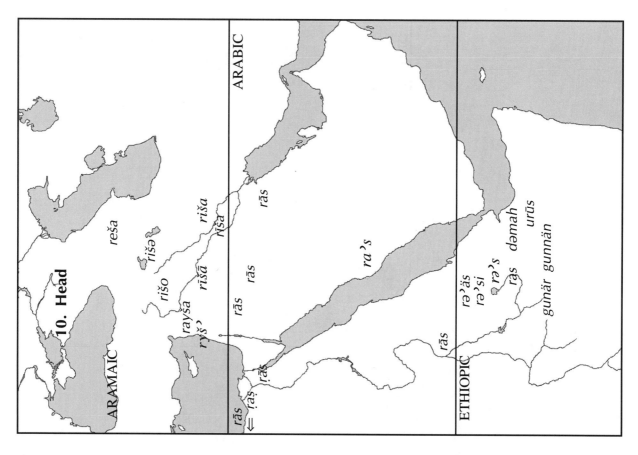

10. Head

ARAMAIC: reša, rišə, rišo, rīša, rīša, rēš, rēšā, rēšā, rēš, rēš, rēš, rēš, rēš

ARABIC: rās, rās, rās, rās, raʾs, rās, rās, ⇐ rās rās

ETHIOPIC: reʾās, reʾsi, reʾs, rās, demah, urūs, gunār gunnān

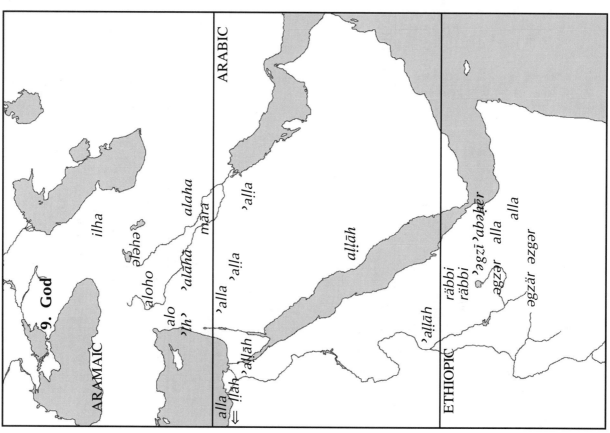

9. God

ARAMAIC: ilha, ʾelohe, ʾaloho, ʾalo ʾlh, ʾalāhā, alaha, māra, ʾalla, ʾalla, alla ⇐ ʾllāh, ʾallāh

ARABIC: ʾalla, ʾalla, allāh, ʾallāh

ETHIOPIC: rābbi, rābbi, ʾegziʾ ʾabəher, agzē, alla, alla, agzār azgar

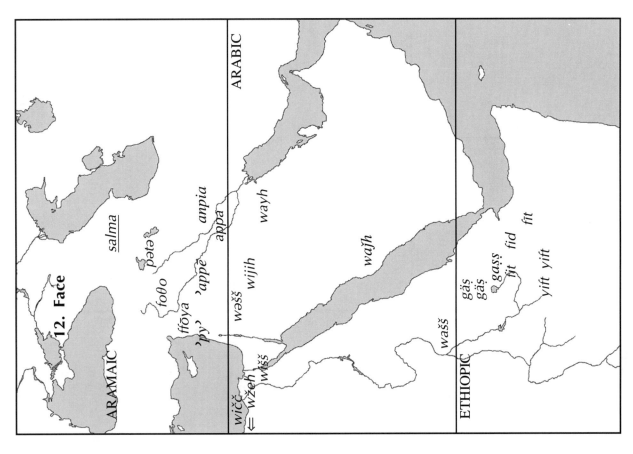

12. Face

ARAMAIC
salma
peṭe
foθo
ffōya
ʾpyʾ
wičč̣
wžeh
ʾappē
ʾappa
anpia

ARABIC
wayh
wajh
wijih
wašš
wēšš
waǰh
wašš

ETHIOPIC
gäṣ
gäṣ
gaṣṣ
fit
fit
fid
fjt
yift yift
yift

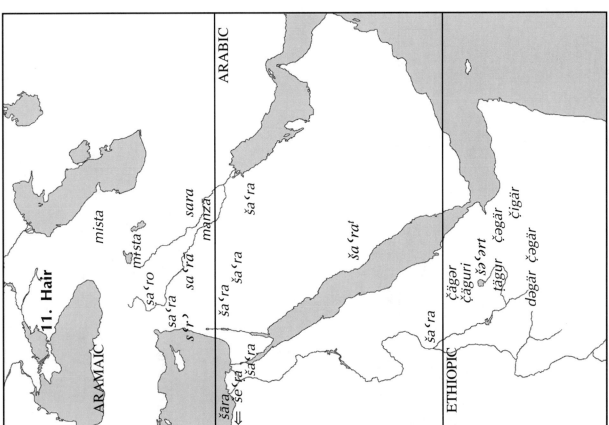

11. Hair

ARAMAIC
mista
miʸsta
saʿro
saʿrā
saʿra
sʾrʾ
sara
manzā
šara
seʿʿra

ARABIC
šaʿra
šaʿra
šaʿra
šaʿrat
šaʿra
šaʿra

ETHIOPIC
čäger
čäguri
tägur
eš eʾert
šeʿart
čegär
čigär
dǝgär čegär
šaʿra

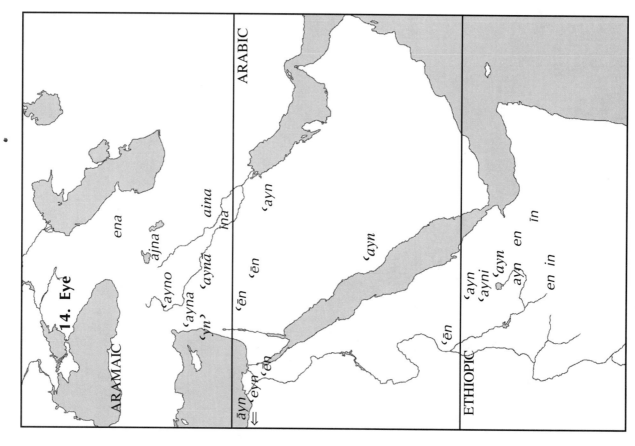

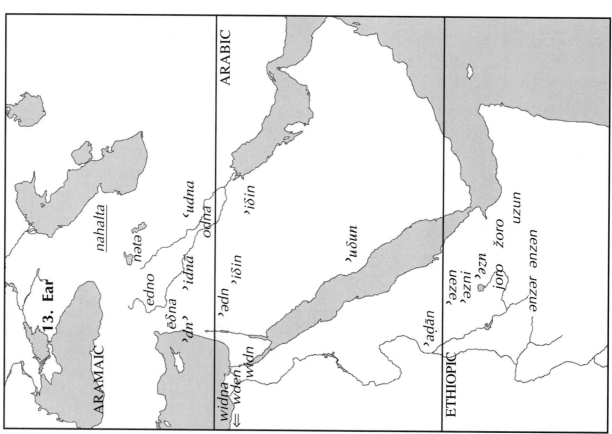

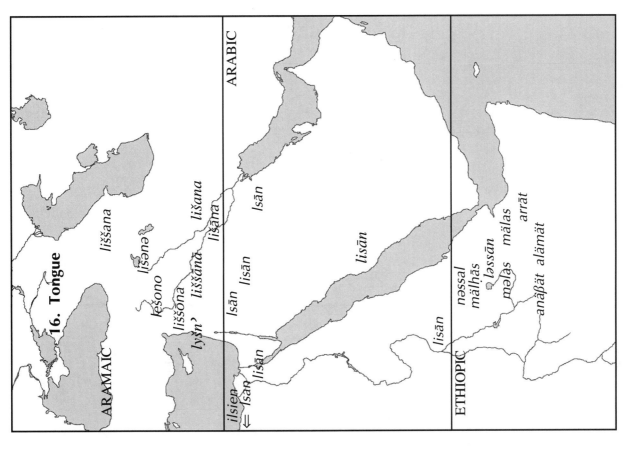

16. Tongue

ARAMAIC

liššana
lišəne
kəšono
liššŏna
lyšn'
lissānā
lišana
lissānā
lišana

ARABIC

lsān
lsān
lisān
lisān
lisān
lisān
lisān
lsān
⇐ lsan
ilsien

ETHIOPIC

nessal
mälḥās
ləssān
mäläs
mäläs
mäläs
arrāt
anäβät alämät

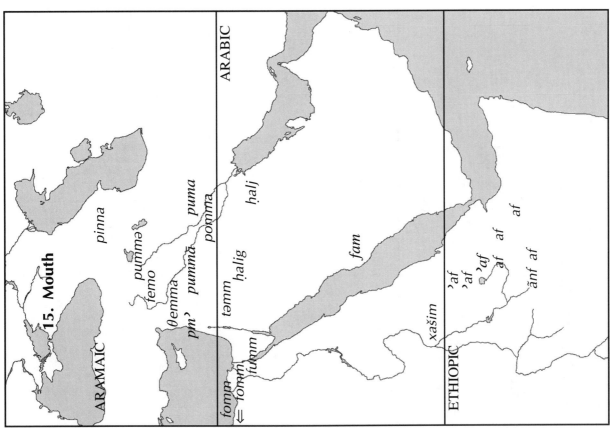

15. Mouth

ARAMAIC

pinna
pumme
femo
θemma
pm'
pummā
puma
puma
pomma

ARABIC

təmm
ḥalig
ḥalj
fam
xašim
⇐ fomm
fomm
fumm

ETHIOPIC

'af
'af
'af
af
af
af
af
änf af

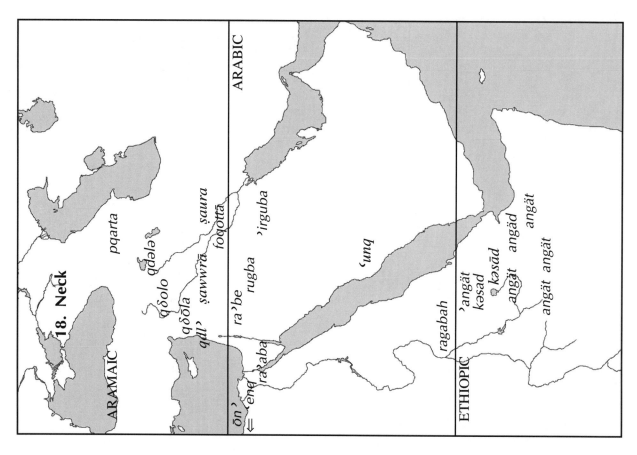

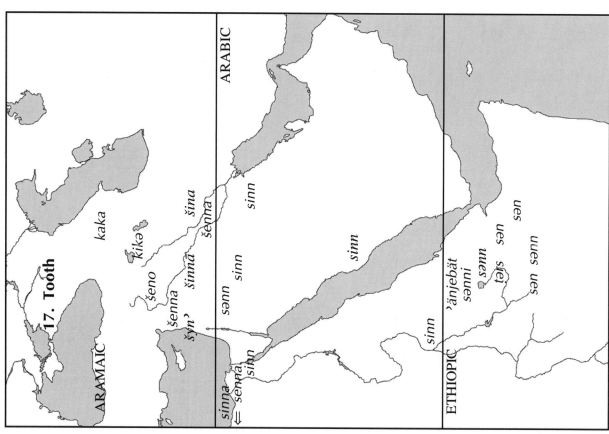

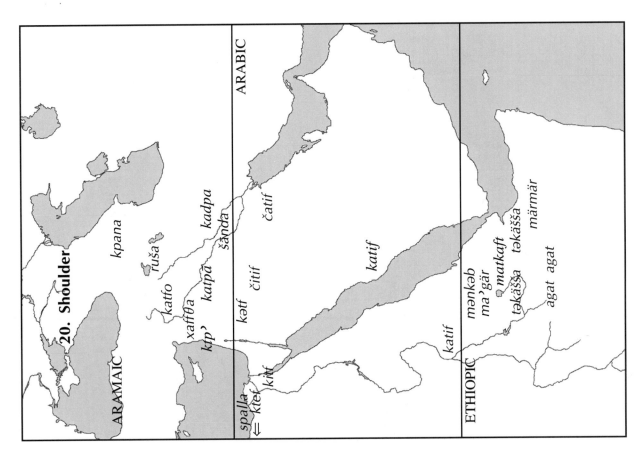

20. Shoulder

ARAMAIC

kpana
ruša
katfo
xatθa
ktp'
katpā
kadpa
šānda

ARABIC

čatif
čitif
kotf
ktf
ktef
spalla ⇐
katif
katif

ETHIOPIC

mӕnkӕb
ma'gär
matkaft
tӕkӓšša
tӕkӓšša
märmär
agat agat

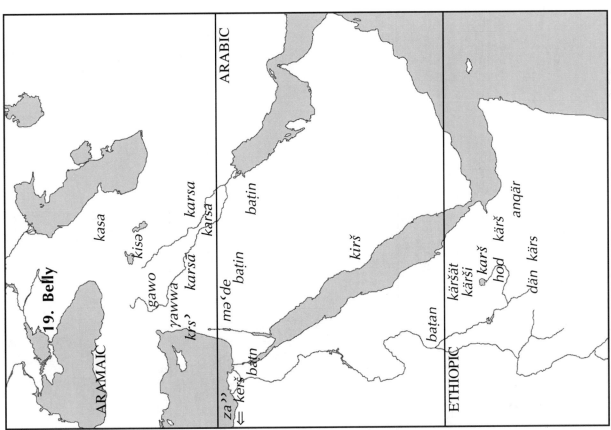

19. Belly

ARAMAIC

kasa
kise
gawo
yawwa
karsā
krs'
karsa
karsa

ARABIC

batin
batin
me'de
batn
kirš
batin ⇐ za''
kerš

ETHIOPIC

kӓršät
kärši
karš
hod
kärš
anqär
dän kärs
batan

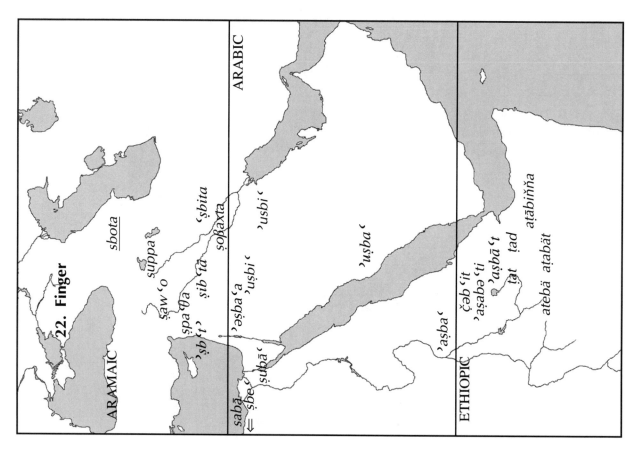

22. Finger

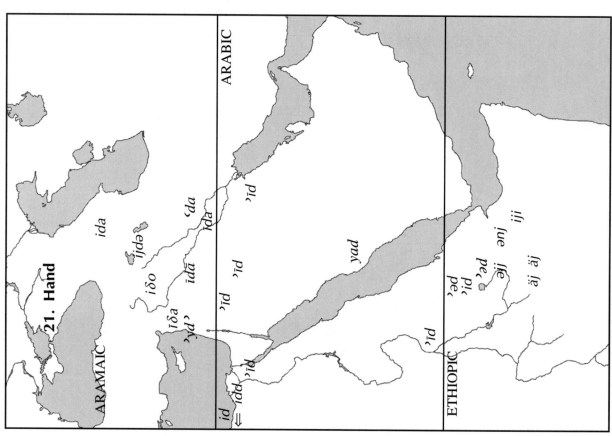

21. Hand

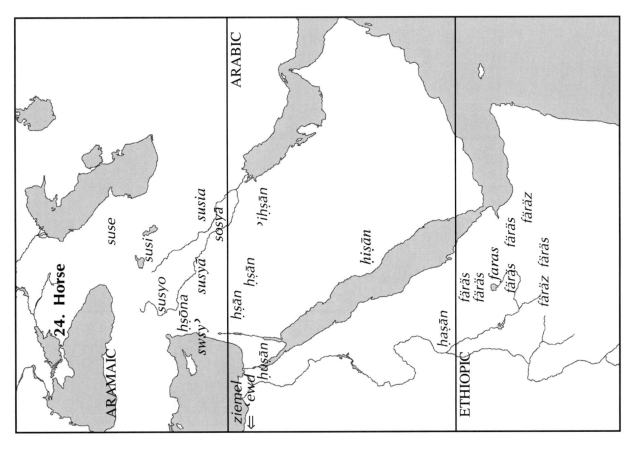

24. Horse

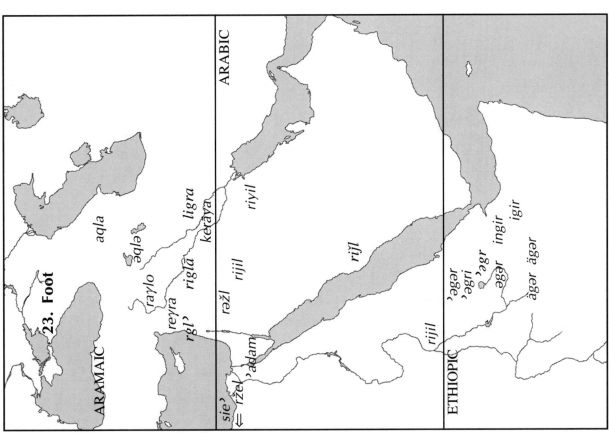

23. Foot

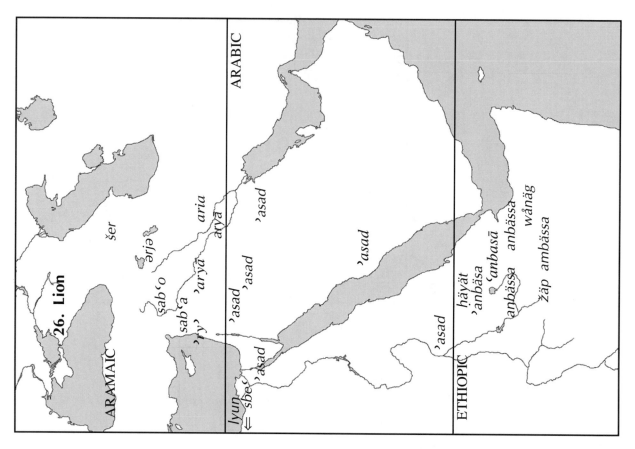

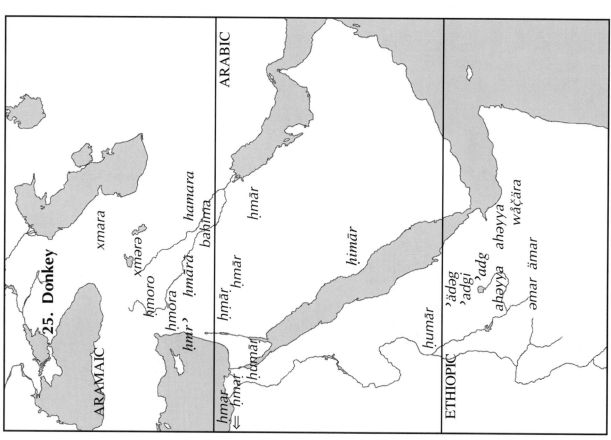

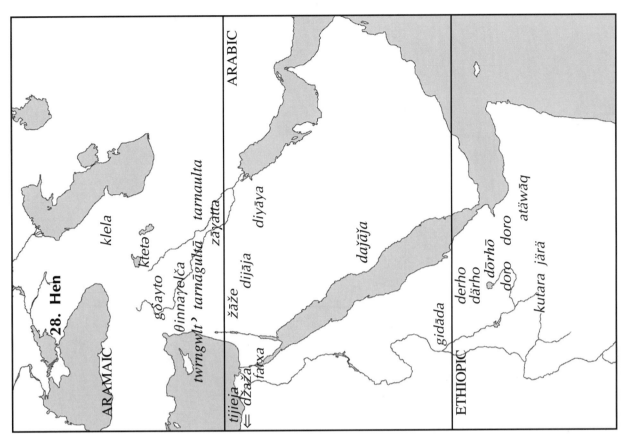

28. Hen

ARAMAIC

klela

ktete

gðayto

θinnaʔelča

twrngwlt> tarnāgultā tarnaulta

tarnaulta

zāχatta

ARABIC

žāže

dijāja

diyāya

dajāja

tījieja ⇐ džažā

farxa

gidāda

ETHIOPIC

derho

dārho

dōrhō

doro

doro

atāwāq

kutara jārā

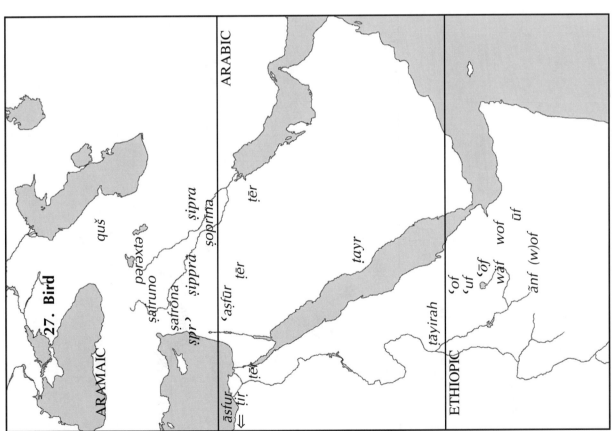

27. Bird

ARAMAIC

quš

pelexe

safruno

safrōna

ṣipr>

ṣipprā

ṣipra

ṣoprīna

ARABIC

ʕasfūr

tēr

tēr

tayr

tēr

āsfur ⇐ tīr

tāyirah

ETHIOPIC

ʕof

ʕuf

ʕōf

wāf

wof

ūf

ānf (w)of

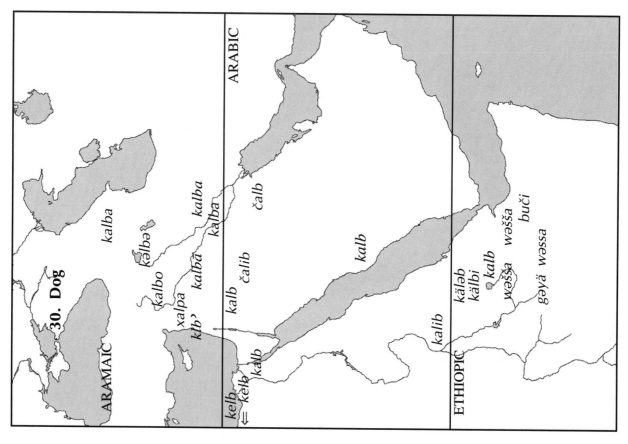

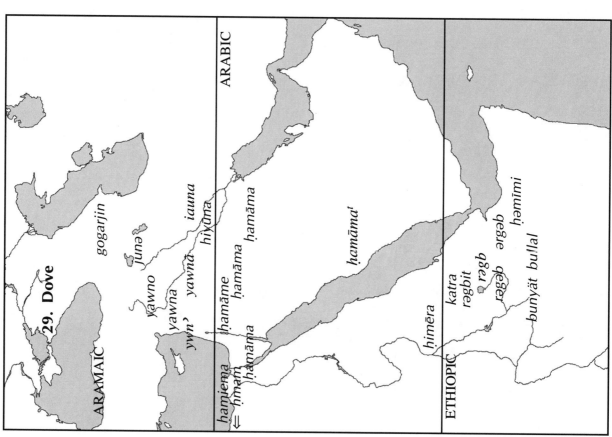

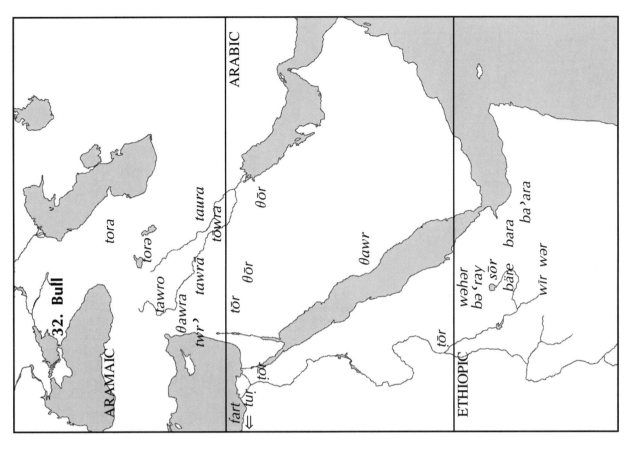

32. Bull

ARAMAIC

tora
tore
tawro
θawra
twrʾ
tawrā
tawrā
taura
tōwra

ARABIC

θōr
tōr *θōr*
θawr
tōr
tōr

fart ⇐ *tuṯ tōr*

ETHIOPIC

weḥer
baʿray *sōr*
bāṯe *bara*
wīr wər
baʾara

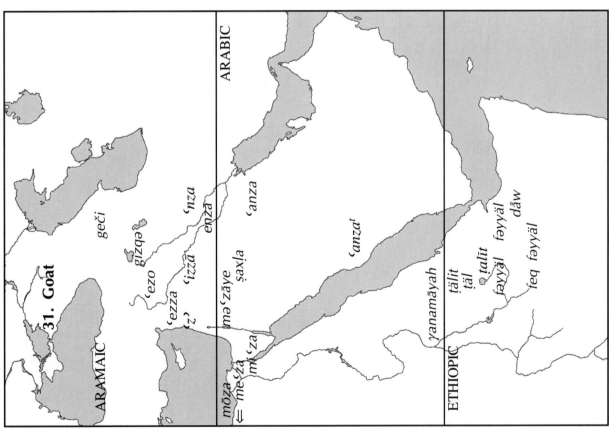

31. Goat

ARAMAIC

geči
gizboza
ʿezo
ʿezza
ʿizzā
ʿz
ʿnza
enza
ʿanza

ARABIC

maʿzāye
ṣaxla
meʿza
ʿanzaᵗ

mōza ⇐ *meʿza*

ETHIOPIC

γanamāyah
tālit
tāl *talit*
fəyyāl *fəyyāl* *dåw*
feq fəyyāl

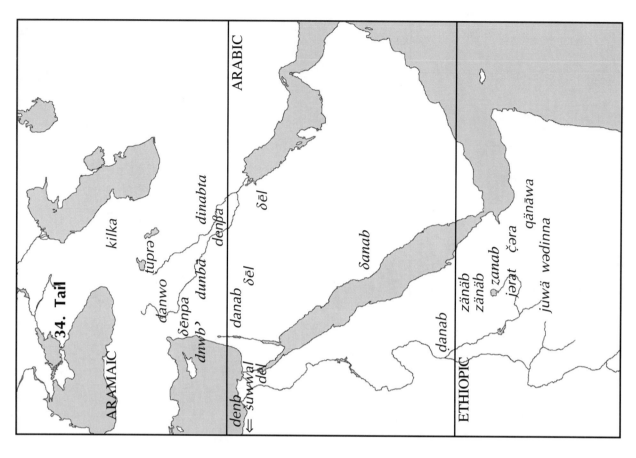

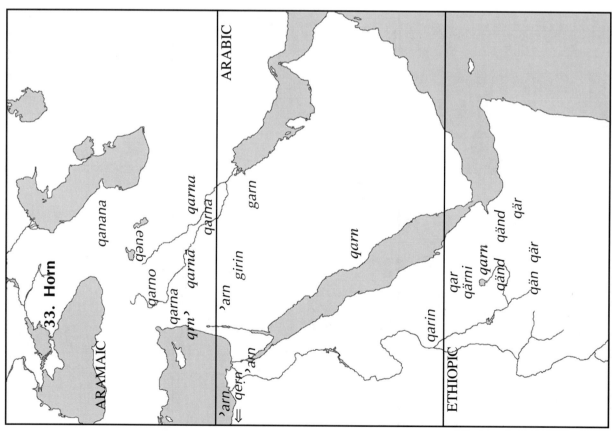

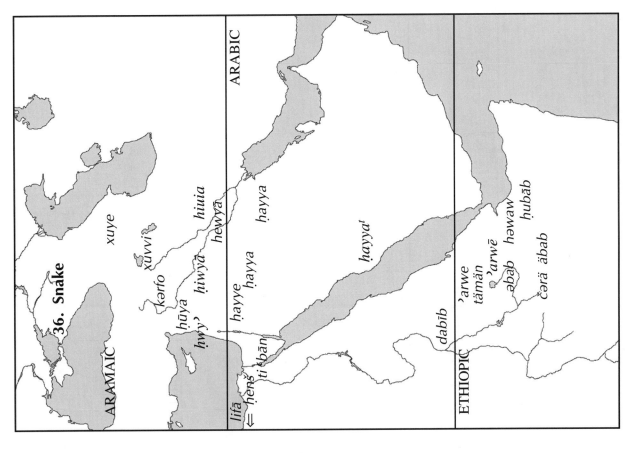

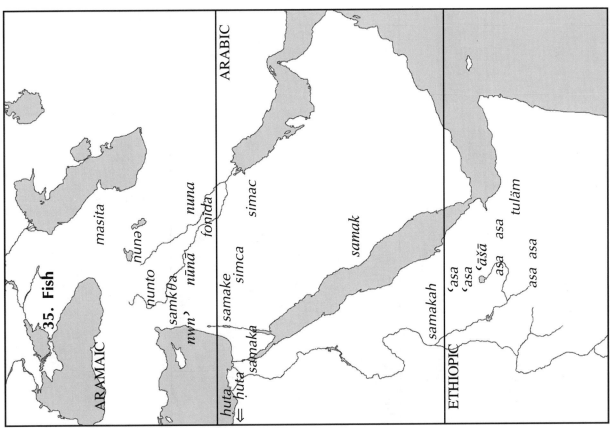

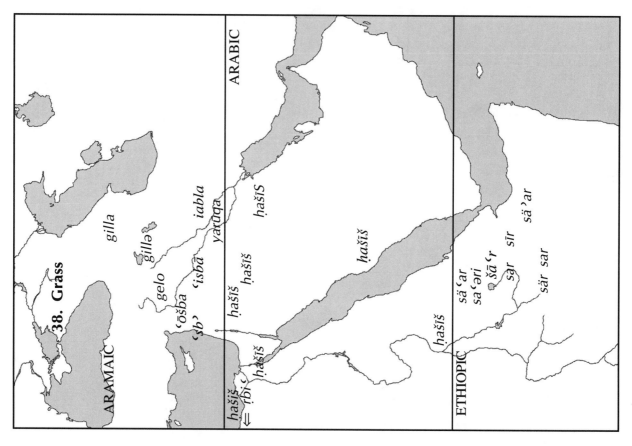

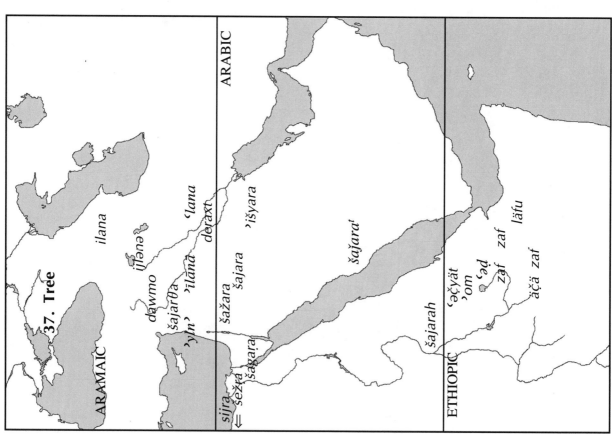

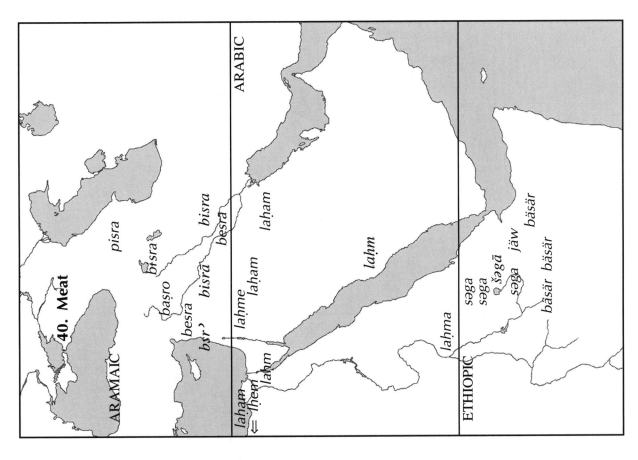

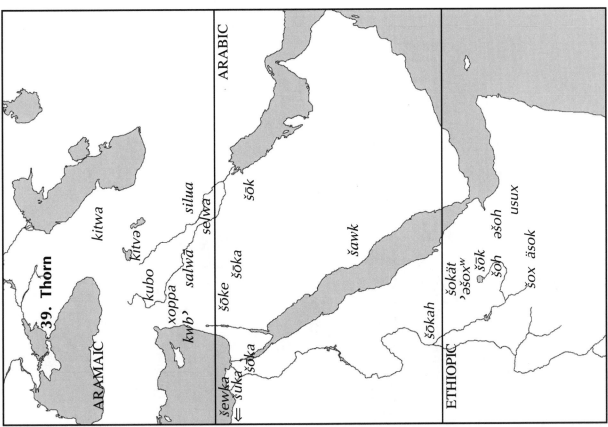

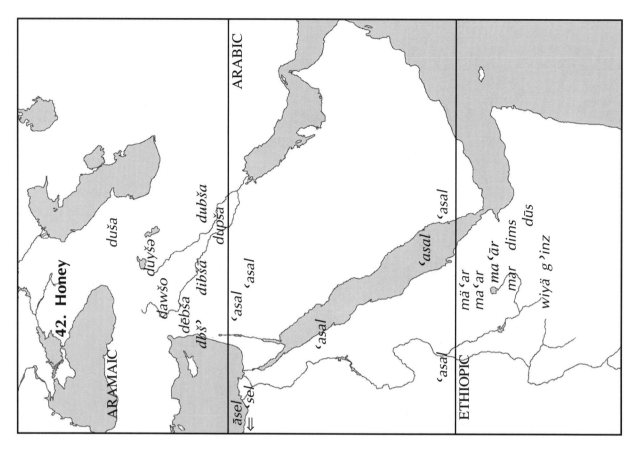

42. Honey

ARAMAIC

duša

duyšə

ḏawšo

dēbsa

dibšā

dubša

dubša

dḇš'

dḇš

duⁱpša

ARABIC

ʿasal

ʿasal

ʿasal

ʿasal

ʿasal

ʿasal

ʿasal

ʿasal

ʿasal

āsel
⇐ *sel*

ETHIOPIC

mä ʿar

ma ʿar

ma ʿār

mạr   *dims*

dūs

wiyä g ʾinz

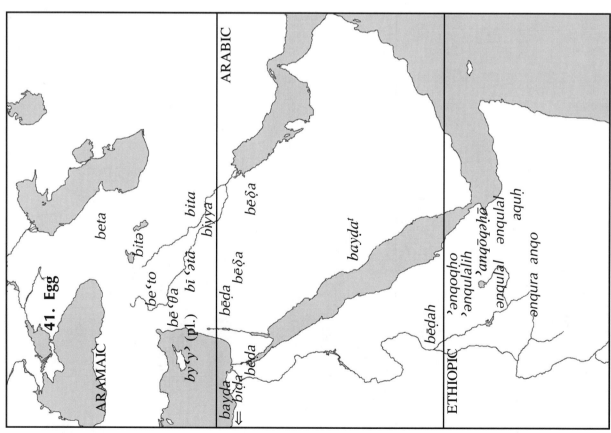

41. Egg

ARAMAIC

beta

bita

bita

beʿto

bē ʿθa

bī ʿtā

biⁱyya

bēḍa

bēḍa

by ʿy' (pl.)

bayḍa
⇐ *biḍa*

bēda

bēda

bēḍa

bēḍa

bayḍạᵗ

ARABIC

bēdah

ETHIOPIC

ʾoḥoḇue, oḥoḇue

ʾanḥoḇue, ʾḥeḇọḥue

ʾanḥalälih

ʾenḥue l aḥuḥ

ʾenḥue l aḥuḥ

ʾenḥue l

ʾanqura anqo

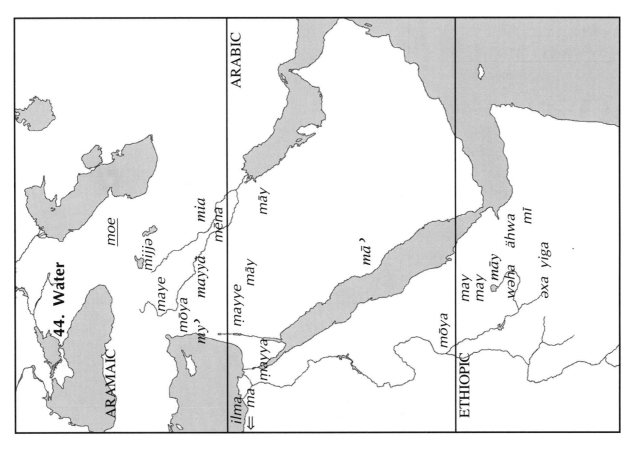

44. Water

ARAMAIC

moe
mijje
maye
mōya
may⁾
mayyā
mayya
mia
mēna
mayye
may

ARABIC
may
mā⁾
mōya
⟸ *ma*
ilma

ETHIOPIC
may
may
māy
weḥa
āhwa
mī
əxa yiga

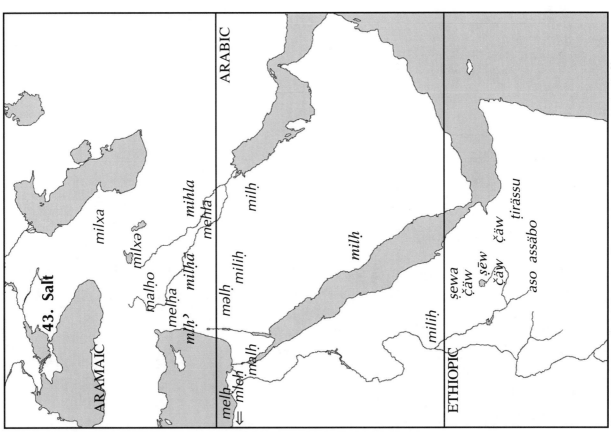

43. Salt

ARAMAIC

milxa
melxu
malho
melḥa
milḥā
mihla
meḥā
mlḥ⁾
melḥ
⟸ *mleḥ*
melḥ
milh
miliḥ

ARABIC
milḥ
milḥ
miliḥ

ETHIOPIC
šewa
čāw
sēw
čāw
čāw
tirāssu
aso assābo

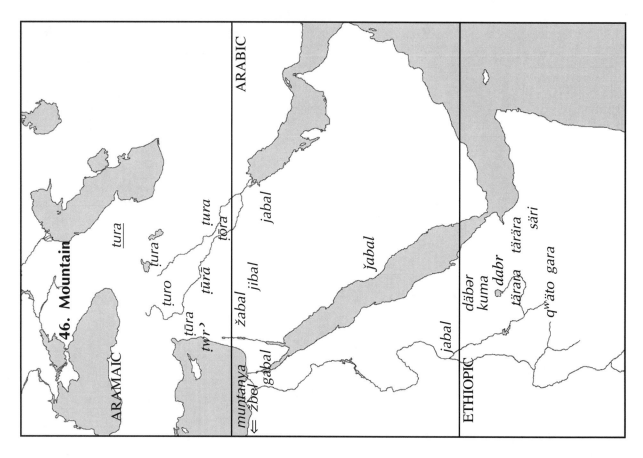

46. Mountain

ARAMAIC

tura
ţura
ţura
turo
tura
tūrā
tūrā
tōra
tūra
ṭwrʾ
ṭi

ARABIC

jabal
žabal
jibal
ǰabal
ǰabal
gabal
jabal
muntanya
⇐ *žbel*

ETHIOPIC

dābr
dāber
kuma
tārāra
sāri
tāraħa
qʷāto gara

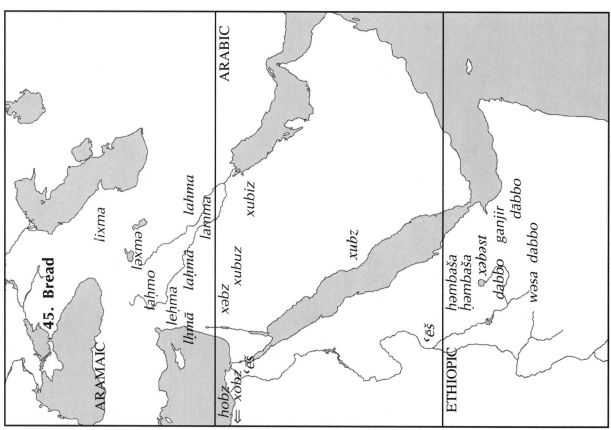

45. Bread

ARAMAIC

lixma
lèxmel
laħmo
lahma
lehma
laħmā
lahma
lḥmā
lanma
hobz
⇐ *xòbz*

ARABIC

xubiz
xubz
xubuz
xəbz
ʿēš
ʿēš

ETHIOPIC

ħembaša
ħembaša
xəbəst
dabbo
ganjir
dābbo
tseqex
wəsa dabbo

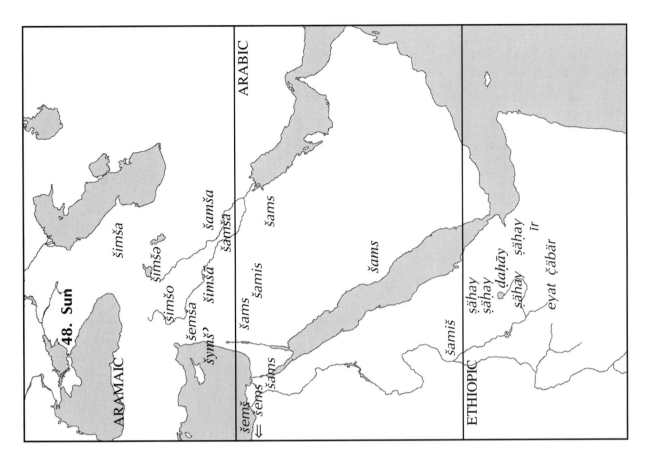

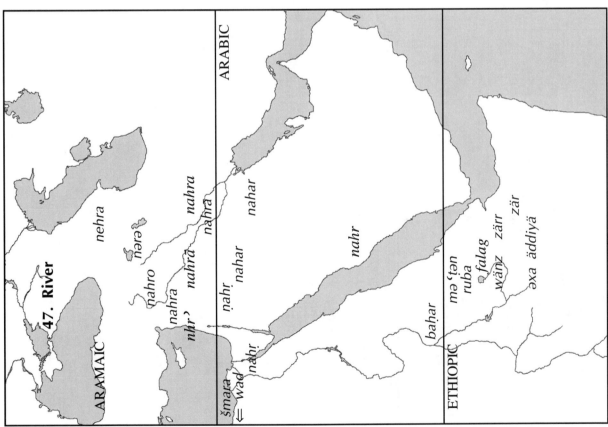

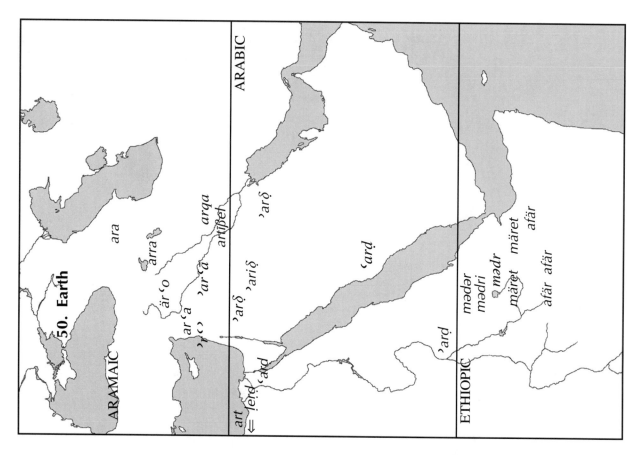

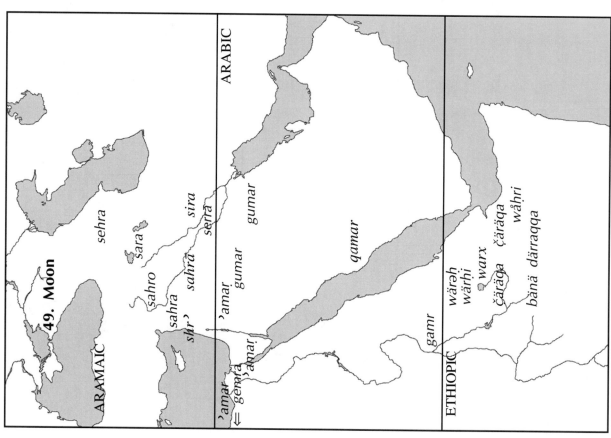

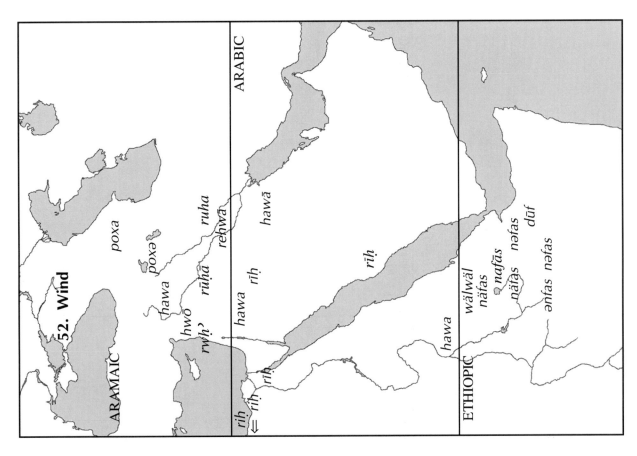

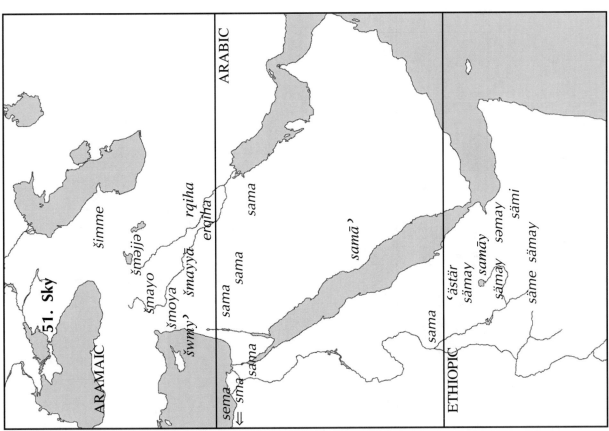

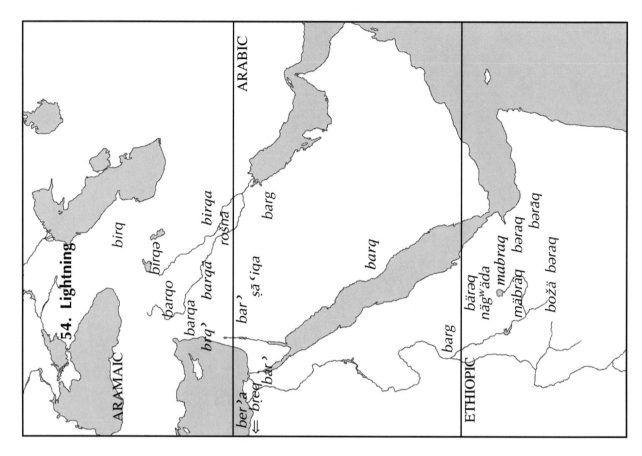

54. Lightning

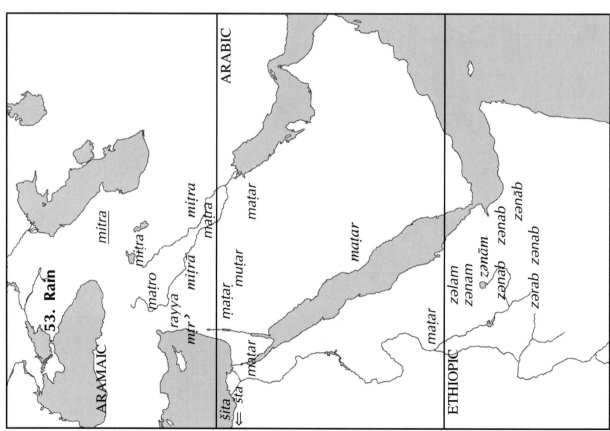

53. Rain

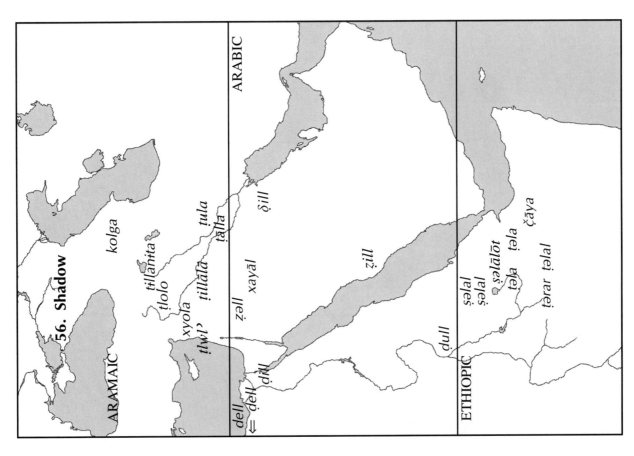

56. Shadow

ARAMAIC

kolga

tïllänita
tïolo
tïllālā tula
xyola tïllālā
tïwlˀ tåĺĺa

zĕll
xayāl

ẟill

⇐ dėll
ḋill

zill

dull

ARABIC

ETHIOPIC

seš selal
seš selal
salālōt
tela tela
terar tela čåya

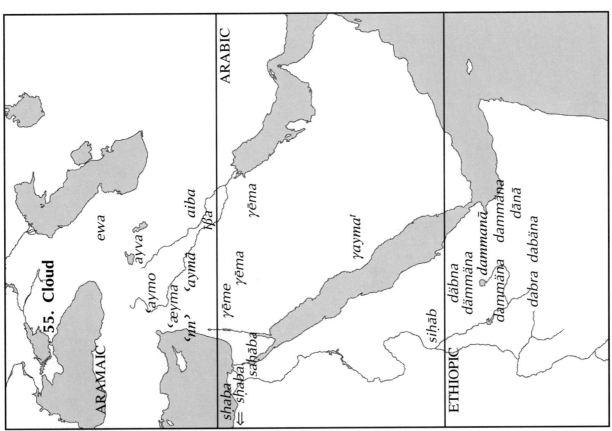

55. Cloud

ARAMAIC

ewa

ʿaymo
ʿæyma
ˀnn ʿaymā aiba
ȶβa

ɣēme
ɣēma

ɣēma

ɣaymaᵗ

⇐ shaba
sihaba sahāba

sihāb

ARABIC

ETHIOPIC

dābna
dämmäna dammanā
dammāna dammāna
dabra dabāna
dānā

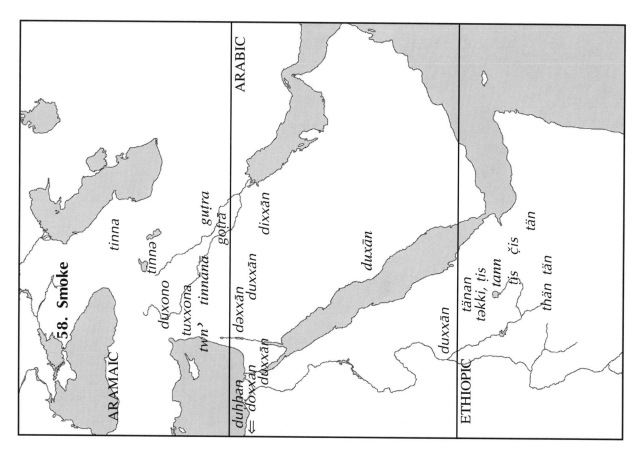

58. Smoke

ARAMAIC

tinna

tinne

duxono

tuxxona

twn⁾

tinnānā

tinnānā

guṭra

goṭra

ARABIC

dexxān

duxxān

dixxān

duxxān

duhhan

doxxān

duxxān

duxxān

ETHIOPIC

tänan

täkki, tis

tann

tis

čis

tän

thän tän

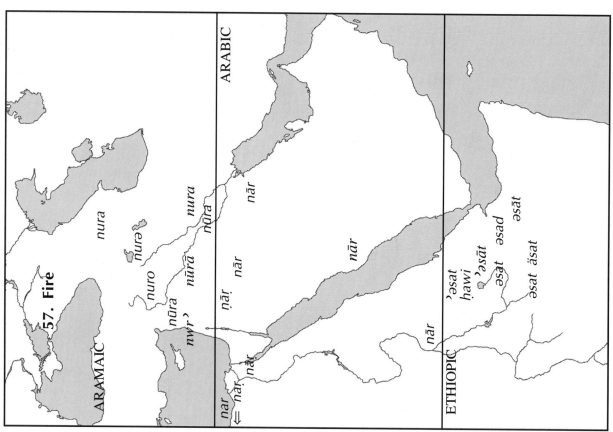

57. Fire

ARAMAIC

nura

nure

nuro

nura

nwr⁾

nūra

nūrā

nura

nūra

ARABIC

nāṛ

nār

nār

nār

nār

nār

nār

ETHIOPIC

⁾əsat

ḥawi

⁾əsāt

əse

əse

pəse

əsāt

əsat äsat

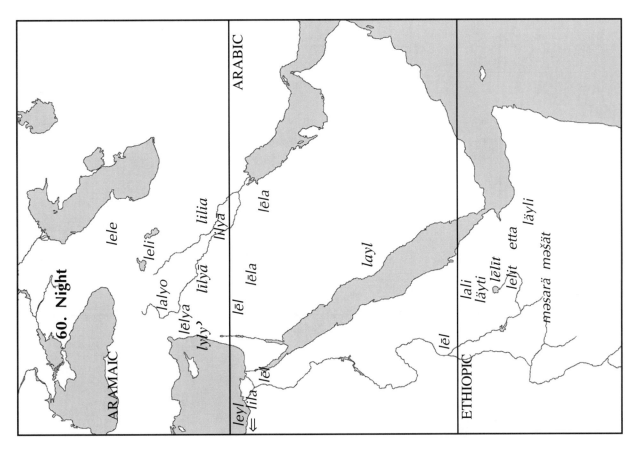

60. Night

ARAMAIC

lele

lalyo

lelî

lēlya

lilyā

lilia

lilya

lyly

ley

lila

ARABIC

lēla

lēl

lēla

lēla

layl

lēl

lēl

ETHIOPIC

lali

lāyti

lēlît

lelit

etta

lāyli

məsarä

məšät

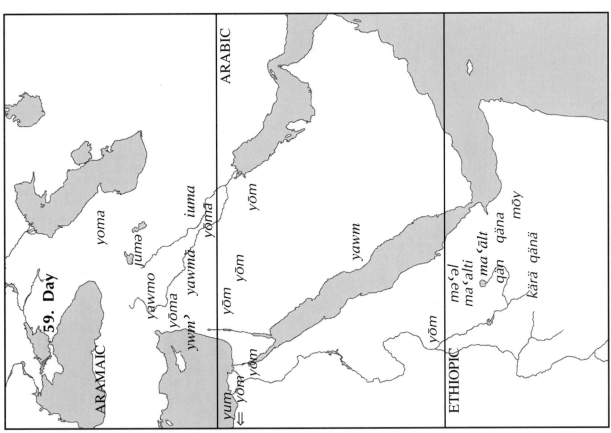

59. Day

ARAMAIC

yoma

ieum

iuma

yawmo

yōma

yawmā

ywm

yawmā

yōmā

yum

yōm

ARABIC

yōm

yōm

yōm

yōm

yawm

yōm

ETHIOPIC

məʿəl

maʿalti

maʿält

qān

qāna

mōy

kärä

qānä

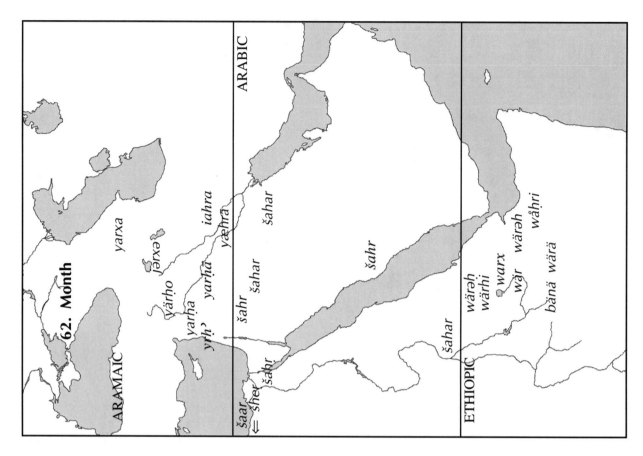

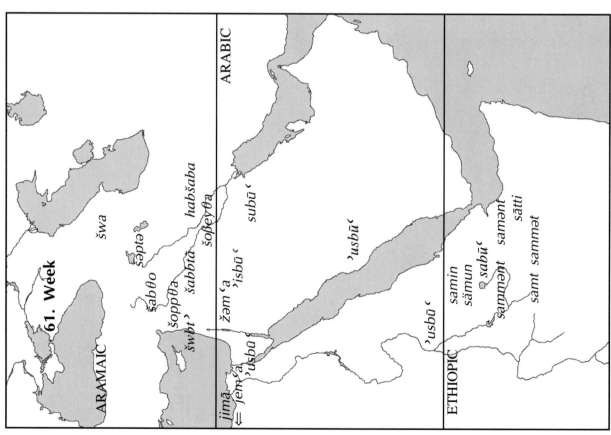

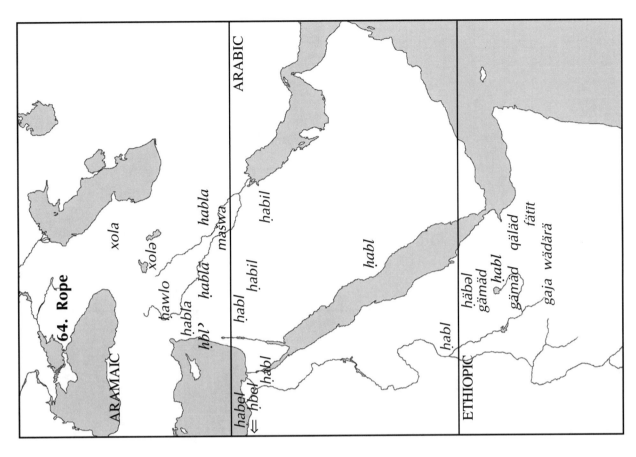

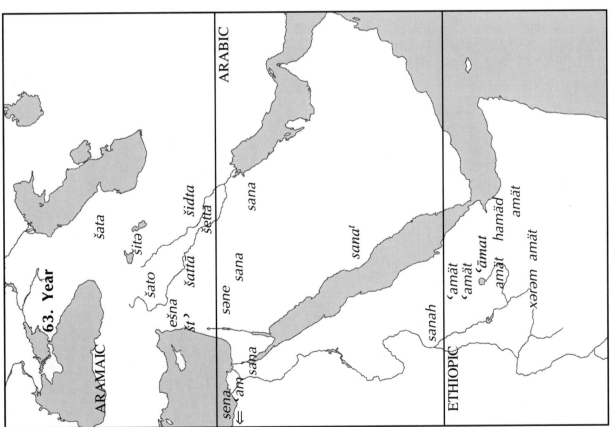

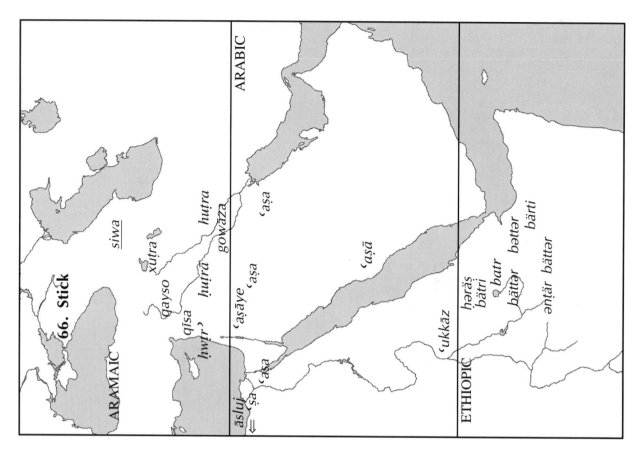

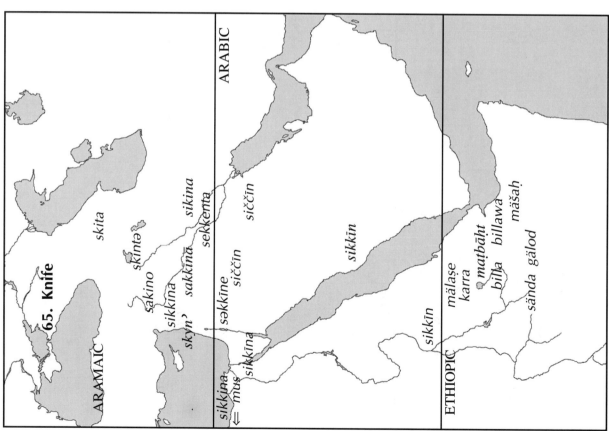

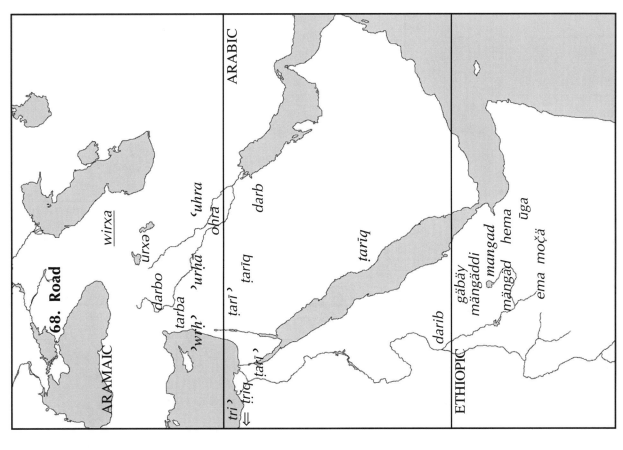

68. Road

ARAMAIC

wirxa

urxeꝑ

darbo

tarba

ꝑwrḥ

ꝑurḥā

tri ꝑ

⟸ ṭrīq

ṭari ꝑ

ṭarīq

ARABIC

ꝑuhra

ohra

darb

ṭarīq

darib

ETHIOPIC

gäbäy

mängäddi

mangad

mängäd

hema

ūga

ema močā

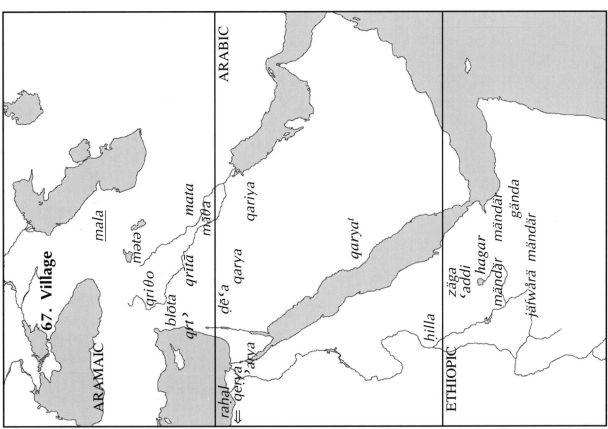

67. Village

ARAMAIC

mala

mete

qriθo

blōta

qrīꝑ

qrītā

mata

māθa

rahal

⟸ qerya

ꝑatya

ARABIC

dēꝏa

qarya

qariya

qarya

qaryat

ETHIOPIC

zäga

ꝏaddi

hagar

mändär

jäfwärä mändär

gända

mändär

hilla

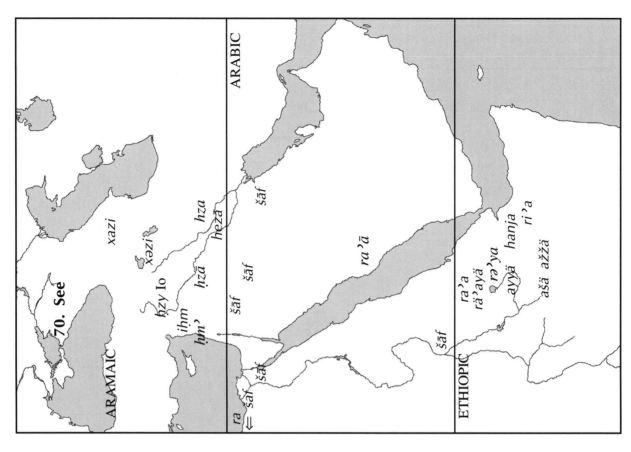

70. See

ARAMAIC

xazi
xəzi
ḥzy Io
ihm
ḥm'
ḥm'
ḥẓa
hza
heza

ARABIC

šaf
šaf
šaf
šaf
ra'ā
šaf
ra ⇐ šaf
šaf

ETHIOPIC

ra'a
rä'ayä
rə'ya
ayyä hanja
ašä ažžä
ri'a

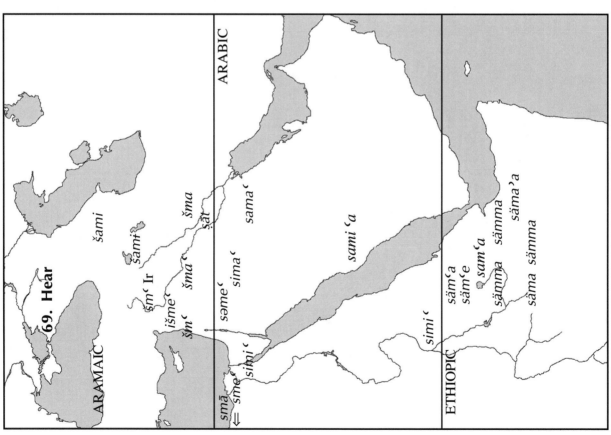

69. Hear

ARAMAIC

šami
šami
šm' Ir
išme'
šm'
šma'
šma'
šma
šat

ARABIC

šeme'
sima'
same'
sama'
sami'a
simi'
smä ⇐ šme'
simi'

ETHIOPIC

säm'a
säm'e
sam'a
sämma
sämma
säma'a
säma sämma

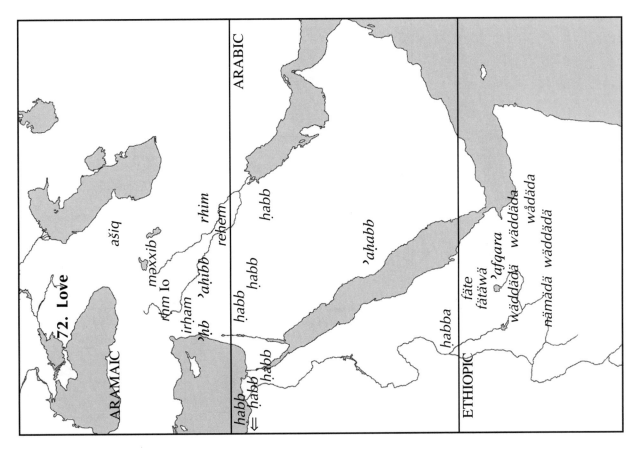

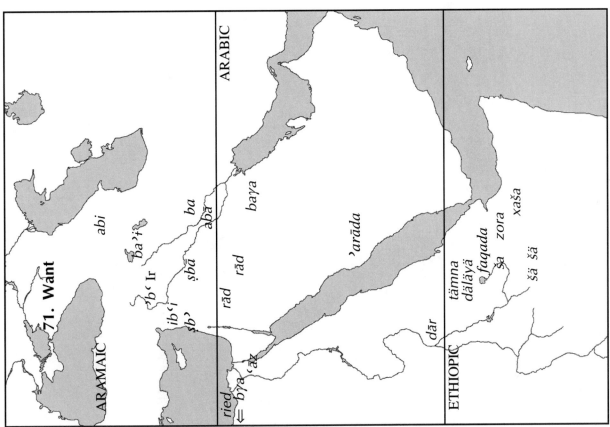

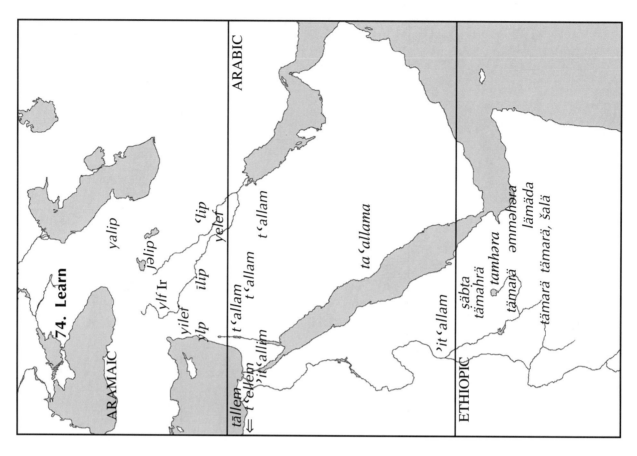

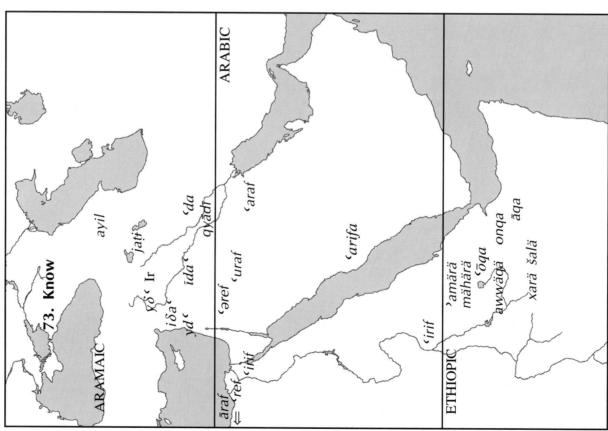

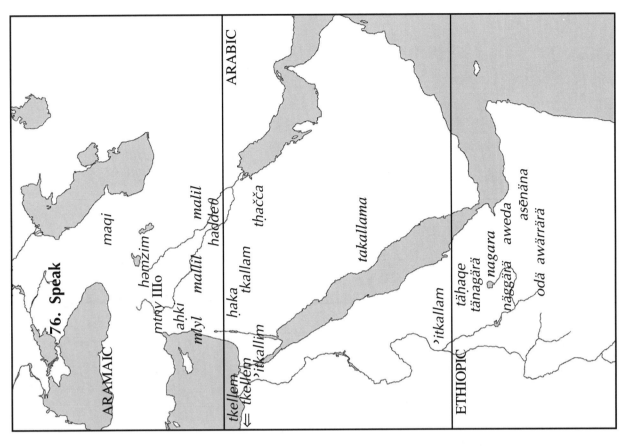

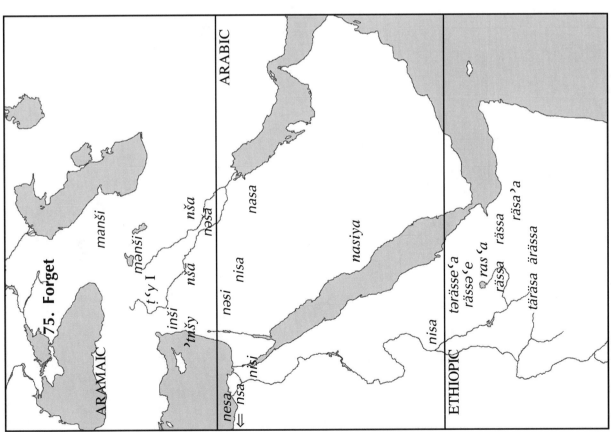

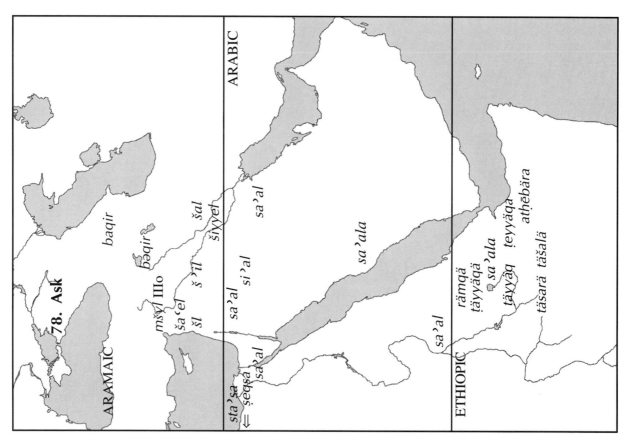

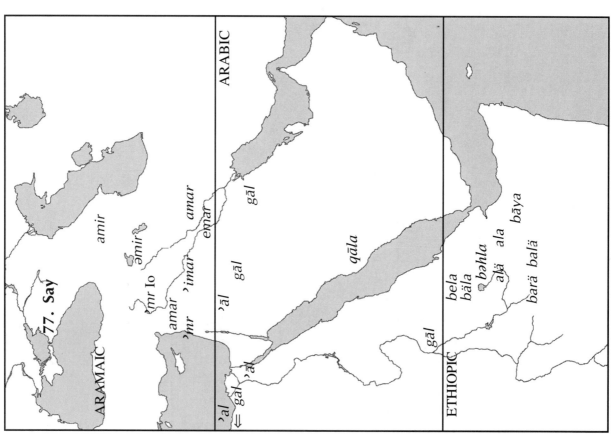

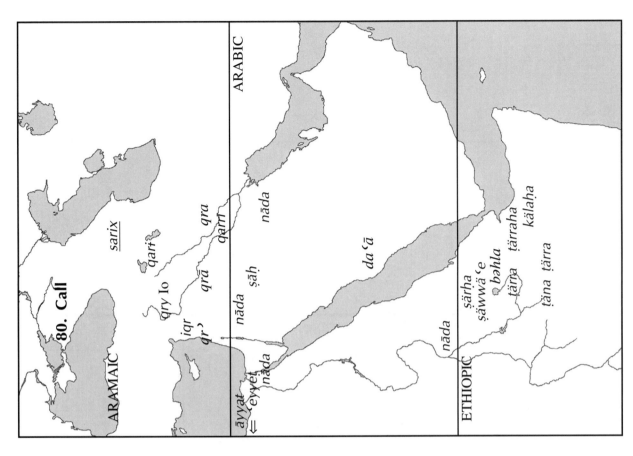

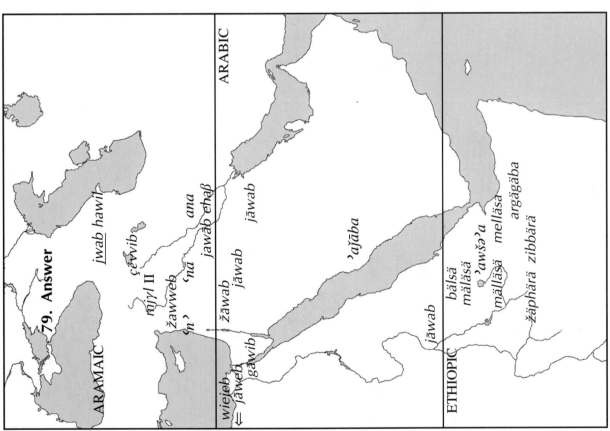

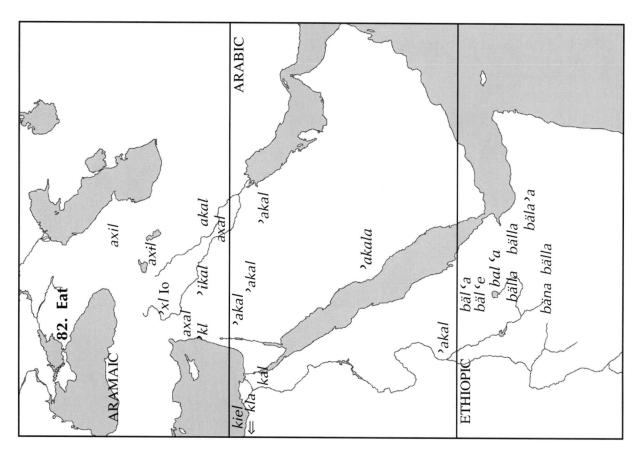

82. Eat

ARAMAIC

axil

axil
axil

ʾxl Io

ʾxl
ʾikal
akal

axal
akat

axal
ʾkl

ʾakal ʾakal

kal kaʾ

kiel
⇐ kla

ARABIC

ʾakal
ʾakal

ʾakala

ʾakal

ETHIOPIC

bälʿa
bälʿe bälʿa

bälla bälla

bäla ʾa

bäna bälla

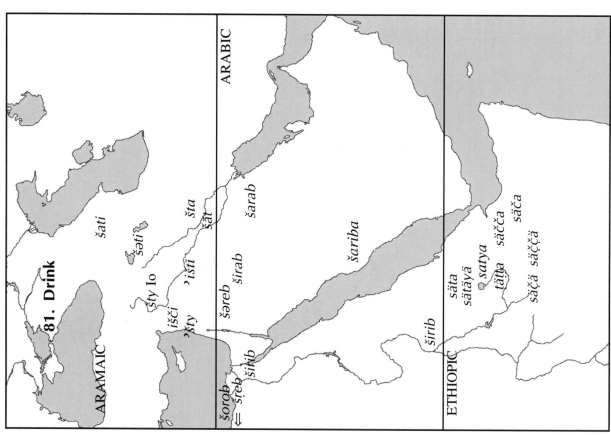

81. Drink

ARAMAIC

šati

šeti

šty Io

ʾištī šta
ʾištī šāt

išči
ʾšty

šəreb
širab

šorob šreb
⇐ šreb šiʾb

ARABIC

šarab

šariba

ETHIOPIC

sāta
sātäyä satya säčča
    tätta säča

širib

säčä säččä

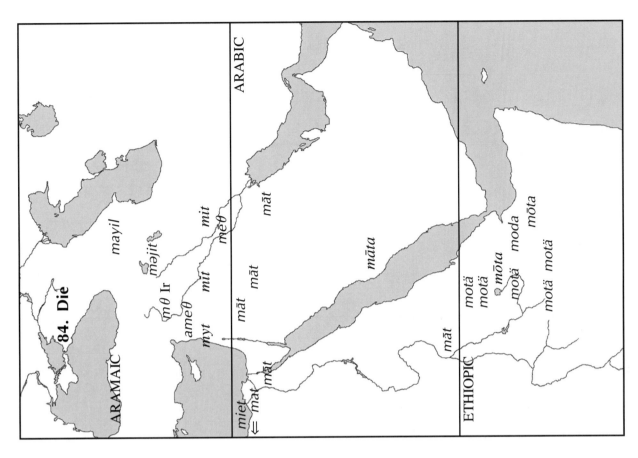

84. Die

ARAMAIC

mayil
məjit
ṃθ Ir
ṃθ
ameθ
mēθ
mit
mīt
mit
mīt
myt
miet ⇐
māt

ARABIC

māt
māt
māt
māt
māt
māt
māta

ETHIOPIC

motä
motä
mōta
motä
moda
mōta
motä
motä motä

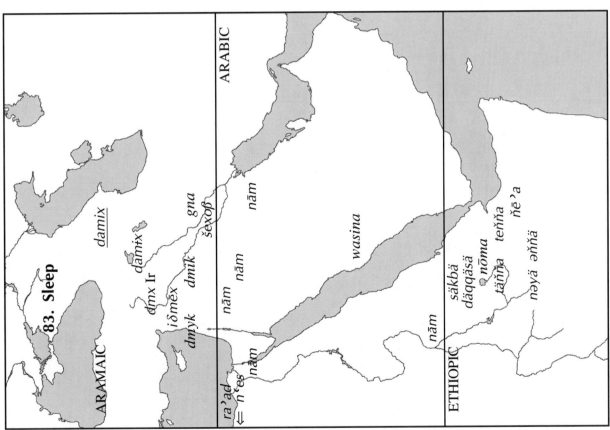

83. Sleep

ARAMAIC

damix
damix
dṃx Ir
iδmēx
dmyk
dmīk
gna
šexoβ
raʾad
nʿes ⇐
nãm

ARABIC

nãm
nãm
nãm
nãm
wasina

ETHIOPIC

säkbä
dãqqäsä
nōma
täñña
teñña
ñēʾa
nǝyä ǝñña

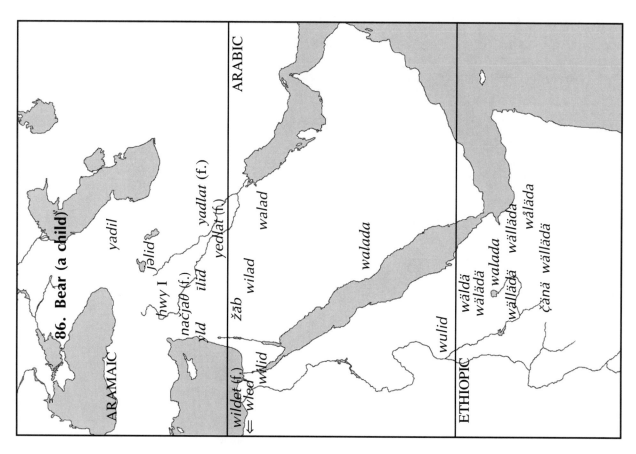

86. Bear (a child)

ARAMAIC

yadil

ʔəlidˀ

ḥwy I

naǧǧaθ (f.)

ʔyld

 īlidˀ

yadlat (f.)

yedlat (f.)

ARABIC

žāb

walad

wilad

walada

walad

wulid

wᵂlid

wildet (f.)
⇐ wled

ETHIOPIC

wäldä

wälläda

walada

wällädä

wällädä

wälädä

čänä wällädä

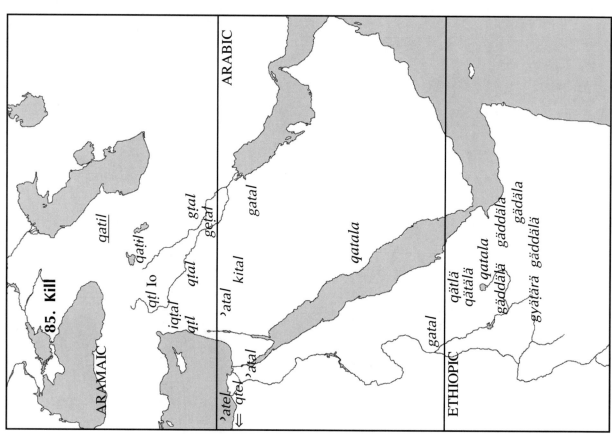

85. Kill

ARAMAIC

qatil

qatil

qṭl Io

iqtal

qṭl

qṭal

qṭal

gṭal

geṭal

ARABIC

ʔatal

kital

gatal

qatala

gatal

ʔatel
⇐ qtel

ʔatal

ETHIOPIC

qätlä

qätälä

qatala

gäddälä

gäddälä

gädälä

gyätärä gäddälä

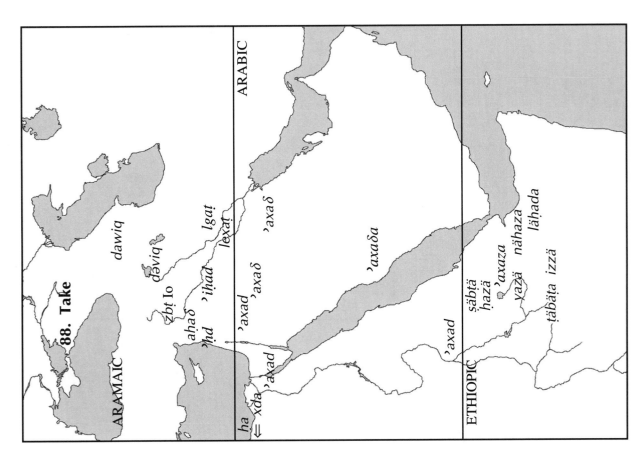

88. Take

ARAMAIC

dawiq

dəwiq

ʿbt Io

ʾahaδ

ʾd

ʾihad

lgat

lexat

ha ⇐ xda

ARABIC

ʾaxad

ʾaxad

ʾaxaδ

ʾaxaδ

ʾaxaδa

ʾaxad

ETHIOPIC

sābtä

ḥazā

ʾaxaza

yazä nähaza

lāhada

tābäta izzā

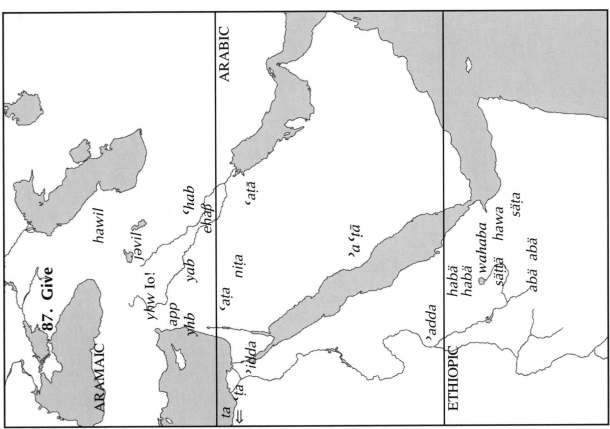

87. Give

ARAMAIC

hawil

jəwil

yhw Io!

ʿhb

app

yhb

yab

ʿhab

eḥaβ

ta ⇐ tä

ʾidda

ARABIC

ʿata

nita

ʿatā

ʿaʿtā

ʾadda

ETHIOPIC

habä

habä

wahaba

sätä hawa

sätä

abä abä

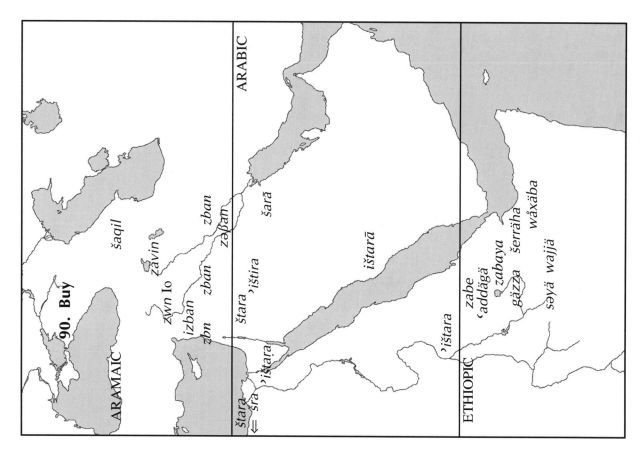

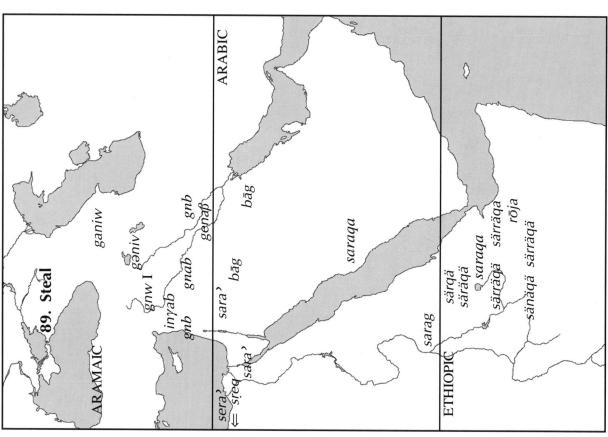

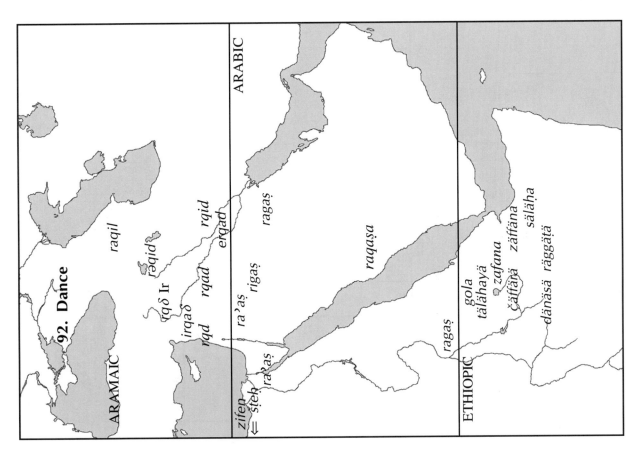

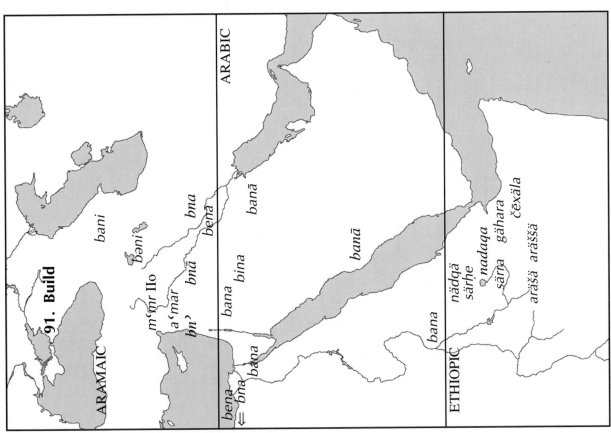

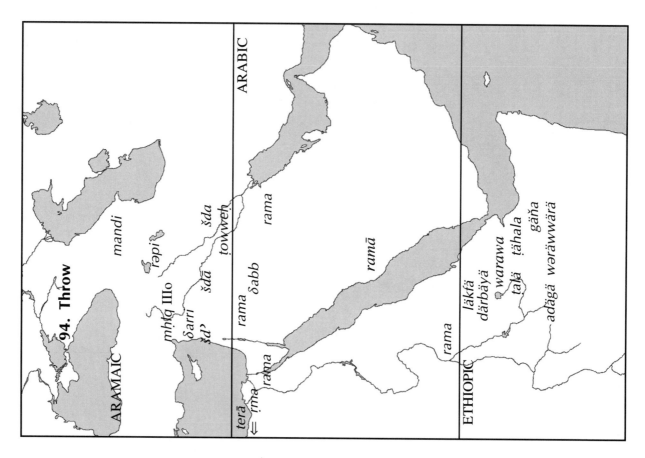

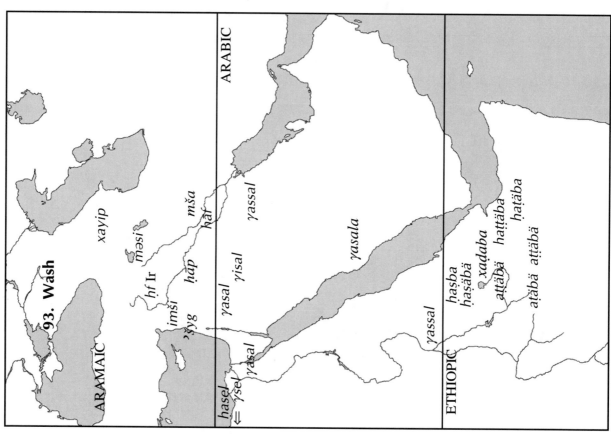

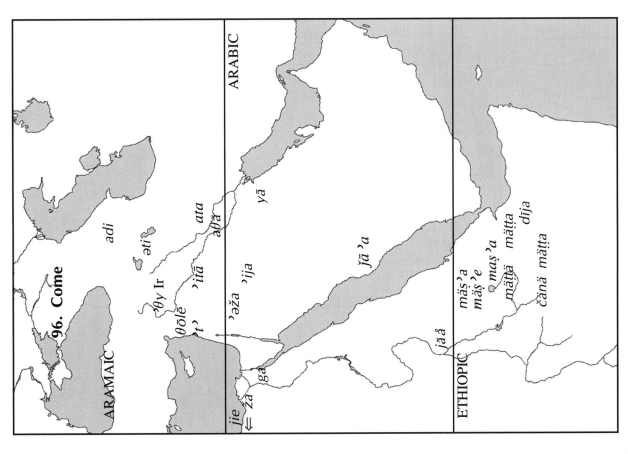

96. Come

ARAMAIC

adi

ēti⁾

θy Ir

ⁿitā

ⁿt⁾

θōlē

ⁿt⁾

ⁿəža

ⁿija

ata

aθā

ARABIC

yā

jā⁾a

jāå

⇐ ža

ga

jie

ETHIOPIC

māṣ⁾a
māṣ⁾e

maṣ⁾a

mättä

mättä

dija

čänä mättä

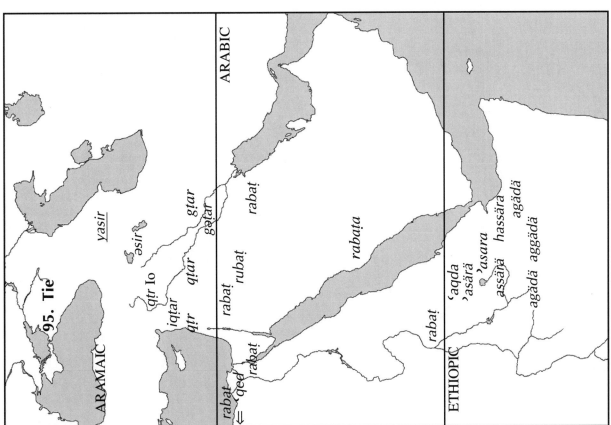

95. Tie

ARAMAIC

yasir

əsir⁾

qṭr Io

iqṭar

qṭr

gṭar

qṭar

gəṭar

ARABIC

rabaṭ

rubaṭ

rabaṭ

rabaṭa

rabaṭ

rabaṭ

⇐ qed⁾

rabaṭ

ETHIOPIC

ⁿaqda

ⁿasärä

ⁿasara

assärä

hassärä

agädä

agädä aggädä

210   *Wordlist E: Isoglosses*

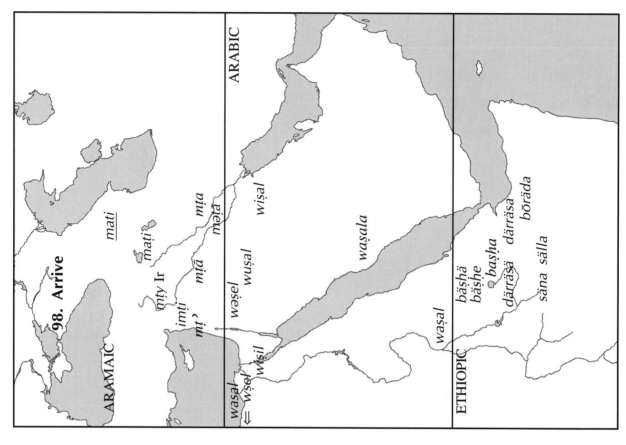

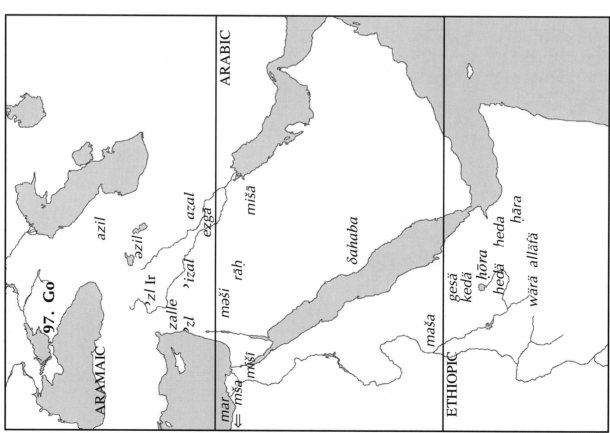

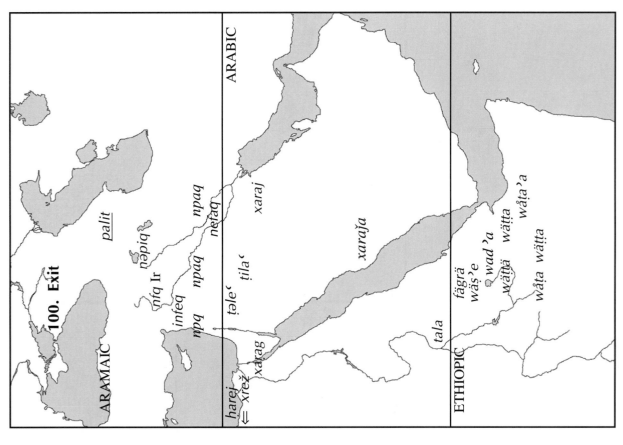

100. Exit

ARAMAIC

palit

nəpēq
Ir *np*
nfq Ir
infeq
npq

npaq
npaq
npaq
nefaq

ARABIC

xaraj

xaraja

tələ‘
ṭila‘

harej
⇐ *xrēž*
xaṛag

tala

ETHIOPIC

fägrä
wäṣ’e
wad’a
wätta
wätta
wåṭa
wåṭa’a
wätta

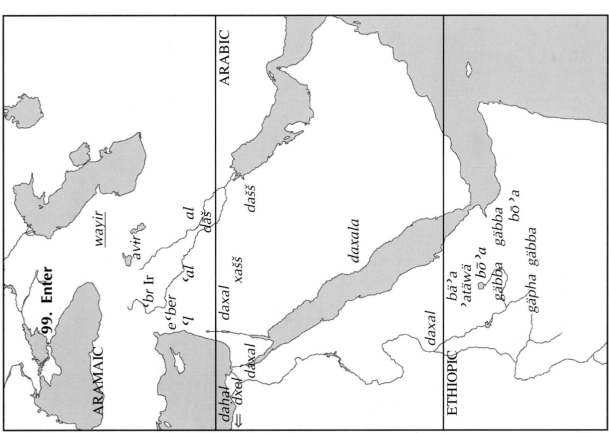

99. Enter

ARAMAIC

wayir

ävir
‘br Ir
e‘ber
‘l

al
‘al

ARABIC

dašš

daxala

daxal
xašš
daš

dahal
⇐ *dxel*
daxal

daxal

ETHIOPIC

bä’a
’atäwä
bō’a
gäbba
gäbba
bō’a
gäpha gäbba

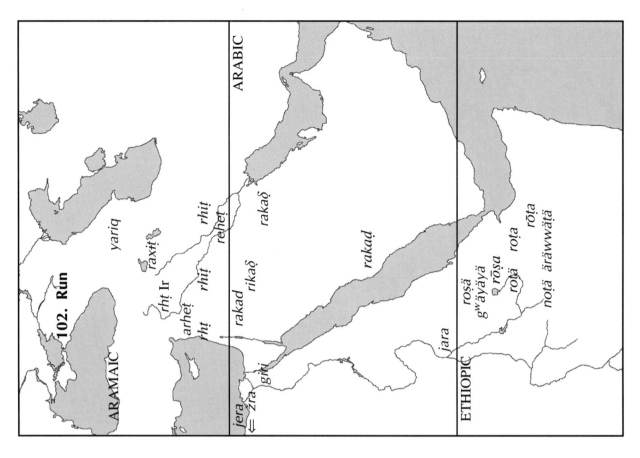

102. Rún

ARAMAIC

yariq

ʾaxiṭ

rḥiṭ Ir

rḥiṭ

rḥiṭ

rḥiṭ

reḥeṭ

arḥeṭ

rḥiṭ

rakad

rikaḏ

rakaḏ

rakaḏ

rakaḏ

ARABIC

jera ⇐ žra

giṭi

jara

ETHIOPIC

roṣä

gʷäyäyä

rōṣa

roṭä

rota

rōṭa

noṭä äräwwäṭä

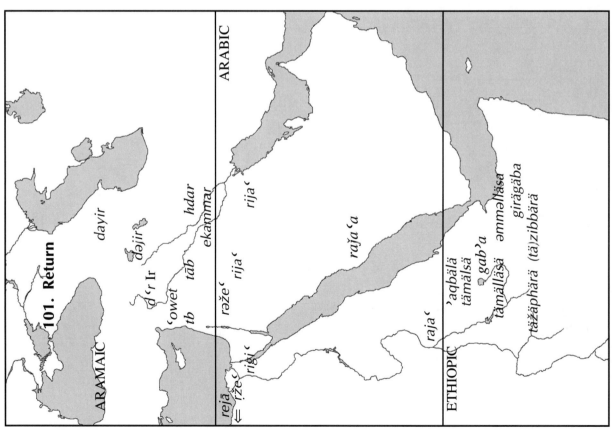

101. Rèturn

ARAMAIC

dayir

dejir

dʿr Ir

ʿowet

tb

tāb

hdar

ekammar

reže

rija

riǧa

riǧaʿa

raǧaʿa

ARABIC

rejā ⇐ řže

riǧiʿ

raja

ETHIOPIC

ʾaqbälä

tämälsä

gabʾa

tämälläsä

emmelläsa

girägäba

täžäphärä (täzibbärä)

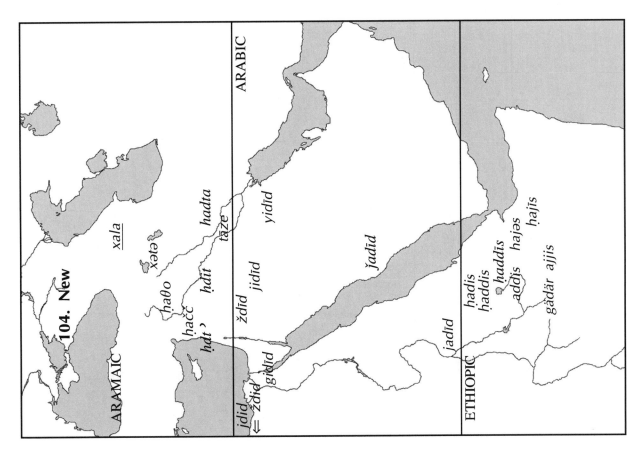

104. New

ARAMAIC

xala

xetex

haθo

hačč

hдtt

hдtt

hдitt

hadta

tāze

ARABIC

ždīd

jidīd

yidīd

jidīd

ǧadīd

jidīd ⇐

ǧidīd

jadīd

ETHIOPIC

hadis

haddis

haddīs

addis

hajes

gädär

ajis

hajīs

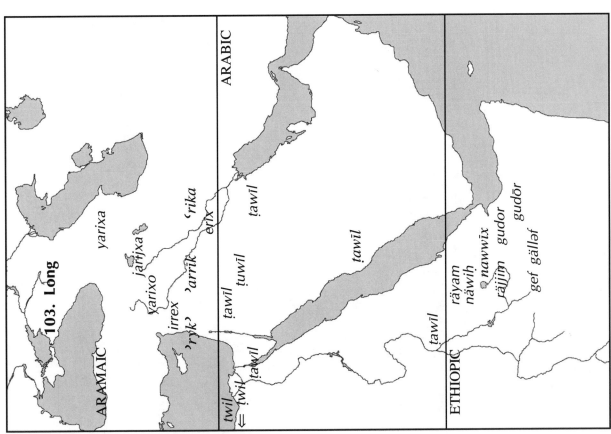

103. Long

ARAMAIC

yarixa

jārỉjxa

yarixo

irrex

ᵓrýkᵓ

ᵓarrīk

ᶜarrīk

ᶜrika

erīx

ARABIC

ṭawīl

tuwīl

ṭawil ⇐

ṭawīl

ṭawīl

ṭawil

ṭawil

ETHIOPIC

räyam

näwiḥ

näwwix

räjjim

gudor

gudōr

gef

gällef

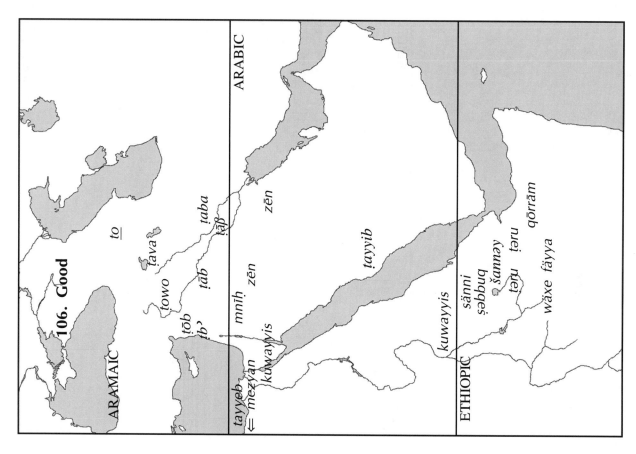

106. Good

ARAMAIC: to, ṭāvā, towo, ṭāḇ, ṭaba, ṭāb, ṭāḇ, ṭōb, ṭb², tayyeb, mezyan, mnīḥ, zēn, kuwayyis

ARABIC: zēn, zēn, tayyib, kuwayyis, kuwayyis

ETHIOPIC: sānni, bnqeš, šannay, ṣebbuq, ṛeꜣi, ṛeꜣi, qōrrām, wāxe, fāyya

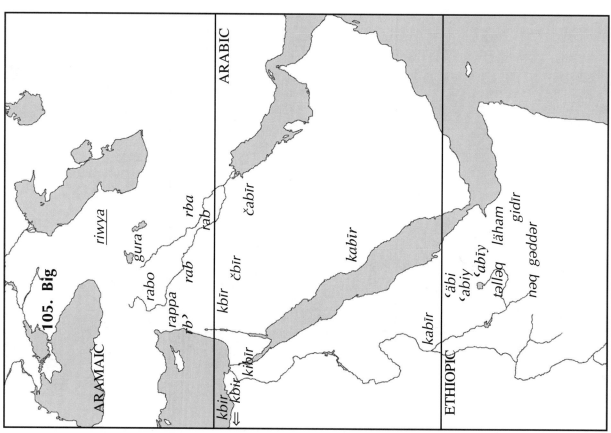

105. Big

ARAMAIC: riwya, gura, rba, rab, rabo, rappa, rab, rb², kbīr, čbīr, kbir, kbir

ARABIC: čabir, kabir, kabir, kabir

ETHIOPIC: ꜥābi, ꜥabiy, ꜥabīy, tälläq, beꜥu, läham, gidir, ṣeppeš

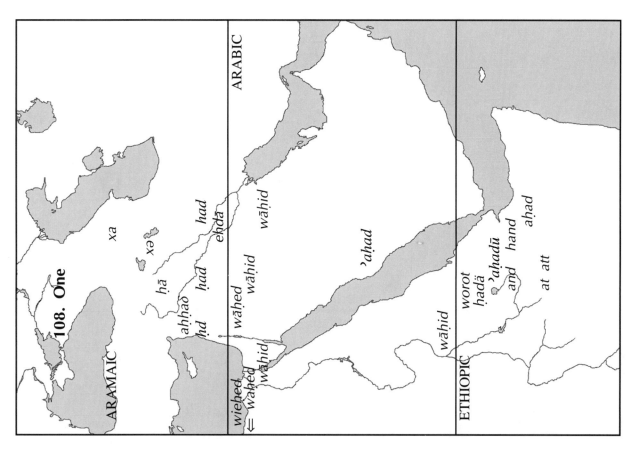

108. One

ARAMAIC

xa

ex

hā

ahhað

ḥd

ḥd

ahhað

ḥd

ḥad

ḥad

had

eḥdā

ARABIC

wiehed
⇐ waḥed

wāḥed

wāḥed

wāḥid

wāḥid

wāḥid

wāḥid

ʔaḥad

wāḥid

ETHIOPIC

worot

hadā

ʔaḥadū

and

hand

aḥad

at att

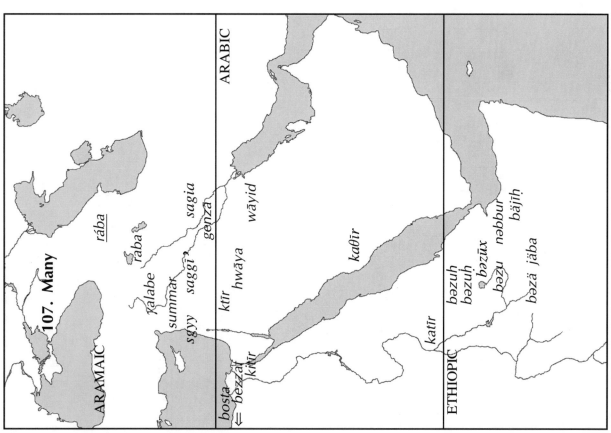

107. Many

ARAMAIC

rába

raba

ʕalabe

summar

saggi

sgyy

sagia

genzā

ARABIC

bosṭa
⇐ bezzat

ktīr

kitīr

hwāya

wāyid

katīr

katīr

kaθīr

ETHIOPIC

bəzuḥ

bəzuḥ

bəzxūeq

nzeq

nəbuʔ

bāǰiḥ

bəzā ǰāba

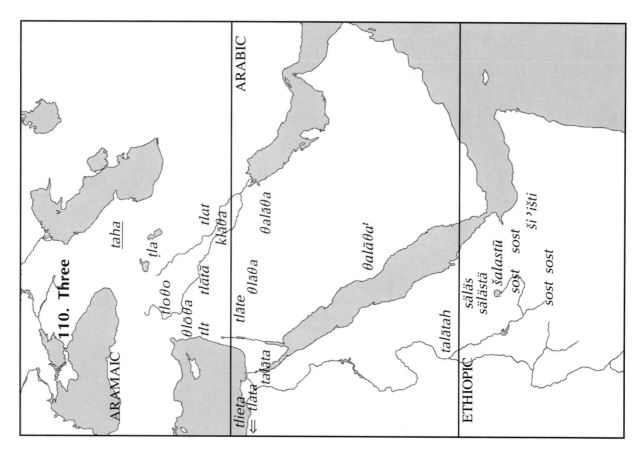

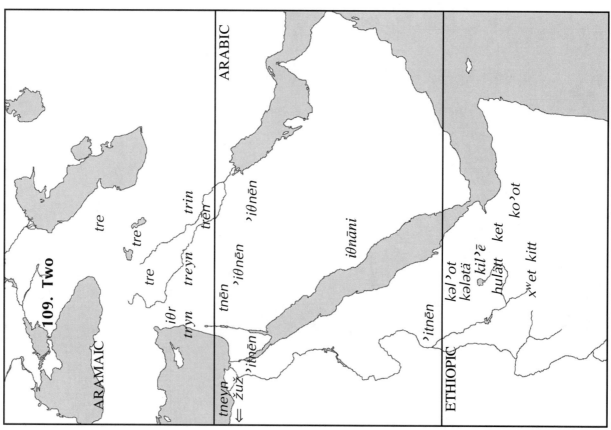

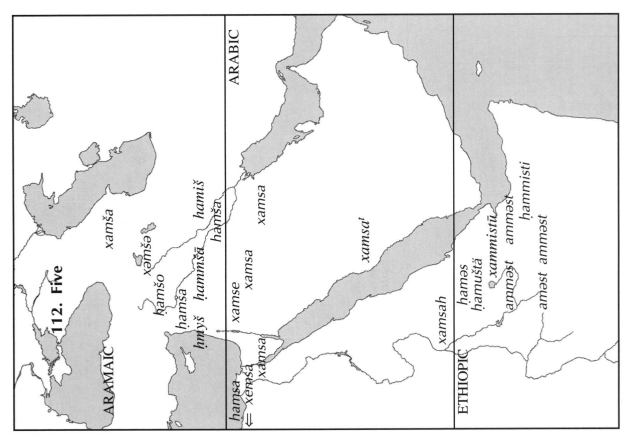

112. Five

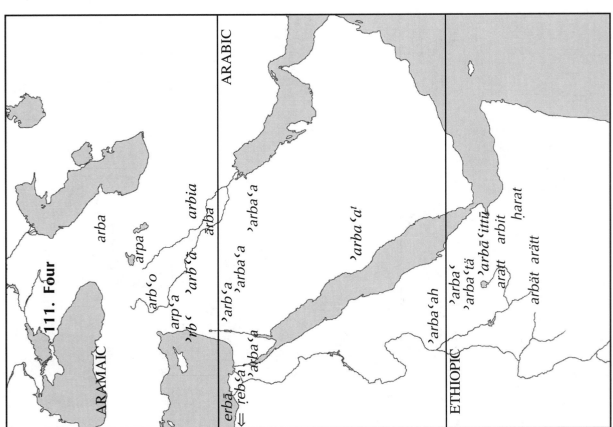

111. Four

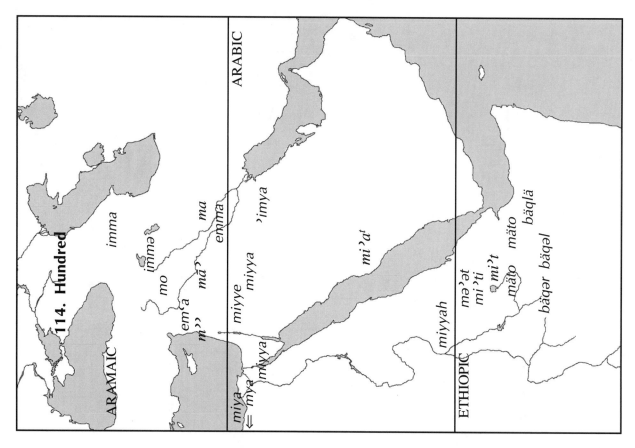

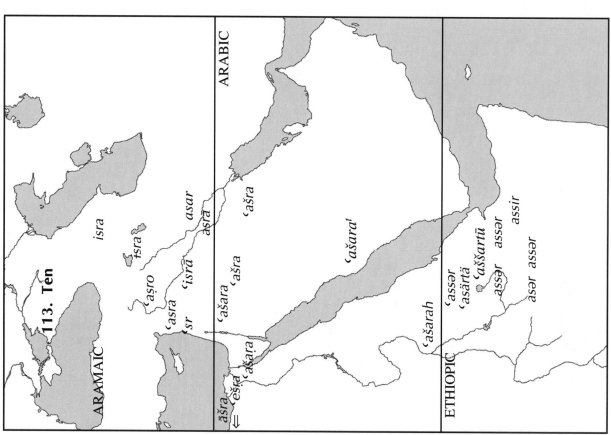

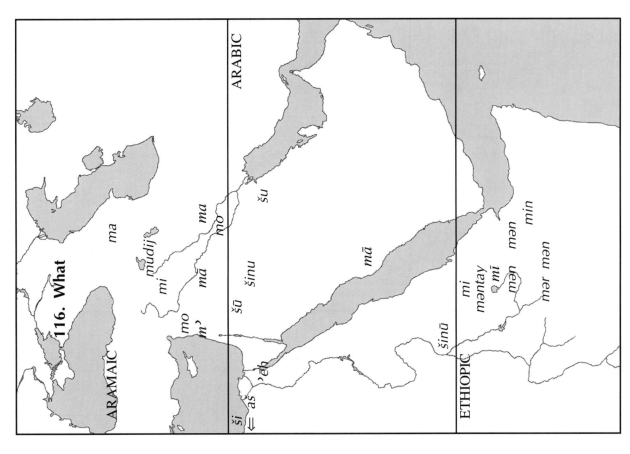

116. What

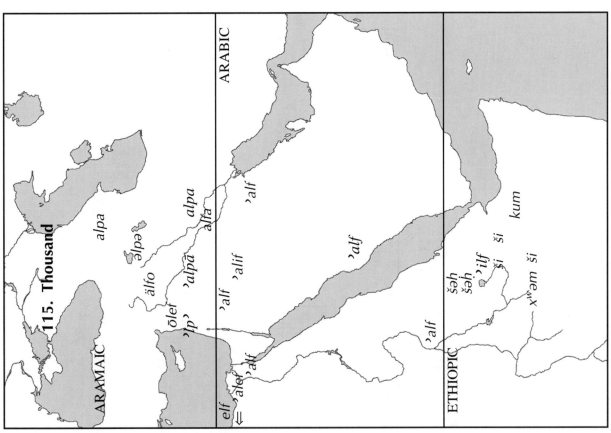

115. Thousand

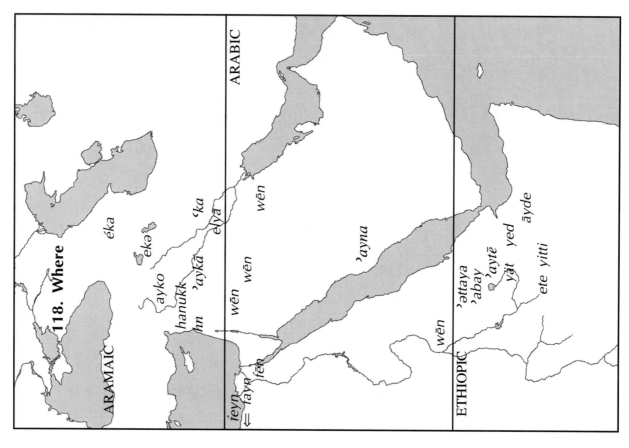

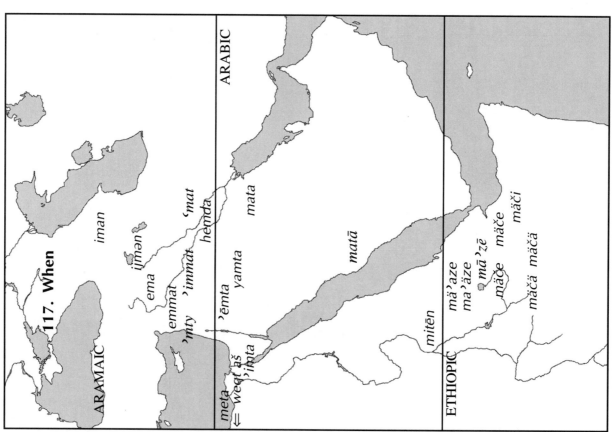

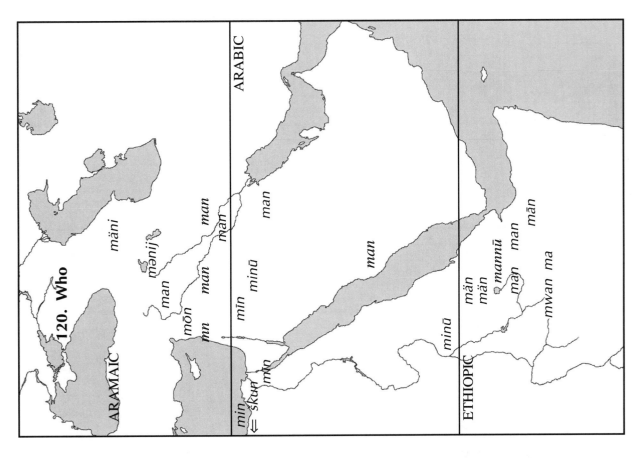

120. Who

ARAMAIC: mǟni, mǟnī, mänīf, man, mōn, mn, man, man, man, man

ARABIC: min ⇐ škūn, mn, mīn, minū, man, man, man, minū

ETHIOPIC: män, män, mannū, man, man, man, mmän, mwan ma

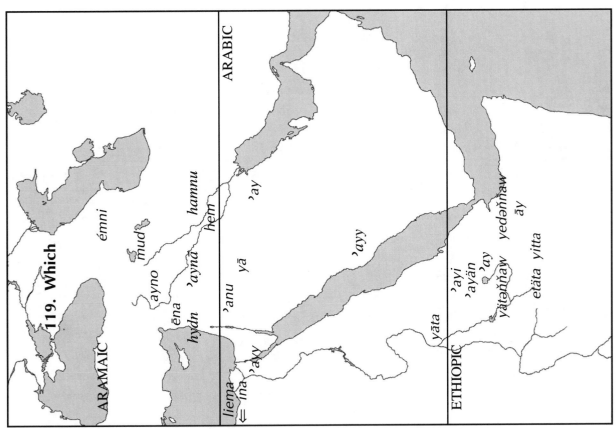

119. Which

ARAMAIC: émni, mud, ayno, ᵓaynā, hamnu, ēna, hem, hydn

ARABIC: ᵓanu, ᵓay, yā, yā, ᵓayy, ᵓay, liema ⇐ ina

ETHIOPIC: ᵓayi, ᵓayän, ᵓay, yätäññaw, yedäññaw, āy, etäta, yitta, yāta

Wordlist F

Berber and Semitic
Exercise 21

Berber				Semitic			
JN	Jebel Nefusa	AS	Ayt Seghrouchen	Ak	Akkadian	Ar	Classical Arabic
Gh	Ghadamsi	Ka	Kabyle	Ug	Ugaritic	Ge	Geʻez
Wa	Wargla	Sh	Shilḥa	Sy	Syriac	Ji	Jibbali

	1. All	2. Answer	3. Arm	4. Arrive	5. Ask	6. Axe
JN	kul:	žawb	aɣɛl:	awṭ	nšd	taglzimt
Gh	kūl:u	s:ədmər	āɣil	awəḍ	æθ:ər	agʻælzim
Wa	kul:	wažb	aɣil	awḍ	t:r	š:aquṛ
AS	q:aḥ	wajb	aɣil	awḍ	sal	ayz:im
Ka	Kul	wajb	iɣil	awḍ	T:r	aglzim
Sh	kul:u	wažb	iɣil	awḍ	s:qsa	aglzim
Ak	kalū	turru, apālu	idu, āxu	kašādu	šālu	pāštu
Ug	kl	ʻny	δrʻ	gly, mɣy	šål	pδ
Sy	kull	ʻnā	drāʻā	mṭā	šʾil	nārgā, pustā
Ar	kull	ʾajāba	δirāʻ	waṣala	saʾala	faʾs, balṭaᵗ
Ge	kʷillū	ʾawšiʾa	mazrāʻt	baṣha	saʾala	maḥsē
Ji	kɔl	ŝəgēb	δέraʻ	ésəl	ŝxəbér	fɔs

	7. Back	8. Barley	9. Be	10. Bear (child)	11. Beard	12. Beat
JN	akrum	tamẓin	l:a	aru	tumɛrt	awet
Gh	akorm	təmẓēn	ili	ārəw	tōmært	æwət
Wa	tikrmin	timẓin	ili	aru	tmart	wt
AS	tiwa	timẓin	ili	aṛw	tmart	w:t
Ka	azagur	timẓin	ili	arw	tamart	wt
Sh	akrum	tumẓin	ili	aru	tamart	ut
Ak	ṣēru	šeʾu	ewū	walādu	ziqnu	maxāṣu
Ug	ẓr	šʻr	kn	yld	dqn	hlm
Sy	ḥaṣṣā	sʻārtā	hwā	īlid	daqnā	mḥā
Ar	ḍahr	šaʻīr	kāna	walada	liḥyaᵗ, δaqn	ḍaraba
Ge	zabān	sagam	kōna, hallawa	walada	sihm	zabaṭa
Ji	šɔ̄	šiʻír	kun	bíri	ləḥyét	gɔ́lɔ́d

	13. Big	14. Bird	15. Bite	16. Blood	17. Bone	18. Bread
JN	amoqrån	ṭ:īr	drm	idm:n	iɣas:	aɣrūm
Gh	mæq:or (v.)	ag'aḍiḍ	æmbər	dæm:æn	ɣæs:	tawag'e
Wa	amq:ṛan	ažḍiḍ	d:d	idam:n	iɣs	aɣṛum
AS	amq:ṛan	ajḍiḍ	qṛ:š	idam:n	iɣṣ:	aɣṛum
Ka	amqʷṛan	afrux	gʷrš	idam:n	iɣs	aɣṛum
Sh	anmɣur	agḍiḍ	b:i	idam:n	iɣs	aɣṛum
Ak	rabū	iṣṣūru	našāku	dāmu	eṣemtu	kurummatu
Ug	gdl, rabbu	ʿuṣṣūru, ʿp	nθk	dm	ʿẓm	lḥm
Sy	rab	ṣipprā	nkat	dmā	garmā	laḥmā
Ar	kabīr	ṭayr, ʿuṣfūr	ʿaḍḍa	dam	ʿaẓm	xubz
Ge	ʿabīy	ʿōf	nasaka	dam	ʿaḍm	xibist
Ji	ʾéb	ʿɛsférɔ́t	źaʿár	δɔhr	ʿíźéź	xabzét

	19. Breast	20. Brother	21. Build	22. Bull	23. Buy	24. Camel
JN	bib:iš	rum:u	bna	funas	esaɣ	alɣom
Gh	admār	aruma	ōsək	afunas	æsæʿ	āḷæm
Wa	if:	m:ʷa	ṣk	afunas	sɣ	aḷm
AS	if:	uma	bna	afunas	sɣ	alɣm
Ka	if:	gma	bnu	afunas	aɣ	alɣʷm
Sh	tab:ušt	gʷma	bnu	afunas	sɣ	aṛam
Ak	tulū	axu	banū	šūru, lū	šāmu	udru
Ug	θd	ȧx	bny	θr	qny	ủdr
Sy	tdā	ʾaḥā	bnā	tawrā	zban	gamlā
Ar	ṣadr, θady	ʾax	banā	θawr	ištarā	jamal
Ge	ṭib	ʾixw	ḥanaṣa	biʿr, sōr	zabaya	gamal
Ji	θɔ́dɛʾ	ʾaɣá	ební	ɣɔźəb	śɔ́tém	gũl

	25. Cheek	26. Child	27. Come	28. Cow	29. Cry	30. Dance
JN	yel:i	bušil	ased	tfunast	ʿayyeṭ	erqås
Gh	ag'æz:	ara	ās	tafunast	æz:əf	dīz
Wa	tmag:aẓt	ara	as	tlbgra	ṛu	drz, rks
AS	madl, anbuẓ	aslmya	ṛaḥd:	tafunast	ru	šṭ:ḥ
Ka	amayg	aqšiš	as	tafunast	ru	šḍḥ
Sh	amadl	ar:aw	aškd	tafunast	al:	siy:s
Ak	lētu	māru, līdu	kašādu	arxu, lītu	bakū	sāru, raqādu
Ug	lḥ	yld ~ wld	ȧtw, bȧ	ȧrx, ypt	bky	xl, rqd
Sy	pakkā	ṭalyā, yaldā	ʾitā, mṭā	tawrtā	bkā	rqad
Ar	xadd	walad	jāʾa, ʾatā	baqaraᵗ	bakā	raqaṣa
Ge	maltāḥt	wald, ʾigwāl	maṣʾa, ʾatawa	lāhm	bakaya	zafana
Ji	xad	əmbéré̀ʾ	zaḥám	léʾ	béké	ɛrqɔ́d

	31. Daughter	32. Day	33. Die	34. Do	35. Dog	36. Donkey
JN	yel:i	as:	em:et	eg	yudi	aziảṭ
Gh	alæt	āsæf	əm:ət	æg′	ēde	azēḍ
Wa	il:i	kl, as:	m:t	g	aydi	aγ:ul
AS	il:i	as:	m:t	ij	aydi	aγyul
Ka	yl:i	as:	m:t	g	aydi	aγyul
Sh	il:i	as:	m:t	g	aydi	aγyul
Ak	mārtu	ūmu	mātu	epēšu	kalbu	imēru
Ug	bt	ym	mt	ʿšy	klb	ḥmr
Sy	bartā	yawmā	mīt	ʿbad	kalbā	ḥmārā
Ar	bint	yawm	māta	ʿamila	kalb	ḥimār
Ge	walatt	maʿālt	mōta	gabra	kalb	ʾadg
Ji	brit	yum	xárɔ́g	ʿɔ̄l	kɔb	qéráḥ

	37. Door	38. Dove	39. Dream	40. Dress	41. Drink	42. Ear
JN	elbab	dbir	etxartel	erwoṭ	ɛsu	tmej:it
Gh	taβ:urt	adaber	βərg′	æls	æsw	ēsəm
Wa	tawurt	atbir	tiržt (n.)	ksa, irḍ	sw	tamž:it
AS	lbab	adbir	irjit	irḍ	sw	amẓ:uγ
Ka	tab:urt	itbir	arGu	ls	sw	amẓ:uγ
Sh	tiflut	atbir	warga	ls	su	amẓ:uγ
Ak	daltu, bābu	summatu	šuttu (n.)	labāšu	šatū	uznu
Ug	ptḥ, dlt	ynt	ḥlm	lbš	šty	ủdn
Sy	tarʿā	yawnā	ḥlam	lbiš	ʾištī	ʾidnā
Ar	bāb	ḥamāmaᵗ	ḥalima	labisa	šariba	ʾuδun
Ge	xōxt, ʾanqaṣ	rigb	ḥalama	labsa	satya	ʾizn
Ji	ʾɔb	ḥõt, ʿeŝyét	ḥélm	lɔ̄s	šúṣ̌i	ʾiδén

	43. Earth	44. Eat	45. Eight	46. Enter	47. Exit	48. Eye
JN	tamurt	ec:	tmanya	ekem	ef:ảγ	tiṭ
Gh	tam:urt	æš:	tām	ātəf	æf:əʿ	awæl:
Wa	tamuṛt	š:	tam, tmnya	atf	f:γ	tiṭ:
AS	tamurt	tš	tmnya	adf	f:γ	tiṭ:
Ka	tamurt	c:	tmanya	kçm	f:γ	tiṭ
Sh	akal	š:	tam	kšm	f:γ	ṭiṭ:
Ak	erṣetu	akālu, taʾū	samānat	erēbu	waṣū	īnu
Ug	ʾarṣu	ảkl, spả	θmn	bả, ʿrb	yṣả	ʿn
Sy	ʾarʿā	ʾikal	tmānyā	ʿal	npaq	ʿaynā
Ar	ʾarḍ	ʾakala	θamāniyaᵗ	daxala	xaraja	ʿayn
Ge	midr	balʿa	samānītū	bō̄ʾa	waḍʾa	ʿayn
Ji	ʾɛrẓ̌	té	θīnə́t	égaḥ	ŝxəníṭ	ʿíhn

	49. Face	50. Fall	51. Fat (n.)	52. Father	53. Fill	54. Finger
JN	*udem*	*uṭa*	*tadunt*	*baba*	*ec:ur*	*tuk:åd*
Gh	*ælwəž:*	*ūḍu*	*tas:əmt*	*dæd:a*	*əṭkur*	*aḍək:əd*
Wa	*udm*	*uḍa*	*tadunt*	*bada, dad:a*	*š:aṛ*	*ḍaḍ*
AS	*udm*	*uḍa*	*tadunt*	*ib:a*	*ʿm:ṛ*	*ḍaḍ*
Ka	*udm*	*γli*	*tas:mt*	*baba*	*c:aṛ*	*aḍad*
Sh	*udm*	*ḍr*	*tadunt*	*baba*	*ktur*	*aḍad*
Ak	*pānū*	*maqātu*	*šamnu*	*abu*	*malū*	*ubānu*
Ug	*pnm*	*npl, ql*	*šmt*	*åb, ʾadānu*	*mlả*	*ủṣbʿ*
Sy	*ʾappē*	*npal*	*tarbā*	*ʾabā*	*mlā*	*ṣibʿtā*
Ar	*wajh*	*waqaʿa*	*šaḥm, duhn*	*ʾab*	*malaʾa*	*ʾuṣbaʿ*
Ge	*gaṣṣ*	*wadqa*	*šibḥ*	*ʾab*	*malʾa*	*ʾaṣbāʿt*
Ji	*fếnɛ, ếgh*	*gaʿár, hē*	*mašḥ, śabḥ*	*ʾiy*	*mízi*	*ʾiṣbáʿ*

	55. Fire	56. Fish	57. Five	58. Flour	59. Fly (v.)	60. Foot
JN	*tfawt*	*taḥotit*	*xamsa*	*aren*	*ṭår, far*	*ṭår*
Gh	*ofa*	*olisma*	*səm:əs*	*aβærn*	*æk:əd*	*aḍar*
Wa	*timsi*	*lḥut*	*sm:s, xmsa*	*arn*	*afr*	*ḍar*
AS	*tims:i*	*aslm*	*xmsa*	*arn*	*afrw*	*ḍaṛ*
Ka	*tims:*	*aslm*	*xmsa*	*awrn*	*f:rfr*	*aḍaṛ*
Sh	*lʿafit, takat*	*aslm*	*sm:us*	*ag:ʷrn*	*frfr*	*aḍaṛ*
Ak	*išātu*	*nūnu*	*xamšat*	*qēmu*	*naprušu, šāʾu*	*šēpu*
Ug	*ʾišītu, nr*	*dg*	*xmš*	*qmḥ*	*dả*	*riglu, pʿn*
Sy	*nūrā*	*nunā*	*ḥammšā*	*qamḥā*	*praḥ*	*riglā*
Ar	*nār*	*samak, nūn*	*xamsaᵗ*	*ṭaḥīn, daqīq*	*ṭāra*	*rijl*
Ge	*ʾisāt*	*ʿāšā*	*xammistū*	*ḥarīd*	*sarara*	*ʾigr*
Ji	*śɔ́ṭ*	*ḥut, ṣod*	*xɔ̃š*	*ṭqíq*	*ferr*	*faʿm, śɛf*

	61. Four	62. Friend	63. Give	64. Go	65. Goat	66. God
JN	*arbʿa*	*aḥbib*	*efk*	*ugur*	*tγåṭ*	*ṛåb:i*
Gh	*aq:oz*	*akawat*	*ækf*	*ās, rar*	*tēʿaṭ*	*al:a*
Wa	*rbʿa*	*amd:ukl*	*uš*	*raḥ, iguṛ*	*tixsi*	*ṛb:i*
AS	*ṛbʿa*	*amd:akʷ:l*	*uš*	*ṛaḥ*	*tγaṭ:*	*ḷ:ah, ṛb:i*
Ka	*ṛbʿa*	*amd:akʷ:l*	*fK*	*d:u, ruḥ*	*taγaṭ*	*ṛb:i*
Sh	*k:uẓ*	*amd:akʷ:l*	*fk*	*d:u*	*taγaṭ:*	*aḷ:ah*
Ak	*erbet*	*ibru, ruʾu*	*nadānu*	*alāku*	*enzu*	*ilu*
Ug	*ảrbʿ*	*rʿ*	*ytn*	*hlk*	*ʿz*	*ʾilu*
Sy	*ʾarbʿā*	*rāḥmā, ḥabrā*	*yab*	*ʾizal*	*ʿizzā, gadyā*	*ʾalāhā*
Ar	*ʾarbaʿaᵗ*	*ṣadīq*	*wahaba, ʾaʿṭā*	*ðahaba*	*ʿanzaᵗ*	*aḷḷāh*
Ge	*ʾarbāʿittū*	*ʿark*	*wahaba*	*ḥōra*	*ṭalīt*	*igzīʾa-biḥēr*
Ji	*ɛrbəʿɔ́t*	*ʿáśər, sudq*	*ezúm*	*aγád*	*ʾɔz*	*ʾɔ́ź, ʾallāh*

	67. Good	68. Grass	69. Grind	70. Hair	71. Hand	72. Hare
JN	aza ͨim	tiga	ezḍ	zaw (coll.)	ufes	tirz̧åzt
Gh	ͨažib (qual.)	aš:əβ	æzəd	azaw	ōfəs:	tag'ærzizt
Wa	awḥdi	tuga	zḍ	zaw (coll.)	fus	agrziz̧
AS	awḥdi	tuja	zḍ	anzḍ, az:ar	fus	awtul
Ka	lḥu (v.)	lḥšiš	zḍ	anzad	afus	awtul
Sh	ͨadl (v.)	tugʷa	zḍ	az:ar	afus	awtil
Ak	ṭābu, damqu	dīšu	samādu, ṭēnu	pērtu, šārtu	qātu	arnabu
Ug	ṭābu, nͨm	ʾmt	ṭhn	ͨq, š ͨrt	yd	ȧnhb
Sy	ṭāb	ͨisbā	ṭhin	saͨrā, minntā	īdā	ʾarnbā
Ar	ṭayyib	ͨušb, ḥašīš	ṭahana	šaͨraᵗ	yad	ʾarnab
Ge	šanniy, xēr	šāͨr	ṭahana	šiͨirt, ṣagwr	ʾid	ʾarnab
Ji	xár, ɛrḥím	rɔγɔd, śáͨər	ṭahán	śfét	éd	ʾɛrní

	73. Head	74. Hear	75. Heart	76. Honey	77. Horn	78. Horse
JN	iγɛf	esel	ul	tamemt	aš:aw	agmär
Gh	ēγæf	æsl	ōg'əm	taməmt	aškaw	ag'mar
Wa	iγf	sl:	ul	tam:imt	aš:aw	lḥsan
AS	ixf, azl:if	sl:	ul	tamnt	iš:	yis
Ka	aqṛ:u	sl	ul	tamnt	iš:	aͨawdiw
Sh	agayu	sl:	ul	tam:mt	isk	agmar, ay:is
Ak	rēšu	šemū	libbu	dišpu	qarnu	sisū
Ug	rʾš	šmͨ	lb	nbt	qrn	ssw
Sy	rīšā	šmaͨ	libbā	dibšā	qarnā	susyā
Ar	raʾs	samiͨa	qalb	ͨasal	qarn	ḥiṣān
Ge	riʾs	samͨa	libb	maͨār, dibs	qarn	faras
Ji	réš	šīͨ	ub, qɛlb	dɛbš	qun	ḥaṣún

	79. House	80. Hunger	81. Iron	82. Kid	83. Kidney	84. Kill
JN	tad:art	låz	z:el	γid	težižilt	enaγ
Gh	daž, ax:yam	lāz	wəz:āl	aͨīd	tag'æz:ult	æn:
Wa	tad:art	l:az̧	lḥdid, uz:al	iγid	taž:lt	nγ
AS	tad:art	ḷaz̧	uz:al, lḥdid	iγid	tiyzlt	nγ
Ka	ax:am	laz̧	uz:al	iγid	tigz:lt	nγ
Sh	tigm:i	ḷaz̧	uz:al	iγid	tigz:lt	nγ
Ak	bītu	būru, bubūtu	parzillu	unīqu, lalū	kalītu	dāku, nēru
Ug	bt, dr	rγbn	brðl	gdy, llủ	klyt	mxš, hrg
Sy	baytā	kapnā	parzlā	gadyā	kulītā	qṭal
Ar	bayt	jūͨ	ḥadīd	jady	kulyaᵗ	qatala
Ge	bēt	raxab	xaṣīn	māḥsiͨ	kwilīt	qatala
Ji	bot	tɔf	ḥádíd	məðkér	kuʓ́ét	létəγ

	85. King	86. Knife	87. Know	88. Lamb	89. Laugh	90. Left
JN	elmelk	elmusi	es:en	zumɛr	eḍs	el:isar
Gh	ašæl:id	taβæṣ:	æs:ən	ælxəruf	æḍs	azəlmaḍ
Wa	ažl:id	lmusi	s:n	aˁl:uš	ḍṣ	azlmaḍ
AS	ajl:id	ajnwi	isin	aˁl:uš	ṭṣ	azlmaḍ
Ka	agl:id	ažnwi, lmus	is:in	izimr	ḍṣ	azlmaḍ
Sh	agl:id	ažnwi	s:n	alq:aγ	ḍṣ:a	azlmaḍ
Ak	šarru	naglābu	edūa	kalūmu	ṣiāxu	šumēlu
Ug	malku	ḥrb, yˁr	ydˁ	imr, kr	ṣḥq, gmž	šmal
Sy	malkā	sakkīnā	īdaˁ	ʾimrā, parrā	gḥak	simmālā
Ar	malik	sikkīn	ˁarifa	xarūf, ḥamal	ḍaḥika	šimāl, yasār
Ge	nigūš	maṭbāḥt	ʾaʾmara, ˁōqa	māḥsiˁ	šaḥaqa	ḍagām
Ji	mélík	skín	édaˁ, γárɔb	kɔbś	źaḥák	śəmlí

	91. Lion	92. Live	93. Liver	94. Long	95. Love	96. Man
JN	eṣ:id	ed:er	tusa	azegrar	γes:	ater:as
Gh	aβōr	æd:ər	tōsa	zəgʹrət (v.)	əβr	wügʾ:id
Wa	ar, aṣ:id	d:r	tsa	azgrar	xs, ˁšq	argaz
AS	izm	d:r	t:sa	azira	ˁšq	aryaz
Ka	izm	d:r	tasa	aγ^wzfan	ḥib:	arGaz
Sh	izm	d:r	tasa	aγ^wz:af	ḥub:u	argaz
Ak	lābu, nēšu	balāṭu	amūtu	arku	rāmu	zikāru
Ug	lbủ	ḥwy	kbd	årk (v.)	åḥb	mt
Sy	ʾaryā	ḥyā	kabdā	ʾarrīk	ʾaḥibb	gabrā
Ar	ʾasad, sabˁ	ḥayiya, ˁāša	kabid	ṭawīl	ʾaḥabb	rajul
Ge	ˁanbasā	ḥaywa	kabd	nawwīx	ʾafqara	ˁid, biʾsī
Ji	ʾaséd	ˁɛ̄ś	šubdét	rihm	ˁágəb, ḥebb	γég

	97. Meat	98. Milk	99. Month	100. Moon	101. Morning	102. Mother
JN	isan	elḥalib	ešhar	tziri	eṣ:baḥ	em:i
Gh	aksəm	yæf:	ōyær	ōyær	əṣ:āla	mā
Wa	aysum	adγs, aγi	yur	yur, taziri	ṣbḥ	l:a, n:a
AS	aysum	aγi	šḥṛ, yur	yur, tziri	ṣ:baḥ	im:a
Ka	aksum	ayfKi	š:huṛ	ag:ur	ṣ:bḥ	ym:a
Sh	aksum	akfay	ay:ur	ay:ur	ṣbaḥ	im:a
Ak	šīru	šizbu	warxu	warxu	šēru	ummu
Ug	bšr, šiʾru	ḥlb	yrx	yrx	šḥr	ủm
Sy	bisrā	ḥalbā	yarḥā	sahrā	ṣaprā	ʾimmā
Ar	laḥm	laban, ḥalīb	šahr	qamar	ṣabāḥ	ʾumm
Ge	šigā	ḥalīb	warx	warx	ṣibāḥ	ʾimm
Ji	téʾ	ḥɔ́lɔ̄b, núśub	ɔ́rx	ʾɛ́rət	kḥáṣṣáf	ʾém

	103. Mountain	104. Mouth	105. Name	106. Night	107. Nine	108. Nose
JN	drar	imi	isəm	iṭ	tesaˁ	tinzert
Gh	adurar	ame	ism	ēβæḍ	təṣō	tənzart
Wa	agrgub	imi	ism	iḍ	tṣ:, tsˁa	tinzrt
AS	lˁari	aq:mu, imi	ism	xyiḍ	tsˁa, tsˁud	tinzar
Ka	adrar	imi	ism	iḍ	Tsˁa	tinzrt
Sh	adrar	imi	ism	iḍ	tsˁa	tinxaṛ
Ak	šadū	pū	šumu	mūšu, līliātu	tišet	appu
Ug	gbl, γr, δd	p	šm	ll	tšˁ	ʾappu
Sy	ṭūrā	pummā	šmā	līlyā ~ laylē	tišˁā	ʾappē, nḥīrā
Ar	jabal	fam	ism	layl	tisˁaᵗ	ʾanf
Ge	dabr	ʾaf	sim	lēlīt	tisˁattū	ʾanf
Ji	giέl	xɔh	šum	ˁáṣər	saˁét	naxrér

	109. Oil	110. One	111. Pass	112. Rain	113. Return	114. Ride
JN	di	ujun	exṭåm	anẓar	wel:a	en:i
Gh	ude	yōn	æxṭəm	anaẓar	ækri	æni
Wa	z:it	ig:n	k:	amẓar	dwl, ali	n:i
AS	z:it	idj	k:	anẓaṛ	ˁid	ny
Ka	z:it	yiwn	fat	agf:ur	ržˁ	rKb
Sh	z:it	ya	k:	anẓaṛ	aḍud	s:udu
Ak	šamnu	ištēnu	etēqu	zunnu	tāru	rakābu
Ug	šmn	åḥd	ˁbr	mṭr	θb	rkb
Sy	mišḥā	ḥad	gāz	miṭrā	tāb	rkib
Ar	zayt	ʾaḥad	marra	maṭar	rajaˁa, θāba	rakiba
Ge	qibʾ	ʾaḥadū	xalafa	zinām	gabʾa	rakaba
Ji	ḥahl	ṭad	xɔ́ṭɔ́f	raḥmέt	régaˁ, redd	rékəb

	115. Road	116. Root	117. Rope	118. Run	119. Salt	120. Say
JN	brid	lˁårq	zukɛr	az:el	tisent	emel
Gh	abrīd	aẓur	tazara	æz:əl	tēsənt	æn
Wa	abrid	aẓur	γan	az:l	tisnt	ini
AS	abrid, aˁlad	aẓuṛ	asγun, izišṛ	az:l	tisnt	ini
Ka	abrid	aẓaṛ	asγʷn, izikr	az:l	lmlḥ	ini
Sh	aγaras	aẓuṛ, azγr	asγun, izikr	az:l	tisnt	ini
Ak	padānu	šuršu	ašlu	rāṣu	ṭābtu	qabū
Ug	ntb	šrš	ḥbl	lsm	mlḥt	rgm
Sy	ʾurḥā	širšā, ˁiqārā	ḥablā, nīnāyā	rhiṭ	milḥā	ʾimar
Ar	ṭarīq	ʾaṣl, ˁirq	ḥabl	jarā, rakaḍa	milḥ	qāla
Ge	finōt, mangad	širw	ḥabl	rōṣa	ṣēw	bihla
Ji	ʾɔrm	šíróx, ˁarq	qod	šaˁé	mízḥót	ˁõr

	121. Sea	122. See	123. Send	124. Seven	125. Shadow	126. Short
JN	lebḥar	ešbaḥ	enki	sebʕa	eṭːål:	agezlal
Gh	ælbəhər	æl:əm, æẓər	āzən	sā	tēle	gʼəz:əl (qual.)
Wa	lbḥr	ẓṛ	azn	sa, sbʕa	tili	aqz:ul
AS	lbḥṛ	ẓṛ	azn	sbʕa	tili	ašṭ:wan
Ka	lbḥṛ	ẓṛ	azn	sbʕa	tili	awzlan
Sh	lbḥar	ẓṛ, an:ay	ṣ:afḍ	sa	asklu	agʷz:al
Ak	tāmtu	amāru	šapāru	sebet	ṣillu	kurū
Ug	ym	åmr, ḥdy, ʕn	lik, šlḥ	šbʕ	ẓl	qṣr
Sy	yammā	ḥzā	šlaḥ	šabʕā	ṭillālā	zʕurā, karyā
Ar	baḥr	ra'ā	'arsala	sabʕaᵗ	ẓill	qaṣir
Ge	bāḥr	ri'ya	la'aka	sabʕattū	ṣilālōt	xaṣīr
Ji	rémnɛm	śíní	ebláɣ	šəbʕə́t	gófɛ'	qéṣír

	127. Shoulder	128. Silver	129. Sing	130. Sister	131. Sit	132. Six
JN	taɣrut	elfežret	ɣɛn:a	weltmu	gaʕmez	set:a
Gh	taɣurəṭ	ælfiṭ:æt	ɣən:u	alætma	qēm	ṣuz
Wa	taɣruḍt	lfḍ:t	ɣan:a	wtma	q:im	sẓ:, st:a
AS	aɣir	n:qṛt	nš:d	ultma	q:im	st:a
Ka	tayts	lft:a	šnu, ɣn:i	wltma	q:im	stsa
Sh	iɣir	n:qʷ:rt	ɣan:u	ultma	qim	st:a
Ak	būdu	kaspu	zamāru	axātu	wašābu	šeššet
Ug	ktp	ksp	šr	'axātu	yθb	θθ
Sy	katpā	kispā	zmar	ḥātā	ītib	štā
Ar	katif, minkab	fiḍḍaᵗ	ɣannā	'uxt	qaʕada	sittaᵗ
Ge	matkaf(t)	birūr	zammara	'ixt	nabara	siddistū
Ji	kənséd, kɛtf	fíẓ́ẓ́át	ɛhbéb	ɣit	skɔf	štət

	133. Skin (n.)	134. Sky	135. Sleep (v.)	136. Small	137. Smoke	138. Snake
JN	uglim	es:əma	eṭ:ås	ameškan	dux:an	telifsa
Gh	ēlæm	ažən:a	nəd:əm	əmtit (qual.)	oβu	tolifsa
Wa	aglim	ažn:a	ṭ:s	akšiš	d:ux:an	fiɣr
AS	ahiḍuṛ	ajn:a	jn	amẓ:yan	d:x:an	alfsa, ifiɣṛ
Ka	agʷlim	ign:i	gn, ṭ:ṣ	amẓ:yan	ab:u, d:ux:an	azrm
Sh	ilm	ign:a	ṭ:ṣ	imzi (v.)	ag:u	algʷmaḍ
Ak	mašku	šamū	ṣalālu	ṣexru	qutru	ṣerru
Ug	ʕōru	šamūma	yšn	ṣɣr, dq, θrr	qṭr	bθn, tunnanu
Sy	gildā	šmayyā	dmik, nām	zʕūrā, daqdqā	tinnānā	ḥiwyā
Ar	jild	samā'	wasina, nāma	ṣaɣīr	duxān	ḥayyaᵗ
Ge	mā's	samāy	nōma	ni'ūs, ḥiṣūṣ	ṭīs, tann	'arwē
Ji	gód	siɛ̄h	ŝéf	nísán	məndɔ́x	ɣuẓ́t, hɔ̄t

	139. Son	140. Soul	141. Speak	142. Spit	143. Star	144. Stomach
JN	tarwa	iman	aḥka	eskufs	tri	ed:ist
Gh	tarwa	iman	sməg':i	sūfəs	iri	tadist
Wa	m:i	iman	s:iwl	s:kufs	itri	adan, aʕd:is
AS	arba	ṛ:uḥ, n:fs	s:iwl	s:ufs	itri	tadist, lmʕda
Ka	m:i	ṛ:uḥ	siwl	susf	itri	lmʕda, aʕb:uḍ
Sh	yu	ṛuḥ, iman	sawl	s:ufs	itri	adis
Ak	māru	napištu	zakāru	xaxū, tabāku	kakkabu	karšu
Ug	bn	npš	rgm	wpθ	kbkb	krs
Sy	brā	napšā	mallil	raqq	kawkbā	karsā
Ar	ibn	nafs	takallama	tafala	kawkab, najm	miʕda^t, kirš
Ge	wald	nafs	nagara	tafʔa, waraqa	kōkab	karš, kabd
Ji	bɛr	nəfsét	hérɔg	féṣəɣ, tfɔl	kəbkéb	ŝírŝ

	145. Stone	146. Sun	147. Sweat	148. Tail	149. Take	150. Tear
JN	tɣåɣåṭ	tufut	tidi	afet:al	aɣ	mäṭ:iw
Gh	ērəg'	tōfət	tidi	tabaḥṣuṣ:	āβæʕ	aməṭ:a
Wa	adɣaɣ	tfit	l'ʕrg	tazṇḍiḍt	aɣ	imt:ṛawn (pl.)
AS	azṛu	tafuyt	tidi	ajlal	asy, awy	imṭ:awn (pl.)
Ka	azṛu	tafukt	tidi	ažḥniḍ	aɣ	imṭ:i
Sh	azṛu	tafukt	l'ʕɑrg	ašṭ:ab	aɣ	amṭ:a
Ak	abnu	šamšu	zūtu	zibbatu	axāzu, leqū	dimtu
Ug	åbn	šapšu	dʕt	δnbt	åxδ, lqḥ	dmʕ
Sy	kīpā, ʔabnā	šimšā	duʕtā	dunbā	ʔiḥad	dimʕtā
Ar	ḥajar	šams	ʕaraq	δanab	ʔaxaδa	damʕa^t
Ge	ʔibn	ḍaḥāy, ʔamīr	hāf	zanab	ʔaxaza, našʔa	ʔanbiʕ
Ji	fúdún	yum	naɣlt	δúnúb	ḥõl	dəmʕát

	151. Ten	152. Three	153. Throw	154. Tie	155. Tongue	156. Tooth
JN	ʕašra	tlata	low:aḥ	åq:ån	iles	sin
Gh	maraw	kāræd	æg'ər	ækrəd, æq:ən	ēləs	asēn
Wa	mraw, ʕšra	šarḍ, tlata	gr	q:n, drs, kms	ils	tiɣmst
AS	ʕšṛa	tlata	jr	q:n, šrs, as:	ils	tiɣmst
Ka	ʕšṛa	tlata	ḍgr	q:n, arz	ils	tuɣmst
Sh	mraw	kṛaḍ	gr	q:n, as:	ils	axʷs
Ak	ešeret	šalāšat	nadū	rakāsu	lišānu	šinnu
Ug	ʕšr	θlθ	yry	rks, åsr	lašānu	šn
Sy	ʕisrā	tlātā	šdā, rmā	ʔisar	liššānā	šinnā, kakkā
Ar	ʕašara^t	θalāθa^t	ramā	rabaṭa	lisān	sinn
Ge	ʕaššartū	šalastū	warawa	ʔasara	lissān	sinn
Ji	ʕəŝírét	ŝɔθét	ɛrdé	ʕɔṣɔ́b, rɔ́ṭ	ɛlŝén	šnin

	157. Two	158. Urine	159. Village	160. Want	161. Wash	162. Water (n.)
JN	*sen*	*ibeziḍen*	*tmura*	*γεs:*	*sired*	*amεn*
Gh	*sən*	*alwāgʾæn*	*amæzdæ*ʿ	*əβr*	*sīrəd*	*āman*
Wa	*sn*	*ibz:ḍn*	*amzdaγ*	*k:r, xs*	*s:ird*	*aman*
AS	*snat*	*ibš:išn*	*aγṛm, lfilaj*	*bγa, štha*	*s:ird*	*aman*
Ka	*sin*	*ibzḍan*	*tad:art*	*bγu*	*s:ird*	*aman*
Sh	*sin*	*ibzḍan*	*lmuḍa*ʿ	*iri*	*s:ird*	*aman*
Ak	*šina*	*šināti*	*ālu, kapru*	*erēšu*	*ramāku, mesū*	*mū*
Ug	*θn*	*θnt*	*qarītu,* ʿ*r*	*ȧrš*	*rḥṣ*	*my*
Sy	*treyn*	*tune*	*qrītā*	*ṣbā*	*ʾašīg, ḥāp*	*mayyā*
Ar	*iθnāni*	*bawl*	*qarya*ᵗ	*ʾarāda*	*γasala*	*māʾ*
Ge	*kilʾē*	*šint*	*hagar*	*faqada*	*xaḍaba, riḥḍa*	*māy*
Ji	*θroh*	*ðaḥyɔ́l*	*ṣ̂írέt*	ʿ*ágəb*	*raḥáẓ́*	*míḥ*

	163. Water (v.)	164. Well	165. What	166. Wheat	167. Where	168. White
JN	*sεsu*	*tanut*	*may*	*yerden*	*mani*	*amel:al*
Gh	*səsw*	*ānu*	*me*	*ayærd*	*din*	*mləl* (qual.)
Wa	*s:wrd*	*tala*	*ma*	*imndi*	*mani*	*aml:al*
AS	*s:u*	*anu*	*ma(y), mi*	*ird, imndi*	*mani*	*aml:al*
Ka	*s:w*	*lbir*	*ašu*	*irdn*	*ani*	*aml:al*
Sh	*s:u*	*anu*	*ma*	*irdn*	*mani*	*umlil*
Ak	*šaqū*	*būru*	*mīnū*	*kibtu*	*ayyānu*	*peṣū*
Ug	*šqy*	*nabku ~ napku*	*mn*	*ḥṭṭ*	*ỉy*	*labanu*
Sy	*ʾašqī*	*bīrā*	*mā*	*ḥiṭṭā*	*ʾaykā*	*ḥiwwār*
Ar	*saqā*	*biʾr*	*mā*	*qamḥ, ḥinṭa*ᵗ	*ʾayna*	*ʾabyaḍ*
Ge	*saqaya*	ʿ*azaqt*	*mī, mint*	*širnāy*	*ʾaytē*	*ṣiʿdiw*
Ji	*šέqέ*	*γɔ̄r*	*ʾínέ*	*bohr*	*hútun, hun*	*lūn*

	169. Who	170. Wind	171. Wing	172. Woman	173. Wood	174. Write	175. Year
JN	*mam:o*	*aṭu*	*afriw*	*tmȧṭ:ut*	*isγaren*	*ari*	*sug:es*
Gh	*an:o*	*aḍo*	*afraw*	*talta*	*asγēr*	*ōrəβ*	*azæg:as*
Wa	*mam:o*	*aḍu*	*afr*	*tamṭ:ut*	*asγar*	*ari*	*asg:as*
AS	*may, mi*	*aḍu*	*afr*	*tamṭ:uṭ:*	*asγaṛ, ayš:uḍ*	*ari*	*asgʷ:as,* ʿ*am*
Ka	*wi*	*aḍu*	*ifr:*	*tamṭ:ut*	*asγaṛ*	*aru*	*asgʷ:as*
Sh	*ma*	*aḍu*	*ifr*	*tamγart*	*asγar*	*ara*	*asgʷ:as*
Ak	*mannu*	*šāru*	*agappu, abru*	*sinništu*	*iṣu*	*šaṭāru*	*šattu*
Ug	*my*	*rḥ*	*knp*	*ȧθt*	ʿ*ṣ*	*ktb, spr*	*šnt*
Sy	*man*	*rūḥā*	*gippā, kinpā*	*ʾattətā*	*qaysā*	*ktab*	*šattā*
Ar	*man*	*rīḥ*	*kanaf, janāḥ*	*imraʾa*ᵗ	*xašab*	*kataba*	ʿ*ām, sana*ᵗ
Ge	*mannū*	*nafās*	*kinf*	*ʾanist*	ʿ*iḍ*	*ṣaḥafa*	ʿ*ām(at)*
Ji	*mun*	*h(i)yέ*	*génaḥ, qaṭf*	*teθ*	*ðarb*	*ktɔb*	ʿ*ónút*

Wordlist G

Proto-Semitic A
Exercise 25

		Hebrew		Syriac		Arabic		Ge'ez	
1.	After	ʾaḥar	אחר	bātar	ܒܵܬܲܪ	baʿda	بعد	dəxra	ድኅረ፡
2.	All	kōl	כל	kull	ܟܠ	kull	كل	kʷəllū	ኩሉ፡
3.	Answer	ʿānā	ענה	ʿnā	ܥܢܐ	ʾajāba	أجاب	ʾawšəʾa	አወሥአ፡
4.	Approach	qārab	קרב	qrib	ܩܪܒ	qāraba	قارب	taqārbō	ተቃርቦ፡
5.	Arm	zrōʿ	זרוע	drāʿā	ܕܪܵܥܐ	δirāʿ	ذراع	mazrāʿt	መዝራዕት
6.	Arrive	higgīʿ	הגיע	mṭā	ܡܛܐ	waṣala	وصل	baṣḥa	በጽሐ፡
7.	Ask	šāʾal	שאל	šʾil	ܫܐܠ	saʾala	سأل	saʾala	ሰአለ፡
8.	Back	gab, šekem	גב, שכם	ḥaṣṣā	ܚܨܐ	ḍahr	ظهر	zabān	ዘባን፡
9.	Barley	śʿōrīm	שערים	sʿārtā	ܣܥܵܪܬܐ	šaʿīr	شعير	sagam	ሰገም፡
10.	Be	hāyā	היה	hwā	ܗܘܐ	kāna	كان	kōna, hallawa	ኮነ፡ ሀለወ፡
11.	Bear (child)	yālad	ילד	īlid	ܝܠܕ	walada	ولد	walada	ወለደ፡
12.	Beard	zāqān	זקן	daqnā	ܕܩܢܐ	liḥyaʿ, δaqn	لحية، ذقن	ṣəḥm	ጽሕም፡
13.	Beat	hikkā	הכה	mḥā	ܡܚܐ	ḍaraba	ضرب	zabaṭa	ዘበጠ፡
14.	Between	bēn	בן	baynāt	ܒܝܢܬ	bayna	بين	bayna	በይነ፡
15.	Big	gādōl	גדול	rab	ܪܒ	kabīr	كبير	ʿabīy	ዐቢይ፡
16.	Bird	ʿōp, ṣippōr	עוף, צפר	ṣipprā	ܨܦܪܐ	ṭayr, ʿuṣfūr	طير، عصفور	ʿōf	ዖፍ፡

232

Wordlist H

Proto-Semitic B
Exercise 25

Wordlist I

Proto-Semitic C
Exercise 25

Akkadian		Ugaritic			Maʕlula	Jibbali
warki	𒀀𒅈𒆠	ȧxr, ȧθr		1. After	bōθar	baʕd, mən ðér
kalū		kl		2. All	uxxul	kɔl
turru, apālu		ʕny		3. Answer	žawweb	ŝəgēb
qerēbu		qrb		4. Approach	qarreb	əqətéréb
idu, āxu		ðrʕ		5. Arm	ðrōʕa	ðɛraʕ
kašādu		gly, mγy		6. Arrive	imṭi	éṣəl
šālu		šȧl		7. Ask	mšaʕʕlille	ŝxəbér
ṣēru		ẓr		8. Back	ḥaṣṣa	šɔ̄
šeʾu		šʕr		9. Barley	sʕarō	šiʕír
ewū		kn		10. Be	wōb	kun
walādu		yld		11. Bear (child)	nacjaθ (fem. sg.)	bíri
ziqnu		dqn		12. Beard	ðaqna	ləḥyét
maxāṣu		hlm		13. Beat	imḥ	gɔ́lɔ́d
bīri		bn		14. Between	baynōθ	mən mún
rabū		gdl, rabbu		15. Big	rappa	ʾéb
iṣṣūru		ʕuṣṣūru, ʕp		16. Bird	ṣafrōna, ṭayra	ʕɛsférɔ́t

		Hebrew		Syriac		Arabic		Ge'ez	
17.	Bite	nāšak	נשך	nkat	ܢܟܬ	ʿaḍḍa	عض	nasaka	ነሰከ ፡
18.	Bless	bērak	ברך	barrik	ܒܪܟ	bāraka	بارك	bāraka	ባረከ ፡
19.	Blood	dām	דם	dmā	ܕܡܐ	dam	دم	dam	ደም ፡
20.	Bone	ʿeṣem	עצם	garmā	ܓܪܡܐ	ʿaẓm	عظم	ʿaḍm	ዐጽም ፡
21.	Bread	lehem	לחם	laḥmā	ܠܚܡܐ	xubz	خبز	xəbəst	ኅብስት ፡
22.	Breast	šad	שד	tdā	ܬܕܐ	ṣadr, θady	صدر ، ثدي	ṭəb	ጥብ ፡
23.	Brother	ʾāḥ	אח	ʾaḥā	ܐܚܐ	ʾax	أخ	ʾəxw	እኅው ፡
24.	Build	bānā	בנה	bnā	ܒܢܐ	banā	بنى	ḥanaṣa, nadaqa	ሐነጸ ፡ ነደቀ ፡
25.	Bull	šōr	שור	tawrā	ܬܘܪܐ	θawr	ثور	baʿr, sōr	ብዕር ፡ ሶር ፡
26.	Buy	qānā	קנה	zban	ܙܒܢ	ištarā	اشترى	zabaya	ዘበየ ፡
27.	Calf	ʿēgel	עגל	ʿiglā	ܥܓܠܐ	ʿijl	عجل	ʾəgwalt	እጕልት ፡
28.	Call	qārāʾ	קרא	qrā	ܩܪܐ	daʿā	دعى	bəhla	ብህለ ፡
29.	Camel	gāmāl	גמל	gamlā	ܓܡܠܐ	ǰamal	جمل	gamal	ገመል ፡
30.	Chair	kissē	כסה	kursyā	ܟܘܪܣܝܐ	kursīy	كرسي	manbar	መንበር ፡
31.	Child	yeled	ילד	ṭalyā, yaldā	ܛܠܝܐ، ܝܠܕܐ	walad	ولد	wald, ʾəgwāl	ወልድ ፡ እጓል ፡
32.	Come	ʾātā, bāʾ	אתה, בא	ʾitā, mtā	ܐܝܬܐ، ܡܛܐ	ǰāʾa, ʾatā	جاء ، أتى	maṣʾa, ʾatawa	መጽአ ፡ አተወ ፡
33.	Cow	pārā	פרה	tawrtā	ܬܘܪܬܐ	baqaraᵗ	بقرة	lāhm	ላህም ፡
34.	Cry	bākā	בכה	bkā	ܒܟܐ	bakā	بكى	bakaya	ነከየ ፡
35.	Dance (v.)	ḥāl, rāqad	חל, רקד	rqad	ܪܩܕ	raqaṣa	رقص	zafana	ዘፈነ ፡
36.	Daughter	bat	בת	bartā	ܒܪܬܐ	bint	بنت	walatt	ወለት ፡
37.	Day	yōm	יום	yawmā	ܝܘܡܐ	yawm	يوم	maʿālt	መዓልት ፡
38.	Die	māt	מת	mīt	ܡܝܬ	māta	مات	mōta	ሞተ ፡
39.	Dog	keleb	כלב	kalbā	ܟܠܒܐ	kalb	كلب	kalb	ከልብ ፡
40.	Donkey	ḥmōr	חמר	ḥmārā	ܚܡܪܐ	ḥimār	حمار	ʾadg	አድግ ፡
41.	Door	delet, peteḥ	דלת, פתח	tarʿā	ܬܪܥܐ	bāb	باب	xōxt, ʾanqaṣ	ኆኅት ፡ አንቀጽ ፡
42.	Dove	tōr, yōnā	תור, יונה	yawnā	ܝܘܢܐ	ḥamāmaᵗ	حمامة	rəgb	ርግብ ፡
43.	Dream (v.)	ḥālam	חלם	ḥlam	ܚܠܡ	ḥalima	حلم	ḥalama	ሐለመ ፡
44.	Dress	lābaš	לבש	lbiš	ܠܒܫ	labisa	لبس	labsa	ለብሰ ፡

Akkadian		Ugaritic		#	English	Maʕlula	Jibbali
našāku	𒀹	nθk	𒀹	17.	Bite	inxac	ẓaʕár
karābu	𒀹	brk	𒀹	18.	Bless	bōrex	ōrək
dāmu	𒀹	dm	𒀹	19.	Blood	eδma	δɔhr
eṣemtu	𒀹	ʕzm	𒀹	20.	Bone	γerma	ʕíẓéẓ
kurummatu	𒀹	lḥm	𒀹	21.	Bread	leḥma	xabzέt
tulū	𒀹	θd	𒀹	22.	Breast	bezzō, maḥalbō	θɔ́dɛ
axu	𒀹	ȧx	𒀹	23.	Brother	ḥōna	ʾaγá
banū	𒀹	bny	𒀹	24.	Build	aʕmar	ební
šūru, lū	𒀹	θr	𒀹	25.	Bull	θawra	γɔ́ẓəb
šāmu	𒀹	qny	𒀹	26.	Buy	izban	śɔ́tέm
būru	𒀹	ʕgl	𒀹	27.	Calf	ʾakkūša	šɔ́ṭər
šasū	𒀹	qrȧ	𒀹	28.	Call	iqr	ṣaʕáq
udru	𒀹	ȧdr	𒀹	29.	Camel	γamla	gūl
kussū	𒀹	ksȧ, kḥθ	𒀹	30.	Chair	kūrsa	kərsí
māru, ṣexru, līdu	𒀹	y/wld	𒀹	31.	Child	bsōna, ṭefla	əmbérέ
kašādu	𒀹	ȧtw, bȧ	𒀹	32.	Come	θōlē	zaḥám
arxu, lītu	𒀹	ȧrx, ypt	𒀹	33.	Cow	θawarcca	léʾ
bakū	𒀹	bky	𒀹	34.	Cry	ibx	béké
sāru, raqādu	𒀹	xl, rqd	𒀹	35.	Dance	irqaδ	ɛrqɔ́d
mārtu	𒀹	bt	𒀹	36.	Daughter	berca	brit
ūmu	𒀹	ym	𒀹	37.	Day	yōma	yum
mātu	𒀹	mt	𒀹	38.	Die	ameθ	xárɔ́g
kalbu	𒀹	klb	𒀹	39.	Dog	xalpa	kɔb
imēru	𒀹	ḥmr	𒀹	40.	Donkey	ḥmōra	qéráḥ
daltu, bābu	𒀹	ptḥ, dlt	𒀹	41.	Door	θarʕa	ʾɔb
summatu	𒀹	ynt	𒀹	42.	Dove	yawna	ḥõt, ʕeẓyét
šuttu (n.)	𒀹	ḥlm	𒀹	43.	Dream	ḥelma (n.)	ḥélm
labāšu	𒀹	lbš	𒀹	44.	Dress	ilpas	lɔ́s

		Hebrew		Syriac		Arabic		Geʿez	
45.	Drink	šātā	שתה	ʾištī	ܐܫܬܝ	šariba	شرب	satya	ሰትየ ፡
46.	Ear	ʾōzen	אוזן	ʾiδnā	ܐܕܢܐ	ʾuδun	أذن	ʾəzn	እዝን ፡
47.	Earth	ʾereṣ	ארץ	ʾarʿā, midrā	ܐܪܥܐ, ܡܕܪܐ	ʾarḍ	أرض	mədr	ምድር ፡
48.	Eat	ʾākal	אכל	ʾikal	ܐܟܠ	ʾakala	أكل	balʿa	በልዐ ፡
49.	Eight	šmōnā	שמונה	tmānyā	ܬܡܢܝܐ	θamāniyaᵗ	ثمانية	samānītū	ሰማኒቱ ፡
50.	Enter	bāʾ	בא	ʿal	ܥܠ	daxala	دخل	bōʾa	ቦአ ፡
51.	Exit	yāṣāʾ	יצא	npaq	ܢܦܩ	xaraǰa	خرج	waḍʾa	ወዕአ ፡
52.	Eye	ʿayin	עין	ʿaynā	ܥܝܢܐ	ʿayn	عين	ʿayn	ዐይን ፡
53.	Face	pānīm	פנים	ʾappē	ܐܦܐ	waǰh	وجه	gaṣṣ	ገጽ ፡
54.	Fall	nāpal	נפל	npal	ܢܦܠ	saqaṭa, waqaʿa	سقط، وقع	wadqa	ወድቀ ፡
55.	Far	rāḥōq	רחוק	raḥḥīqā	ܪܚܝܩܐ	baʿīd	بعيد	rəḥūq	ርሑቅ ፡
56.	Fat	šemen	שמן	tarbā	ܬܪܒܐ	šaḥm, duhn	شحم، دهن	šəbḥ	ሥብሕ ፡
57.	Father	ʾāb	אב	ʾabā	ܐܒܐ	ʾab	أب	ʾab	አብ ፡
58.	Fill	mālēʾ	מלא	mlā	ܡܠܐ	malaʾa	ملأ	malʾa	መልአ ፡
59.	Finger	ʾeṣbaʿ	אצבע	ṣibʿtā	ܨܒܥܬܐ	ʾuṣbaʿ	أصبع	ʾaṣbāʿt	አጽባዕት ፡
60.	Fire	ʾēš	אש	nūrā	ܢܘܪܐ	nār	نار	ʾəsāt	እሳት ፡
61.	Fish	dāg	דג	nunā	ܢܘܢܐ	samak, nūn	سمك، نون	ʿāšā	ዓሣ ፡
62.	Five	ḥmiššā	חמשה	ḥammšā	ܚܡܫܐ	xamsaᵗ	خمسة	xamməstū	ኃምስቱ ፡
63.	Flour	qemaḥ	קמח	qamḥā	ܩܡܚܐ	ṭaḥīn, daqīq	طحين، دقيق	ḥarīḍ	ሐሪ� ፡
64.	Fly	ʿāp	עף	praḥ	ܦܪܚ	ṭāra	طار	sarara	ሰረረ ፡
65.	Foot	regel, paʿam	רגל, פעם	riglā	ܪܓܠܐ	riǰl	رجل	ʾəgr	እግር ፡
66.	Four	ʾarbāʿā	ארבעה	ʾarbʿā	ܐܪܒܥܐ	ʾarbaʿaᵗ	أربعة	ʾarbāʿəttū	አርባዕቱ ፡
67.	Friend	yādīd, ḥābēr, rēʿ	ידיד, חבר, רע	rāḥmā, ḥabrā	ܪܚܡܐ, ܚܒܪܐ	ṣadīq	صديق	ʿark	ዐርክ ፡
68.	From	min	מן	min	ܡܢ	min	من	ʾəm	እም ፡

Akkadian	Ugaritic		Maʿlula	Jibbali
šatū	*šty*	45. Drink	*išci*	*šúŝi*
uznu	*ůdn*	46. Ear	*ēδna*	*ʾiδén*
erṣetu	*ʾarṣu*	47. Earth	*arʿa*	*ʾɛrẓ́*
akālu, *taʾū*	*åkl,* *spå*	48. Eat	*axal*	*té*
samānat	*θmn*	49. Eight	*θmōnya*	*θĩnə́t*
erēbu	*bå,* *ʿrb*	50. Enter	*eʿber*	*égaḥ*
waṣū	*yṣå*	51. Exit	*infeq*	*ŝxəníṭ*
īnu	*ʿn*	52. Eye	*ʿayna*	*ʿíhn*
pānū	*pnm*	53. Face	*ffōya*	*fénɛ,* *ɛ́gh*
maqātu	*npl,* *ql*	54. Fall	*iqlab,* *isqaṭ*	*gaʿár,* *hē*
rēqu	*rḥq*	55. Far	*baʿʿeδ*	*raḥq*
šamnu	*šmt*	56. Fat	*šobna* (butter)	*mašḥ,* *śabḥ*
abu	*åb,* *ʾadānu*	57. Father	*ōb*	*ʾiy*
malū	*mlå*	58. Fill	*iml*	*míẓ́i*
ubānu	*ůṣbʿ*	59. Finger	*ṣpaʿθa*	*ʾiṣbáʿ*
išātu	*ʾišitu,* *nr*	60. Fire	*nūra*	*śɔ́ṭ*
nūnu	*dg*	61. Fish	*samkθa*	*ḥut,* *ṣod*
xamšat	*xmš*	62. Five	*ḥamša*	*xõš*
qēmu	*qmḥ*	63. Flour	*qamḥa*	*ṭqíq*
naprušu, *šāʾu*	*då*	64. Fly	*aṭar*	*ferr*
šēpu	*riglu,* *išd,* *pʿn*	65. Foot	*reγra*	*faʿm,* *śɛf*
erbet	*årbʿ*	66. Four	*arpʿa*	*ɛrbəʿɔ́t*
ibru, *ruʾu*	*rʿ*	67. Friend	*ṣtīqa,* *rfīqa*	*ʿáśər,* *sudq*
ištu	*l-*	68. From	*m(n)*	*m(ən)*

		Hebrew		Syriac		Arabic		Ge'ez	
69.	Give	*nātan,* *yāhab*	נתן, יהב	*yab*	ܝܗܒ	*wahaba,* *ʾaʿṭā*	وهب، أعطى	*wahaba*	ወሀበ ፡
70.	Go	*hālak*	הלך	*ʾizal*	ܐܙܠ	*ðahaba*	ذهب	*ḥōra*	ሖረ ፡
71.	Goat	*ʿēz*	עז	*ʿizzā,* *gadyā*	ܥܙܐ، ܓܕܝܐ	*ʿanzaᵗ,* *maʿzaᵗ*	عنزة، معزة	*ṭalīt*	ጠሊት ፡
72.	God	*ʾlōhīm*	אלהים	*ʾalāhā*	ܐܠܗܐ	*allāh*	الله	*ʾəgzīʾa-bəḥēr*	እግዚአብሔር ፡
73.	Gold	*zāhāb*	זהב	*dahəbā*	ܕܗܒܐ	*ðahab*	ذهب	*warq*	ወርቅ
74.	Good	*ṭōb*	טב	*ṭāb*	ܛܒ	*ṭayyib*	طيب	*šannāy,* *xēr*	ሠናይ, ኄር
75.	Grass	*ʿēśeb,* *deše'*	עשׂב, דשא	*ʿisbā*	ܥܣܒܐ	*ʿušb,* *ḥašīš*	عشب، حشيش	*šāʿr*	ሣዕር
76.	Grind	*ṭāḥan*	טחן	*ṭḥin*	ܛܚܢ	*ṭaḥana*	طحن	*ṭaḥana,* *ḥaraḍa*	ጠሐነ ፡ ሐረፀ ፡
77.	Hair	*śēʿār*	שׂער	*saʿrā,* *minntā*	ܣܥܪܐ، ܡܢܬܐ	*šaʿraᵗ*	شعرة	*šəʿrt,* *ṣagʷr*	ሥዕርት ፡ ጸጕር
78.	Hand	*yād*	יד	*īdā*	ܐܝܕܐ	*yad*	يد	*ʾəd*	እድ ፡
79.	Hare	*ʾarnab*	ארנב	*ʾarnbā*	ܐܪܢܒܐ	*ʾarnab*	أرنب	*ʾarnab*	አርነብ ፡
80.	Head	*rōš*	ראש	*rīšā*	ܪܝܫܐ	*raʾs*	رأس	*rəʾs*	ርእስ ፡
81.	Hear	*šāmaʿ*	שמע	*šmaʿ*	ܫܡܥ	*samiʿa*	سمع	*samʿa*	ሰምዐ ፡
82.	Heart	*lēb*	לב	*libbā*	ܠܒܐ	*qalb*	قلب	*labb*	ልብ ፡
83.	He-Goat	*tayiš*	תיש	*tayšā,* *barḥā*	ܬܝܫܐ، ܒܪܚܐ	*tays*	تيس	*ṭalī*	ጠሊ ፡
84.	Honey	*dbaš*	דבש	*dibšā*	ܕܒܫܐ	*ʿasal*	عسل	*maʿār,* *dəbs*	መዓር ፡ ድብስ ፡
85.	Horn	*qeren*	קרן	*qarnā*	ܩܪܢܐ	*qarn*	قرن	*qarn*	ቀርን ፡
86.	Horse	*sūs*	סוס	*susyā*	ܣܘܣܝܐ	*ḥiṣān*	حصان	*faras*	ፈረስ ፡
87.	House	*bayit*	בית	*baytā*	ܒܝܬܐ	*bayt*	بيت	*bēt*	ቤት ፡
88.	Hundred	*mēʾā*	מאה	*māʾ*	ܡܐܐ	*miʾaᵗ*	مائة	*məʾt*	ምእት ፡
89.	Hunger	*rāʿāb*	רעב	*kapnā*	ܟܦܢܐ	*ǰūʿ*	جوع	*raxab*	ረኀብ ፡
90.	Hunt	*ṣād*	צד	*ṣād*	ܨܕ	*ṣāda*	صاد	*naʿawa*	ነዐወ
91.	Iron	*barzel*	ברזל	*parzlā*	ܦܪܙܠܐ	*ḥadīd*	حديد	*xaṣin*	ኀጺን ፡
92.	Kid	*gdī*	גדי	*gadyā,* *ṣiprāyā*	ܓܕܝܐ، ܨܦܪܝܐ	*ǰady*	جدي	*māḥsəʿ*	ማሕስዕ
93.	Kidney	*kilyā*	כליה	*kulītā*	ܟܘܠܝܬܐ	*kulyaᵗ*	كلية	*kʷəlīt*	ኵሊት ፡

Akkadian	Ugaritic			Maʕlula	Jibbali
nadānu	ytn	69.	Give	app	ezúm
alāku	hlk	70.	Go	zalle, allex	aɣád
enzu	ʕz	71.	Goat	ʕezza	ʔɔz
ilu	ʾilu	72.	God	alo	ʾɔ́ź, ʾallāh
xurāṣu	xrṣ	73.	Gold	δahba	ṭíb
ṭābu, damqu	ṭābu, nʕm	74.	Good	ṭōb	xár, ɛrḥím
dīšu	ỉmt	75.	Grass	ʕōšba, ḥašiša	rɔɣɔ́d, šáʾər
samādu, ṭēnu	ṭḥn	76.	Grind	ṭaḥnulle	ṭaḥán
pērtu, šārtu	ʕq, šʕrt	77.	Hair	saʕra	śfét
qātu	yd	78.	Hand	īδa	éd
arnabu	ảnhb	79.	Hare	arnba	ʾɛrní
rēšu	rỉš	80.	Head	rayša	réš
šemū	šmʕ	81.	Hear	išmeʕ	šĩʕ
libbu	lb	82.	Heart	leppa	ub, qɛlb
atūdu	gd	83.	He-Goat	caysa	tuš
dišpu	nbt	84.	Honey	δēbša	dɛbš
qarnu	qrn	85.	Horn	qarna	qun
sisū	ssw	86.	Horse	ḥṣōna	ḥáṣún
bītu	bt, dr	87.	House	payθa	bot
meʾat	miʾtu	88.	Hundred	emʕa	mút
būru, bubūtu	rɣbn	89.	Hunger	xafna	tɔf
ṣādu	ṣd	90.	Hunt	ṣayyat	əṣtɔ́d
parzillu	brδl	91.	Iron	ḥatīta	ḥádíd
unīqu, lalū	gdy, llủ	92.	Kid	ɣaδδya	mədkér
kalītu	klyt	93.	Kidney	xulīθa	kuźét

		Hebrew		Syriac		Arabic		Ge'ez	
94.	Kill	hārag, qāṭal	הרג, קטל	qṭal	ܩܛܠ	qatala	قتل	qatala	ቀተለ፥
95.	King	melek	מלך	malkā	ܡܠܟܐ	malik	ملك	nəgūš	ንጉሥ፥
96.	Knee	berek	ברך	burkā	ܒܘܪܟܐ	rukba'	ركبة	bərk	ብርክ፥
97.	Know	yāda'	ידע	īda'	ܝܕܥ	'arifa	عرف	'a'mara, 'ōqa	አእመረ፥ ዖቀ
98.	Lamb	kebeš, ṭāle	כבש, טלה	'imrā, parrā	ܐܡܪܐ, ܦܪܐ	xarūf, ḥamal	خروف، حمل	māḥsə'	ማሕሰዕ፥
99.	Laugh	ṣāḥaq	צחק	ghak	ܓܚܟ	ḍaḥika	ضحك	šaḥaqa	ሠሐቀ፥
100.	Lion	'ri	ארי	'aryā	ܐܪܝܐ	'asad, sab'	أسد، سبع	'anbasā	ዐንበሳ፥
101.	Lip	śāpā	שפה	siptā	ܣܦܬܐ	šifa'	شفة	kanfar	ከንፈር፥
102.	Live	ḥāyā	חיה	ḥyā	ܚܝܐ	ḥayiya, 'āša	حيي، عاش	ḥaywa	ሐይወ፥
103.	Long	'ārok	ארך	'arrīk	ܐܪܝܟ	ṭawīl	طويل	nawwīx	ነዊኅ፥
104.	Lord	'ādōn, ba'al	אדון, בעל	ba'lā, mārā	ܒܥܠܐ, ܡܪܐ	sayyid, ba'l	سيد، بعل	'əgzī'	እግዚ፥
105.	Love	'āhēb	אהב	'aḥibb	ܐܚܒ	'aḥabb	أحب	'afqara	አፍቀረ፥
106.	Make	'āśā	עשה	'bad	ܥܒܕ	'amila, fa'ala	عمل، فعل	gabra	ገብረ፥
107.	Man	'īš, geber	איש, גבר	gabrā	ܓܒܪܐ	rajul	رجل	'əd, bə'sī	ዕድ፥ ብእሲ፥
108.	Many	rabbīm	רבים	rabbā, saggī'ā	ܪܒܐ, ܣܓܝܐ	kaθīr	كثير	bəzūx	ብዙኅ፥
109.	Meat	bāśār	בשר	bisrā	ܒܣܪܐ	laḥm	لحم	šəgā	ሥጋ፥
110.	Milk	ḥālāb	חלב	ḥalbā	ܚܠܒܐ	laban, ḥalīb	لبن، حليب	ḥalīb	ሐሊብ፥
111.	Month	ḥōdeš	חודש	yarḥā	ܝܪܚܐ	šahr	شهر	warx	ወርኅ፥
112.	Moon	yārēḥ, lbānā	ירח, לבנה	sahrā	ܣܗܪܐ	qamar	قمر	warx	ወርኅ፥
113.	Morning	bōqer, šaḥar	בקר, שחר	ṣaprā	ܨܦܪܐ	ṣabāḥ	صباح	ṣəbāḥ	ጽባሕ፥
114.	Mother	'ēm	אם	'immā	ܐܡܐ	'umm	أم	'əmm	እም፥
115.	Mountain	har	הר	ṭūrā	ܛܘܪܐ	jabal	جبل	dabr	ደብር፥
116.	Mouth	pe	פה	pummā	ܦܘܡܐ	fam	فم	'af	አፍ፥

Akkadian		Ugaritic				Ma'lula	Jibbali
dāku,	𒀭	*mxš,*	𒀭	94.	Kill	*iqṭal*	*létəγ*
nēru	𒀭	*hrg*	𒀭				
šarru	𒀭	*malku*	𒀭	95.	King	*malka*	*mélík*
birku	𒀭	*brk*	𒀭	96.	Knee	*rḥōbθa*	*bɛrk*
edū	𒀭	*ydʿ*	𒀭	97.	Know	*iδaʿ*	*édaʿ,*
							γárɔb
kalūmu,	𒀭	*imr,*	𒀭	98.	Lamb	*qarqōra*	*kɔbś*
puxādu	𒀭	*kr*	𒀭				
ṣiāxu	𒀭	*ṣḥq,*	𒀭	99.	Laugh	*iδḥek*	*ẓaḥak*
		gmẓ	𒀭				
lābu,	𒀭	*lbủ*	𒀭	100.	Lion	*sabʿa*	*ʾasɛ́d*
nēšu	𒀭						
šaptu	𒀭	*špt*	𒀭	101.	Lip	*sefθa*	*qəfrér*
balāṭu	𒀭	*ḥwy*	𒀭	102.	Live	*eḥi*	*ʿɛ́ś*
arku	𒀭	*ảrk* (v.)	𒀭	103.	Long	*irrex*	*rihm*
bēlu	𒀭	*bʿl,*	𒀭	104.	Lord	*mōra*	*báʿal*
		ảdn	𒀭				
rāmu	𒀭	*ảhb*	𒀭	105.	Love	*irḥam*	*ʿágəb,*
							ḥebb
epēšu	𒀭	*ʿšy*	𒀭	106.	Make	*išwi*	*ʿõl*
zikāru	𒀭	*mt*	𒀭	107.	Man	*γabrōna*	*γég*
mādu	𒀭	*mỉd,*	𒀭	108.	Many	*summar,*	*mɛ́kən*
		ʿẓm	𒀭			*baḥar*	
šīru	𒀭	*bšr,*	𒀭	109.	Meat	*besra*	*téʾ*
		šiʾru	𒀭				
šizbu	𒀭	*ḥlb*	𒀭	110.	Milk	*ḥalpa*	*ḥɔ́lɔ́b,*
							núśub
warxu	𒀭	*yrx*	𒀭	111.	Month	*yarḥa*	*ɔ́rx*
warxu	𒀭	*yrx*	𒀭	112.	Moon	*sahra*	*ʾɛ́rɔ́t*
šēru	𒀭	*šḥr*	𒀭	113.	Morning	*ṣofra*	*kḥássǎf*
ummu	𒀭	*ủm*	𒀭	114.	Mother	*emma*	*ʾɛ́m*
šadū	𒀭	*gbl,*	𒀭	115.	Mountain	*ṭūra*	*giɛ́l*
		γr,	𒀭				
		δd	𒀭				
pū	𒀭	*p*	𒀭	116.	Mouth	*θemma*	*xɔh*

		Hebrew		Syriac		Arabic		Ge'ez
117.	Name	šēm	שם	šmā	ܫܡܐ	ism	اسم	səm	ስም ፡
118.	New	ḥādāš	חדש	ḥatā	ܚܰܬ݂ܳܐ	ǧadīd, ḥadīθ	جديد، حديث	ḥaddīs	ሐዲስ ፡
119.	Night	laylā	לילה	līlyā	ܠܺܠܝܳܐ	layl	ليل	lēlīt	ሌሊት ፡
120.	Nine	tišʿā	תשעה	tišʿā	ܬܶܫܥܳܐ	tisʿaᵗ	تسعة	təsʿattū	ትስዕቱ ፡
121.	Nose	ʾap	אף	ʾappē, nḥīrā	ܐܰܦܳܐ، ܢܚܺܝܪܳܐ	ʾanf	أنف	ʾanf	አንፍ ፡
122.	Oil	šemen	שמן	mišḥā	ܡܶܫܚܳܐ	zayt	زيت	qəbʾ	ቅብእ ፡
123.	On	ʿal	על	ʿal	ܥܰܠ	ʿalā	على	lāʿla	ላዕለ ፡
124.	One	ʾeḥād	אחד	ḥad	ܚܰܕ	ʾaḥad	أحد	ʾaḥadū	አሐዱ ፡
125.	Or	ʾō	או	ʾaw	ܐܰܘ	ʾaw	أو	ʾaw	አው ፡
126.	Person	ʾādām	אדם	nāšā	ܐܢܳܫܳܐ	ʾinsān	إنسان	bəʾsī	ብእሲ ፡
127.	Pig	ḥzīr	חזיר	ḥzīrā	ܚܙܺܝܪܳܐ	xinzīr	خنزير	xanzīr, ḥarāwəyā	ጎንዚር ፡ ሐራውያ ፡
128.	Rain	māṭār, gešem	מטר, גשם	miṭrā	ܡܶܛܪܳܐ	maṭar	مطر	zənām	ዝናም ፡
129.	Return	šāb	שב	tāb	ܬܳܒ	raǧaʿa, θāba	رجع، ثاب	gabʾa	ገብአ ፡
130.	Rib	ṣēlaʿ	צלע	ʾilʿā	ܐܶܠܥܳܐ	ḍilʿ	ضلع	gabō	ገቦ ፡
131.	Ride	rākab	רכב	rkib	ܪܟܶܒ	rakiba	ركب	rakaba	ረከበ ፡
132.	Right	yāmīn	ימין	yammīnā	ܝܰܡܺܝܢܳܐ	yamīn	يمين	yamān	የማን ፡
133.	River	nāhār	נהר	nahrā	ܢܰܗܪܳܐ	nahr	نهر	falag, wəḥīz	ፈለግ ፡ ዉሒዝ ፡
134.	Road	derek, šbīl	דרך, שביל	ʾurḥā	ܐܽܘܪܚܳܐ	ṭarīq	طريق	fənōt, mangad	ፍኖት ፡ መንገድ ፡
135.	Root	šōreš	שרש	širšā, ʿiqqārā	ܫܶܪܫܳܐ، ܥܶܩܳܪܳܐ	ʾaṣl, ʿirq, širš	أصل، عرق، شرش	šərw	ሥርው ፡
136.	Rope	ḥebel	חבל	ḥablā, nīnāyā	ܚܰܒܠܳܐ، ܢܺܝܢܳܝܳܐ	ḥabl	حبل	ḥabl	ሐብል ፡
137.	Run	rāṣ	רץ	rhiṭ	ܪܗܶܛ	ǧarā, rakaḍa	جرى، ركض	rōṣa	ሮጸ ፡
138.	Salt	melaḥ	מלח	milḥā	ܡܶܠܚܳܐ	milḥ	ملح	ṣēw	ጼው ፡
139.	Say	ʾāmar	אמר	ʾimar	ܐܶܡܰܪ	qāla	قال	bəhla	ብህለ ፡
140.	Sea	yām	ים	yammā	ܝܰܡܳܐ	baḥr	بحر	bāḥr	ባሕር ፡

Akkadian		Ugaritic				Maʕlula	Jibbali
šumu	𒈬𒌑	šm	𒊹𒋾	117.	Name	ešma	šum
eššu	𒀸𒈬	ḥdθ	𒄭𒐊𒌋	118.	New	ḥacc	ʔódín
mūšu, līliātu	𒈬𒈬 𒆠𒉌𒆠𒉌𒈨𒈬	ll	𒐼𒐼	119.	Night	lēlya	ʕáṣər
tišet	𒋾𒐈𒈬𒁹	tšʕ	𒊹𒋗𒌋	120.	Nine	ṭešʕa	saʕét
appu	𒀊𒈬	ʔappu	𒀊𒈬	121.	Nose	manxra	naxrér
šamnu	𒐊𒈨𒅆𒌋	šmn	𒊹𒋾𒈬	122.	Oil	mešḥa	ḥahl
eli	𒂖𒆠𒐊	ʕl	𒍵𒐈	123.	On	ʕal	ðér
ištēnu	𒅖𒋼𒌋	aḥd	𒄷𒄭𒐊	124.	One	aḥḥað	ṭad
ū	𒌋𒆠𒐊	u	𒐈	125.	Or	yā	mən
awīlu	𒇽𒌋𒈨𒐊	adm, bunušu	𒄩𒐈𒋾 𒍵𒌋𒈬	126.	Person	barnāš	bírdém
xuzīru, šaxū	𒄷𒍝𒍣𒊑 𒐊𒄷𒍝𒄷	xnzr xuzīru	𒄷𒄯𒍝 𒄷𒍝𒍣𒊑	127.	Pig	ḥzīra	xanzír
zunnu	𒍪𒌋𒀭	mṭr	𒈬𒀴𒈨	128.	Rain	rayya	raḥmét
tāru	𒆳𒆠𒐈𒊺	θb	𒌋𒉡	129.	Return	ʕowet	edōr, régaʕ, redd
ṣēlu	𒅖𒐈𒈨	ṣlʕ	𒐕𒐈𒍵	130.	Rib	ʕalʕa	ḻ̣alʕ, gɛśf
rakābu	𒊑𒐈𒆳𒍝	rkb	𒊑𒅗𒉡	131.	Ride	irxab	rékəb
imnu	𒄀𒐊𒀭	ymn	𒐊𒈨	132.	Right	yīmen	émlí
nāru	𒀭𒐊𒊏	nhr	𒈨𒂖𒐊	133.	River	nahra	félég
padānu	𒉺𒐊𒀭	ntb	𒈨𒐈𒉡	134.	Road	tarba	ʔɔrm
šuršu	𒋩𒈬	šrš	𒊹𒊑𒊹	135.	Root	šerša	síróx, ʕarq
ašlu	𒀾𒐊	ḥbl	𒄷𒉡𒐊	136.	Rope	ḥabla	qod
rāṣu	𒊑𒐈𒍝	lsm	𒐈𒌋𒋾	137.	Run	arheṭ	šaʕé
ṭābtu	𒌅𒐊	mlḥt	𒈨𒐈𒋫	138.	Salt	melḥa	míẓḥót
qabū	𒋡𒈬	rgm	𒊑𒄀	139.	Say	amar	ʕõr
tāmtu	𒆳𒈨𒋫𒐊	ym	𒐊𒋾	140.	Sea	bahra, yamm	rémnɛm

		Hebrew		Syriac		Arabic		Geʿez	
141.	See	*rāʾā*	ראה	*ḥzā*	ܚܙܐ	*raʾā*	رأى	*rəʾya*	ርእየ ፡
142.	Seed	*zeraʿ*	זרע	*zarʿā*	ܙܪܥܐ	*baδraᵗ*	بذرة	*zarʾ,* *bəzr*	ዘርእ ፡ ብዝር ፡
143.	Send	*šālaḥ*	שלח	*šlaḥ*	ܫܠܚ	*ʾarsala*	أرسل	*laʾaka,* *fannawa*	ለአከ ፡ ፈነወ ፡
144.	Seven	*šibʿā*	שבעה	*šabʿā*	ܫܒܥܐ	*sabʿaᵗ*	سبعة	*sabʿattū*	ሰብዐቱ ፡
145.	Shadow	*ṣēl*	צל	*ṭillālā*	ܛܠܠܐ	*ẓill*	ظل	*ṣəlālōt*	ጽላሎት ፡
146.	Sheep	*śe*	שה	*niqyā*	ܢܩܝܐ	*šāʾ,* *γanam*	شاء، غنم	*baggəʿ*	በግዕ ፡
147.	Shepherd	*rōʿe*	רועה	*rāʿyā*	ܪܥܝܐ	*rāʿⁱⁿ*	راع	*raʿāyī*	ረዓዪ ፡
148.	Short	*qāṣār*	קצר	*zʿurā,* *karyā*	ܙܥܘܪܐ، ܟܪܝܐ	*qaṣir*	قصير	*xaṣir*	ኀጺር ፡
149.	Shoulder	*kātēp*	כתף	*katpā*	ܟܬܦܐ	*katif,* *minkab*	كتف، منكب	*matkaf(t)*	መትከፍ ፡
150.	Silver	*kesep*	כסף	*kispā*	ܟܣܦܐ	*fiḍḍaᵗ*	فضة	*bərūr*	ብሩር ፡
151.	Sing	*šār,* *zimmer*	שר, זמר	*zmar*	ܙܡܪ	*γannā*	غنى	*ḥalaya,* *zammara*	ሐለየ ፡ ዘመረ ፡
152.	Sister	*ʾāḥōt*	אחות	*ḥātā*	ܚܬܐ	*ʾuxt*	أخت	*ʾəxt*	እኅት ፡
153.	Sit	*yāšab*	ישב	*ītib*	ܝܬܒ	*qaʿada*	قعد	*nabara*	ነበረ ፡
154.	Six	*šiššā*	ששה	*štā*	ܫܬܐ	*sittaᵗ*	ستة	*səddəstū*	ስድስቱ ፡
155.	Skin	*gēled*	גלד	*gildā*	ܓܠܕܐ	*ǰild*	جلد	*māʾs*	ማእስ ፡
156.	Sky	*šāmayim*	שמים	*šmayyā*	ܫܡܝܐ	*samāʾ*	سماء	*samāy*	ሰማይ ፡
157.	Slave	*ʿebed*	עבד	*ʿabdā*	ܥܒܕܐ	*ʿabd*	عبد	*bāryā,* *gabr*	ባርያ ፡ ገብር ፡
158.	Sleep (v.)	*yāšēn,* *nām*	ישן, נם	*dmik,* *nām*	ܕܡܟ، ܢܡ	*wasina,* *nāma*	وسن، نام	*nōma*	ኖመ ፡
159.	Small	*qāṭān,* *ṣāʿir*	קטן, צעיר	*zʿūrā,* *daqdqā*	ܙܥܘܪܐ، ܕܩܕܩܐ	*ṣaγir*	صغير	*nəʾūs,* *ḥəṣūṣ*	ንኡስ ፡ ሕጹጽ ፡
160.	Smoke (n.)	*ʿāšān,* *qīṭōr*	עשן, קיטר	*tinnānā*	ܬܢܢܐ	*duxān*	دخان	*ṭīs,* *tann*	ጢስ ፡ ተን ፡
161.	Snake	*nāḥāš*	נחש	*ḥiwyā*	ܚܘܝܐ	*ḥayyaᵗ*	حية	*ʾarwē*	አርዌ ፡
162.	Son	*bēn*	בן	*brā*	ܒܪܐ	*ibn*	ابن	*wald*	ወልድ ፡
163.	Soul	*nepeš*	נפש	*napšā*	ܢܦܫܐ	*nafs*	نفس	*nafs*	ነፍስ ፡
164.	Speak	*millēl*	מלל	*mallil*	ܡܠܠ	*takallama*	تكلّم	*nagara*	ነገረ ፡

Akkadian	Ugaritic		Maʿlula	Jibbali
amāru	*ảmr*, *ḥdy*, *ʿn*	141. See	*eḥmi*	*šíní*
zēru	*drʿ*	142. Seed	*zarʿa*	*bέðər*
šapāru, *ṭarādu*	*lỉk*, *šlḥ*	143. Send	*šattar*	*ebláγ*
sebet	*šbʿ*	144. Seven	*šobʿa*	*šəbʿə́t*
ṣillu	*ẓl*	145. Shadow	*xyola*	*gɔ́fɛʾ*
immeru, *šū*	*š*, *θảt*	146. Sheep	*xarōfa*	*θēt*
rēʾū	*rʿy*	147. Shepherd	*rōʿya*	*réʿi*
kurū	*qṣr*	148. Short	*qūṣṣur*	*qéṣír*
būdu	*ktp*	149. Shoulder	*xaffθa*	*kənséd*, *kɛtf*
kaspu	*ksp*	150. Silver	*xesfa*	*fíżżát*
zamāru	*šr*	151. Sing	*ʿanni*	*ɛhbéb*
axātu	*ʾaxātu*	152. Sister	*ḥōθa*	*γit*
wašābu	*yθb*	153. Sit	*qʿōle*	*skɔf*
šeššet	*θθ*	154. Six	*šecca*	*štət*
mašku	*ʿōru*	155. Skin	*γelta*	*gɔ́d*
šamū	*šamūma*	156. Sky	*šmoya*	*siɛ̃h*
wardu	*ʿabdu*	157. Slave	*ʿapta*	*ʾɔʾgɔ́r*
ṣalālu	*yšn*	158. Sleep (v.)	*iðmēx*	*ŝéf*
ṣexru	*sγr*, *dq*, *θrr*	159. Small	*izʿur*, *əzʿūṭ*	*níṣán*
qutru	*qṭr*	160. Smoke	*tuxxona*	*məndɔ́x*
ṣerru	*bθn*, *tunnanu*	161. Snake	*ḥūya*	*γuźt*, *hɔ́t*
māru	*bn*	162. Son	*ebra*	*bɛr*
napištu	*npš*	163. Soul	*nefša*	*rəqbét*, *nəfsét*
zakāru	*rgm*	164. Speak	*aḥki*	*hérɔ́g*

		Hebrew		Syriac		Arabic		Ge'ez	
165.	Star	kōkāb	כוכב	kawkbā	ܟܘܟܒܐ	kawkab, najm	كوكب، نجم	kōkab	ኮከብ ፡
166.	Stick	šēbeṭ	שבט	ḥuṭrā	ܚܘܛܪܐ	ʿaṣā	عصا	batr	በትር ፡
167.	Stomach	qēbā, kārēś	קבה, כרש	karsā	ܟܪܣܐ	miʿdat, kirš	معدة، كرش	karš, kabd	ከርሥ ፡ ከብድ ፡
168.	Stone	ʾeben	אבן	kīpā, ʾabnā	ܟܐܦܐ ܐܒܢܐ	ḥajar	حجر	ʾəbn	እብን ፡
169.	Sun	šemeš	שמש	šimšā	ܫܡܫܐ	šams	شمس	ḍaḥāy, ʾamir	ፀሐይ ፡ አሚር ፡
170.	Sweat	zēʿā	זעה	duʿtā	ܕܘܥܬܐ	ʿaraq	عرق	ḥāf	ሃፍ ፡
171.	Tail	zānāb	זנב	dunbā	ܕܘܢܒܐ	ðanab	ذنب	zanab	ዘነብ ፡
172.	Take	lāqaḥ	לקח	ʾiḥad	ܐܣܒ	ʾaxaða	أخذ	ʾaxaza, našʾa	አኀዘ ፡ ነሥአ ፡
173.	Ten	ʿśārā	עשׂרה	ʿisrā	ܥܣܪܐ	ʿašarat	عشرة	ʿaššartū	ዐሠርቱ ፡
174.	Thousand	ʾelep	אלף	ʾalpā	ܐܠܦܐ	ʾalf	ألف	ʾəlf	አልፍ ፡
175.	Three	šlōšā	שלשה	tlātā	ܬܠܬܐ	θalāθat	ثلاثة	šalastū	ሠለስቱ ፡
176.	Throw	yārā	ירה	šdā, rmā	ܫܕܐ، ܪܡܐ	ramā	رمى	warawa, ramaya	ወረወ ፡ ረመየ ፡
177.	Tie	ʾāsar, qāšar	אסר קשר	ʾisar, qṭar	ܐܣܪ، ܩܛܪ	rabaṭa	ربط	ʾasara, qʷaṣara	አሰረ ፡ ቈጸረ ፡
178.	Tomb	qeber	קבר	qabrā	ܩܒܪܐ	qabr	قبر	maqbar	መቅበር ፡
179.	Tongue	lāšōn	לשון	liššānā	ܠܫܢܐ	lisān	لسان	ləssān	ልሳን ፡
180.	Tooth	šēn	שן	šinnā, kakkā	ܫܢܐ، ܟܟܐ	sinn	سن	sənn	ስን ፡
181.	Tree	ʿēṣ, ʾilān	עץ, אילן	ʾilānā	ܐܝܠܢܐ	šajarat	شجرة	ʿəḍ, ʿōm	ዕፅ ፡ ዖም ፡
182.	Two	šnayim	שנים	treyn	ܬܪܝܢ	iθnāni	اثنان	kəlʾē	ክልኤ ፡
183.	Under	taḥtī	תחתי	tḥēt	ܬܚܝܬ	taḥt	تحت	tāḥta	ታሕተ ፡
184.	Want	ʾābā	אבה	ṣbā	ܨܒܐ	ʾarāda	أراد	faqada	ፈቀደ ፡
185.	Wash	rāḥaṣ	רחץ	ʾašīg, ḥāp	ܐܫܝܓ، ܣܚ	ɣasala, raḥaḍa	غسل، رحض	xaḍaba, rəḥḍa	ኀፀበ ፡ ርሕፀ ፡
186.	Water (n.)	mayim	מים	mayyā	ܡܝܐ	māʾ	ماء	māy	ማይ ፡
187.	Water (v.)	hišqā	השקה	ʾašqī	ܐܫܩܝ	saqā	سقى	saqaya	ሰቀየ ፡
188.	Well	bʾēr	באר	bīrā	ܒܝܪܐ	biʾr	بئر	ʿazaqt	ዐዘቅት ፡
189.	West	maʿrāb	מערב	maʿrbā	ܡܥܪܒܐ	ɣarb, maɣrib	غرب، مغرب	ʿarab, məʿrāb	ዐረብ ፡ ምዕራብ ፡
190.	What	mah	מה	mā	ܡܐ	mā	ما	mī, mənt	ሚ ፡ ምንት ፡

Akkadian		Ugaritic				Maʕlula	Jibbali
kakkabu	𒃷𒃷	kbkb	𒃷𒃷	165.	Star	xawkæbθa	kəbkéb
xaṭṭu	𒃷	xṭ	𒃷	166.	Stick	qīsa	xɔṭrɔ́q
karšu	𒃷	krs	𒃷	167.	Stomach	ɣawwa	ŝírŝ
abnu	𒃷	ảbn	𒃷	168.	Stone	xēfa	fúdún
šamšu	𒃷	šapšu	𒃷	169.	Sun	šimša	yum
zūtu	𒃷	dʕt	𒃷	170.	Sweat	daʕθa	naɣlt
zibbatu	𒃷	δnbt	𒃷	171.	Tail	δēnpa	δúnúb
axāzu, leqū	𒃷	ảxδ, lqḥ	𒃷	172.	Take	aḥaδ	ḥōl
ešeret	𒃷	ʕšr	𒃷	173.	Ten	ʕasra	ʕəŝírét
līmu	𒃷	ảlp	𒃷	174.	Thousand	ōlef	ʾɔf
šalāšat	𒃷	θlθ	𒃷	175.	Three	θlōθa	ŝɔθét
nadū	𒃷	yry	𒃷	176.	Throw	δarri	ɛrdé
kaṣāru, rakāsu	𒃷	rks, ảsr	𒃷	177.	Tie	iqṭar	ʕɔ́ṣɔ́b, rɔ́ṭ
qabru	𒃷	qbr	𒃷	178.	Tomb	qabra	qɔ̄r
lišānu	𒃷	lašānu	𒃷	179.	Tongue	liššōna	ɛlŝén
šinnu	𒃷	šn	𒃷	180.	Tooth	šenna	šnin
iṣu	𒃷	ʕṣ	𒃷	181.	Tree	šajarθa	hérúm
šina	𒃷	θn	𒃷	182.	Two	iθr	θroh
šaplānu	𒃷	tḥt	𒃷	183.	Under	cuḥc	lxin
erēšu	𒃷	ảrš	𒃷	184.	Want	ibʕi	ʕágəb
ramāku, mesū	𒃷	rḥṣ	𒃷	185.	Wash	imši	raḥáẓ
mū	𒃷	my	𒃷	186.	Water (n.)	mōya	míh
šaqū	𒃷	šqy	𒃷	187.	Water (v.)	ašqi	šéqé
būru	𒃷	nab/pku	𒃷	188.	Well	bīra	ɣɔ̄r
erbu	𒃷	ʕrb	𒃷	189.	West	maʕrba	múɣrub, qəblét
mīnū	𒃷	mn	𒃷	190.	What	mō	ʾíné

	Hebrew		Syriac		Arabic		Ge'ez	
191. Wheat	ḥiṭṭā	חטה	ḥiṭṭtā	ܚܛܬܐ	qamḥ, hinṭaᵗ	قمح، حنطة	šərnāy	ሥርናይ ፡
192. Where	ʾayyēh	איה	ʾaykā	ܐܝܟܐ	ʾayna	عين	ʾaytē	አይቴ ፡
193. White	lābān	לבן	ḥiwwār	ܚܘܪ	ʾabyaḍ	أبيض	ṣəʿdəw	ጸዕድው ፡
194. Who	mī	מי	man	ܡܢ	man	من	mannū	መኑ ፡
195. Wind (n.)	rūḥ	רוח	rūḥā	ܪܘܚܐ	rīḥ	ريح	nafās	ነፋስ ፡
196. Wine	yayin	יין	ḥamrā	ܚܡܪܐ	xamr	خمر	wayn	ወይን ፡
197. With	ʿim	עם	ʿam	ܥܡ	maʿa	مع	məsla	ምስለ ፡
198. Woman	ʾiššā	אשה	ʾattətā	ܐܢܬܬܐ	imraʾaᵗ	امرأة	bəʾsīt, ʾanəst	ብእሲት ፡ አንስት ፡
199. Write	kātab	כתב	ktab	ܟܬܒ	kataba	كتب	ṣaḥafa	ጸሐፈ ፡
200. Year	šānā	שנה	šattā	ܫܢܬܐ	ʿām, sanaᵗ	عام سنة	ʿāmat	ዓመት ፡

Akkadian		Ugaritic				Maʕlula	Jibbali
kibtu	𒆳𒆳	*ḥṭt*	𒐏𒐏𒐏	191.	Wheat	*ḥeṭṭθa*	*bohr*
ayyānu	𒀭𒀭𒀭	*iy*	𒐏𒐏	192.	Where	*hanukk*	*hútun, hun*
peṣū	𒐏𒐏𒐏	*labanu*	𒐏𒐏𒐏	193.	White	*ḥūwwar*	*lūn*
mannu	𒐏𒐏	*my*	𒐏𒐏	194.	Who	*mōn*	*mun*
šāru	𒐏𒐏	*rḥ*	𒐏𒐏	195.	Wind (n.)	*hwō, riḥa*	*h(i)yɛ́*
karānu	𒐏𒐏𒐏	*yn, xmr*	𒐏𒐏 𒐏𒐏	196.	Wine	*ḥamra*	*xɛ̃r*
itti	𒐏𒐏	*ʕm*	𒐏𒐏	197.	With	*ʕemm*	*k-*
sinništu, iššu	𒐏 𒐏𒐏	*aθt*	𒐏𒐏	198.	Woman	*eccθa, šunīθa*	*teθ*
šaṭāru	𒐏𒐏𒐏	*ktb, spr*	𒐏𒐏 𒐏𒐏	199.	Write	*ixθab*	*ktɔb*
šattu	𒐏𒐏	*šnt*	𒐏𒐏	200.	Year	*ešna*	*ʕónút*

Appendix

Classical Semitic Scripts*

by Peter T. Daniels

The writing systems used for the Semitic languages are traditionally said to encompass the three principal kinds: alphabetic, syllabic, and logographic-syllabic. According to the typology introduced by this author, to categorize the Semitic scripts two additional types must be recognized, called "abjad" and "abugida."

A Bit of History

The scripts in which the West Semitic literary languages are written, and all alphabets everywhere, are descended from a common ancestor, often said to be attested in the graffiti of Canaanite mine workers in the Sinai from about the 16th century B.C.E. and first certainly found in the "proto-Canaanite" inscriptions of a somewhat later date. While the interpretation of proto-Sinaitic is far from certain, the next stages of the script, found in Phoenician and Aramaic inscriptions from about 1300 B.C.E. on, are well understood and the principal difficulties in interpretation stem from poor preservation of the materials and from the fact that at various eras various pairs of characters came to resemble each other more than is optimal for differentiating them. All the scripts mentioned here are *abjad*s—they denote consonants only. By the sixth century B.C.E. there could be distinguished a Canaanite and an Aramaic script. The former died out almost entirely (surviving only in Samaritan), to be replaced by the latter, which by the time of the Qumran documents (as early as 200 B.C.E.), if not the Egyptian Aramaic ones (up to 400 B.C.E.), had nearly achieved the shape of today's square Hebrew letters. A striving for ease and speed in writing led, in separate developments, to cursive Syriac (by 400 C.E.) and Arabic (by 500), among other varieties. Puzzling is the relationship between the main stream of abjadic systems and the Ugaritic abjad (14th century B.C.E.): some of its letters, which are cuneiform signs (see below), resemble the Phoenician counterparts, while a

---

* Adapted from Appendix B of G. Bergsträsser, *Introduction to the Semitic Languages: Text Specimens and Grammatical Sketches* (translated and annotated by Peter T. Daniels; Copyright © Eisenbrauns [Winona Lake, Indiana], 1983, 1995); used by permission.

251

connection is difficult to perceive for others; but the abjad of the South Arabian inscriptions (from at least 500 B.C.E.) is closest in letterforms to the Ugaritic. The earliest Arabic-language graffiti (Safaitic, 1st century B.C.E. – 3d century C.E.; Thamudic, perhaps 5th century B.C.E. – 5th century C.E.) are in a South Arabian script. The Ethiopic script is derived from the South Arabian abjad.

Abjads

Table 37. Northwest Semitic Scripts

Value	Ugaritic	Hebrew	Estrangelo	Serto	Nestorian	Numeric Value
ʾ (å)	⊢	א	ܐ	ܐ	ܐ	1
b	⊞	ב	ܒ	ܒ	ܒ	2
g	Ⲧ	ג	ܓ	ܓ	ܓ	3
(ḫ)	⚇					
d	⅏	ד	ܕ	ܕ	ܕ	4
h	☰	ה	ܗ	ܗ	ܗ	5
w	⊱	ו	ܘ	ܘ	ܘ	6
z	⚓	ז	ܙ	ܙ	ܙ	7
ḥ	⚘	ח	ܚ	ܚ	ܚ	8
ṭ	⚛	ט	ܛ	ܛ	ܛ	9
y	⧻	י	ܝ	ܝ	ܝ	10
k	⊷	ךכ	ܟ ܟ	ܟ ܟ	ܟ ܟ	20
(š)	⟁					
l	Ⲙ	ל	ܠ	ܠ	ܠ	30
m	Ⲩ	םמ	ܡ ܡ	ܡ ܡ	ܡ ܡ	40
(δ)	◇					
n	⊶	ןנ	ܢ ܢ	ܢ ܢ	ܢ ܢ	50
ẓ	⬓					
s	⚥	ס	ܣ	ܣ	ܣ	60
ʿ	⟨	ע	ܥ	ܥ	ܥ	70
p	⊨	ףפ	ܦ	ܦ	ܦ	80
ṣ	⫴	ץצ	ܨ	ܨ	ܨ	90
q	⊢⟨	ק	ܩ	ܩ	ܩ	100
r	⊢⊢	ר	ܪ	ܪ	ܪ	200
ś		שׂ				
š (θ)	⟨	שׁ	ܫ	ܫ	ܫ	300
(γ)	⊬					
t	⊢—	ת	ܬ	ܠ	ܬ	400
(ì)	☰					
(ù)	⅏					
(ṡ)	⬚					

Where two forms are shown, the one on the right occurs at the end of a word. Ugaritic values are given in parentheses.

Table 38. Vocalization Systems of the Abjads

Value		Hebrew		East Syriac		West Syriac		Arabic	
i	ī	בִ	בִי	ܒܹ	ܒ݂	ܒ	ܒ	ـِ بِ	بِي ـِي
e	ē	בֶ	בֵ		ܒ	ܒ	ܒ		
a	ā	בַ	בָ	ܒ	ܒ	ܒ	ܒ	ـَ بَ	بَا ـَا
o	ō	בָ	בֹ	ܒܘ ܒ		ܒ	ܒ		
u	ū	בֻ	בוּ	ܒܘ ܒ		ܒܘ ܒ		ـُ بُ بُـ	بُو بُـو
∅		בְ						ـْ بْ	
ĕ		בֱ							
ă		בֲ							
ŏ		בֳ							

Each symbol is shown alone and following b-.

The order of the abjad is fundamentally the same for all that are in use today (Table 37).

With the devising of marks to indicate vowels, complete and adequate alphabets have been achieved for each of the literary languages (Ge'ez excepted). Actually, only in Phoenician and South Arabian is there absolutely no indication of vowel quality.[1] Ugaritic, otherwise vowel-less, has three separate characters for *ȧ*, *i̇*, and *u̇* (the treatment of V'C is less clear), which makes possible considerable confidence in reconstructing the vocalism, particularly conjugation patterns, when roots containing ' are studied. Early in the history of recorded Aramaic, the letters for the semivowels *w* and *y* in effect stood for the diphthongs *aw* and *ay*, and later were retained to mark *o* and *e* as contractions of the diphthongs, and then also *ū* and *ī*. Perhaps by analogy ' was used for *a*, and *h* (particularly finally) also entered the system.

The other scripts have adopted versions of this system. Arabic, the most regular, indicates all long vowels with *w*, *y*, or *alif*. Hebrew shows considerable freedom in using vowel letters or not; Syriac employs an intermediate system.

Hebrew, Syriac, and Arabic can all add signs indicating vowel quality, and other phonological features, to the basic consonantal text; the vowel sign denotes the vowel following the consonant to which it is appended. The three scripts have different systems, Syriac and Hebrew more than one (Table 38).

All three read from right to left. In books where they are combined with a Western language (grammars, dictionaries, commentaries, etc.), the individual words in a series of examples are usually to be taken one at a time from left to right. If a sentence or other long example does not fit on a single line in a primarily left-to-right text, the quotation begins at the right end of the first line, occupies the space to the middle of that line, and continues from as far to the right of the next line as necessary, reading to the left margin. The English, etc., text then resumes at the middle of the line in which the quotation ends. For example:

---

1. Fortunately, at a late stage some Phoenician texts were written in the Greek alphabet and careful study allows the determination of some of the vowels; the South Arabian pattern *qtlw* may represent *qatalaw* or possibly *qatalu*.

These words from the Palestinian Talmud summarize the Rabbis' attitude toward their languages: ארבע לשונות נאה לעולם שישתמשו בהם לעז לזמר רומי לקרב סורסי לאילייא עברי לדיבור: 'There are four tongues worthy of common use: Greek for song, Latin for war, Syriac for lamentation, and Hebrew for ordinary speech'. (Megilloth iv 4)

The letters of the alphabets can also be used as numerals. Arabic normally uses its own decimal notation; the digits of a number are then read from left to right.

Hebrew

Certain letters of the Hebrew alphabet have distinctive forms word-finally.

The vowel signs are placed above, below, and beside the letters. The values indicated for Hebrew vowels in Table 38, and used throughout this book, follow what Joseph L. Malone (*Tiberian Hebrew Phonology*, Appendix B) calls a "5-color interpretation" of the system. While we take no stance on the correct interpretation of the Tiberian system, a "5-color" reading yields a vocalization whose relationship to other Semitic languages is easier to recognize.

A dot inside *b d g p t k* indicates nonspirantized (stop rather than fricative) pronunciation; inside final *h* it marks it as consonantal rather than a vowel letter; in other letters it indicates a long consonant. Long *b d g p t k* are never spirantized. A dash above a letter verifies the absence of the dot.

A "hyphen" joins particles to their head words and other closely connected items. A "colon" marks the end of a verse of the Bible.

Syriac

Three forms of the Syriac alphabet are in common use, the Estrangelo (στρογγύλη 'round,' or perhaps Arabic سطر الإنجيلية *saṭr anğīliyya* 'gospel writing'), the Serto (Syriac ܣܪܛܐ *serṭā* [*pšīṭta*] '[simple] stroke'), and the Nestorian. The Nestorian script is primarily found in Modern Aramaic texts in such Christian dialects as Urmi and Tell Kepe; the Serto is used for the Ṭuroyo dialect of Modern Aramaic and in scholarly works; the Estrangelo, the oldest, is now generally limited to scholarly works. Because the script is a cursive one, many letters are joined with those that precede and follow, though some may not join on one side or the other. There are up to three different forms of each letter; only final *k* and *n* differ greatly from the basic form, however. There are ligatures for *lʾ* ܠܐ and *ʾl* ܐܠ; *k* and *n* standing alone (as when being cited qua letters) are doubled: ܟܟ, ܢܢ. Nestorian can substitute ܠ for final ܐܠ and ܗ for ܗܘ, as space dictates; a diacritic produces ܓ and ܙ for modern *ǰ* and *č*, respectively.

Vowels are added in three ways, one using single dots, two with an individual sign for each vowel. A dot above or below a word or suffix distinguishes homographs. The principle is that the dot above marks a fuller vowel—usually *a/ā*—while the dot below indicates a closer vowel—*i*, *u*, or vowellessness; some words have more than one. This system has to some extent been "lexicalized" so that the pointing used for weak verbs (with vowels different from those of corresponding strong verbs) reflects the strong pattern rather than the actual vowels, and a final *-h* with point above represents a feminine singular suffix, whatever its vowel. The two explicit systems of vowels are shown in Table 38. The East Syriac signs, developed from the dot system, are used with the Nestorian alphabet. The West Syriac system is used with Serto; its signs are based on Greek letters and may appear indifferently above or below their letters, as there is room.

In Syriac-script materials, we have followed normal scholarly practice in using the Serto alphabet with West Syriac pointing. However, in most cases an East Syriac vocalization has been followed in transcriptions, so that رجلا 'leg' is transcribed *riglā* rather than *reglō*. While neither tradition necessarily reflects the pronunciation of the oldest Syriac, a compromise rooted primarily in the Eastern values gives a vocalization that is probably close to the ancestral pronunciation and one that is unquestionably easier to use in comparative work.

A point above *b d g p t k* indicates non-spirantized; below, spirantized pronunciation. Two dots above some letter of a word (or   if possible—over   they replace its dot,) mark the word as a plural form. A stroke over a letter marks it as silent. Certain suffixes are written with final, etymological, vowel letters, but they are not pronounced: ه-, ـ-, ـهو-; in this manual we transcribe silent ه-, ـ- with superscript -*w*, -*y*. The enclitic verb forms are written as separate words, even in Modern Aramaic.

Arabic

In Arabic there may be as many as four forms of each letter, according as they are joined on both sides, left, right, or neither (Table 39). Note that a number of letters turn into mere spikes in the line, distinguished only by the dots above or below them. Ligatures include *lā* لا, *kā* كـ, *kl* كل.

The glottal stop is not indicated by *alif*, as in Syriac, but by ء *hamza*. This sits on a *y*, *w*, *alif*, or nothing, according to the vowels on either side: a *yā*-seat indicates an *i*/*ī* on one side or both, a *waw*-seat an *u*/*ū* but no *i*, etc. Initially it goes above *alif* for *'a* and below it for *'i*. To avoid writing double consonants, a *hamza* beside a long vowel has no seat at all, nor has it one when it ends a word-final cluster.

Vowels are – a, – i, and – u; final nunation is indicated by doubling the vowel sign, –, –, –, and never by adding the letter *n*. -*an*, however, is supported by a final *alif*. Nunation is generally not noted in our transcriptions of nouns and adjectives. Long vowels are marked by vowel letters, except that in a few common words *ā* is not written. In vocalized texts it is then indicated by –. Where two *alif*s would be adjacent (in the combination *'ā*) they are written آ. A long consonant is marked –. A vowelless consonant has –.

Certain morphophonemic (sandhi) phenomena are noted at the beginnings and ends of words. The definite article is written ال even before dentals etc., but its assimilation is indicated by – over the following consonant. After the preposition *l*- the *alif* is omitted. The initial *alif* of *ibn* 'son' is omitted when the word conjoins name and patronymic. The feminine ending -*a(tun)* is written ة-, and not ت-; -*atan* is ة-. The feminine-singular ending is transcribed in this manual -*a^t*. The weak ending -*ā* is ى. The plural -*ūna* when it loses its -*na* takes a merely decorative *alif*. A prothetic vowel supporting an initial cluster is written with *alif* without *hamza*; when this vowel is supplanted by the final vowel of the preceding word, its sign is replaced by – on the alif.

Maltese

The modern Maltese alphabet comprises the following 29 letters: a, b, ċ (= *č*), d, e, f, ġ (= *ǧ*), g, h (silent except finally [= *ḥ*] and in the digraphs għh and ħh [= *ḥḥ*]), ħ (= *ḥ*), i, j (= *y*), k, l, m, n, għ (silent, representing Classical Arabic ʿ; replaced by ' finally after a), o, p, q (= *'*), r, s, t, u, v, w, x (= *š*), ż (= *z*), z (= *c*). The letters ħ and għ lengthen neighboring vowels. Spelling is largely phonemic, with some etymological admixture.

Table 39. Arabic

Value	Alone	Final	Medial	Initial	Numerical Value
a	ا	ـا			1
b	ب	ـب	ـبـ	بـ	2
t	ت	ـت	ـتـ	تـ	400
θ	ث	ـث	ـثـ	ثـ	500
ǰ	ج	ـج	ـجـ	جـ	3
ḥ	ح	ـح	ـحـ	حـ	8
x	خ	ـخ	ـخـ	خـ	600
d	د	ـد			4
δ	ذ	ـذ			700
r	ر	ـر			200
z	ز	ـز			7
s	س	ـس	ـسـ	سـ	60
š	ش	ـش	ـشـ	شـ	300
ṣ	ص	ـص	ـصـ	صـ	90
ḍ	ض	ـض	ـضـ	ضـ	800
ṭ	ط	ـط	ـطـ	طـ	9
ẓ	ظ	ـظ	ـظـ	ظـ	900
ʿ	ع	ـع	ـعـ	عـ	70
γ	غ	ـغ	ـغـ	غـ	1000
f	ف	ـف	ـفـ	فـ	80
q	ق	ـق	ـقـ	قـ	100
k	ك	ـك	ـكـ	كـ	20
l	ل	ـل	ـلـ	لـ	30
m	م	ـم	ـمـ	مـ	40
n	ن	ـن	ـنـ	نـ	50
h	ه	ـه	ـهـ	هـ	5
w	و	ـو			6
y	ي	ـي	ـيـ	يـ	10
lā	لا	ـلا			

Ethiopic

Table 40. Geʿez

	a	ū	ī	ā	ē	ə	ō
h	ሀ	ሁ	ሂ	ሃ	ሄ	ህ	ሆ
l	ለ	ሉ	ሊ	ላ	ሌ	ል	ሎ
ḥ	ሐ	ሑ	ሒ	ሓ	ሔ	ሕ	ሖ
m	መ	ሙ	ሚ	ማ	ሜ	ም	ሞ
š	ሠ	ሡ	ሢ	ሣ	ሤ	ሥ	ሦ
r	ረ	ሩ	ሪ	ራ	ሬ	ር	ሮ
s	ሰ	ሱ	ሲ	ሳ	ሴ	ስ	ሶ
q	ቀ	ቁ	ቂ	ቃ	ቄ	ቅ	ቆ
qʷ	ቈ		ቊ	ቋ	ቌ	ቍ	
b	በ	ቡ	ቢ	ባ	ቤ	ብ	ቦ
t	ተ	ቱ	ቲ	ታ	ቴ	ት	ቶ
x	ኀ	ኁ	ኂ	ኃ	ኄ	ኅ	ኆ
xʷ	ኈ		ኊ	ኋ	ኌ	ኍ	
n	ነ	ኑ	ኒ	ና	ኔ	ን	ኖ
ʾ	አ	ኡ	ኢ	ኣ	ኤ	እ	ኦ
k	ከ	ኩ	ኪ	ካ	ኬ	ክ	ኮ
kʷ	ኰ		ኲ	ኳ	ኴ	ኵ	
w	ወ	ዉ	ዊ	ዋ	ዌ	ው	ዎ
ʿ	ዐ	ዑ	ዒ	ዓ	ዔ	ዕ	ዖ
z	ዘ	ዙ	ዚ	ዛ	ዜ	ዝ	ዞ
y	የ	ዩ	ዪ	ያ	ዬ	ይ	ዮ
d	ደ	ዱ	ዲ	ዳ	ዴ	ድ	ዶ
g	ገ	ጉ	ጊ	ጋ	ጌ	ግ	ጎ
gʷ	ጐ		ጒ	ጓ	ጔ	ጕ	
ṭ	ጠ	ጡ	ጢ	ጣ	ጤ	ጥ	ጦ
p̣	ጰ	ጱ	ጲ	ጳ	ጴ	ጵ	ጶ
ṣ	ጸ	ጹ	ጺ	ጻ	ጼ	ጽ	ጾ
ḍ	ፀ	ፁ	ፂ	ፃ	ፄ	ፅ	ፆ
f	ፈ	ፉ	ፊ	ፋ	ፌ	ፍ	ፎ
p	ፐ	ፑ	ፒ	ፓ	ፔ	ፕ	ፖ

Ethiopic is read from left to right.

The earliest Ethiopic inscriptions do not indicate vowels. From the middle of the reign of Ezana, ca. 350 C.E., the letters were modified to express the 7 vowel phonemes of the Ethiopic languages. The *abugida*—the word refers to a script type where the basic shape stands for C*a* (Table 40)—provides each of the 26 consonants with 7 shapes, listed in conventional sequence as 1st through 7th orders. The basic sign shape is the 1st order; the 2d order appends a stroke on the middle right to represent Cū; 3d order has a similar stroke at bottom right for Cī. The 4th order marks Cā by lengthening a right-hand leg, or by bending a single leg to the left. The 5th order represents Cē by altering Cī's stroke to a circle; likewise the 7th order changes Cū's stroke to a ring for Cō, or else lengthens a left leg. The 6th order ambiguously stands for C∅ or Cə and has no consistent graphic device. 6th-order signs do often involve a break in a stroke.

Furthermore, when the four velars *q x k g* are labialized, their forms are modified; there are no signs for the labiovelars + rounded vowels, because these are neutralized. Additional letters for Amharic and other languages of Ethiopia have been created using diacritics.

The ambiguity of the sixth order of vowels makes for difficulty in determining word structure; consonant length is not indicated. A colon separates words; a double colon is a punctuation mark.

Some of the signs are easily confused. Vowel marks that do not represent what the principles suggest they do are ዮ *yō* not *yū*; ወ *wə* not *wū*; ዎ *wō* not *wā*; መ *mə* not *mā*; ሠ *šə* not *šā*. *r* and *f* do not lend themselves to the overall system but at least resemble each other in vowel-modification. The ʷī and ʷə series are especially similar to each other; the horizontal marking ʷī is broken, and ʷə's is straight.

Akkadian

The earliest cuneiform documents (ca. 3200 B.C.E.) bear fairly recognizable, representational pictures. It is not until nearly 1000 years later that Akkadian texts appear; by then the signs had evolved to more abstract shapes. These cuneiform signs are composed of marks that were impressed in wet clay tablets with a square-ended stylus that characteristically produced wedge-shaped indentations (Latin *cuneus* 'wedge'). (The clay hardens upon drying and may thus survive the millennia to be excavated and read; additionally the tablets might be baked, either in antiquity intentionally or accidentally [in a conflagration] or else in the modern museum workshop, whereupon they become virtually indestructible.) The wedges may be horizontal, vertical, or diagonal. Modern lists of signs include about 600, but only a couple hundred were in everyday use at any one time.

Akkadian is read from left to right.

A cuneiform sign usually stands for a vowel, a consonant plus vowel or vice versa, or a vowel with consonant on each side. But because the writing system was used first for Sumerian and only later for Akkadian, many signs have more than one value, typically reflecting both the Sumerian word(s) represented by the original picture and the Akkadian equivalent. Thus the same sign ⊷╪ may be read both a n ('heaven' in Sumerian) or d i n g i r ('god'), and *il* (from *ilu* 'god' in Akkadian). Further polyphony arises in part because typically a sign containing *i* may also be read with *e* and because the sound system of Akkadian is richer than that of Sumerian: the triplets of voiced, voiceless, and emphatic consonants may indifferently be represented by the same sign. There is also considerable homophony, whereby several different characters may have a common reading. Thus several different signs can be read *šu*. Normally, however, at any one place and epoch only one sign with a particular value was common.

Assyriologists have developed a number of conventions for transliterating cuneiform signs so that the original sequence is immediately recoverable (*transliteration*: unambiguous replacement of one set of signs by another, for mere typographic or other convenience; *transcription*: interpretation of the original writing into words according to a particular understanding of the grammar, etc.).[2] Akkadian is presented in italics, Sumerian preferably in letterspaced roman. The signs making up a word are joined in Akkadian by hyphens and in Sumerian by periods. Logograms (in Akkadian context, see below) are written with the appropriate Sumerian value in small capitals; determinatives designating proper names and the dual number are superscript: ^{d} = god's name; ^{f} = woman's name; ^{I} = man's name; ^{II} (dual number); ^{ki} = place name; ^{kur} = country name; ^{uru} = city name. Names are written with an initial capital. When it is uncertain which value of a sign is the appropriate one or when a sign is mentioned qua sign, the name of the sign in the modern lists (usually the most common of its values) is given in small capitals. Homophonous signs are distinguished by numerical subscripts, assigned many years ago in the supposed order of frequency overall in cuneiform documents, except that the most common sign for a particular reading has no index, and the subscripts $_2$ and $_3$ are replaced by acute and grave accents respectively. Thus the first five šU signs are transliterated $šu$, $šú$, $šù$, $šu_4$, $šu_5$. In a transcription, ordinarily not included in the publication of a text, features like vowel and consonant length, not always consistently indicated in the original, are added, while full information on the signs in the text is sacrificed.

Akkadian words may be written either (1) phonetically, e.g., *u-lam-mi-da-an-ni* = *ulammidannī* 'he has reported to me', or (2) logographically (Greek λόγος 'word' + γπάφω 'write'), in which a single sign is understood to represent the meaning rather than the sound, e.g., É 'house' not é (Sumerian) or *bīt* (Akkadian); GIŠ 'wood' not giš (Sumerian) or *iṣ* (Akkadian); KUR 'mountain' not kur (Sumerian) or *šad* (Akkadian). A common use of logograms is as semantic determinatives, where they precede (or in a few cases follow) a word and mark it as denoting something classified among, e.g., buildings or wooden objects or lands. The two principles (logographic and phonetic) may be combined, when a logogram with several readings—both noun and verb, say—is disambiguated by a "phonetic complement" read in Akkadian, e.g., KUR-*u* = *šadū* 'mountain', KUR-*tim* = *māt(āt)im* 'land(s)' (genitive), KUR-*ud* = *i/akšud* 'he/I conquered', KUR-*ad* = *i/akaššad* 'he/I conquer(s)' (occasionally a phonetic complement is supplied to help with the reading of a rare Akkadian sign, e.g., *ak-šud*^{ud}); or when a grammatical meaning is indicated by a logogram attached to a phonetically written word. The most common of these is MEŠ, marking plurality (of either noun or verb—i.e., the iterative stem); plurality may also be indicated by repeating the word's logogram. Another sort of grammatical logogram arises when a particular sign is read phonetically but its use is virtually confined to representing a particular morpheme, e.g., -*šú* used for the third-person masculine singular possessive suffix (but almost never for other syllables with that phonetic value) or *ù* used only for 'and'. Idiosyncratically, the sequence -*a-a*- can stand for -*ayya*-.

Space precludes presenting a complete sign list; a chart of the most basic phonetic signs has been compiled (Table 41, page 260).

It is customary to present a pen-and-ink copy of the signs on a tablet when publishing a text; formerly, cuneiform type, as seen here, could be used; and now photographs of the tablet may suffice.

---

2. However, even transliteration involves interpretation, choosing from the numerous possible combinations of letters and type styles (italics, small capitals, superscripts, letterspacing) the ones required by the context.

Table 41. Phonetic Arrangement of Neo-Assyrian Cuneiform Syllabary

Ca	Ce	Ci	Cu		aC	eC	iC	uC
𒀀				—				
				m				
				b				
				p				
				w				
				y				
				d				
				ṭ				
				t				
				z				
				ṣ				
				s				
				š				
				n				
				l				
				r				
				g				
				q				
				k				
				x				
				ʾ				

The table gives the most common monoconsonantal signs. The intersections of vowel columns and consonant rows are sometimes subdivided to include more than one homophonous sign. The "q row" thus reads qa qá qe/i qé/í qu qú aq e/iq uq *(where* qá *is* GA, qé/í *is* KI, *and* qú *is* KU).

Index 1

Languages of Glosses

A

Achaemenid Aramaic   *See* Aramaic, Achaemenid
Akkadian   15, 17, 28, 32, 35–36, 42–44, 46,
     49–50, 69, 75, 95–97, 130–42, 222–31,
     233–49
Amharic   29, 130–42, 143–52, 161–221
Arabic, Classical   10–11, 13–17, 25, 27–29, 31–
     32, 42–43, 45, 48–51, 62–63, 71, 82–83,
     104–6, 127–29, 130–42, 153–248
Arabic, Egyptian   47, 57, 72, 84–85, 107–8,
     127–42, 161–221
Arabic, Iraqi   47, 130–42, 161–221
Arabic, Kuwaiti   161–221
Arabic, Moroccan   13, 42, 47, 130–42, 153–221
Arabic, Sudanese   127–29
Arabic, Syrian   161–221
Aramaic, Achaemenid   130–142
Aramaic, Azerbaijan Jewish   161–221
Aramaic, Christian Palestinian   161–221
Aramaic, Maʕlula   13, 42–43, 130–42, 161–221,
     233–49
Aramaic, Ṭur ʕAbdin   161–221
Aramaic, Urmi   11, 43, 70, 78, 100, 130–42,
     161–221
Argobba   161–221
Ayt Seghrouchen   153–60, 222–31
Azerbaijan Jewish Aramaic   *See* Aramaic,
     Azerbaijan Jewish

B

Berber   49

C

Chaha   143–52, 161–221
Christian Palestinian Aramaic   *See* Aramaic,
     Christian Palestinian
Classical Arabic   *See* Arabic, Classical
Coptic   91, 115–16

E

Egyptian Arabic   *See* Arabic, Egyptian.

G

Geʕez   14, 16, 18, 29, 31, 35–36, 42, 44–45, 49–
     50, 63, 72, 86–87, 109–10, 127–52, 161–
     248
Ghadamsi   92–93, 117–18, 153–60, 222–31

H

Harari   13, 130–42, 143–152, 161–221
Hebrew   11, 13–15, 17, 27, 30–32, 44, 49–50, 52,
     63, 71, 80–81, 102–3, 130–42, 232–48

I

Iraqi Arabic   *See* Arabic, Iraqi

J

Jebel Nefusa   222–31
Jibbali   11, 13, 27–28, 42, 45–46, 49–50, 73, 90,
     113–14, 130–42, 222–31, 233–49

261

K

Kabyle   222–31
Kuwaiti Arabic   *See* Arabic, Kuwaiti

M

Maʿlula   *See* Aramaic, Maʿlula
Maltese   153–221
Mandaic   161–221
Mandaic, Modern   13, 130–42, 161–221
Meḥri   13, 130–42
Moroccan Arabic   *See* Arabic, Moroccan

P

Phoenician   130–42
Proto-Semitic   68

S

Sabean   49–50, 130–42
Senhayi   153–60
Shilḥa   222–31
Soddo   161–221

Soqoṭri   13, 35–36, 59, 130–42
Sudanese Arabic   *See* Arabic, Sudanese
Syriac   11, 13–15, 18, 27–32, 35–36, 43–44,
            46, 49–50, 59, 63, 69, 76–77, 98–99,
            130–42, 161–248
Syrian Arabic   *See* Arabic, Syrian

T

Tigre   73, 88–89, 111–12, 127–29, 143–52,
            161–221
Tigrinya   13, 42, 127–52, 161–221
Ṭur ʿAbdin   *See* Aramaic, Ṭur ʿAbdin

U

Ugaritic   42, 49, 70, 79, 101, 130–142, 222–31,
            233–49
Urmi   *See* Aramaic, Urmi

W

Wargla   222–31

Index 2

Glosses

A

above   143
abundant   50
after   43, 130, 232
all   130, 143, 153, 222, 232
altar   43
and   30
anoint   143
answer   143, 153, 201, 222, 232
ant   153
appoint   110
approach   46, 97, 232
arm   143, 153, 222, 232
arrive   143, 153, 210, 222, 232
arrow   143
ash   143, 153
ask   43, 97, 110, 130, 143, 153, 200, 222, 232
axe   46, 143, 153, 222

B

back   143, 153, 222, 232
bad   143
bandage   45
bark   64
barley   143, 153, 222, 232
be   97, 130, 143, 153, 222, 232
bear   29, 47–48, 110, 112, 131, 143, 153, 204, 222, 232
bear (animal)   29
beard   29, 31, 144, 153, 222, 232
beat   97, 153, 222, 232
beautiful   18
bee   127, 144
belch   144

believe   110
bell   144
bellows   45
belly   43, 45, 171
bend   114
between   232
big   50, 131, 144, 153, 214, 223, 232
bind up   14, 44
bird   127, 144, 154, 175, 223, 232
bitch   14
bite   31, 44, 64, 144, 154, 223, 234
black   144, 154
bleed   114
bless   131, 234
blind   144, 154
blood   11, 28, 29, 50, 144, 154, 223, 234
blow   64, 144
boast   52
body   46, 144
bone   144, 154, 223, 234
book   11, 46, 127
bosom   44, 45
bow   144
boxing   57
boxwood   57
brave   43, 50
bread   154, 184, 223, 234
break   30, 144
break off   45
breast   29, 127, 144, 154, 223, 234
brother   17, 127, 131, 144, 154, 165, 223, 234
build   17, 47–48, 63, 97, 131, 144, 154, 207, 223, 234
bull   44–45, 127, 144, 154, 177, 223, 234
bunch   50

bury   46
buy   144, 154, 206, 223, 234

C

calf   47, 48, 127, 144, 234
call   106, 131, 144, 154, 201, 234
camel   127, 144, 154, 223, 234
capture   43, 144
careful   28
carpet   50
cave   144
chain   62
chair   127, 144, 234
cheek   11, 144, 154, 223
chew   144, 154
chicken   127, 144, 154
chief   50
chieftain   50
child   29, 144, 154, 163, 223, 234
chop   63, 65
city   131, 145
cloud   145, 154, 189
coagulate   145
comb   100
come   18, 114, 131, 145, 209, 223, 234
compose   114
conquer   18
consecrate   45
consecrated   44
cook   43, 50
cooked   45, 50
cough   31, 46, 145
cow   127, 145, 154, 223, 234
co-wife   44, 45
cross   43, 45, 114
cry   47, 48, 110, 145, 154, 223, 234
cultivate   117
curse   11, 44
cut   28, 63, 64, 65
cut off   63, 65
cut off hair   63, 65
cut open   65

D

dam   114
dance   145, 154, 207, 223, 234
date   154
date honey   46
daughter   127, 132, 145, 154, 224, 234

day   128, 132, 145, 154, 191, 224, 234
decide   97
demand pay   45
devour   43
die   10, 18, 47–48, 110, 112, 132, 145, 154, 203,
     224, 234
dig   114, 154
dip   45
divide   43
do   224
dog   11, 60, 128, 145, 154, 176, 224, 234
donkey   128, 145, 154, 174, 224, 234
door   47–48, 132, 145, 154, 224, 234
dove   145, 155, 176, 224
dream   47–48, 64, 145, 155, 224, 234
dress   15, 46, 155, 224, 234
drill   63
drink   108, 145, 155, 202, 224, 236
drive   28
drug   43, 46
drum   46
dry   112
duck   57
dumb   114
dwell   11
dye   43

E

ear   27, 29, 128, 145, 155, 168, 224, 236
earth   13, 28, 132, 145, 155, 186, 224, 236
eat   97, 99, 112, 145, 155, 202, 224, 236
egg   28, 44–45, 47–48, 145, 155, 182
eggplant   57
eight   28, 132, 145, 155, 224, 236
elbow   145
elder   50
elephant   128
embrace   145
emerge   63
enemy   44
enter   43, 97, 132, 145, 155, 211, 224, 236
evening   145
excel   63
exit   132, 145, 155, 211, 224, 236
eye   128, 133, 145, 155, 168, 224, 236

F

face   145, 155, 167, 225, 236
fall   28, 64, 97, 103, 108, 145, 155, 225, 236

far   236
fat   50, 146, 155, 225, 236
father   133, 146, 155, 163, 225, 236
fear   99, 110
feather   47–48, 146, 155
feces   146, 155
feed   43
field   43, 45, 133
fill   43, 45, 97, 133, 146, 155, 225, 236
find   108
fine   44
finger   46, 146, 155, 172, 225, 236
fire   146, 155, 190, 225, 236
firstborn   146
fish   146, 155, 179, 225, 236
five   35, 43, 45, 133, 146, 155, 217, 225, 236
flea   31–32, 57, 62, 146
flee   146
flour   146, 155, 225, 236
fly   29, 146, 155, 225, 236
foot   128, 133, 146, 155, 173, 225, 236
footprint   45
forbidden   64
forget   64, 146, 155, 199
four   35, 46, 133, 146, 155, 217, 225, 236
fox   62
free   63
friend   128, 133, 146, 155, 165, 225, 236
frog   28, 156
from   16, 30, 134, 236
future marker   16

G

garlic   30
gather   28
gazelle   28
get up   108
give   97, 134, 146, 156, 205, 225, 238
gnaw   45
go   112, 134, 146, 156, 210, 225, 238
goat   128, 134, 146, 156, 177, 225, 238
god   134, 146, 156, 166, 225, 238
gold   29, 49, 50, 134, 146, 156, 238
good   18, 106, 134, 146, 156, 214, 226, 238
grandchild   50
grass   146, 156, 180, 226, 238
grave   46, 128
graves   46
graze   44–45

great   50, 52
green   49
grind   28, 43–45, 146, 156, 226, 238
grindstone   146
guard   28, 44, 64
guest   47, 48, 146

H

hair   146, 156, 167, 226, 238
hammer   147
hand   15, 128, 134, 147, 156, 172, 226, 238
hang   29, 147
hare   147, 156, 226, 238
harness   44
hate   147
he   30
head   128, 135, 147, 156, 166, 226, 238
healer   11
hear   30, 47–48, 115, 135, 147, 156, 196, 226, 238
heart   46, 135, 147, 156, 226, 238
heavy   103
he-goat   156, 238
help   156
hen   175
hide   156
high   97
hit with stick   50
hobble   45
honey   46, 147, 156, 182, 226, 238
honored   50
horn   128, 147, 156, 178, 226, 238
horse   128, 135, 147, 156, 173, 226, 238
hot   10, 64
house   14, 16, 46, 128, 135, 147, 226, 238
how many   147
hundred   135, 147, 218, 238
hunger   147, 156, 226, 238
hunt   147, 238
hyena   28, 31, 44–45, 60, 147

I

in   62, 115
incise   44
increase   52
inherit   147
invoke god   57
iron   135, 147, 156, 226, 238

J

jaundice   49
judge   11

K

kick   29, 147
kid   29, 156, 226, 238
kidney   147, 156, 226, 238
kill   99, 103, 110, 112, 147, 156, 204, 226, 240
king   18, 128, 135, 147, 156, 227, 240
knee   128, 147, 156, 240
knife   147, 156, 194, 227
know   114, 136, 147, 157, 198, 227, 240

L

lamb   136, 147, 157, 227, 240
land   18
laugh   13, 147, 157, 227, 240
leaf   28, 49, 128, 147
leafy   49
learn   147, 198
leave   63, 99
leech   148
left   43, 45, 148, 157, 227
leg   46–48, 128, 136, 148, 157
lend   114
leopard   28, 128, 148
library   17
lie   29, 114, 157
light   11, 14, 31
lightning   28, 31, 148, 188
like   44
lion   129, 148, 157, 174, 227, 240
lip   31, 148, 157, 240
live   136, 157, 227, 240
liver   148, 157, 227
load   112, 148
locust   148
long   148, 157, 213, 227, 240
long ago   50
look   44, 45
lord   15, 50, 52, 136, 240
lot   148
louse   148
love   64, 136, 148, 157, 197, 227, 240
lowly   11
lung   148, 157

M

mail   57
mailman   57
make   100, 136, 157, 240
male   157
man   15, 129, 136, 148, 157, 162, 227, 240
many   50, 52, 137, 148, 157, 215, 240
mare   148, 157
mash   45
master   52
meat   31, 137, 148, 157, 181, 227, 240
medicine   46
mention   44
mighty   18, 50
milk   29, 31, 46–48, 148, 157, 227, 240
mix   28
molar   28
month   43, 129, 137, 148, 157, 192, 227, 240
moon   43, 45, 148, 186, 227, 240
morning   157, 227, 240
mosquito   148
moss   49
mother   137, 148, 157, 164, 227, 240
mother-in-law   148
mountain   47–48, 129, 137, 148, 184, 228, 240
mourn   100
mouth   137, 148, 157, 169, 228, 240
mule   148

N

nail   28, 31, 44–45, 129, 148, 157
name   62, 137, 149, 157, 228, 242
narrow   44, 149
navel   149, 157
near   114
neck   149, 157, 170
needle   129, 149
new   149, 213, 242
news   11
night   31, 137, 149, 191, 228, 242
nine   149, 157, 228, 242
nip   65
nip off   44
nose   31, 43, 149, 158, 228, 242
nostril   31, 43

O

office   17
oil   47–48, 149, 158, 228, 242

older 50
on 30, 138, 242
one 29, 31, 35, 138, 149, 158, 215, 228, 242
onion 31, 46, 149, 158
open 43, 45, 97
open country 63
oppress 28
or 138, 242
outside 63

P

palace 43
pale 49
palm (of hand) 11
paper 49
parable 30–31, 44–45
pasha 57
pass 149, 158, 228
peace 138
peel 63, 65
person 129, 138, 149, 158, 242
pick 64
pick at 65
pick up 64
pierce 64–65
pig 242
pity 64
place 43
plant 64
plow 45
plowshare 57
pluck 65
plum 57
pointed rod 50
poison 43, 45–46
pray 44–45
precede 64
promise 114
publication 11
pus 149
put 97, 108

R

raid 99
rain 31, 149, 188, 228, 242
raise 15
ram 158
rat 149, 158
ready 50

reap 65
red 149, 158
remember 45
resemble 149
return 30, 106, 149, 158, 212, 228, 242
reveal 99, 103
rib 28, 129, 149, 242
rich 110
ride 158, 228, 242
right 149, 158, 242
ripe 50
rise 15
river 31, 43, 45, 149, 158, 185, 242
road 138, 158, 195, 228, 242
roast 149
root 46, 129, 138, 149, 158, 228, 242
rope 149, 158, 193, 228, 242
rub 149
rudder 43, 45
rule 97
run 43, 45, 149, 158, 212, 228, 242

S

sabbath 46
sacrifice 50
saliva 63, 149
salt 149, 158, 183, 228, 242
sand 150
saturday 46
say 50, 114–15, 150, 158, 200, 228, 242
say *bi-smi-llāhi* 62
saying 50
scepter 50
scrape off 63
scratch 150
sea 138, 150, 158, 229, 242
seal 64
see 17, 47–48, 139, 150, 158, 196, 229, 244
seed 43, 150, 244
seize 150
sell 108
send 139, 158, 229, 244
sense 43
set 64
set up 64
seven 27, 46, 139, 150, 158, 229, 244
sew 29, 150
shadow 44–45, 150, 158, 189, 229, 244
shear 65

sheep   129, 139, 150, 158, 244
shepherd   244
short   150, 229, 244
shoulder   47–48, 150, 158, 171, 229, 244
show   11
silence   50
silent   50, 108
silver   139, 158, 229, 244
silver coin   49
sin   28
sing   158, 229, 244
sister   129, 139, 158, 229, 244
sit   97, 99, 103, 139, 159, 229, 244
six   139, 159, 229, 244
skin   150, 229, 244
sky   31, 140, 150, 159, 187, 229, 244
slander   150
slave   50, 129, 150, 244
sleep   63, 106, 150, 159, 203, 229, 244
slice   44
slumber   64
small   44, 103, 118, 140, 159, 229, 244
smell   159
smite   50
smoke   150, 159, 190, 229, 244
snake   129, 150, 159, 179, 229, 244
sneeze   150
snort   64
soak   43
soldier   18
son   31, 129, 140, 150, 164, 230, 244
soot   150
soul   140, 159, 230, 244
sow   44–45, 150
spark plug   57
speak   14, 150, 159, 199, 230, 244
spear   150
spider   150, 159
spit   63, 150, 159, 230
splinter   150
split open   65
squeeze   44–45
staff   50
stand   63–64, 99, 103, 106
star   62, 129, 151, 159, 230, 246
steal   114, 151, 159, 206
stick   50, 151, 159, 194, 246
stomach   43, 151, 159, 230, 246
stone   64, 129, 140, 151, 159, 230, 246
stooped   45

strangle   151
straw   10
strike   50
suck   151
summer   159
sun   14, 17, 28, 46, 140, 151, 159, 185, 230, 246
surround   103
swallow   151, 159
sweat   151, 159, 230, 246
sword   129
syrup   46

T

tail   151, 159, 178, 230, 246
take   29, 44–45, 140, 159, 205, 230, 246
taste   43, 45, 64, 151
teacher   17, 52
tear   151, 159, 230
temple   43, 45
ten   43–45, 140, 151, 159, 218, 230, 246
ten thousand   52
the   15
thigh   159
thin   44
think   151
this   16
thorn   151, 159, 181
thousand   141, 151, 219, 246
three   30, 35, 44–45, 141, 151, 159, 216, 230, 246
throw   106, 108, 151, 159, 208, 230, 246
tie   43, 141, 159, 209, 230, 246
tomb   28, 246
tomorrow   151, 160
tongue   141, 151, 160, 169, 230, 246
tooth   129, 151, 160, 170, 230, 246
tower   17, 57
tree   129, 151, 160, 180, 246
tribe   50
trim   64, 65
truce   50
trust   97
twin   151
two   35, 59, 62, 141, 151, 160, 216, 231, 246

U

uncle, maternal   160
uncle, paternal   160
uncover   114

under   151, 246
understand   114
urine   151, 160, 231

V

vegetables   49
village   151, 160, 195, 231
voice   50
vomit   151
vow   44

W

wander   114
want   151, 160, 197, 231, 246
war   152, 160
wash   47–48, 112, 152, 160, 208, 231, 246
watch   28, 64
water   28, 141, 152, 160, 183, 231, 246
wear   15, 46, 106
week   152, 192
well   47–48, 141, 160, 231, 246
west   142, 246
wet   114
what   142, 152, 160, 219, 231, 246
wheat   152, 160, 231, 248

when   152, 220
where   152, 160, 220, 231, 248
which   152, 221
white   44, 152, 160, 231, 248
who   142, 152, 160, 221, 231, 248
widow   152
wind   47–48, 152, 160, 187, 231, 248
wine   11, 248
wing   31, 152, 160, 231
wish   152
with   62, 142, 248
wolf   31, 60
woman   129, 142, 152, 160, 162, 231, 248
wood   142, 152, 160, 231
word   50
work   110, 112
worry   100
write   10–11, 17, 25, 106, 108, 142, 152, 160, 231, 248
writing   46

Y

year   142, 152, 160, 193, 231, 248
yesterday   152
yoke   44